DeMARK ON
DAY TRADING OPTIONS

DeMARK ON DAY TRADING OPTIONS

Using Options to Cash In
on the Day Trading Phenomenon

Thomas R. DeMark

Thomas R. DeMark, Jr.

Boston, Massachusetts   Burr Ridge, Illinois
Dubuque, Iowa   Madison, Wisconsin   New York, New York
San Francisco, California   St. Louis, Missouri

Library of Congress Cataloging-in-Publication Data

DeMark, Thomas R., date.
    DeMark on day trading options : using options to cash in on the day trading phenomenon / by Thomas R. Demark and Thomas R. DeMark Jr.
      p. cm.
    Includes index.
    ISBN 0-07-135059-4
    1. Options (Finance)—United States. I. DeMark, Thomas R., Jr. II. Title.
HG6024.U6D46   1999
332.63'228—dc21
                                          99-21299
                                           CIP

McGraw-Hill

A Division of The McGraw·Hill Companies

    4 5 6 7 8 9 BKM BKM   0 9 8 7 6 5 4

ISBN 0-07-135059-4

The sponsoring editor for this book was Stephen Isaacs and the production supervisor was Tina Cameron. It was set in Times New Roman by North Market Street Graphics of Lancaster, Pennsylvania.

This publication is designed to provide accurate and authoritative information in regard to the subject matter covered. It is sold with the understanding that neither the author nor the publisher is engaged in rendering legal, accounting, or other professional service. If legal advice or other expert assistance is required, the services of a competent professional person should be sought.

—From a Declaration of Principles jointly adopted by a Committee of the American Bar Association and a Committee of Publishers.

Although both the authors and the publisher believe the information, data, and contents presented are accurate, they neither guarantee their accuracy and completeness nor assume any liability. It should not be assumed that the methods, techniques, or indicators presented in this book will be profitable or that they will not result in losses. Trading involves the risk of loss, as well as the potential for profit. Past performance is not a guarantee of future results.

Options involve risk and are not suitable for all investors.

To my namesake and partner (T.J.) for his exceptional writing talents and organizational skills, as well as thorough knowledge of options and trading.

To my wife Nancy and our other children, Carrie, Meghan, Rocke, Evan, and Dominic for enriching my life.

To Steve Cohen, a market magician and professional trader who excels at every aspect of the business, for his support and commitment to market timing, as well as his friendship.

To Bruce Hauptman for his interest in the indicators and his friendship.

To Rick Knox, Matt Storz, Duane Davis, Larry McMillan, Chris Evans, John Hill, John Snyder, Rick Bensignor, and Mark Ellingson for their friendship and support.

To the management and software developers at Aspen Graphics, Bloomberg, Bridge, CQG, Data Transmission (DTN), Dow Jones Markets, FutureSource, Omega Research, Option Vue, Quote.Com, and Window on Wall Street.

Thomas Sr.

To my father Thomas whose name, birthday, and passion for trading I share.

To my mother Nancy who has taught me what is important in life. For the morals she has instilled in me and my siblings, as well as her incredible kindness, understanding, love, and friendship.

To my brothers and sisters for their encouragement and love.

To John DiFrancesca, my floor trading partner, for his attitude, humor, and friendship.

To Rich Rovetto and Tim Slater for taking a chance on me and introducing me into the trading and seminar communities.

To my roommate and friend Matt Stauffer for his inspiration and for teaching me to live life to its fullest, each and every day.

To Dan Davis, the Maddens (Rob and Scott), Doug Jansen, Joe Gits, Sr., Jason Perl, Thomas Stridsman, Leslie Richman, Brian Walls, Pat Raffalovich, Kathy Simpson, Drew Bryant, Marshall Persky, Martha Arriaga, Bruce McDonald, Bob Hendrickson, Trippe Lonian, Landon Stone, Mayeti Gametchu, Greg Forbes, Kris Kahn, Brad Murray, Mark Torres, Jeff Walsh, Sean Ladley, Dave Jones, Terry Kaufman, Mike Dillard, and Mindy Rozak for their friendship and support throughout the years.

Thomas Jr. (T.J.)

Contents

Foreword

DERIVATIVES HAVE TAKEN ON an ever increasing importance in the markets. The broad definition of *derivatives* includes options, futures, and many more exotic instruments that are conjured up by the leading investment banks. For most traders, though, *derivatives* means options—stock options, futures options, or index options. The virtual explosion in trading volume of options of all types attests to their importance. Moreover, there has been an increased interest in short-term trading—even day trading. This work by the DeMarks addresses both issues with a degree of professionalism reflective of their experience as traders and system designers.

This is not a get-rich-quick book. The setups, signals, and concepts described herein will require some study by even the most astute trader in order to use them successfully. But that is good news. So many books on day trading are published that seem to tout the concept as an easy road to riches. Any serious day trader—and I consider myself among them—knows that day trading is hard work, which is difficult on the psyche, and the concomitant rewards are available only to those who are willing to "pay the toll," so to speak. This book should appeal to both the aspiring trader and the experienced trader as well, for it lays out nontrivial concepts that can lead to excellent profits.

Most of the systems in this book are a continuation of the ones described in DeMark's earlier works—they deal with the timing of the purchase or sale of the underlying security. Options can, of course, be used in place of the underlying in any trading system—buying calls instead of taking a bullish signal on the underlying stock, index or futures, or buying puts instead of shorting the same. However, there is one very interesting new twist present here: the TD % F system. In this instance, DeMark lays out an option trading system that depends only on the price of the option itself! There is no consideration of what the underlying is doing—although the movements of the underlying, of course, influence the price of the option. I have often been a proponent of using options as a technical indicator to predict the movement of the underlying security—option volume spikes, sudden increases in the expensiveness of options, and put-call ratios are all accepted ways of doing this. Now, perhaps, another indicator has been introduced that may help in determining prices reversals by the underlying security.

Options are very useful as sentiment indicators. Unfortunately, most of our fellow option traders are wrong in their market opinions most of the time. That's why the put-call ratios—which measure option volume—are important contrary sentiment market indicators. This book describes a new sentiment indicator. It uses the dollar-weighted values of puts and calls *during* a trading day or at the close of trading. This indicator is similar to the put-call ratio that is commonly used for measuring sentiment, but because it uses price as well as volume *and* open interest, it may truly represent a new way of looking at sentiment. As always, though, the astute contrarian will want to be in a position opposite to that of the majority of traders.

TD % F is only one of many indicators presented in this book. It is important to understand that these are indicators—not *systems*. A *system* has specific entry and exit points and an exact track record can be constructed using them. However, most systems are hard to use for individual traders because somewhere along the line they conflict with the trader's own penchant for trading. The DeMarks, on the other hand, have given us *indicators*—rules for determining when a market is ready to be bought or sold, but which stop short of the dictatorial rules of a system. The good news is that this method gives the trader some room to use reason and logic in the way he or she employs the indicator; the bad news is that inexperienced traders might not be able to "reason" very well.

There is little mention in this book of terms you would find in a conventional option book—such as *implied volatility, delta, gamma, theta,* or *vega.* But that's okay. This isn't an option theory book—rather it is designed primarily as a trading book and it recommends that you use options to do that trading. When I am trading options for a short-term trade, I prefer to use near-term, in-the-money options, for they have little time value premium and most closely reflect the movements in the underlying security. The DeMarks espouse the same philosophy. You want to be able to capture quick price movements without having to worry a lot about time decay or possibly a change in the volatility pricing structure of the options—that is, how expensive the options are. Day traders of options don't have to worry much about either one—there is little time decay in the course of a single day, and options don't normally have a significant change in their pricing level in one day's time. Moreover, options limit your risk if something especially untoward should happen, but they allow for almost unlimited rewards.

In addition, the beauty of the DeMarks' approach is that these systems are geared toward option buyers. Forget spreads, covered writes, strangles, and so forth. If you can identify the likelihood of a swift movement by the underlying security—and that's what this book is all about—then you can concentrate on buying options as your trading vehicle. There is no need for the hedged strategies. In fact, it's a myth that option writers make all of the money in option trading. Anyone who has written covered or uncovered calls on the major stocks—especially the technology stocks—during the ongoing bull market has suffered the consequences. Even those who have employed bull spreads have found their profits reduced because they limited their profit potential. So the DeMarks' approach— and it is a valid one—is to forsake the exotic and stick with the basic: buy calls if the underlying is going to rise, and buy puts if it's going to fall. Of course, determining what the underlying is going to do is a difficult endeavor, but the indicators presented herein are very useful for that purpose.

While many setups and indicators are presented in this book, my favorite is the TD Camouflage. It is simple, seems to have excellent results, and can be quickly understood by even the most novice trader. If you come away with nothing else, learn this one concept. It should improve your short-term trading results.

Another very interesting concept that is stressed in this book is that of using the current day's opening price as the point from which to measure net change for the day. Not a single pricing service approaches the markets in this way—from newspapers to the most sophisticated and expensive real-time data services. Yet, as the DeMarks stress throughout, the most important thing for a trader to know about a stock, future, or index is how it is doing *relative to today's opening price.* I won't get into examples—the DeMarks do that—but suffice it to say that I agree with this concept and perhaps this book's greatest contribution to investment theory will be the realization of that ideology.

Readers who are familiar with Tom DeMark's previous works will find these systems to be similar to ones you have previously discovered. New traders will be intrigued by them as well, and should learn a lot. Again, I stress that this is not a trivial, "make-a-million" (while you lie on the beach) book. It is a serious endeavor and requires study and concentration. But from the myriad of examples and charts that point out how these indicators work, you should be able to see that any serious time spent studying these techniques should prove profitable to you in your trading.

If you want to keep track of these indicators yourself, you will need software to do it. There are just too many calculations and too many markets to expect that you can do it by hand. The DeMarks address this problem, though, by providing a list of potential software solution providers in the appendix. This, of course, necessitates having a computer and a pricing service so that you can monitor these setups at all times. However, for the trader who is interested in only a market or two—and these indicators appear to work well on the biggest market: S&P futures (and OEX traders can be included as well)—it *would* be possible to keep the information updated by hand, at least on a daily basis.

The summary chapter is extremely well done, for it ties together the concepts laid out in the more detailed portions of the body of the work. In fact, it is *so* good in describing what the book is about, that you might want to glance at the summary chapter first and *then* delve into the detail of the book.

Overall, I think you will find this book interesting and will also find that it contributes to your profitability, whether you are a day trader using five-minute, ten-minute, or hourly charts, or if you are a short-term trader using daily charts and planning to hold for several days at a time.

Lawrence G. McMillan

Preface

WELL, I STAND CORRECTED. After the completion of each of my first two books, I vowed never again to submit to such an ordeal. Articles, yes; seminars, maybe; but books, no, never. So, now that this work has been completed, I shall make the same statement once more: "never again." I promise—I think. I suppose I knew all along that I would write just one more book. I always felt as if I had so much to say and too little space and time in which to say it, which is probably not a surprise to many of you who know me. But what is different about this book? Why options and why now? You might say my son's involvement in floor trading and then in managing funds, as well as his keen interest in this area of the market were certainly catalysts.

To some of you already familiar with our work, a few of the indicators in this book may seem to be simply a rehash of our previous books and articles, only this time applied to option trading. Believe us, this is not the case. We've developed several option rules and indicators which we are sharing with you for the very first time and have added several additional settings, qualifiers, and applications to our existing library of indicators, all of which have enhanced their efficacy. The indicators discussed in Chaps. 6, 7, 8, and 9 apply to the underlying asset as opposed to the option itself. From these indicators, a trader can apply the results to option trading to identify low risk call buying and put buying opportunities. To other readers unfamiliar with our work or to beginning traders, this is a great place to start. One of the biggest complaints regarding our previous written works has been the perceived complexity of the techniques presented and discussed. We understand this concern; after all, accepting new and unorthodox approaches to market analysis is just plain difficult. Fortunately, this book is a departure from the highly detailed technical writings of the past. Although the ideas discussed in this book have been an ongoing collaborative effort between father and son, the organization and writing skills that T.J. has provided have simplified the descriptions and the explanations of the material. Although unexpected, should you experience difficulty with any aspect of this book, don't be discouraged—just like learning to ride a bicycle, once the skill is acquired, it becomes second nature.

We refer to the information in this book as market timing indicators, not turnkey systems intentionally. The reason for this distinction is that our techniques lack precise entry and exit levels and instead concentrate upon trading opportunity zones. Our goal is simply to provide the components from which traders can select, design, and build their own trading models with which there exists a level of comfort. Our contribution is the various trading concepts and the assortment of trading methodologies from which to choose. We encourage your research and experimentation with the various indicator settings, as well as indicator combinations. It is only through experience and testing that you will acquire an aptitude with these methods.

Now to answer the question many have posed throughout the years. Why does *TD* preface each of our indicators? Believe us when we say it is neither our intentions to promote our initials, nor is there some underhanded mercenary motivation at work here. Our legal counsel advised us to trademark our indicators to ensure proper control of their distribution and to limit our liability should others offer facsimiles for sale and distribution and misrepresent their effectiveness or intended application.

We do not profess to be experts in the intricacies of various option-writing programs and mathematical models. Since being introduced to option trading almost three decades ago, we have been fascinated by these markets. The purchase of options has served as a poor traders' alternative to trading stocks and futures. Most of the techniques we developed specifically for option trading were tested by closely following both the intraday and the daily price activity reported by quote services, as well as option charts we created ourselves. Not until we decided to write this book did we realize that there existed a serious data deficiency within this industry. There was a lack of uniform option data and some of the data which was provided proved to be inconsistent and riddled with errors. Data reliability and availability are two serious industrywide problems. Unfortunately, the data providers with whom we had success specialized in only equity or only futures information, but not both. Fortunately, the occasional errors in data reporting even by these services while conducting tests proved to be tolerable. Consequently, we recommend you observe and monitor closely, the integration of the various data and the techniques before you commence trading.

While we have personally traded and used these indicators successfully over the last 30 years, we feel it is important that you not assume they are infallible. Extraneous factors, such as money management and discipline, also contribute to one's trading success. Each trader has his or her own trading pain threshold and as a result, the location of one's stop losses and profit levels may be different from other traders who may be more or less emotional. Therefore, we stress the importance of not only paper trading each indicator, but also the proper integration of those you especially like into your trading regimen.

Since the majority of our indicators are designed to anticipate trend exhaustion or trend reversals, they may appear unorthodox to some readers of conventional technical analysis. I stress that we are not trend followers; to be one and, at the same time, day trade options is incongruous. We prefer to buck the prevailing market sentiment, intending to anticipate the inflection point where the trend reverses. We believe that this is the only way to day trade options properly. We feel that, at the very least, the market-timing techniques presented in this book will improve a trader's ability to identify ideal low-risk entry levels.

Individually, these indicators may appear intimidating and seem unsuitable for your style of trading. However, given the variability and the diversity of this suite of market-timing tools, inevitably at least a few should comfortably complement various aspects of your trading style. We encourage you to apply them and to experiment with variations of these tools and settings. We've never meant to imply that we are blessed with the Holy Grail of trading indicators; however, we do believe we are on the right track. Assuming your appetite for market-timing research is as voracious as ours, our experience and ideas should enable you to trade more profitably.

Introduction

BEFORE A BABY CAN WALK, it must first learn to crawl. Before the walls of any building can be erected, architectural plans must be prepared and carefully followed to insure a sound foundation is in place. Likewise, before any discussion of techniques to day trade options can be presented, it must be preceded by an explanation of what options are; where and how they are traded; what filters or screens can be used to select option trading candidates and then, once purchased, what techniques can be applied to predict and monitor their price activity; what types of market orders can be placed to execute option trades; what methods can be used to lock in profits and exit trading positions; and what contingencies exist to protect against the inevitable—trading losses. These factors, together with an acute awareness and appreciation for the risks and the rewards associated with trading options, should prepare a prospective trader for this exciting and financially rewarding form of trading.

Within the investment industry, there is a commonly held belief that more than 90 percent of option buyers lose money. The majority of books and courses devoted to the subject of option trading have been written by authors who are convinced that the only way to trade profitably is not to buy options, but rather to write or to sell them based upon a series of complex, mathematical pricing models and strategies. Unfortunately, most of these writers are theoreticians and not active option traders. They fail not only to address the reasons why most option buyers consistently lose money but also to provide methods which can improve a buyer's chances of trading success. Were these authors traders themselves, they would be more inclined to develop option-trading methods that concentrate upon the timely purchase of options with the potential of open-ended profits, rather than merely to rely upon complicated formulas that are designed to control option-trading risk but, at the same time, limit reward. Our experience indicates that these complex approaches serve to intimidate and confuse most traders, discouraging their participation and therefore preventing their chances for trading profits.

Although some option-writing techniques may be profitable, the degree of success traders enjoy is limited to the value of the option at the time the trade is initiated which is a function of market volatility, the underlying security price, and the time remaining before an option's expiration, among other considerations as well. In actuality, trading defensively and adhering to option models and complicated option-writing strategies contradicts the goal of most option traders, which is to leverage their investments and make a significant amount of money within a short period of time. They perceive, we believe incorrectly, that this selling methodology is a safer and a more profitable means of trading than the outright purchase of options. Similarly, we could present theoretical price valuation models that describe option price behavior given various levels of price activity of the underlying security along a specified time spectrum. After all, models are helpful since they are designed to provide a trader with an option-pricing road map. On the other hand, how often has real-time trading conformed to a market model? Not often and especially not in those instances in which traders have relied heavily upon a specific game plan to trade their own accounts aggressively.

We're certain there are a number of excellent books that discuss how to write or sell options and lock in respectable returns. Unfortunately, the option-investing public is often precluded from participating in these trading strategies because the implementation of these techniques requires either a large capital commitment or the possession of the underlying security. As a result, an undercapitalized trading novice is forced to either buy options outright or forego participation in this potentially rewarding trading opportunity. Fortunately, we believe that what may be perceived by some as an inferior and riskier approach to option trading is in reality a preferable form of trading, provided proper guidelines are followed. In other words, we feel that buying options outright without the requirement of, or concern for, complex formula-ridden and capital-intensive methods of writing or selling options can be more rewarding, both financially and emotionally. If you are like we are, you prefer limited risk and unlimited gains and that is precisely the focus of our book.

Despite the multitude of formidable barriers to successful trading, there exist numerous strategies which enable traders to buy and to sell options, even intraday, profitably. These methods are a reasonable and a practical alternative to the sophisticated, hypothetical trading techniques which require large account balances and complex computer-driven market models. We believe all that is required is a basic understanding of the operation of the options markets and a measure of trading discipline and money management skills. This book concentrates upon the presentation of simple, easily understood methods to identify option-trading opportunity zones. Our methodology deemphasizes the commonly accepted practice of selling an option in anticipation of the premium value's decline to zero as time lapses into option expiration. Rather we attempt to provide a disciplined option trader with an open-ended profit potential, since our basic approach merely requires buying and then liquidating an option position at the appropriate time.

Although this book may occasionally describe or refer to various option-writing strategies or trading models, they are incidental to the thrust of our discussion which is to present a number of approaches to successfully buy and day trade options. Certainly, there is nothing to prevent a trader from employing the day-trading techniques presented in this book and then electing to extend the holding period longer than the conclusion of the entry day's trading. The important consideration is to adhere to the application of a mechanical and disciplined approach to both the selection of option-trading candidates and the timing of their purchase.

You've heard the expressions "you're only as good as your last trade," "trading opportunities are like city buses—if you miss one, another will appear shortly," and the ever quoted market nemesis "coulda, woulda, shoulda." (As in, "I *coulda* bought it; if I had, I *woulda* made a lot of money; now that I know this, I *shoulda* bought it.") Each phrase emphasizes the importance of two critical factors often neglected by most traders; namely, discipline and money management. Without proper respect for these elements of successful trading, one is doomed to failure. Obviously, not all trades will be profitable and unless contingencies exist to preserve one's capital against such unforeseen events, trading becomes gambling. Having a systematic approach or a mechanized set of indicators to time entry clearly provides a trader with a distinct advantage over discretionary and emotional trading. This is the basis of our focus. Discipline is an extension of one's psyche and personality, and, although it can be acquired, we view it as more innate. Money management, on the other hand, is a skill which can be taught, but its mastery usually comes with market maturity and experience. This book is not intended to concentrate upon the mechanics of money management or the psychology of a trader but rather to impart a defined set of option-trading rules which should provide the framework required to trade options successfully.

It appears to happen all the time to the uninitiated, inexperienced option trader. Some lucky trader purchases an option anticipating a forthcoming news announcement or development. The expected event occurs and while the underlying security may double in price, the option's value may increase many multiples of that amount. Examples such as these, however, are the exceptions rather than the rule. History confirms that it is much more likely that the value of an option will expire worthless than produce lofty gains such as those described. Just as playing slot machines is usually a losing proposition and the casino's odds of winning are greater than those of the gambler, so too the frequency of failure is much greater than success for option buyers as opposed to option sellers or writers. Unless an option buyer's timing is precise and option-trading methodology is disciplined, trading losses are a foregone conclusion. That is exactly why our emphasis is upon introducing effective methods that will tip the scales in favor of the option buyer.

It's amazing how people will foolishly spend their hard-earned, after-tax dollars on a whim or market rumor. Many traders part with their money without a thorough understanding of how options behave. We believe most option buyers' selection processes are random and driven primarily by emotion. To trade options profitably, it's important that a buyer have an edge over the writers or sellers of options, as well as other option buyers. With the proper trading tools and mindset, a trader should be equipped to establish just such a trading advantage. The techniques we present are certainly not a panacea for all the ailments afflicting option traders. Nevertheless, they should help eliminate the commonly held perception that buying options is a nonreturnable or a nonrefundable form of securities trading. The indicators and option-trading techniques we describe will provide a new, fresh perspective in which to view option trading, all of which should contribute to your trading success. Best wishes for trading profits.

Acknowledgments

THE RESEARCH AND composition of this book have been a joint endeavor, father and son. However, the project would never have been completed were it not for the efforts of Mssrs. Stephen Isaacs and Jeffrey Krames, McGraw-Hill's "good cop, bad cop" team. Their encouragement and direction were a positive influence. The book's copy editor, Christina Palaia from North Market Street Graphics, was instrumental in providing the necessary continuity and editing.

Window on Wall Street (800-998-8439) and CQG (800-525-7082) generously supplied the charts and data presented throughout this book. Deltasoft (Option Oracle)—800-250-7866—was a reliable resource for option data and for the implementation of option trading strategies, as were CSI (800-274-4727) and More Research (514-484-7256).

Once again Duane Davis and his team of programmers and support staff at Financial Software Systems (FSI) (714-731-3384) were invaluable in their support and direction.

Trademarks

ALL OF THE FOLLOWING indicators are registered trademarks and are protected by U.S. Trademark Law. Any unauthorized use without the express written permission of Market Studies, Inc. or Tom DeMark is a violation of the law. They are as follows: TD Absolute Retracement, TD Breakout Qualifiers, TD Camouflage, TD CLOP, TD CLOPWIN, TD Combo, TD Countdown, TD Critical Price, TD Critical Qualifier, TD Demand Line, TD Differential, TD Dollar-Weighted Options, TD Double Retracement, TD Exit One, TD Fibonacci Range, TD Line, TD Magnet Price, TD Open, TD Percentage Factor (TD % F), TD Point, TD Price Oscillator Qualifier (TD POQ), TD Range Expansion Index (TD REI), TD REBO, TD Reverse REBO, TD Relative Retracements, TD Sequential, TD Setup Trend (TDST), TD Supply Line, TD Termination Count, and TD Trap.

1

BACKGROUND

ACLASSMATE INTRODUCED ME to option trading quite by accident over 30 years ago. As a diversion while in law school, our luncheon discussions would inevitably revolve around the stock market. He was a more active trader and was more well-versed in the nuances of trading than I. Usually I would defer to his trading decisions. In one instance, however, I uncovered an attractive trading opportunity that I was confident would produce a sizable profit in a very short period of time. I alerted my friend to its potential and I then placed an order to purchase 1000 shares of stock. I leveraged the purchase of my stock on what I believed to be the best terms possible—entering the trade on margin by writing a check to the brokerage house for approximately 60 percent of the purchase price and financing the balance directly from the broker. Unbeknownst to me, my friend's broker had convinced him to purchase call options, believing that the anticipated news event would be announced in a matter of days and that buying options would maximize his profit in the trade. With approximately the same investment of funds as myself, he bought 100 call options which enabled him to control 10,000 shares of stock. Within days, the stock's price soared 9 points and I realized a profit of $9000. Upon informing my friend of the good news, he indicated that he likewise made a profit in the trade but his return was in excess of $65,000! I was confused by his revelation. I was under the impression that he had not bought the stock outright and he said that my assumption was correct. He indicated that he had purchased call options. I quizzed him regarding the mechanics of trading the option market and his understanding proved to be somewhat vague and unclear. But what did it matter to him? After all, he was able to make a lot of money in a short period of time—over seven times the profit I had realized, having invested approximately the same amount of money as I.

That episode served as a catalyst, inspiring me to acquire as much information about options as possible in order to enable me to participate in this mysterious and profitable form of trading. The dearth of option information was alarming and the little I did uncover was from a different perspective than I had sought. The books in the local library described how to sell or write options on stocks already owned in order to lock in incremental income, as well as for purposes of portfolio insurance against unanticipated moves in stock prices, either upside or downside. However, this was not the trading approach I was seeking. I wanted to acquire methods to evaluate and distinguish between an assortment of option opportunities and then, once selected, to time their purchases. Since no information was available, I was forced to conduct my own research.

The ensuing years of option trading were a period of on-the-job training with the activity of my personal option-trading account playing an important role in this learning process. Countless hours of poring over limited option data brought into focus market tendencies which in turn were reduced to a series of trading rules. Next, a number of trading methods were developed and aggressively applied within the most stringent and unforgiving laboratory conditions imaginable, the marketplace.

During this period of time, option trading was quite primitive. All option trades were conducted over the telephone in what was commonly referred to as the "over-the-counter" option market. The over-the-counter market did not lend itself well to trading. The process of placing option orders was cumbersome and the various methods used to value an option position were incomplete. Prior to 1973, the buyers and the sellers were brought together by a broker since there existed no public marketplace to trade stock options. Once a potential option trade was identified, a broker had to be contacted to locate someone who was willing to take the opposite side of the transaction at the stated conditions. Oftentimes, a broker charged an exorbitant commission to complete this transaction. The expiration period for the option was usually unacceptable since there were only a few fixed choices from which to select. In addition, to liquidate an option, one had to make deep concessions in price or retain a position and exercise it on expiration day, thereby incurring an unnecessary commission expense.

The year 1973 marked the formation of an entirely new public marketplace for the trading of options. The Chicago Board of Options Exchange (CBOE) established a standardized format for trading options and provided a common meeting place where buyers and sellers could agree upon a transaction price. The CBOE changed the casual, ineffective method of trading options and opened a new and modern avenue for trading options. No longer was it necessary to pay the high commissions required to match a buyer and a seller and the need to commit to unacceptable terms was eliminated as well. Market makers served to facilitate customer orders by providing liquidity to the various markets, much like the activity specialists on the major stock exchanges do. After years of studying and actively trading options in the over-the-counter market, I was excited about this fledgling exchange's potential and even applied for trading membership in 1973. Unfortunately, at the time I was employed by a large financial institution and the partners frowned upon my participation in what was perceived by many to be a speculative investment. Consequently, I had to abandon any aspirations I may have had to trade these markets from the floor of the exchange. I was relegated to the same status as any off-the-floor trader who was obligated to operate through a broker.

From its modest beginnings, the CBOE has grown from a marketplace for a small list of call options, strike prices, and expiration months representing 16 major corporations to a massive list of companies with call options, put options, and a full calendar of expiration months and strike prices. Initially, the CBOE listed call options on only a handful of the country's largest companies, such as AT&T, Eastman Kodak, and Avon Products, and only with limited strike prices and an expiration series of January, April, July, and October. Things quickly grew, with the majority of the New York Stock Exchange (NYSE) companies soon represented on the exchange. Eventually, other stocks listed on the American Stock Exchange and on the NASDAQ were added to the growing list of option names. Other option series with alternating expiration months of February, May, August, and November and March, June, September, and December were included to complement the original calendar of expirations and complete the full year. About the same time, the American Stock Exchange, the Pacific Stock Exchange, and the Philadelphia Stock Exchange began to introduce their own listed options in an effort to compete with the CBOE and capitalize on the growing success and acceptance of options trading. Competition among these exchanges produced a quick and massive overhaul within the options market. Option expirations were extended years into the future; the selection of strike prices was increased; the population and the variety of options available were increased; the option pool was expanded from simply individual stocks to industry groups and market indices; and exchanges experimented with new products, such as currency, financial, and commodity options. Eventually, practically all actively traded markets had listed options. The reception by the trading community and the growth of these exchanges exceeded traders' most optimistic forecasts. The initial expectation that option trading was too risky and would not attract a serious following was dispelled quickly. Large and well-respected financial institutions removed the political and regulatory barriers which had previously existed and precluded their involvement in the options market and they immediately became a formidable force in selling and writing options. These large traders viewed option writing or selling as a way to enhance the performance of their portfolios with incremental gains and as a low-cost means to protect their portfolios from unexpected news events. However, despite the tremendous response and the enormous appetite for option trading expressed by both the public and large traders alike, investment literature was still short on information on how to best utilize options as a trading vehicle.

Throughout the subsequent years, a handful of books were written by noted experts in the field of options. In particular books authored by Larry McMillan have provided an excellent overview of the options markets, as well as specific information as to how to compile a library of effective option-writing programs. His books are directed toward the professional audience and draw upon Mr. McMillan's vast experience in dealing with options, both as a trader and as an instructor over the past 30 years. The information he provides is invaluable to the large institutional option writers who wish to increase market performance and buy cheap insurance protection for their portfolios against unexpected financial disasters. He does acknowledge the plight of the small individual option trader by addressing various trading strategies intended for this trading segment of the market but the methods he suggests are not specifically designed for intraday and very short term trading. Furthermore being aware of the enormous risks associated with option trading, his approach is more subdued and defensive in nature than our more aggressive quick "in-and-out" trading posture. We prefer to concentrate our attention upon a series of methods we have developed to time the intraday purchase and liquidation of options. We're convinced that if the proper rules and techniques are followed and applied, the most difficult part of day trading options—the timing of purchases—can be simplified immensely.

The majority of our indicators are anti-trend or trend-anticipatory methods which will enable an alert option buyer to enter a market just as an existing trend is about to reverse and a new trend is about to begin. For those indicators that are not, when various trades are qualified, the techniques we present can be viewed as objective refinements to traditional trend-following approaches. The methods we present can be used individually or in combination with one another. Although effective in identifying low-risk trend-following opportunities, we stress their value in predicting pending price reversals. Once the concepts have been fully understood, the only obstacle to trading success becomes an option trader's ability to combine the methods and to introduce a level of discipline into his or her trading regimen.

OPTION BASICS

2

OPTION BASICS

*F*OR MANY YEARS, *options have been a means of conveying rights from one party to another at a specified price on or before a specific date. Options to buy and sell are commonly executed in real estate and equipment transactions, just as they have been for years in the securities markets. There are two types of option agreements: calls and puts. A* call *option is a contract that conveys to the owner the right, but not the obligation, to purchase a prescribed number of shares or futures contracts of an underlying security at a specified price before or on a specific expiration date. A* put *option is a contract that conveys to the owner the right, but not obligation, to sell a prescribed number of shares or futures contracts of an underlying security at a specified price before or on a specific expiration date. Consequently, if the market in a security were expected to advance, a trader would purchase a call and, conversely, if the market in a security were expected to decline, a trader would purchase a put. With the advent of listed options, the inconvenience and difficulties originally associated with transacting options have been greatly diminished.*

INTRODUCTION TO BASICS

We all know many opportunities exist in trading today. Everywhere you turn, someone is waiting to inform you of the tremendous profits to be realized in the stock and futures markets. However, many people are unaware of the derivative trading possibilities which are available within and across several different markets. Option trading is just one of the many ways to participate in these secondary markets. And contrary to popular belief, this potential trading arena is not limited strictly to the practice of selling or writing options.

Options are an important element of investing in markets, serving a function of managing risk and generating income. Unlike most other types of investments today, options provide a unique set of benefits. Not only does option trading provide a cheap and effective means of hedging one's portfolio against adverse and unexpected price fluctuations, but it also offers a tremendous speculative dimension to trading. One of the primary advantages of option trading is that option contracts enable a trade to be leveraged, allowing the trader to control the full value of an asset for a fraction of the actual cost. And since an option's price mirrors that of the underlying asset at the very least, any favorable return in the asset will be met with a greater percentage return in the option. Another major benefit of outright buying options is that an option provides limited risk and unlimited reward. With options, the buyer can only lose what was paid for the option contract, which is a fraction of what the actual cost of the asset would be. However, the profit potential is unlimited because the option holder possesses a contract that performs in sync with the asset itself. If the outlook is positive for the security, so too will the outlook be for that asset's underlying options. Options also provide their owners with numerous trading alternatives. Options can be customized and combined with other options and even other investments to take advantage of any possible price dislocation within the market. They enable the trader or investor to acquire a position that is appropriate for any type of market outlook that he or she may have, be it bullish, bearish, choppy, or silent.

While there is no disputing that options offer many investment benefits, option trading involves risk and is not for everyone. For the same reason that one's returns can be large, so too can the losses—leverage. Also, while the potential for financial success does exist in option trading, the means of realizing such opportunities are often difficult to create and to identify. With dozens of variables, several pricing models, and hundreds of different strategies to choose from, it is no wonder that options and option pricing have been a mystery to the majority of the trading public. Most often, a great deal of information must be processed before an informed trading decision can be reached. Computers and sophisticated trading models are often relied upon to select trading candidates. However, as humans, we like things to be as simple as possible. This often creates a conflict when deciding what, when, and how to trade a particular investment. It is much easier to buy or sell an asset outright than to contend with the many extraneous factors of these derivative markets.* If an investor thinks an asset's value will appreciate, he or she can simply buy the security; if an investor thinks an asset's value will depreciate, he or she can simply sell the security. In these scenarios, the only thing an investor must worry about is the value of the investment relative to the value of the prevailing market. If only options were that easy!

---

* A *derivative security* is any security, in whole or in part, the value of which is based upon the performance of another (underlying) instrument, such as an option, a warrant, or any hybrid securities.

Typically, option trading is more cumbersome and complicated than stock trading because traders must consider many variables aside from the direction they believe the market will move. The effects of the passage of time, variables such as delta, and the underlying market volatility on the price of the option are just some of the many items that traders need to gauge in order to make informed decisions. If one is not prudent in one's investment decisions, one could potentially lose a lot of money trading options. Those who disregard careful consideration and sound money management techniques often find out the hard way that these factors can quickly and easily erode the value of their option portfolios.

Because of these risks and benefits, options offer tremendous profit potential above and beyond trading in any other instrument, including the underlying security itself. This is the juncture at which option theoreticians enter the picture. Once the benefits have been defined, it is now a matter of determining how to best attain them. Up to now, the vast majority of option techniques have been elaborate mathematical models designed to help identify when option-writing or -selling opportunities exist. However, we hope to break new ground by introducing simple market-timing techniques that will enable traders to buy options with greater confidence and with greater success.

WHAT IS AN OPTION?

Before we devote our attention to more sophisticated option applications, it is important that we introduce a basic option foundation. While this introduction to options will be descriptive in its scope, its coverage will by no means be exhaustive. The sheer magnitude of option terminology and strategy could comprise an entire book on its own, and that is not our primary focus. We understand you did not buy this book to read the DeMarks on basic option definitions. For us to give our interpretation of existing material is much like making an entire career out of singing covers of popular songs of the past. And while it may work for Michael Bolton, we don't feel it works for us. Therefore, we will only be addressing the items necessary to understanding option basics and the techniques we will be presenting throughout the book. This simple introduction is tailored to those who are unfamiliar with options; for many, this chapter will simply be a review.

Whether they apply to stocks, indices, or futures, all options work in the same manner. Simply stated, an *option* is a financial instrument that allows the owner the right, but not the obligation, to acquire or to sell a predetermined number of shares of stock or futures contracts in a particular asset at a fixed price on or before a specified date. With each option contract, the holder can make any of three possible choices: exercise the option and obtain a position in the underlying asset; trade the option, closing out the trader's position in the contract by performing an offsetting trade; or let the option expire if the contract lacks value at expiration, losing only what was paid for the option. We will discuss the benefits and implications of each action later in this chapter.

Option contracts are identified using quantity, asset, expiration date, strike price, type, and premium. With the exception of the option's premium, each of these items is standardized upon issuance of a listed option contract. In other words, once an option contract is created, its rights are static; the price that one would pay for those rights is not; it is dynamic and determined by market forces. Seeing as there are many items which make up the definition of an option contract, it is important that each be addressed before moving on.

The first aspect of an option contract is the option's *quantity*. The number of shares or contracts that can be obtained upon exercising an exchange-listed option contract is standardized. Each stock option contract allows the holder of that option to control 100 shares of the underlying security while each futures option contract can be exercised to obtain one contract in the underlying futures contract.*

Another item that identifies the option contract is the asset itself. The *asset* refers to the type of investment that can be obtained by the option holder. This asset could be a futures contract, shares of stock in a company, or a cash settlement in the case of an index contract.

The *type* of option is critical in determining the trader's market outlook. Unlike trading stocks or futures themselves, option trading is not simply being long a particular market or short a particular market. Rather, there are two types of options, *call options* and *put options,* and two sides to each type, long or short, allowing the trader to take any of four possible positions. One can buy a call, sell a call, buy a put, sell a put, or any combination thereof. It is important to understand that trading call options is completely separate from trading put options. For every call buyer there is a call seller; while for every put buyer there is a put seller. Also keep in mind that option buyers have rights, while option sellers have obligations. For this reason, option buyers have a defined level of risk and option sellers have unlimited risk.

A *call option* is a standardized contract that gives the buyer the right, but not the obligation, to purchase a specific number of shares or contracts of an underlying security at the option's strike price, or exercise price, sometime before the expiration date of the contract. Buying a call contract is similar to taking a long position in the underlying asset, and one would purchase a call option if one believed that the market value of the asset was going to appreciate before the date the option expires. The most a trader can lose by purchasing a call option is simply the price that he or she pays for the option; the most the trader can make is unlim-

---

* Futures are leveraged assets typically representing a large, standardized quantity of an underlying security which expire at some predetermined date in the future. Each futures option contract allows the holder to control the total number of units that comprise the futures contract until the option is liquidated, but no later than its expiration date.

ited. On the other side of the transaction, the seller, or writer, of a call option has the obligation, not the right, to sell a specific number of shares or contracts of an asset to the option buyer at the strike price, if the option is exercised prior to its expiration date. Selling a call contract acts as a proxy for a short position in the underlying asset, and one would sell a call option if one expected that the market value of the asset would either decline or move sideways. (See Payoff Diagram 2.1.) The most an option seller can make on the trade is the price he or she initially receives for the option contract; the most the trader can lose is unlimited. In order to offset a long position in a call option contract, one must sell a call option of the same quantity, type, expiration date, and strike price. Similarly, in order to offset a short position in a call option contract, one must buy a call option of the same quantity, type, expiration date, and strike price.

A *put option* is a standardized contract that gives the buyer the right, but not the obligation, to sell a predetermined number of shares or contracts of an under-lying security at the option's strike price, or exercise price, sometime before the expiration date of the contract. A put contract is similar to taking a short position in the underlying asset, and one could purchase a put option contract if one believed that the market price of the asset was going to decline at some point before the date the option expires. The most a trader can lose by purchasing a put option is simply the price that he or she pays for the option; the most the trader can make is unlimited (in reality, it is the full value of the underlying asset which is realized if its price declines to zero). Conversely, the seller, or writer, of a put option has the obligation, not the right, to buy a specific number of shares or con-tracts of an asset to the option buyer at the strike price, assuming the option is exer-cised prior to its expiration date. Selling a put contract acts as a substitute for a long position in the underlying asset, and a trader would sell a put contract if he or she expected the market value of the asset to either increase or move sideways. Again, the most an option seller can make on the trade is the price he or she initially receives for the option contract; the most the seller can lose is unlimited (in reality, the most one can lose is the full value of the underlying asset which is realized if its price declines to zero). (See Payoff Diagram 2.2.) In order to offset a long posi-tion in a put option contract, one must sell a put option of the same quantity, type, expiration date, and strike price. Similarly, in order to offset a short position in a put option contract, one must buy a put option of the same quantity, type, expira-tion date, and strike price.

Just remember, call buyers want the market price of the underlying security to go higher so the option will gain in value and they can make money; and call writ-ers want the market to go sideways or lower so the option will expire worthless and they can make money. Put buyers want the market price of the underlying security to go lower so the option can gain in value and they can make money; and put sell-ers want the market price to go higher or sideways so the option will expire worth-

PAYOFF DIAGRAM 2.1   Profit diagrams for a long call and a short call.

LONG CALL

OUTLOOK = BULLISH
S = STRIKE PRICE
BEP = BREAK-EVEN POINT = S + DR
DR = DEBIT = INITIAL OPTION COST = MAXIMUM LOSS
MAXIMUM GAIN = UNLIMITED

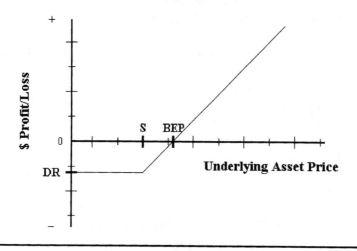

SHORT CALL

OUTLOOK = BEARISH
S = STRIKE PRICE
BEP = BREAK-EVEN POINT = S + CR
CR = CREDIT = INITIAL OPTION PAYMENT RECEIVED = MAXIMUM GAIN
MAXIMUM LOSS = UNLIMITED

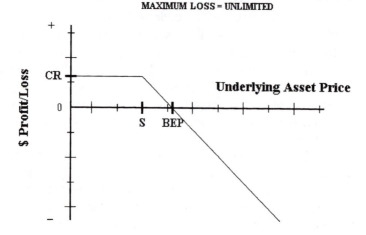

PAYOFF DIAGRAM 2.2   Profit diagrams for a long put and a short put.

LONG PUT

OUTLOOK = BEARISH
S = STRIKE PRICE
BEP = BREAK-EVEN POINT = S − DR
DR = DEBIT = INITIAL OPTION COST = MAXIMUM LOSS
MAXIMUM GAIN = UNLIMITED

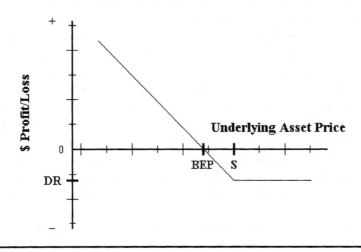

SHORT PUT

OUTLOOK = BULLISH
S = STRIKE PRICE
BEP = BREAK-EVEN POINT = S − CR
CR = CREDIT = INITIAL OPTION PAYMENT RECEIVED = MAXIMUM GAIN
MAXIMUM LOSS = UNLIMITED

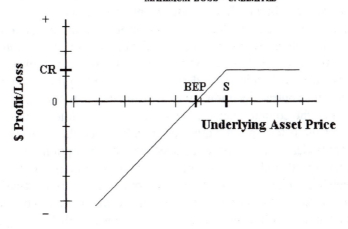

less and they can make money. Also remember, option buyers can choose whether they wish to exercise their options; option sellers cannot.

The *strike price* or exercise price is simply the price at which the underlying security can be obtained or sold if one were to exercise the option. For a call option, the strike price is the price at which the holder can buy the security from the option writer upon exercising the option. For a put option, the strike price is the price at which the holder can sell the security to the option writer upon exercising the option. These option strike prices are standardized, with the strike increments determined by the asset's price. For most stocks with a market value between $25 and $200, listed option strike prices are issued in 5-point increments nearest to the price of the stock. For stocks that trade below $25, option strike prices are separated into 2½-point increments; for those that trade above $200, strike prices are graduated into 10-point intervals. Newly created contracts can only be issued with strike prices that straddle the current market price of the security; however, at any one time, several different previously existing strike prices trade on the open option market. Which of the standardized strike prices the trader chooses depends upon his or her investment needs and capital outlay. Obviously, depending upon the prevailing underlying market price, the rights to some option strike prices will cost more than others.

Strike prices for futures options contracts are different than those for stock options. Much like options on stock, the trader can choose from any of the standardized futures option strike prices that are issued. However, the strike prices that are set for the futures options are more contract-specific, contingent upon the market price of the underlying contract, how the future is priced, and how it trades. For obvious reasons, the issued strike prices for Treasury bond options will be different than those for soybean options. Because strikes vary depending on the commodity, it is important that traders familiarize themselves with the option contract and the underlying security before they initiate an option position.

The *expiration date* refers to the length of time through which the option contract and its rights are active. At any time up to and including the expiration date, the holder of an option is entitled to the contract's benefits, which include exercising the option (taking a position in the underlying asset), trading the option (closing one's position in the contract by trading it away to another individual), or letting it expire worthless (if the contract lacks value at expiration). While the trader can choose from any of the listed option expiration months he or she wishes to purchase (or sell), the trader cannot choose the specific date the option will expire. This date is standardized and is determined when the option is listed on the exchange on which it is traded. For most options on equity securities, the final trading day occurs on the third Friday of each month. The actual expiration occurs the following day, the Saturday following the third Friday of the month. The expiration date for futures options is more complicated than that for stock options and depends upon the contract that is being traded. Some futures option contracts expire the Saturday before the third Wednesday of the expiration month while others expire the month before the expiration month. Since an option's expiration date depends upon the type of asset that is traded, it is important for a trader to know the specific date the contract will expire before investing in the option.

The majority of listed options are issued with expiration dates approximately nine months into the future. In addition to these standard options, there are also options that possess a longer life than the nine-month maximum for regular stock options. These are called *long-term equity anticipation options,* or LEAPS. LEAPS are issued each January with an expiration up to 36 months into the future. LEAPS allow traders to position themselves for market movement that is expected over a longer period of time: weeks, months, even years. They are more expensive than standard options because the added life increases the likelihood that the option will have value at some point prior to expiration. However, LEAPS can be traded only on stocks, indices, and interest rate classes and not every security offers them.

There are also two option styles that are important in determining when a trader can exercise the option contract to obtain a position in the underlying instrument: European-style and American-style options. *European-style* options are options that can only be exercised at the end of their life. They can be traded at any time, but they cannot be exercised until the contract's final trading day. The more common type of option in the U.S. markets is *American-style* options. These options can be traded or exercised at any point during their lifetime. As you can see, American-style options allow the trader more flexibility and freedom.

There is one additional factor that is crucial to determining the value of an option contract called the option's premium. The *premium* is simply the price the option buyer must pay to the option seller for the rights to the option contract. Premium is the only variable of an option and is determined by the forces of supply and demand for both the underlying instrument and for the option itself. As the market price of the underlying asset fluctuates, the premium adjusts to reflect the change in value. Premium is quoted on a unit basis and the dollar equivalent is determined by the number of units that make up the contract. The option premium trades in the same units as the underlying security but typically at a much lower price than that of the asset (for example, an equity option might cost $5 per share, while the underlying stock is trading at a price of $75 per share); please note that an option premium's price per unit will always be less than the asset's price per unit because the premium is the amount the trader must pay for the rights to the option contract, not for the rights to the asset itself. This premium is simply the value of the option. This feature of options allows the trader to control the full value of the underlying asset for a fraction of the actual cost.

In the case of stock options, the premium is quoted on a dollar-per-share amount. Since each stock option contract allows the option holder to control 100 shares of the stock, the cost of an option would be the number of shares multiplied by the premium's price quote. Therefore, if a stock option has a premium of 5, or $5 per share, the cost to the option purchaser would be $500 ($5 × 100). Stock premiums less than 3 points are quoted in one-sixteenths of a point, while premiums above 3 points are quoted in one-eighths of a point.

Calculating the total cost of a futures option contract is more complicated and is a function of the commodity in question and the number of units that comprise each contract. As is the case with equity options, the premium for a futures option is also quoted on a dollar-value-per-unit basis. To arrive at the total cost of the option to the trader one must multiply the cost per unit by the total number of units in the futures contract. Remember that each futures option contract entitles the option holder to one futures contract upon exercising the option and each contract represents a much greater number of units. Wheat futures option premiums, for example, are quoted in cents per bushel with each wheat futures contract (and therefore wheat futures option contract) made up of 5000 bushels. If a trader were quoted a premium of 12½, or 12½ cents per bushel, for the option contract, the total cost to the option buyer would be $625 ($0.125 × 5000). The increments in which futures option premiums are quoted also depend upon the futures option contract that is being traded.

In order to complete an option transaction, an option buyer must pay the option seller a premium for the rights to the contract. Without this premium, there exists no incentive for the seller to take on the risk of departing with the underlying security. Once this payment is made by the option buyer, the funds belong to the option writer and the transaction between them is irrevocable. Whether the option expires worthless or is exercised, the option buyer is unable to recover any portion of his or her option payment from the writer. However, an option buyer does possess the ability to trade the option's rights to another purchaser. The premium that the individual would receive by selling these rights to another would be enough to cover some, all, or more than the initial cost for the option. An easy way to look at things is to treat an option like most other physical goods. Once the buyer pays for the good, the buyer owns it for the rest of its lifetime and, for the most part, cannot get his or her money back. The only way for the individual to recover any of the initial cost is to sell the good to someone else.

Now that we have addressed each option factor thoroughly, let's bring this information together and examine a call scenario and a put scenario with the information we have presented thus far. An example of a stock option order would be something like, "Buy 1 MSFT Dec 90 Call @ $6." In this example, the customer wishes to purchase one Microsoft call contract with a $90 strike price and a December expiration month at a price of $6 per option, for a total of $600. In other words, by paying $600 for the option contract, the option buyer has obtained the right but not the obligation to purchase 100 shares of Microsoft stock at a price of

$90 any time before the contract expires in December, regardless of the price at which Microsoft stock is trading. The perspective of the option writer is different from that of the option buyer. The option writer's order would read, "Sell 1 MSFT Dec 90 Call @ $6." By writing the option, the trader agrees to sell one Microsoft call contract with a $90 strike price and a December expiration month at a price of $6 per option, for a total of $600, to the call buyer. The $600 that the seller receives for the transaction is payment for relinquishing the rights of the option contract. If the owner of the option chooses to exercise the contract sometime before its expiration date in December, the writer is now obligated to sell the buyer 100 shares of Microsoft stock at a price of $90, regardless of where Microsoft stock is currently trading. Obviously, the option holder would choose to exercise the option if it were profitable for him or her to do so, meaning the contract has value and the individual wishes to take a long position in the underlying security. (See Payoff Diagram 2.3.) If either trader's market outlook were to change, they could offset their position by taking the opposite side of their initial trade.

A futures option order would look something like, "Buy 2 Soybean Nov 550 Puts @ 17." In this case, the customer wishes to purchase two soybean put option contracts with a $5.50 per bushel strike price and a November expiration month at a price of 17 cents per bushel. Since each soybean futures contract is made up of 5000 bushels, the cost to the option buyer is $850 per contract ($0.17 × 5000), or $1700 total ($850 × 2). By paying $1700 to the option seller, the option holder has the right, not the obligation, to sell two soybean futures contracts to the option writer at a price of $5.50 per bushel at any time before the option expires in November, regardless of the price at which the soybean market is trading.* The opposite side of this order would be, "Sell 2 Soybean Nov 550 Puts @ 17." Here the option writer agrees to sell two soybean put option contracts with a $5.50 strike price and a November expiration month to the option buyer at a price of $1700. If the option is exercised prior to expiration in November, the writer is obligated to purchase two soybean futures contracts from the put option buyer at $5.50 per bushel, regardless of where the soybean market is trading at the time. For offering this benefit, the option writer receives a payment of $1700. Again, the holder would only choose to exercise the option if it were profitable to do so and either party can offset their position by trading the opposite side of their initial transaction. (See Payoff Diagram 2.4.)

OPTION PRICING

As we mentioned earlier, an option's price, or premium, is the only option value that can fluctuate. And as is the case with any investment, price varies according to

---

* For those of you unfamiliar with futures, they are highly leveraged assets which trade on margin. The investor is not responsible for putting up the full dollar value of the futures contract, just a small portion of the full value.

PAYOFF DIAGRAM 2.3   Profit diagrams for the Microsoft Dec 90 call example.

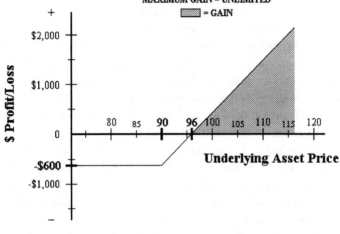

LONG CALL
BUY 1 MSFT DEC 90 CALL @ 6
OUTLOOK = BULLISH
S = STRIKE PRICE = $90
BEP = BREAK-EVEN POINT = $96
DR = DEBIT = MAXIMUM LOSS = $600
MAXIMUM GAIN = UNLIMITED
▨ = GAIN

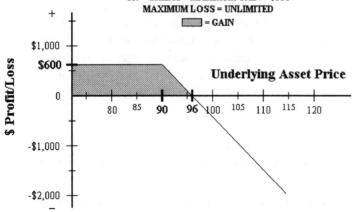

SHORT CALL
SELL 1 MSFT DEC 90 CALL @ 6
OUTLOOK = BEARISH
S = STRIKE PRICE = $90
BEP = BREAK-EVEN POINT = $96
CR = CREDIT = MAXIMUM GAIN = $600
MAXIMUM LOSS = UNLIMITED
▨ = GAIN

PAYOFF DIAGRAM 2.4   Profit diagrams for the soybean Nov 550 put example.

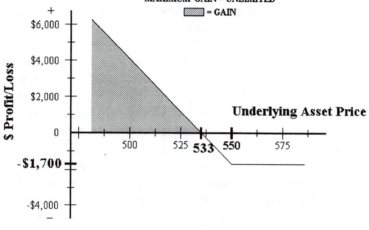

LONG PUT

BUY 2 SOYBEAN NOV 550 PUTS @ 17

OUTLOOK = BEARISH
S = STRIKE PRICE = $5.50
BEP = BREAK-EVEN POINT = $5.33
DR = DEBIT = MAXIMUM LOSS = $1,700
MAXIMUM GAIN = UNLIMITED

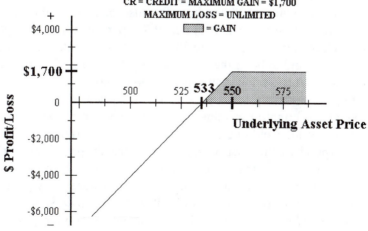

SHORT PUT

SELL 2 SOYBEAN NOV 550 PUTS @ 17

OUTLOOK = BULLISH
S = STRIKE PRICE = $5.50
BEP = BREAK-EVEN POINT = $5.33
CR = CREDIT = MAXIMUM GAIN = $1,700
MAXIMUM LOSS = UNLIMITED

market information and other external factors that affect supply and demand. Pricing of an option is somewhat different than the pricing of other investments. An option's price is defined as

$$\text{Option Premium} = \text{Intrinsic Value} + \text{Time Value}$$

Although this seems to be a simple and straightforward mathematical equation, you'd be surprised to learn that pricing options is a very complicated task, what with the many factors that make up these two components. While it may not be crucial to know the exact value of each factor that affects an option's price, it is important to understand the impact they have upon the value of the contract over time.

Intrinsic value and time value are most influenced by such factors as the time to option expiration, asset volatility, dividend rates, interest rates, delta and gamma, and the difference between the strike price and the underlying price. Of the two components of option pricing, intrinsic value is an objective measure while time value is more subjective, encompassing everything that intrinsic value doesn't.

The first component of an option's price is its *intrinsic value* or what is also known as fair value. An option's intrinsic value is the only pricing factor that is discernible; it is simply the difference between the strike price and the market price of the underlying asset. This comparison indicates whether the option is considered in-the-money, at-the-money, or out-of-the-money. An option is *in-the-money* if it has intrinsic value and *out-of-the-money* if it does not have intrinsic value.

In the case of a call option, if the strike price is less than the market price of the underlying asset, then the call option has intrinsic value and is said to be in-the-money. The intrinsic value is the amount that the option is considered to be in-the-money. Premium will always be worth the intrinsic value of the option at the very least. The portion of an option's premium that is left unexplained by intrinsic value is devoted to time value. For example, suppose a trader buys 1 DIS July 30 Call @ $5 when Disney stock is trading at $33 per share. Because the option holder has the right to buy 100 shares of Disney stock at a price of $30 per share from the option writer when the stock is worth $33 per share, the call option has intrinsic value of $3 per share and is also said to be in-the-money by $3. The other $2 of premium that is unexplained by intrinsic value is attributed to time value.

When a call option's strike price is greater than the price of the underlying asset, then the option has no intrinsic value and is said to be out-of-the-money. In this case, the intrinsic value would be zero because the option rights provide no benefits—one could purchase the asset at a higher price than the prevailing market. Intrinsic value will never be less than zero because a long option position cannot have a negative value. In cases when an option is out-of-the-money, any premium is considered to be time value. If a trader buys 1 DIS July 30 Call @ $2 when Disney stock is trading at $27 per share, the call would be out-of-the-money because it enables the trader to purchase 100 shares of Disney stock at $30 per share while the stock is trading at a lower price of $27 per share. Because there is no intrinsic value, the $2 premium is devoted entirely to time value.

When the call option's strike price is equal to the market price of the underlying security, the option is said to be *at-the-money.* In this scenario, the option has no intrinsic value and any premium is due to time value. Suppose a trader buys 1 DIS July 30 Call @ $3 when Disney stock is trading at $30 per share. The option gives the holder the right to buy 100 shares of Disney stock at $30 per share when the market is trading at $30 per share, so the option is trading at-the-money. In this example, the intrinsic value would be zero and the time value would be $3.

In the case of a put option, if the strike price is greater than the market price of the underlying security, then the put option has intrinsic value and is said to be in-the-money. Again, the intrinsic value is the nominal amount by which the option is in-the-money. Also, to reiterate, premium will always be worth at least the intrinsic value of the option and the portion of the premium that is left unexplained by intrinsic value is devoted to time value. For example, suppose a trader buys 1 DIS July 30 Put @ $5 when Disney stock is trading at $27 per share. Because the option holder can sell 100 shares of Disney stock at $30 per share to the option writer while the stock is trading at a lower price of $27 per share, the put option has intrinsic value of $3. The option is also said to be $3 in-the-money. The $2 of premium that is unexplained by intrinsic value is attributed to time value.

When a put option's strike price is less than the price of the underlying market price, then the option has no intrinsic value and the option is said to be out-of-the-money. In this case, the intrinsic value would be zero because if one were to exercise the option at that time, one would be entitled to sell the asset at a lower price than the prevailing market. In cases where a put option is out-of-the-money, all of the option's premium is considered to be time value. If a trader buys 1 DIS July 30 Put @ $2 when Disney stock is trading at $33 per share, the call would be out-of-the-money because there is no intrinsic value. The put enables the trader to sell 100 shares of Disney stock at $30 per share while the stock is trading at a higher price of $33 per share. Since there is no intrinsic value, the full $2 premium is time value.

Finally, when a put option's strike price is equal to the market price of the underlying security, the option is said to be at-the-money. In this case, the option has no intrinsic value and all of the option premium is derived from time value. Suppose a trader buys 1 DIS July 30 Put @ $3 when Disney stock is trading at $30 per share. The option gives the holder the right to sell 100 shares of Disney stock at $30 per share when the market is trading at $30 per share, so the option is trading at-the-money. In this example, the intrinsic value would be zero and the time value would account for the full value of the premium.

Bear in mind that in-the-money, out-of-the-money, and at-the-money are all stated from the option holder's perspective. Also, as a contract moves in-the-money, an option's premium will increase to reflect the increase in value. As a contract moves out-of-the-money, an option's premium will decrease to reflect the decrease in value. Intrinsic value is very important to an option's price and must always be equivalent to its premium, at the very least. If it were not, investors would recognize the arbitrage possibility and the option could be used to create an instant profit with no risk, whatsoever.

As we mentioned, an option's premium will change with fluctuations in the price of the underlying asset. How much of an increase or a decrease in the premium that can be expected with these changes in intrinsic value depends upon an option's delta and gamma. While delta and gamma are important to many traders, they are not crucial to the information we will present throughout the book, and for that reason we will simply cover the bare essentials. Delta and gamma provide a rough measurement of how sensitive option price movements are to price changes in the underlying security. *Delta* is defined as the amount by which the price of an option changes for every dollar move in the underlying asset. *Gamma,* on the other hand, is defined as the degree by which the delta changes in response to changes in the underlying instrument's price. Therefore, when the price of an asset changes, delta explains what should happen to the option's premium while gamma explains what should happen to the option's delta. Between delta and gamma, delta is the more important and telling of the two. In general, delta increases as an option moves in-the-money and decreases as an option moves out-of-the-money.

The delta of a call option is a number that fluctuates between 0.00 and 1.00. Also, the greater the delta, the more the option premium will react to a given move in the underlying asset. If one were to follow the tendencies of options with different values, one would find that delta increases as an option goes from deeply out-of-the-money to deep in-the-money. Very deep out-of-the-money call options have a delta of 0.00, meaning that even if the price of the underlying asset were to rise by one point, the option's value would be unaffected. Call options that are out-of-the-money, but not dramatically so, have smaller deltas, such as 0.25. This means that for every one-point move in the price of the underlying asset, the price of the option should increase by ¼ of a point. Call options that are at-the-money have deltas that are slightly larger than the middle of the range because the assets they cover can move more to the upside than they can to the downside. These options have deltas somewhere around 0.55 to 0.60, which means that for every one-point move in the price of the underlying asset, the price of the option should increase by a little more than ½ of a point. Call options that are in-the-money, but not dramatically so, have larger deltas around 0.75 and behave more like the underlying asset. In this case, for every one-point move in the price of the underlying asset, the price of the option should increase by ¾ of a point. Finally, for very deep in-the-money call options, delta equals 1.00, meaning for every one-point move in the price of the underlying asset, the option premium will move by one point. As you could imagine, strike prices that are much higher than the prevailing asset price (which would be out-of-the-money) will have a lower delta because they have less chance of expiring in-the-money.

The delta of a put option is just the opposite of that for a call option and is a number that fluctuates between 0.00 and −1.00. In this case, the lower or more negative the delta, the more the option premium will react to a given move in the underlying asset. Again, if one were to follow the tendencies of options that possess different values, one would find that delta increases as an option goes from deeply out-of-the-money to deep in-the-money. Very deep out-of-the-money put options have a delta of 0.00, meaning that even if the price of the underlying asset were to decline by one point, the option's value would not change. Put options that are out-of-the-money, but not dramatically so, have smaller deltas, such as −0.25. This means that for every one-point decline in the price of the underlying asset, the price of the option should increase by ¼ of a point. Put options that are at-the-money have deltas that are slightly less than the middle of the range because the assets they cover can move more to the upside than they can to the downside. These options have deltas somewhere around −0.40 to −0.45. This means that for every one-point decline in the price of the underlying asset, the price of the option should rise by a little less than ½ of a point. Put options that are in-the-money, but not dramatically so, have larger deltas around −0.75 and, again, behave more like the underlying asset. In this case, for every one-point decline in the underlying asset, the price of the option should increase by ¾ of a point. Finally, for very deep in-the-money put options, delta equals −1.00, meaning for every one-point decline in the price of the underlying asset, the option premium will increase by one point. As you could imagine, strike prices that are much lower than the prevailing asset price (which would be out-of-the-money) will have a lower delta because they have a lower chance of expiring in-the-money.

One should also understand that as time passes, the delta of an out-of-the-money option will move toward zero. Conversely, as time passes, the delta of an in-the-money option will move toward its maximum of 1.00 for call options and −1.00 for put options.

The second major component of an option's price is referred to as *time value* or time premium. These may be slight misnomers in the premium equation because, in reality, many factors are lumped together into this variable. Time value accounts not only for the amount of time that is left before an option expires, but for everything else that intrinsic value does not. In this sense, time value can be explained as the amount that option buyers are willing to pay for the protective benefits provided by the option. Taken by itself, time premium is the effect that time has upon the value of an option contract. The greater the *time to expiration,* the greater the chance that the option will move in-the-money. Buyers will be willing to pay more for the rights to an option with a distant expiration month because they are entitled to the benefits for a longer period of time, and writers will be willing to sell an option with a distant expiration month at a higher premium because they face a longer period of risk. Therefore, the more time remaining until expiration, the greater the price. Naturally, an option with a closer expiration date will have less time to move in-the-money and will therefore command a lower premium.

As time passes, an option's time value will decrease. One important thing to keep in mind is that time decay is not linear. As an option approaches expiration, its time value erodes more and more quickly because there is less time for the option to move in-the-money. Clearly, losing one day when the contract has six months to expiration will have a much lower negative impact upon the premium than losing one day when the option has one week to expiration. At expiration, an option's time value will be equal to zero, with any premium remaining due to intrinsic value. One of the ways traders measure the rate of this decay is by examining an option's *theta*. Theta acts much like delta and gamma do for intrinsic value. With theta, traders can get a general idea as to how an option's value will erode as time passes.

Another factor that affects the time value of an option contract is the *volatility* of the underlying instrument. Of all the factors that justify an option's time premium, volatility and time to expiration are certainly two of the most important. Yet, while volatility is significant in determining an option's price, it is quite difficult to quantify. If an asset is experiencing dramatic price swings over a relatively short period of time, then the asset is said to be volatile. With greater volatility comes a greater possibility that the asset will move in-the-money. In addition, because less time is needed for the option to move, the option will retain more of its time value; conversely, if a market is static, it takes more time for the market to move in-the-money, thereby wasting valuable time. Lastly, with greater volatility comes greater trading risk; if the underlying market is unusually volatile, people may be reluctant to trade the asset and instead turn to options in the hope of limiting their downside risk. Option buyers would be willing to pay more for this protection and option writers would require more for providing this protection, both of which would drive option premiums upward. Therefore, in all cases, the greater the market volatility, the greater the time premium.

Measuring past volatility is relatively simple; what is difficult is predicting future volatility. By applying mathematical formulas to an asset's prior trading activity, investors can measure that asset's historical volatility, and from that value can obtain a useful benchmark as to how the asset should trade and perform over time. However markets are constantly changing and it is impossible to know how much price will move in the future. One way that investors predict and anticipate future volatility is by trading options with various expiration dates and strike prices. Some traders examine an option's *vega* to determine the effect that volatility will have upon the option's premium. Vega acts very much like an option's delta and gamma when examining intrinsic value. It is defined as the amount by which an option's price changes when the volatility in the underlying security changes. Vega basically states that any increase in an asset's volatility will be met with an increase in the price of the option while any decrease in an asset's volatility will be met with a decrease in the price of the option.

One common index that many traders utilize to gauge anticipated market volatility is the Chicago Board of Options Exchange's Volatility Index, known by its ticker symbol as VIX. The Volatility Index is calculated by taking a weighted average of the implied volatilities of eight at-the-money OEX calls and puts which have at least eight days to expiration and an average time to expiration of one month. Traders refer to this index to determine how future volatility will be affected, and therefore how the price of most stock options will be influenced as option expiration approaches. When the VIX value is high, it indicates that stock option volatility as a whole is high, and therefore premium levels for both calls and puts have expanded; when this VIX value is low, it indicates that stock option volatility is low, and therefore premium levels for both calls and puts have declined.

The level of *interest rates* is an additional factor that indirectly influences time value. As interest rates fluctuate, so too does option participation. As a general rule, when interest rates are low, option premiums are low; and when interest rates are high, option premiums are high. This can be explained by the fact that as interest rates rise, it becomes more attractive for individuals to invest a larger proportion of their money in these higher interest–bearing accounts. Because individuals are committing more of their funds to these safer investments, they have less with which to trade other assets. Obviously, with the large capital requirements that are necessary to obtain an actual position in an asset itself, it becomes more sensible to invest in options. The smaller capital outlay and lower risk that options provide enable traders to control the same asset and the same quantity of that asset with a smaller financial commitment. As an alternative to purchasing an asset, traders will buy call options; and as an alternative to selling an asset, traders will purchase put options. Therefore, an increase in interest rates should cause an increase in option trading as opposed to trading in the underlying asset itself. Furthermore, the increase in demand for options should also be met with a commensurate increase in option premiums.

The *dividend rate* is the final factor that influences the time value of an option. One of the most important things to understand with options on securities is that they do not entitle the option holder to cash dividends—dividends are paid only to those who own the security itself.* But the effect that cash dividends have on the price of the underlying security are felt by all those who own the option. This means that when a stock goes ex-dividend, an option's premium value can be negatively or positively affected, depending upon whether the option is a call or a put.

---

* However, an option contract's strike price and quantity are adjusted to reflect stock dividends.

When the cash dividend rate of a security is high, the price adjustment that occurs in the option will be more significant. Those with call options on the security will experience a decrease in the value of their contract when a stock goes ex-dividend, while those who own the asset outright will not lose any value, as what they will lose in price per share they will receive in the dividend. In this instance, it makes more sense to own the asset, not to control it. For this reason, as a stock's dividend rate increases, the demand for that security's call option will decrease, thereby decreasing its premium. Those with put options on the security will experience an increase in the value of their contract when a stock goes ex-dividend, while those who sell the security short will experience no change in the value of their investment, as what they are required to pay to the lender of the stock in dividends is equal to the amount they will realize with the price decrease. In this case, it makes more sense to control a short position in the asset with a put option than it does to actually obtain a short position in the asset. For this reason, as a stock's dividend rate rises, the demand for that security's put options will increase, which will thereby increase its premium.

This scenario for cash dividends differs from those for stock splits, reverse splits, stock dividends, and fractional splits. In these cases, a stock's market price will change but will have no effect upon an option's premium. Instead, the option's strike price and quantity are adjusted to reflect the change in the underlying asset. With stock splits, an option holder will receive a larger quantity of the option contract at a lower strike price; with reverse splits, an option holder will receive a smaller quantity of the option contract at a higher strike price. With stock dividends and fractional splits, the option's strike price is reduced and the number of option contracts will remain the same, with each contract now covering more shares than before.

One last term that is important to know when discussing option premium is *parity*. An option is said to be trading at parity when the premium is equal to the intrinsic value of the contract. For example, a GM March 70 Call @ $4 is at parity when General Motors stock trades at $74 per share. A GM March 70 Put @ $4 is at parity when General Motors stock is trading at $66 per share. Keep in mind that if the premium is equal to the intrinsic value, then that means there is no time value assigned to the price. This situation arises when the option has just about expired and does not have enough time to make a dramatic move in or out of the money. If an option's premium is trading at a value below the intrinsic value of the contract, the option is said to be trading below parity. If an option's premium is trading at a value that is greater than the intrinsic value of the contract, the option is said to be trading above parity.

In summary, by combining all of these factors, we can understand how an option's premium is generated. Premium is greatly affected by the intrinsic value of the option as well as the time value of the option. Either of the two can have a noticeable impact upon the price of the option. However, when both variables work together, an option's price can move dramatically, creating substantial returns. With the lower capital commitment that is required to purchase an option contract, returns are most often far greater than those realized by owning the asset outright, providing more bang for your buck. But the opposite holds true as well. When both of these variables work against the option holder's position, it can decrease the option's value significantly. Although the trader has the advantage of having invested less to control the desired amount, or paid the equivalent amount to control much more, adverse changes in these variables can decrease the value of one's option by a much greater percentage than what would be experienced with a position in the underlying asset. The impetus behind these greater returns is an option's delta, gamma, theta, and vega. These values dictate the degree to which an option's premium will respond to changes in intrinsic value, theta, time decay, and underlying volatility, respectively.

Obviously, premium is an ever changing variable. Over time, intrinsic value will change and traders will form new opinions as to the significance of each variable of time value, all of which will continually adjust the price of the option. Remember that, as a general rule, as intrinsic value, an option's time to expiration, asset volatility, and the level of interest rates increase, so will the price of both call and put options. And as dividend rates increase, put premiums will rise and call premiums will decline.

Now that we know the components of an option's valuation, we can turn our attention to the various alternatives available to traders with respect to options and how a trader can apply what was discussed in this section.

OPTIONS WITH OPTIONS

As we briefly touched upon earlier, an option contract holder is bestowed with three choices—exercise the option, let the option expire, or trade the option. But how does a trader decide which of the three alternatives to choose? A large portion of this decision is contingent upon the value of the option contract (or lack thereof) as well as the amount of time remaining before the option expires. When an option lacks value, meaning it is out-of-the-money, the trader can simply let the option expire worthless. When an option has value, meaning it is in-the-money, the trader can choose whether to trade the contract to another individual or exercise the contract and obtain the underlying asset. The ultimate decision that is made depends upon the individual investor, his or her trading style, his or her trading needs, and the situation at hand.

Exercise the Option

As we just mentioned, one will only exercise a long option contract when one stands to make money from that position, otherwise one could simply let the option expire and lose the premium.* When an option buyer exercises an option, he or she is choosing to take a position in the underlying instrument. Naturally, the position is determined by the option type and whether it is a call or a put. In exercising a stock or futures call option, the holder agrees to purchase the standardized quantity of the underlying asset from the option writer at the predetermined strike price. Because of their contract, the writer is obligated to sell the asset to the buyer at the strike price, regardless of the price at which the market is currently trading. This transaction gives the buyer a long position in the asset and gives the writer a short position in the asset.†

In exercising a stock or futures put option, the option holder agrees to sell the standardized quantity of the underlying asset to the option writer at the predetermined strike price. Because of their contract, the writer must purchase the asset from the option holder at the strike price, regardless of the price at which the market is currently trading. This transaction gives the buyer a short position in the asset and gives the seller a long position in the asset.

Exercising an index option, be it a call or a put, is handled differently because index options are settled in cash as opposed to the physical asset. When a call option buyer or a put option buyer exercises an index option, the holder is simply credited the amount by which the option is in-the-money, less any commission that applies. On the other hand, the call option writer or the put option writer is debited the amount by which the option is in-the-money, plus any commission that applies. For obvious reasons, an index option holder would choose to exercise his or her position only if it were profitable to do so, meaning the contract were in-the-money.

The majority of index options today are European-style options, meaning that exercise can only occur at the end of the contract's life. However, the most widely traded index option, the OEX Index option which covers the S&P (Standard & Poor's) 100, is an American-style contract, meaning exercise can occur at any point during the life of the option.

On the whole, most traders choose not to exercise an option prior to expiration. Doing so only entitles the investor to the intrinsic value of the option and sacrifices the added effect of time value. Exercising one's option before the expiration date is not common when it comes to futures. Unless the option is deep in-the-money, where time value has a much lower impact, it generally makes more sense to trade out of the position. Exercising before the expiration date does occur more frequently when it comes to equity call options. Because option holders are not entitled to cash dividends, call options are usually exercised right before a stock goes ex-dividend so no contract value will be lost.

---

* There are instances in which this is not necessarily the case, such as when an investor is exercising a large quantity in an illiquid market, but such cases are rare.

† Please note that while options provide the right to acquire the underlying instrument, the owner must still produce the necessary funds for the asset itself.

Defining the profit.   In each of these cases, exercise will only occur when it is profitable to do so—when the option is in-the-money. However, any time an individual exercises an option, that individual loses the full cost of the premium. Because of this, any gains on the trade will be offset by the losses on the cost of the option. does not really make a profit on the transaction until the premium is recove Therefore, there is a break-even point that occurs with options that are exercisec

With call options, the break-even point occurs when the underlying asset increased in price to a point where the intrinsic value is equal to the initial cos the option—in other words, the strike price of the option plus the call premi Any price above this break-even point would produce a profit on the transactio exercised, and any price below this break-even point would produce a loss on transaction, if exercised. For example, if the premium for 1 Compaq (CPQ) Dec Call is $5, then the break-even point is achieved when the underlying securit trading at $55. In this case, if the holder exercised the option, that individual co purchase the stock for $50 and immediately sell it at $55, for a $5 profit per share or total of $500 profit on the stock trade. However, the trader had to pay $500 for the rights to the option. This means that on the entire transaction, the trader broke even. If the stock were trading at $60 per share, the trader would make $1000 on the stock trade and would lose $500 on the cost of the option, for a gain of $500 on the transaction. If the stock were trading at $52 per share, he or she would make $200 on the stock trade and would lose $500 on the cost of the option, for a net loss of $300 on the transaction. It is a loss, but not as much as the total cost of the premium. If the stock were trading at $45, the option would not be exercised and the total loss would be that of the $500 premium.

With put options, the break-even point occurs when the underlying asset has decreased in price to a point where the intrinsic value is equal to the initial cost of the option—in other words, the strike price of the option minus the put premium. Any price below this break-even point would produce a profit on the transaction, if exercised, and any price above this break-even point would produce a loss on the transaction, if exercised. For example, if the premium for 1 Compaq (CPQ) Dec 50 Put is $5, then the break-even point is achieved when the underlying security is trading at $45. In this case, if the holder exercised the option, that individual could sell the stock for $50 and immediately buy it back at $45, for a $5 profit per share or total of $500 profit on the stock trade. However, the trader had to pay $500 for the right to the put. This means that on the entire transaction, the trader broke even. If the stock were trading at $40 per share, he or she would make $1000 on the stock trade and would lose $500 on the cost of the option, for a gain of $500 on the transaction. If the stock were trading at $48 per share, he or she would make $200 on the stock trade and would lose $500 on the cost of the option, for a net loss of $300 on the transaction. It is a loss, but not as much as the total cost of the premium. If the stock were trading at $55, the option would not be exercised and the total loss would be that of the $500 premium.

Because the trader must lose money in order to lock-in profits, some people choose to forego the exercising of their options and instead turn to the second option alternative.

Trade the Option

The second choice the holder of an option can make is to trade out of the option position before the option expires. Trading one's option is exactly the same as trading any other asset. To close out a position, one must perform the opposite side of the trade in the same asset. To offset a long option position, be it a call or a put, the holder must sell an option of the same type, expiration month, and strike price. To offset a short option position, be it a call or a put, the holder must buy an option of the same type, expiration month, and strike price. When one initiates a long option trade, the premium that is paid for the option is the entry price and when one liquidates a long option trade, the premium that is received for the option is the exit price. Obviously, if the exit price is greater than the entry price, the holder will profit on the trade. When one initiates a short option trade, the premium that is received for the option is the entry price and the premium that is paid for the option is the closing price. In this case, if the exit price is less than the entry price, the writer will profit on the trade.

To illustrate, if a trader initially purchases a call option for $5 per share and later sells that call option at $8 per share, the trader would realize a profit of $3 per share, or $300. If that same trader sold the option at $2 per share, he or she would have a loss of $3 per share, or $300. Likewise, if a trader were to initially sell a put option at $5 per share and later purchase that put option for $2.50 per share, the trader would realize a profit of $2.50 per share, or $250. If that same trader purchased the option at $8 per share, he or she would experience a loss of $3 per share, or $300.

Trading versus exercising.   There is a common misconception that the most profitable way to make money with options is by exercising the contract when it is in-the-money, when in reality, trading out of one's option can be far more lucrative. There are three reasons why this is so. The primary reason is that exercising an option can only provide the investor with the intrinsic value of the trade, while trading an option position can entitle the investor to the intrinsic value as well as additional time value. How much more the time value will provide is determined by the factors we mentioned earlier, such as time to expiration, volatility, dividend rates, and interest rates. A second reason is that trading one's position does not force the option buyer to incur the full cost of the premium, which is what occurs when one exercises an option. Since the gains from trading an option are not used to cover the cost of the premium, there is no break-even point, there is simply the entry price and the exit price. Finally, by trading out of one's option(s), the trader saves on commission costs. This is particularly helpful when a trader has a large option position.

Let the Option Expire

A final alternative available to the option holder is to let the option expire. Simply put, the trader can do nothing with the option and lose only what he or she paid in premium. Naturally, an option buyer will only let the contract expire if it lacks value at expiration, meaning it is out-of-the-money. Once the expiration occurs, the option buyer no longer controls the underlying asset and loses all rights conveyed by the contract. Doing nothing is a luxury that is afforded only to option traders. This eliminates the necessity of offsetting a losing position, thereby serving as an inherent stop loss on the trade. Trading any other type of asset obligates the investor to eventually offset the position, regardless of whether it is profitable to do so.

Example of Exercising versus Trading

Let's look at an option example and the alternatives an option buyer possesses. In February, a trader buys 1 IBM May 110 Call at $5 when IBM is trading at $108 per share. In late April, when the option is nearing expiration, IBM stock is trading around $120 per share and the option's premium has increased to $11½. In this example, because the option is in-the-money, the option holder has the choice of either exercising the option contract or trading out of the long call position. If the trader decides to exercise the IBM May 110 Call option contract, he or she must first inform the clearing firm of his or her intentions. The clearing firm then notifies an IBM May 110 call writer that he or she has been exercised and is obligated to sell 100 shares of IBM stock to the option holder at a price of $110 per share.* The option buyer pays the option writer $110 per share for the 100 shares of IBM, for a total of $11,000, giving the trader a long stock position at $110 when the market is trading $10 higher. In exercising the long call contract, the trader paid $500 for the rights to the option and $11,000 for the 100 shares of IBM stock, for a total cost of $11,500 on the transaction. If the trader were to immediately liquidate this long IBM stock position, by selling 100 shares of IBM at $120, the trader would receive a total payment of $12,000. Therefore, on the overall transaction, the trader realizes a total profit of $500 ($12,000 − $11,500), excluding any commission costs necessary to purchase the call option, to purchase the 100 shares of IBM stock, and to sell the 100 shares of IBM stock.

On the other hand, if the trader were to trade out of this long IBM call option position by performing an offsetting transaction, the process would be much simpler. To offset the long IBM May 110 Call option position, the trader must sell 1 IBM May 110 Call option. With the prevailing market prices, the option buyer paid $5, or $500, for the rights to the call option and can sell the option at $11½, or

* The option writer who has been exercised is not necessarily the trader who initiated the option transaction with the option buyer in the first place. The clearing firm decides how it will match option buyers and sellers. It is important that a trader is aware of the method the firm chooses before he or she decides to write an option contract.

$1150. Therefore, the option buyer realizes a total of $650 of profit on the trade, less any commission that applies for purchasing the call option and later liquidating that option.

In comparison, by trading out of the option position the option holder was able to realize a greater profit on the trade. This is usually the case with options. However, the closer to expiration the option gets, the less a trader will be able to retrieve in premium by trading out of his or her position. It is important that a trader compare the two processes before making a decision as to what to do with the option position.

OPTION STRATEGIES

As we described earlier, four possible option selections exist for a trader: (1) long a call, (2) long a put, (3) short a call, and (4) short a put. These four can be used independently, together, or in conjunction with other financial instruments to create a number of option-trading strategies. These combinations enable a trader to develop an option-trading model which meets the trader's specific trading needs, expectations, and style, and enables him or her to anticipate every conceivable situation in the market. This trading structure can be adapted to handle any type of market outlook, whether it be bullish, bearish, choppy, or neutral.

Options are unique trading instruments. They can be used for a multitude of purposes, providing tremendous versatility and utility. Among their multiple applications are the following: to speculate on the movement of an asset; to hedge an existing position in an asset; to hedge other option positions; to generate income by writing option positions against asset positions; and to generate additional income by writing options against different quantities of options or the underlying asset, also known as ratio writing. Due to the numerous option strategies that arise from these applications and the fact that the scope of this book is limited, we will devote coverage to a cursory explanation of two of the most popular strategies which are designed to take advantage of market movement: spreads and straddles.

SPREADS

Option *spreads* are hedged positions that can be utilized to control a trade's risk, while at the same time limiting gains. They accomplish this goal by simultaneously taking positions on both sides of the market. A *call option spread* is the simultaneous purchase and sale of call options with different strike prices, different expiration dates, or with both different strike prices and different expiration dates. Likewise, a *put option spread* is the simultaneous purchase and sale of a put option with different strike prices, different expiration dates, or with both different strike prices and different expiration dates. Spreads with different strike prices are referred to as *price spreads* or *vertical spreads* because the strike prices are stacked vertically on top of each other in financial listings. Spreads with different expiration months are referred to as *calendar spreads, horizontal spreads,* or *time spreads* because the options expire at different times. A spread where both the strike price and the expiration month are different is referred to as a *diagonal spread.*

Option spreads can be used when one has an inclination as to where the underlying market is heading, but is somewhat uncertain. Because the position is hedged, a spread allows the trader to participate in the market while effectively containing risk, sometimes even more so than with single option positions. Option spreads can also be used when a trader has particular price targets in mind—because spreads limit gains as well as losses, spreads can be initiated that will enable the trader to take advantage of these targets while at the same time keeping risk at a minimum.

Vertical Spreads

As is the case with options, any of four possible vertical option spreads can be selected depending on what a trader expects will happen in the market: one can buy a call spread, one can sell a call spread, one can buy a put spread, or one can sell a put spread. A long call spread and a short put spread are considered bull spreads because they are used when a trader's market outlook is positive, or bullish. A short call spread and a long put spread are considered bear spreads because they are used when a trader's outlook is negative, or bearish.

Buying a call spread. If a trader purchases a call option, he or she is looking for the market to rally so the option can expire in-the-money and the trader can profit. Likewise, a long call spread can be initiated to anticipate bullish market conditions. A long call spread requires the purchase of a call option with one strike price and the simultaneous sale of the same call option with a higher strike price. Ultimately, when buying a call spread, the trader wants both call options to expire in-the-money. With call options, the lower the strike price, the greater the premium. Therefore, at the time the long call spread is initiated, the premium that the trader pays for the call option with the lower strike price will be greater than the premium that the trader receives for the call option with the higher strike price. Since the trader must pay a greater premium for the rights to the long call option than what he or she receives for the short call option, the net premium cost is partially offset in a bull call spread. Because the trader must put up some money upon initiating the trade, this is considered a debit spread. To obtain the break-even point of a long call spread, one would add the net cost of the spread to the long call's strike price (the lower strike price)—any value above this break-even point is a gain on the trade and anything below this break-even point is a loss on the trade.

The advantage of buying a call spread is that it provides less risk than if one were to simply purchase a call option outright. The most one can lose on the trade is the total cost (net premium cost) of the spread—if both options of a long call spread were to expire out-of-the-money, then the trader would lose the greater price paid for the long call option position with the lower strike price and would retain the lesser price received for the short call position with the higher strike price. By selling a call option with a higher strike price, the trader receives some additional income, thereby reducing the total cost of the spread and the maximum loss. However, the drawback is that the gains are also limited. This maximum gain is capped at the difference between the two call option strike prices minus the total cost (net premium cost) of the spread. In any case, with a long call spread, the potential gains are greater than the potential losses.

Example
Buy 1 Micron (MU) Jan 50 Call @ 4
Sell 1 Micron (MU) Jan 60 Call @ 1
Market price of Micron stock: $50

In this example, the trader has initiated a long call spread. This trader has purchased one Micron call option with a January expiration and a $50 strike price for $400 and has sold one Micron call option with a January expiration and a $60 strike price for $100, when Micron is trading at $50 per share. Therefore, the total cost of the spread is $300. This payment is a nonrefundable, fixed cost to the trader and cannot be recovered. This $300 is also the most a trader can lose on the transaction—if both calls were to expire out-of-the-money, meaning Micron stock were trading at any price below $50, the trader would lose $400 on the long January 50 call and would make $100 on the short January 60 call. Ideally, the trader would like to see the market rally. If Micron stock were trading at $50 per share, the trader would make nothing on the long Jan 50 call option position that is at-the-money, lose nothing on the short Jan 60 call option position that is out-of-the-money, and lose $300 for the fixed cost to initiate the spread, for a net loss of $300. If Micron stock were trading at $53 per share, the trader would make $300 on the long January 50 call option position that is in-the-money, lose nothing on the short January 60 call option position that is out-of-the-money, and lose $300 in nonrefundable costs to initiate the spread, for a net gain of zero. If Micron stock were trading at $55 per share, the trader would make $500 on the long January 50 call option position that is in-the-money, lose nothing on the short January 60 call option position that is out-of-the-money, and lose $300 in fixed costs necessary to initiate the spread, for a net gain of $200. If Micron stock were trading at $60 per share, the trader would make $1000 on the long January 50 call option position that is in-the-money, lose nothing on the short January 60 call option position that is at-the-money, and lose $300 for the fixed cost to initiate the spread, for a net gain of $700. Finally, if Micron stock were trading at $65 per share, the trader would make $1500 on the long January 50 call option position that is in-the-money, lose $500 on the short January 60 call option position that is in-the-money, and lose another $300 for the nonrefundable cost to initiate the spread, for a net gain of $700. Please note that once both call options are in-the-money, the maximum gains have been attained, as any profits in the long call option are exactly offset by the losses in the short call option. Also, if both calls are exercised when they are in-the-money, the long January 50 call option allows the trader to purchase 100 shares of Micron stock at $50 per share and the short January 60 call option obligates the trader to sell 100 shares of Micron stock at $60 per share.

To summarize, the most the trader could lose in a long call spread would be the cost of the spread ($300), and the most the trader could make in a long call spread would be the difference between the two strike prices minus the cost of the spread ($1000 − $300 = $700). (See Payoff Diagram 2.5.) This differs from the case of a long January 50 call option alone, where the maximum loss is the cost of the contract ($400) and the maximum gains are unlimited.

Selling a call spread.   If a trader sells a call option, he or she is looking for the market to decline so the option can expire out-of-the-money and he or she can profit. Likewise, a short call spread can be initiated to anticipate bearish market conditions. A short call spread entails the sale of a call option with one strike price and the simultaneous purchase of the same call option with a higher strike price. Ultimately, when selling a call spread, the trader wants both calls to expire out-of-the-money. With call options, the lower the strike price, the greater the premium. Therefore, at the time the short call spread is initiated, the premium that the trader receives for the call option with the lower strike price will be greater than the premium that the trader pays for the call option with the higher strike price. Since the trader receives a greater premium by selling a call option than what he or she must pay for the long call option, the net premium cost is more than offset in a bear call spread. Because the trader receives money upon initiating the trade, this is considered a credit spread. To obtain the break-even point of a short call spread, one would add the net premium received on the spread to the short call option's strike price (the lower strike price)—anything below this break-even point would be a gain on the trade and anything above this break-even point would be a loss on the trade.

The advantage of selling a call spread is that it offers less risk than if one were to simply sell a call option outright. Initiating a short call spread provides immediate income to the option writer, although it is less than the amount the trader would have received had he or she simply sold the call option outright. By purchasing a call option with a higher strike price, the trader receives some added protection, thereby creating a finite, as opposed to an unlimited, level of risk. The most one can lose on the trade is capped at the difference between the two call option strike prices minus the total premium received on the spread. However, the drawback is that the maximum gains are defined at the outset of the trade as simply the total (net) premium received on the spread. If both options of a short call spread were to

PAYOFF DIAGRAM 2.5   Profit diagrams for a long call spread and the Micron long call spread example.

LONG CALL SPREAD

OUTLOOK = BULLISH
LS = LOWER STRIKE PRICE
HS = HIGHER STRIKE PRICE
BEP = BREAK-EVEN POINT = LS + DR
DR = DEBIT = INITIAL SPREAD COST = MAXIMUM LOSS
MG = MAXIMUM GAIN = (HS – LS) – DR

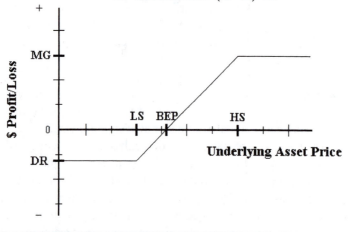

LONG CALL SPREAD

BUY 1 MICRON JAN 50 CALL @ 4
SELL 1 MICRON JAN 60 CALL @ 1

OUTLOOK = BULLISH
LS = LOWER STRIKE PRICE = $50
HS = HIGHER STRIKE PRICE = $60
BEP = BREAK-EVEN POINT = $53
DR = DEBIT = MAXIMUM LOSS = $300
MG = MAXIMUM GAIN = $700
▨ = GAIN

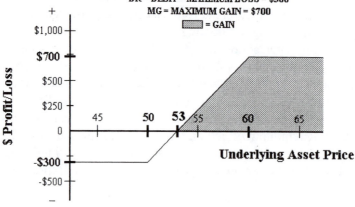

expire out-of-the-money, then the trader would retain the greater price received for the short call option position with the lower strike price, and would lose the lesser price paid for the long call position with the higher strike price. In any case, with a short call spread, the potential gains are less than the potential losses.

Example
Sell 1 Micron (MU) Jan 50 Call @ 4
Buy 1 Micron (MU) Jan 60 Call @ 1
Market price of Micron stock: $50

In this example, the trader has initiated a short call spread. This trader has sold one Micron call option with a January expiration and a $50 strike price for $400 and has purchased one Micron call option with a January expiration and a $60 strike price for $100, when Micron is trading at $50 per share. Therefore, the total premium received by the trader for the spread is $300. This is a nonrefundable, fixed income payment to the trader and cannot be lost. This $300 is also the most a trader can gain on the transaction—if both calls were to expire out-of-the-money, meaning Micron stock were trading at any price below $50, the trader would gain $400 on the short January 50 call and would lose $100 on the long January 60 call. Therefore, the trader would ideally like to see the market decline. If Micron stock were trading at $50 per share, the trader would lose nothing on the short January 50 call option position that is at-the-money, make nothing on the long January 60 call option position that is out-of-the-money, and make $300 for the fixed payment to initiate the spread, for a net gain of $300. If Micron stock were trading at $53 per share, the trader would lose $300 on the short January 50 call option position that is in-the-money, make nothing on the long January 60 call option position that is out-of-the-money, and make $300 for the nonrefundable payment to initiate the spread, for a net gain of zero. If Micron stock were trading at $55 per share, the trader would lose $500 on the short January 50 call option position that is in-the-money, make nothing on the long January 60 call option position that is out-of-the-money, and make $300 for the fixed payment that was necessary to initiate the spread, for a net loss of $200. If Micron stock were trading at $60 per share, the trader would lose $1000 on the short January 50 call option position that is in-the-money, make nothing on the long January 60 call option position that is at-the-money, and make $300 for the fixed payment to initiate the spread, for a net loss of $700. Finally, if Micron stock were trading at $65 per share, the trader would lose $1500 on the short January 50 call option position that is in-the-money, make $500 on the long January 60 call option position that is in-the-money, and make another $300 for the nonrefundable payment necessary to initiate the spread, for a net loss of $700. Please note that once both call options are in-the-money, the maximum losses have been attained, as losses in the short call option are exactly offset by the profits in the long call option. Also, if both calls are exercised when they are in-the-money, the short

January 50 call option obligates the trader to sell 100 shares of Micron stock at $50 per share and the long January 60 call option allows the trader to purchase 100 shares of Micron stock at $60 per share.

To summarize, the most the trader could make in a short call spread would be the payment received for the spread ($300) and the most the trader could lose in a short call spread would be the difference between the two strike prices minus the payment received for the spread ($1000 − $300 = $700). (See Payoff Diagram 2.6.) This differs from the case of a short January 50 call option alone, where the maximum gain is the payment received for the contract ($400) and the maximum losses are unlimited.

Buying a put spread.   If a trader purchases a put option, the trader is looking for the market to decline so the option can expire in-the-money and he or she can profit. Likewise, a long put spread can be initiated to anticipate bearish market conditions. A long put spread requires the purchase of a put option with one strike price and the simultaneous sale of the same put option with a lower strike price. Ultimately, when buying a put spread, the trader wants both put options to expire in-the-money. With put options, the higher the strike price, the greater the premium. Therefore, at the time the long put spread is initiated, the premium that the trader pays for the put option with the higher strike price will be greater than the premium that the trader receives for the put option with the lower strike price. Since the trader must pay a greater premium for the rights to the long put option than what he or she receives for the short put option, the net premium cost is partially offset in a bear put spread. Because the trader must put up the necessary funds upon initiating the trade, this is considered a debit spread. To obtain the break-even point of a long put spread, one would subtract the net cost of the spread from the long put option's strike price (the higher strike price)—anything below this break-even point would be a gain on the trade and anything above this break-even point would be a loss on the trade.

The advantage of buying a put spread is that it provides less risk than if one were to simply purchase a put option outright. The most one can lose on the trade is the total cost (net premium cost) of the spread—if both options of a long put spread were to expire out-of-the-money, then the trader would lose the greater price paid for the long put option position with the higher strike price, and would retain the lesser price received for the short put position with the lower strike price. By selling a put option with a lower strike price, the trader receives additional income, thereby reducing the total cost of the spread and the maximum possible loss. However, the drawback is that gains are also limited. This maximum gain is capped at the difference between the two put option strike prices minus the total cost (net premium cost) of the spread. In any case, with a long put spread, the potential gains are greater than the potential losses.

PAYOFF DIAGRAM 2.6   Profit diagrams for a short call spread and the Micron short call spread example.

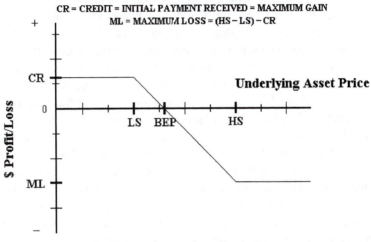

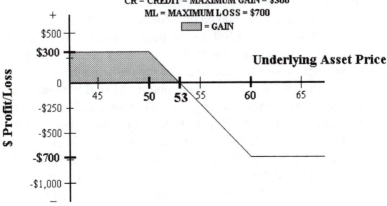

Example
Buy 1 Micron (MU) Jan 60 Put @ 4
Sell 1 Micron (MU) Jan 50 Put @ 1
Market price of Micron stock: $60

In this example, the trader has initiated a long put spread. He or she has purchased one Micron put option with a January expiration and a $60 strike price for
$400 and has sold one Micron put option with a January expiration and a $50 strike
price for $100, when Micron is trading at $60 per share. Therefore, the total cost of
the spread is $300. This payment is a nonrefundable, fixed cost to the trader and
cannot be retrieved. This $300 is also the most a trader can lose on the transac-
tion—if both puts were to expire out-of-the-money, meaning Micron stock were
trading at any price above $60, the trader would lose $400 on the long January 60
put and would make $100 on the short January 50 put. Ideally, the trader would like
to see the market decline. If Micron stock were trading at $60 per share, the trader
would make nothing on the long Jan 60 put option position that is at-the-money,
lose nothing on the short Jan 50 put option position that is out-of-the-money, and
lose $300 for the fixed cost to initiate the spread, for a total loss of $300. If Micron
stock were trading at $57 per share, the trader would make $300 on the long Jan 60
put option position that is in-the-money, lose nothing on the short Jan 50 put option
position that is out-of-the-money, and lose $300 in nonrefundable costs to initiate
the spread, for a net gain of zero. If Micron stock were trading at $55 per share, the
trader would make $500 on the long Jan 60 put option position that is in-the-
money, lose nothing on the short Jan 50 put option position that is out-of-the-
money, and lose $300 in fixed costs necessary to initiate the spread, for a net gain
of $200. If Micron stock were trading at $50 per share, the trader would make
$1000 on the long Jan 60 put option position that is in-the-money, lose nothing on
the short Jan 50 put option position that is at-the-money, and lose $300 for the
fixed cost to initiate the spread, for a net gain of $700. Finally, if Micron stock were
trading at $45 per share, the trader would make $1500 on the long Jan 60 put option
position that is in-the-money, lose $500 on the short Jan 50 put option position that
is in-the-money, and lose another $300 for the nonrefundable cost to initiate the
spread, for a net gain of $700. Please note that once both put options are in-the-
money the maximum gains have been attained, as any profits in the long put option
are exactly offset by the losses in the short put option. Also, if both puts are exercised when they are in-the-money, the long Jan 60 put option allows the trader to
sell 100 shares of Micron stock at $60 per share and the short Jan 50 put option
obligates the trader to purchase 100 shares of Micron stock at $50 per share.
       To summarize, the most the trader could lose in a long put spread would be the
cost of the spread ($300) and the most the trader could make in a long put spread
would be the difference between the two strike prices minus the cost of the spread

($1,000 − $300 = $700). (See Payoff Diagram 2.7.) This differs from the case of a long Jan 60 put option alone, where the maximum loss is the cost of the contract ($400) and the maximum gains are the total value of the underlying contract if it were to decline to zero ($6000 − $400 = $5600).

Selling a put spread.   If a trader sells a put option, he or she is looking for the market to rally so the option can expire out-of-the-money and he or she can profit. Likewise, a short put spread can be initiated to anticipate bullish market conditions. A short put spread entails the sale of a put option with one strike price and the simultaneous purchase of the same put option with a lower strike price. Ultimately, when selling a put spread, the trader wants both puts to expire out-of-the-money. With put options, the higher the strike price the greater the premium. Therefore, at the time the short put spread is initiated, the premium that the trader receives for the put option with the higher strike price will be greater than the premium that the trader pays for the put option with the lower strike price. Since the trader receives a greater premium by selling a put option than what he or she must pay for the long put option, the net premium cost is more than offset in a bull put spread. Because the trader receives money upon initiating the trade, this is considered a credit spread. To obtain the break-even point of a short put spread, one would subtract the net cost of the spread from the short put option's strike price (the higher strike price)—anything above this break-even point would be a gain on the trade and anything below this break-even point would be a loss on the trade.

The advantage of selling a put spread is that it offers less risk than if one were to simply sell a put option outright. Initiating a short put spread provides immediate income to the option writer, although it is less than the amount the trader would have received had he or she simply sold the put option outright. Also, by purchasing a put option with a lower strike price, the trader receives some added protection, thereby creating a finite (as opposed to an unlimited) level of risk. The most one can lose on the trade is capped at the difference between the two put option strike prices minus the total premium received on the spread. However, the drawback is that the maximum gains are defined at the outset of the trade as simply the total (net) premium received on the spread. If both options of a short put spread were to expire out-of-the-money, then the trader would retain the greater price received for the short put option position with the higher strike price, and would lose the lesser price paid for the long put position with the lower strike price. In any case, with a short put spread, the potential gains are less than the potential losses.

Example
Sell 1 Micron (MU) Jan 60 Put @ 4
Buy 1 Micron (MU) Jan 50 Put @ 1
Market price of Micron stock: $60

PAYOFF DIAGRAM 2.7   Profit diagrams for a long put spread and the Micron long put spread example.

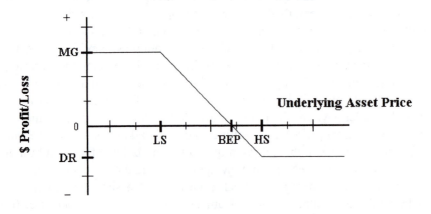

LONG PUT SPREAD

OUTLOOK = BEARISH
LS = LOWER STRIKE PRICE
HS = HIGHER STRIKE PRICE
BEP = BREAK-EVEN POINT = HS − DR
DR = DEBIT = INITIAL SPREAD COST = MAXIMUM LOSS
MG = MAXIMUM GAIN = (HS − LS) − DR

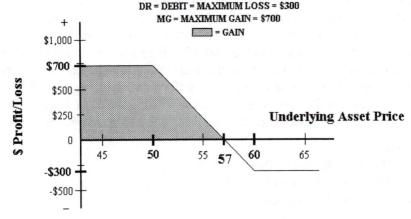

LONG PUT SPREAD

BUY 1 MICRON JAN 60 PUT @ 4
SELL 1 MICRON JAN 50 PUT @ 1

OUTLOOK = BEARISH
LS = LOWER STRIKE PRICE = $50
HS = HIGHER STRIKE PRICE = $60
BEP = BREAK-EVEN POINT = $57
DR = DEBIT = MAXIMUM LOSS = $300
MG = MAXIMUM GAIN = $700

▨ = GAIN

In this example, the trader has initiated a short put spread. The trader has sold one Micron put option with a January expiration and a $60 strike price for $400 and has purchased one Micron put option with a January expiration and a $50 strike price for $100, when Micron is trading at $60 per share. Therefore, the total premium received by the trader for the spread is $300. This is a nonrefundable, fixed income payment to the trader and cannot be lost. This $300 is also the most a trader can gain on the transaction—if both puts were to expire out-of-the-money, meaning Micron stock were trading at any price above $60, the trader would gain $400 on the short January 60 put and would lose $100 on the long January 50 put. Therefore, the trader would ideally like to see the market rally. If Micron stock were trading at $60 per share, the trader would lose nothing on the short Jan 60 put option position that is at-the-money, make nothing on the long Jan 50 put option position that is out-of-the-money, and make $300 for the fixed payment to initiate the spread, for a net gain of $300. If Micron stock were trading at $57 per share, the trader would lose $300 on the short Jan 60 put option position that is in-the-money, make nothing on the long Jan 50 put option position that is out-of-the-money, and make $300 for the nonrefundable payment to initiate the spread, for a net gain of zero. If Micron stock were trading at $55 per share, the trader would lose $500 on the short Jan 60 put option position that is in-the-money, make nothing on the long Jan 50 put option position that is out-of-the-money, and make $300 for the fixed payment that was necessary to initiate the spread, for a net loss of $200. If Micron stock were trading at $50 per share, the trader would lose $1000 on the short Jan 60 put option position that is in-the-money, make nothing on the long Jan 50 put option position that is at-the-money, and make $300 for the fixed payment to initiate the spread, for a net loss of $700. Finally, if Micron stock were trading at $45 per share, the trader would lose $1500 on the short Jan 60 put option position that is in-the-money, make $500 on the long Jan 50 put option position that is in-the-money, and make another $300 for the nonrefundable payment necessary to initiate the spread, for a net loss of $700. Please note that once both put options are in-the-money the maximum losses have been attained, as losses in the short put option are exactly offset by the profits in the long put option. Also, if both puts are exercised when they are in-the-money, the short Jan 60 put option obligates the trader to purchase 100 shares of Micron stock at $60 per share and the long Jan 50 put option allows the trader to sell 100 shares of Micron stock at $50 per share.

To summarize, the most the trader could make in a short put spread would be the payment received for the spread ($300) and the most the trader could lose in a short put spread would be the difference between the two strike prices minus the payment received for the spread ($1000 − $300 = $700). (See Payoff Diagram 2.8.) This differs from the case of a short put option where the maximum gain is the payment received for the contract ($400) and the maximum losses are the total value of the underlying contract if it were to decline to zero ($6000 − $400 = $5600).

Calendar Spreads

The four types of spreads just mentioned were vertical spreads, or price spreads. Another group of spreads is referred to as *horizontal spreads, time spreads,* or *calendar spreads.* Whereas vertical spreads are used to take advantage of price movements in the underlying security, horizontal spreads are used to take advantage of time erosion and the pricing discrepancies that arise from movements in the underlying market. A horizontal spread involves the simultaneous purchase and sale of an option contract of the same asset, type, and strike price but with different expiration dates. As we indicated earlier, the option's time value erodes toward zero as time passes toward option expiration. The erosion occurs more rapidly as the option's life decreases and the expiration date comes into view. A calendar spread is intended to take advantage of this decline in an option's premium. Typically, a trader will sell an option with the closer expiration month and purchase an option with the distant expiration month to take advantage of the fact that the latter position will retain more of its value. Since the near-month option has less time to expiration than the back-month option, the premium the trader receives will be less than the premium the trader must pay for the spread. Therefore, this spread is considered a debit spread. Also, because one option expires before the other, oftentimes one or both legs of the calendar spread are offset by trading out of the position.

> Example
> Sell 1 Intel (INTC) Apr 120 Call @ 6
> Buy 1 Intel (INTC) July 120 Call @ 10
> Market price of Intel stock: $117

In this example, a trader has initiated a short calendar spread. Here, he or she has sold one Intel call option with an April expiration and a $120 strike price at a cost of $600 and has purchased one Intel call option with a July expiration and a $120 strike price at a cost of $1000. Therefore, the net cost to initiate the spread is $400. By selling the April 120 call option, a trader is hoping that the market will move sideways into expiration so that a profit can be realized coincident with the erosion in the time premium. However, to protect him- or herself in the case of an adverse price move, the trader hedges his or her position by purchasing the July 120 call option. This way, if the market were to rally and the trader's short option position were exercised, obligating the trader to sell 100 shares of Intel stock to the option holder at $120 per share, the trader could in turn exercise the long option position to purchase 100 shares of Intel stock at $120 per share. If the market were to move sideways as the trader had hoped, the short option contract would lose much more of its premium value than the long option contract. For example, say that on the April option expiration date both calls are still trading at $117 per share (out-of-the-money) with the new premium for the April 120 call falling to zero and the new premium for the July 120 call falling to $6½. By trading out of the spread

PAYOFF DIAGRAM 2.8   Profit diagrams for a short put spread and the Micron short put spread example.

SHORT PUT SPREAD

OUTLOOK = BULLISH
LS = LOWER STRIKE PRICE
HS = HIGHER STRIKE PRICE
BEP = BREAK-EVEN POINT = HS − CR
CR = CREDIT = INITIAL PAYMENT RECEIVED = MAXIMUM GAIN
ML = MAXIMUM LOSS = (HS − LS) − CR

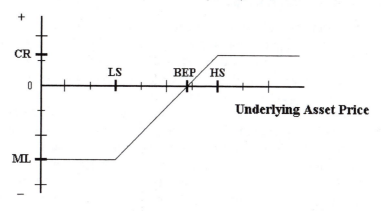

SHORT PUT SPREAD

SELL 1 MICRON JAN 60 PUT @ 4
BUY 1 MICRON JAN 50 PUT @ 1

OUTLOOK = BULLISH
LS = LOWER STRIKE PRICE = $50
HS = HIGHER STRIKE PRICE = $60
BEP = BREAK-EVEN POINT = $57
CR = CREDIT = MAXIMUM GAIN = $300
ML = MAXIMUM LOSS = $700

▨ = GAIN

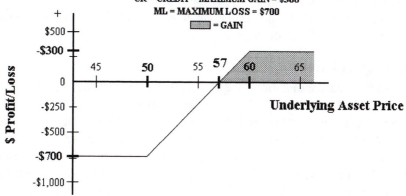

at these prices (by taking the opposite side of each option), the trader would make $600 by selling the April call at $600 and purchasing it at $0 and would lose $350 by purchasing the July call at $1000 and selling it at $650, for a net gain of $250. In this case, the trader could exit the trade with a profit.

Example
Sell 1 Intel (INTC) Apr 120 Put @ 6
Buy 1 Intel (INTC) July 120 Put @ 10
Market price of Intel stock: $123

In this scenario, the trader has again initiated a short calendar spread. Here, the trader has sold one Intel put option with an April expiration and a $120 strike price at a cost of $600 and has purchased one Intel put option with a July expiration and a $120 strike price at a cost of $1000. Therefore, the net cost to initiate the spread is $400. By selling the April 120 put option, the trader is hoping that the market will move sideways into expiration so that a profit can be realized coincident with the erosion in the time premium. However, to protect him- or herself in the case of an adverse price move, the trader hedges his or her position by purchasing the July 120 put option. This way, if the market were to decline and the trader's short option position were exercised, obligating the trader to purchase 100 shares of Intel stock from the option holder at $120 per share, the trader could in turn exercise the long option position to sell 100 shares of Intel stock at $120 per share. If the market were to move sideways as the trader had hoped, the short option contract would lose much more of its premium value than the long option contract. For example, say that on the April option expiration date both puts are still trading at $123 per share (out-of-the-money) with the new premium for the April 120 put falling to zero and the new premium for the July 120 put falling to $6½. By trading out of the spread at these prices (by taking the opposite side of each option), the trader would make $600 by selling the April put at $600 and purchasing it at $0 and would lose $350 by purchasing the July put at $1000 and selling it at $650, for a net gain of $250. In this case, the trader could exit the trade with a profit.

Diagonal spreads work in the same manner as vertical and horizontal spreads and are simply a combination of the two.

STRADDLES AND COMBINATIONS

Option straddles and combinations are a unique way of capitalizing on market activity or market consolidation. Straddles and combinations can be utilized to make money if a trader feels the market will experience a move, but is not certain as to the direction of that move. They can also be utilized to make money if one expects the market to stabilize or consolidate over a specific period of time. Straddles and combinations are very similar. A *straddle* involves the simultaneous purchase of a call and a put, or the simultaneous sale of a call and a put, of the same security, strike price, and expiration date; while a *combination* involves the simultaneous purchase of a call and a put, or the simultaneous sale of a call and a put, of the same security, but with different strike prices, different expiration dates, or both different strike prices and different expiration dates. Unlike spreads, where four possible positions can be taken, there are only two sides to straddles and combinations, long and short.

Long Straddle

In a long straddle, the trader believes the market will make a sizable move, but is uncertain of the direction of that move. This option strategy is especially common when a trader is anticipating that a news release or earnings report will have a dramatic impact on the price of an asset. A long straddle entails the simultaneous purchase of a call option and a put option of the same security, strike price, and expiration date. The long call option allows the trader to gain if it were to expire in-the-money, and the long put option allows the trader to gain if it were to expire in-the-money; if both options were to expire at-the-money, meaning the market neither advances nor declines, then the trader loses what was paid in premium for both the options. Since the trader is purchasing both a call option and a put option, the trader must pay the option writers for both contracts, making this a debit straddle. So, in order to profit on the trade, one must first recoup the total cost of the straddle. To obtain the break-even points of a long straddle, one would add the net cost of the straddle to the long call option's strike price and subtract the net cost of the straddle from the long put option's strike price—anything above the upper (call option's) break-even point would be a profit and anything below the lower (put option's) break-even point would be a profit. Any price in between these two levels would be a loss to the trader. The maximum gain for a long straddle is unlimited, while the maximum loss for a long straddle is simply the total cost of the option premiums.

Example
Buy 1 Exxon (XON) June 70 Call @ 4
Buy 1 Exxon (XON) June 70 Put @ 3
Market price of Exxon stock: $70

In this example, the trader has initiated a long straddle since the security, the strike prices, and the expiration months are all the same. In this instance, one Exxon call option with a June expiration and a $70 strike price for $400 has been purchased and one Exxon put option with a June expiration and a $70 strike price for $300 has been purchased, when Exxon is trading at $70 per share. Therefore, the total cost of the straddle is $700. This is a nonrefundable, fixed cost to the trader and cannot be recovered. This $700 is also the most a trader can lose on the transaction—if both the call and the put option were to expire at-the-money, meaning Exxon stock were trading at $70 per share, the trader would lose $400 on the long June 70 call and would lose $300 on the long June 70 put. Ideally, the trader would like to see the market advance or decline dramatically. If Exxon stock were trading at $75 per share, the trader would make $500 on the long June 70 call option position that is in-the-money, make nothing on the long June 70 put option position that is out-of-the-money, and lose $700 for the fixed cost to initiate the straddle, for a net loss of $200. If Exxon were trading at $65 per share, the trader would make nothing on the long June 70 call option position that is out-of-the-money, make $500 on the long June 70 put option position that is in-the-money, and lose $700 for the fixed cost to initiate the straddle, for a net loss of $200. If Exxon stock were trading at $77 per share, the trader would make $700 on the long June 70 call option position that is in-the-money, make nothing on the long June 70 put option position that is out-of-the-money, and lose $700 in nonrefundable costs to initiate the straddle, for a net gain of zero. If Exxon stock were trading at $63 per share, the trader would make nothing on the long June 70 call option position that is out-of-the-money, make $700 on the long June 70 put option position that is in-the-money, and lose $700 in nonrefundable costs to initiate the straddle, for a net gain of zero. If Exxon stock were trading at $80 per share, the trader would make $1000 on the long June 70 call option position that is in-the-money, make nothing on the long June 70 put option position that is out-of-the-money, and lose $700 in fixed costs necessary to initiate the straddle, for a net gain of $300 on the spread. Finally, if Exxon stock were trading at $60 per share, the trader would make nothing on the long June 70 call option position that is out-of-the-money, make $1000 on the long June 70 put option position that is in-the-money, and lose $700 in fixed costs necessary to initiate the straddle, for a net gain of $300. Please note that a long straddle is simply made up of two regular option contracts. Therefore, as Exxon's market price continues to move in-the-money, either upside or downside, profits continue to grow indefinitely. Long straddles differ from spreads in that the gains are not limited.

To summarize, the most the trader could lose in a long straddle would be the cost of the straddle ($700) and this would occur if the options expired at-the-money ($70). The most the trader could make in a long straddle is unlimited to the upside and restricted to the total value of the underlying contract if it were to decline to zero ($7000 − $700 = $6300) on the downside. Therefore, if the market were to advance or decline, the trader will gain; however, if the market were to move sideways, the trader will experience a loss. (See Payoff Diagram 2.9.)

Long Combination

A long combination is very similar to a long straddle. In a long combination, the trader believes the market will make a sizable move, but is uncertain of the direction of that move. A long combination entails the simultaneous purchase of a call option and a put option of the same security, but with different strike prices, dif-

PAYOFF DIAGRAM 2.9   Profit diagrams for a long straddle and the Exxon long straddle example.

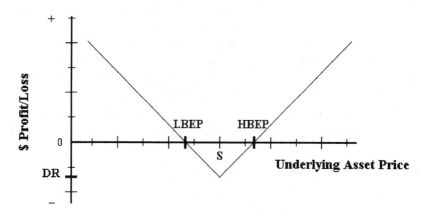

LONG STRADDLE

OUTLOOK = BULLISH OR BEARISH
S = STRIKE PRICE
LBEP = LOWER BREAK-EVEN POINT = S – DR
HBEP = HIGHER BREAK-EVEN POINT = S + DR
DR = DEBIT = INITIAL STRADDLE COST = MAXIMUM LOSS
MAXIMUM GAIN = UNLIMITED

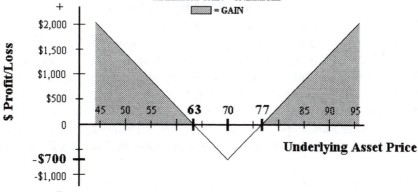

LONG STRADDLE

BUY 1 EXXON JUNE 70 CALL @ 4
BUY 1 EXXON JUNE 70 PUT @ 3

OUTLOOK = BULLISH OR BEARISH
S = STRIKE PRICE = $70
LBEP = LOWER BREAK-EVEN POINT = $63
HBEP = HIGHER BREAK-EVEN POINT = $77
DR = DEBIT = MAXIMUM LOSS = $700
MAXIMUM GAIN = UNLIMITED
■ = GAIN

ferent expiration dates, or both different strike prices and different expiration dates.* The long call option allows the trader to earn a profit if it were to expire in-the-money, and the long put option allows the trader to earn a profit if it were to expire in-the-money; if both options were to expire out-of-the-money, meaning the market neither advances nor declines, then the trader loses what was paid in premium for the options. Since the trader is purchasing both a call option and a put option, the trader must pay the option writers for both contracts, making this a debit combination. Consequently, in order to profit on the trade, one must first recoup the total cost of this combination. To obtain the break-even points of a long combination, one would add the net cost of the combination to the long call option's strike price and subtract the net cost of the combination from the long put option's strike price—anything above the upper (call option's) break-even point would be a profit and anything below the lower (put option's) break-even point would be a profit. Any price in between these two levels would be a loss to the trader. The maximum gain for a long combination is unlimited, while the maximum loss for a long combination is simply the total cost of the option premiums.

Example
Buy 1 Exxon (XON) June 75 Call @ 3
Buy 1 Exxon (XON) June 65 Put @ 2½
Market price of Exxon stock: $70

In this example, the trader has initiated a long combination since the security and the expiration months are the same, but the strike prices are different. The advantage of this long combination is that the premiums will be lower than those for a long straddle because the strike prices are spaced further apart, creating a larger window for losses. Here, the trader has purchased one Exxon call option with a June expiration and a $75 strike price for $300 and has purchased one Exxon put option with a June expiration and a $65 strike price for $250, when Exxon is trading at $70 per share. Therefore, the total cost of the combination is $550. This is a nonrefundable, fixed cost to the trader and cannot be retrieved. This $550 is also the most the trader can lose on the transaction—if both the call and the put options were to expire at-the-money or out-of-the-money, meaning Exxon stock were trading at $65 per share, $75 per share, or somewhere in between, the trader would lose $300 on the long June 75 call and would lose $250 on the long June 65 put. Again, the trader would ideally like to see the market advance or decline dramatically. If Exxon stock were trading at $80 per share, the trader would make $500 on the long June 75 call option position that is in-the-money, make nothing on the long June 65 put option position that is out-of-the-money, and lose $550 on the fixed cost to initiate the combination, for a net loss of $50. If Exxon

* However, long combinations with differing strike prices are the most common.

were trading at $60 per share, the trader would make nothing on the long June 75 call option position that is out-of-the-money, make $500 on the long June 65 put option position that is in-the-money, and lose $550 for the fixed cost to initiate the combination, for a net loss of $50. If Exxon stock were trading at $80½ per share, the trader would make $550 on the long June 75 call option position that is in-the-money, make nothing on the long June 65 put option position that is out-of-the-money, and lose $550 in nonrefundable costs to initiate the combination, for a net gain of zero. If Exxon stock were trading at $59½ per share, the trader would make nothing on the long June 75 call option position that is out-of-the-money, make $550 on the long June 65 put option position that is in-the-money, and lose $550 in nonrefundable costs to initiate the combination, for a net gain of zero. If Exxon stock were trading at $85 per share, the trader would make $1000 on the long June 75 call option position that is in-the-money, make nothing on the long June 65 put option position that is out-of-the-money, and lose $550 in fixed costs necessary to initiate the combination, for a net gain of $450. Finally, if Exxon stock were trading at $55 per share, the trader would make nothing on the long June 75 call option position that is out-of-the-money, make $1000 on the long June 65 put option position that is in-the-money, and lose $550 in fixed costs necessary to initiate the combination, for a net gain of $450. Please note that a long combination is made up of two regular option contracts. Therefore, as Exxon's market price continues to move in-the-money, either upside or downside, profits continue to grow indefinitely. Long combinations differ from spreads in that the gains are not limited.

To summarize, the most the trader could lose in a long combination would be the cost of the combination ($550) and this would occur if the options expired at-the-money or out-of-the-money (greater than or equal to $65 and/or less than or equal to $75). The most the trader could make in a long combination is unlimited to the upside and restricted to the total value of the underlying contract if it were to decline to zero ($6500 − $550 = $5950) on the downside. Therefore, if the market were to advance or decline, the trader will gain; however, if the market were to move sideways, the trader will experience a loss. (See Payoff Diagram 2.10.)

Short Straddle

In a short straddle, the trader believes the market will consolidate or move sideways into the options' expirations. A short straddle entails the simultaneous sale of a call option and a put option of the same security, strike price, and expiration date. The short call option allows the trader to gain if it expires at-the-money, and the short put option allows the trader to gain if it also expires at-the-money; if the market either advances or declines, then the trader loses the amount by which the option is in-the-money. Since the trader is selling both a call option and a put option, the trader initially receives the full option premiums for both contracts, making this a credit straddle. Because he or she is taking on more risk by selling both options, the trader

PAYOFF DIAGRAM 2.10   Profit diagrams for a long combination and the Exxon long combination example.

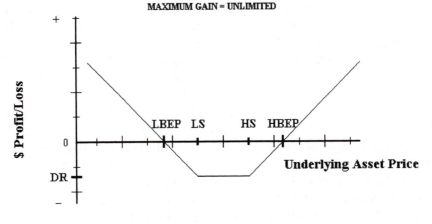

LONG COMBINATION

OUTLOOK = BULLISH OR BEARISH
LS = LOWER STRIKE PRICE
HS = HIGHER STRIKE PRICE
LBEP = LOWER BREAK-EVEN POINT = LS − DR
HBEP = HIGHER BREAK-EVEN POINT = HS + DR
DR = DEBIT = INITIAL COMBINATION COST = MAXIMUM LOSS
MAXIMUM GAIN = UNLIMITED

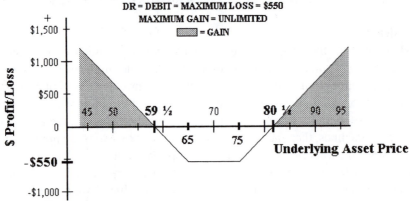

LONG COMBINATION

BUY 1 EXXON JUNE 75 CALL @ 3
BUY 1 EXXON JUNE 65 PUT @ 2 ½

OUTLOOK = BULLISH OR BEARISH
LS = LOWER STRIKE PRICE = $65
HS = HIGHER STRIKE PRICE = $75
LBEP = LOWER BREAK-EVEN POINT = $59 ½
HBEP = HIGHER BREAK-EVEN POINT = $80 ½
DR = DEBIT = MAXIMUM LOSS = $550
MAXIMUM GAIN = UNLIMITED
▨ = GAIN

receives a larger premium. To obtain the break-even points of a short straddle, one would add the net payment received on the straddle to the short call option's strike price and subtract the net payment received on the straddle from the short put option's strike price—anything above the upper (call option's) break-even point would be a loss and anything below the lower (put option's) break-even point would be a loss. Any price in between these two levels would be a gain to the trader. The maximum gain for a short straddle is the initial premium income the trader receives for selling the options, while the maximum loss for a short straddle is unlimited.

Example
Sell 1 Exxon (XON) June 70 Call @ 4
Sell 1 Exxon (XON) June 70 Put @ 3
Market price of Exxon stock: $70

In this example, the trader has initiated a short straddle since the security, the strike prices, and the expiration months are all the same. Here, the trader has sold one Exxon call option with a June expiration and a $70 strike price for $400 and has sold one Exxon put option with a June expiration and a $70 strike price for $300, when Exxon is trading at $70 per share. Therefore, the total premium received by the option writer on the straddle is $700. This is a nonrefundable, fixed income payment to the trader and cannot be lost. This $700 is also the most the seller can make on the transaction—if both the call and the put option were to expire at-the-money, meaning Exxon stock were trading at $70 per share, the trader would owe nothing and keep the $400 on the long June 70 call and the $300 on the long June 70 put. Therefore, the trader would ideally like to see the market move sideways. If Exxon stock were trading at $75 per share, the trader would lose $500 on the short June 70 call option position that is in-the-money, lose nothing on the short June 70 put option position that is out-of-the-money, and make $700 for the fixed cost to initiate the straddle, for a net gain of $200. If Exxon were trading at $65 per share, the trader would lose nothing on the short June 70 call option position that is out-of-the-money, lose $500 on the short June 70 put option position that is in-the-money, and make $700 for the fixed cost to initiate the straddle, for a net gain of $200. If Exxon stock were trading at $77 per share, the trader would lose $700 on the long June 70 call option position that is in-the-money, lose nothing on the long June 70 put option position that is out-of-the-money, and make $700 in nonrefundable costs to initiate the straddle, for a net gain of zero. If Exxon stock were trading at $63 per share, the trader would lose nothing on the short June 70 call option position that is out-of-the-money, lose $700 on the short June 70 put option position that is in-the-money, and make $700 in nonrefundable costs to initiate the straddle, for a net gain of zero. If Exxon stock were trading at $80 per share, the trader would lose $1000 on the short June 70 call option position that is in-the-money, lose nothing on the long June 70 put option position that is out-of-the-money, and make $700 in fixed costs necessary to initiate the straddle, for a net loss of $300 on the spread. Finally, if Exxon stock were trading at $60 per share, the trader would lose nothing on the short June 70 call option position that is out-of-the-money, lose $1000 on the short June 70 put option position that is in-the-money, and make $700 in fixed costs necessary to initiate the straddle, for a net loss of $300. Please note that a short straddle is simply made up of two regular option contracts. Therefore, as Exxon's market price continues to move in-the-money, either upside or downside, losses continue to increase indefinitely. Short straddles differ from spreads in that the losses are unlimited.

To summarize, the most the trader could make in a short straddle would be the full premium received by initiating the straddle ($700) and this would occur if the options expired at-the-money ($70). The most the trader could lose in a short straddle is unlimited to the upside and restricted to the total value of the underlying contract if it were to decline to zero ($7000 − $700 = $6300) on the downside. Therefore, if the market were to move sideways, the trader will gain; however, if the market were to advance or decline, the trader will experience a loss. (See Payoff Diagram 2.11.)

Short Combination

A short combination is very similar to a short straddle. In a short combination, the trader believes the market will consolidate or move sideways into the options' expirations. A short combination entails the simultaneous sale of a call option and a put option of the same security, but with different strike prices, different expiration dates, or both different strike prices and different expiration dates.* The short call option allows the trader to gain if it expires at-the-money or out-of-the-money, and the short put option allows the trader to gain if it also expires at-the-money or out-of-the-money; if the market either advances or declines, then the trader loses the amount by which the option is in-the-money. Since the trader is selling both a call option and a put option, the trader initially receives the full option premiums for both contracts, making this a credit combination. Because the trader is taking on more risk by selling both options, he or she receives a larger premium. To obtain the break-even points of a short combination, one would add the net payment received on the combination to the short call option's strike price and subtract the net payment received on the combination from the short put option's strike price— anything above the upper (call option's) break-even point would be a loss and anything below the lower (put option's) break-even point would be a loss. Any price in between these two levels would be a gain to the trader. The maximum gain for a short combination is the initial premium income the trader receives for selling the options, while the maximum loss for a short combination is unlimited.

---

* However, short combinations with different strike prices are the most common.

PAYOFF DIAGRAM 2.11   Profit diagrams for a short straddle and the Exxon short straddle example.

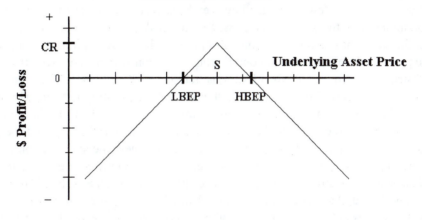

SHORT STRADDLE

OUTLOOK = NEUTRAL
S = STRIKE PRICE
LBEP = LOWER BREAK-EVEN POINT = S − CR
HBEP = HIGHER BREAK-EVEN POINT = S + CR
CR = CREDIT = INITIAL PAYMENT RECEIVED = MAXIMUM GAIN
MAXIMUM LOSS = UNLIMITED

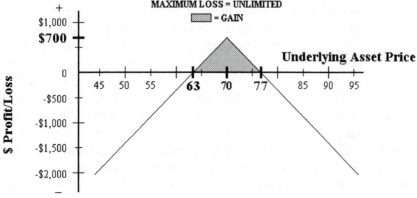

SHORT STRADDLE

SELL 1 EXXON JUNE 70 CALL @ 4
SELL 1 EXXON JUNE 70 PUT @ 3

OUTLOOK = NEUTRAL
S = STRIKE PRICE = $70
LBEP = LOWER BREAK-EVEN POINT = $63
HBEP = HIGHER BREAK-EVEN POINT = $77
CR = CREDIT = MAXIMUM GAIN = $700
MAXIMUM LOSS = UNLIMITED
= GAIN

Example
Sell 1 Exxon (XON) June 75 Call @ 3
Sell 1 Exxon (XON) June 65 Put @ 2½
Market price of Exxon stock: $70

In this example, the trader has initiated a **short** combination since the security and the expiration months are the same, but **the** strike prices are different. The advantage of this short combination is that the strike prices are spaced further apart, creating a larger window for gains; however, because of the widened strike prices, the premiums that the seller receives will be lower than those for short straddles. Here, the trader has sold one Exxon call option with a June expiration and a $75 strike price for $300 and has sold one Exxon put option with a June expiration and a $65 strike price for $250, when Exxon is trading at $70 per share. Therefore, the total premium received by the option writer on the combination is $550. This is a nonrefundable, fixed income payment to the trader and cannot be lost. This $550 is also the most the trader can make on the transaction—if both the call and the put option were to expire at-the-money or out-of-the-money, meaning Exxon stock were trading at $65 per share, $75 per share, or somewhere in between, the trader would owe nothing and keep the $300 on the short June 75 call and the $250 on the short June 65 put. Again, the trader would ideally like to see the market move sideways. If Exxon stock were trading at $80 per share, the trader would lose $500 on the short June 75 call option position that is in-the-money, lose nothing on the short June 65 put option position that is out-of-the-money, and make $550 on the fixed cost to initiate the combination, for a net gain of $50. If Exxon were trading at $60 per share, the trader would lose nothing on the short June 75 call option position that is out-of-the-money, lose $500 on the short June 65 put option position that is in-the-money, and make $550 for the fixed cost to initiate the combination, for a net gain of $50. If Exxon stock were trading at $80½ per share, the trader would lose $550 on the short June 75 call option position that is in-the-money, lose nothing on the short June 65 put option position that is out-of-the-money, and make $550 in nonrefundable costs to initiate the combination, for a net gain of zero. If Exxon stock were trading at $59½ per share, the trader would lose nothing on the short June 75 call option position that is out-of-the-money, lose $550 on the short June 65 put option position that is in-the-money, and make $550 in nonrefundable costs to initiate the combination, for a net gain of zero. If Exxon stock were trading at $85 per share, the trader would lose $1000 on the short June 75 call option position that is in-the-money, lose nothing on the short June 65 put option position that is out-of-the-money, and make $550 in fixed costs necessary to initiate the combination, for a net loss of $450. Finally, if Exxon stock were trading at $55 per share, the trader would lose nothing on the short June 75 call option position that is out-of-the-money, lose $1000 on the short June 65 put option position that is in-the-money, and

PAYOFF DIAGRAM 2.12   Profit diagrams for a short combination and the Exxon short combination example.

SHORT COMBINATION

OUTLOOK = NEUTRAL
LS = LOWER STRIKE PRICE
HS = HIGHER STRIKE PRICE
LBEP = LOWER BREAK-EVEN POINT = LS − CR
HBEP = HIGHER BREAK-EVEN POINT = HS + CR
CR = CREDIT = INITIAL PAYMENT RECEIVED = MAXIMUM GAIN
MAXIMUM LOSS = UNLIMITED

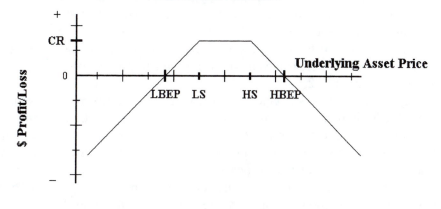

SHORT COMBINATION

SELL 1 EXXON JUNE 75 CALL @ 3
SELL 1 EXXON JUNE 75 PUT @ 2 ½

OUTLOOK = NEUTRAL
LS = LOWER STRIKE PRICE = $65
HS = HIGHER STRIKE PRICE = $75
LBEP = LOWER BREAK-EVEN POINT = $59 ½
HBEP = HIGHER BREAK-EVEN POINT = $80 ½
CR = CREDIT = MAXIMUM GAIN = $550
MAXIMUM LOSS = UNLIMITED
▨ = GAIN

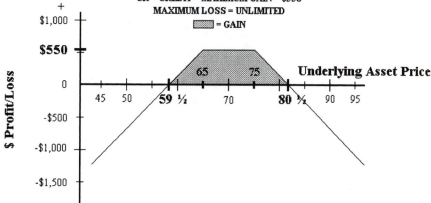

make $550 in fixed costs necessary to initiate the combination, for a net loss of $450. Please note that a short combination is made up of two regular option contracts. Therefore, as Exxon's market price continues to move in-the-money, either upside or downside, losses continue to grow indefinitely. Short combinations differ from spreads in that the losses are unlimited.

To summarize, the most the trader could make in a short combination would be the full premium received by initiating the combination ($550) and this would occur if the options expired at-the-money or out-of-the-money (greater than or equal to $65 and/or less than or equal to $75). The most the trader could lose in a short combination is unlimited to the upside and restricted to the total value of the underlying contract if it were to decline to zero ($6500 − $550 = $5950) on the downside. Therefore, if the market were to move sideways, the trader will gain; however, if the market were to advance or decline, the trader will experience a loss. (See Payoff Diagram 2.12.)

Many possible option strategies can be utilized to anticipate price movement. Before a trader initiates a position, it is important that the trader determine the most advantageous and cost-effective strategy for his or her needs. This depends upon the individual's trading intentions and whether he or she is trading options for hedging, income, or speculative purposes.

If you have any additional questions concerning option basics, consult your broker or any of the option trading literature listed at the end of this book.

C H A P T E R

3

OPTION MECHANICS
AND TRADING

N *OW THAT WE HAVE discussed the basics of options, let's look at some of the important factors a trader must consider before trading options.*

PLACING OPTION ORDERS

Before participating in a market, regardless of which one, it is important that one become familiar with many of the trading nuances and aspects which apply to that specific market. This is especially true when trading options. Once these variables are addressed and an option contract is selected, the trader must then place the order. When placing an option order, a trader must make certain to supply the following trading instructions to the broker:

1. Whether the option order is a buy or a sell
2. The number of option contracts the trader wishes to transact
3. The proper description of the option, including the specific option contract to be traded, the correct month and year, and the exercise price
4. The price at which the trader wishes to buy or sell the option
5. The specific exchange the trader wishes to use to conduct the trade if more than one exchange lists the option
6. The stop loss level, or the price at which the trader wishes to exit an unprofitable trade

7.   The type of option order to be executed, that is, an opening purchase, a
     closing purchase, an opening sale, or a closing sale

There are several types of orders that can be placed with one's broker, depending upon the trader's situation. Some orders are utilized to simply determine the
place or the time to buy or sell an option position, while others are utilized to provide protection on an existing market position. With the exception of Good-Til-
Canceled orders, or GTC orders, all of the following are day orders, meaning if
they are not executed by the end of the trading day, they are canceled. Although not
all order types are available on all exchanges, some of the most common option
orders are presented.

Market orders.   The simplest type of option order is a *market order.* In this case,
as soon as the order arrives on the trading floor, the trade is executed at the best
possible price. Buy orders will be filled at the market's lowest existing offering
price level, and sell orders will be filled at the market's highest existing bid price
level. Therefore, the price at which an order is executed is determined by the forces
of supply and demand. While market orders will always be filled immediately
upon arriving on the trading floor, some price accommodations must be made,
especially when trading large quantities. In some instances when fewer contracts
are offered on the floor than a trader wishes to purchase, or when fewer contracts
are bid on the floor than a trader wishes to offer, certain price concessions must be
made to complete the transaction. In these cases, the bidding and offering price in
the market will be adjusted accordingly to absorb the desired quantity, and any
trader who places a large market order must often be prepared to accept a series of
market fill prices, some progressively worse than others.

Limit orders.   To counteract any market disruption which may be caused by a
market order, it is often prudent to enter a limit order. A *limit order* is entered when
one wishes to purchase or sell an option at a specific price. Buy limit orders can
only be filled when price trades downward to that specified price and can only be
filled at the limit price or better (meaning the buy order is filled at a price that is
lower than the limit price); sell limit orders can only be filled when price trades
upward to that specified price and can only be filled at the limit price or better
(meaning the sell order is filled at a price that is higher than the limit price). Unfortunately, whereas a market order will always be executed, a limit order runs the risk
of going unfilled if the market fails to rally to a sell limit order, or if the market
fails to decline to a buy limit order. In any case, if the market exceeds the limit
order level, it should be filled since the limit becomes a resting bid or offer in the
market place.

Stop order.   Stop orders are useful when one wishes to control one's losses or execute a trade when a price's momentum starts to shift. A stop order is placed away from the current market and becomes effective only when price trades at or through the stop level, whereupon the order is treated as a market order. A buy-stop is placed above the current market and it becomes active once price trades at or above that price level; and a sell-stop is placed below the current market and it becomes active once price trades at or below that price level. However, keep in mind that even when triggered, stop orders cannot guarantee a price, and in situations where the market is fluctuating wildly there is a greater likelihood that one's fill will be worse than one would like.

Stop-limit order.   Stop-limit orders are useful when one wishes to control one's losses or execute a trade when a price's momentum starts to shift, and obtain a specific price. A stop-limit order is placed away from the current market and becomes effective only when price trades at or through the stop level, whereupon the order is treated as a limit order. A buy-stop limit order is placed above the current market and it becomes active once price trades at or above that price level. Once the stop-limit level is hit, the buy order must be executed at the stated price or better; also, once this level is touched, the buy limit becomes a standing order until it is filled or until the end of the day's trading, whichever comes first. A sell-stop limit order is placed below the current market and it becomes active once price trades at or below that price level. Once the stop-limit level is hit, the sell order must be executed at the stated price or better; also, once this level is touched, the sell limit becomes a standing order until it is filled or until the end of the day's trading, whichever comes first. However, keep in mind that even when triggered, stop-limit orders cannot guarantee a price, and in situations where the market is fluctuating wildly there is a chance that one's order may not be executed.

There can be some confusion between limit orders and stop orders, especially when a trader is forced to make a quick trading decision. Just remember that buy limits are placed below the market because a trader wants to pay as little for the instrument as possible; sell limits are placed above the market because a trader wants to receive as much for the instrument as possible; buy stops are placed above the market because a trader only wants to purchase the instrument if price exhibits strength; and sell stops are placed below the market because a trader only wants to sell the instrument if price exhibits weakness.

Market-if-touched (MIT) order.   A market-if-touched order is similar to a stop order only with the levels placed on the opposite side of the market. Once price trades to a specific level, a MIT order becomes a market order and is executed at the best possible price. A market-if-touched buy order is placed below the market and is filled at the lowest offer price available once price trades to that level. A market-if-touched sell order is placed above the market and is filled at the highest bid price available once price trades to that level. These orders can be placed if a trader wishes to wait for price to move to a certain level, but wants to ensure that his or her order will be filled.

Limit- or market-on-open (MOO) order.   Like their names sound, a market-on-open and a limit-on-open order are used to execute a trade sometime during the trading day's opening period (typically within the first minute of trading). In the case of a market-on-open order, the trader's order is filled at the best available price at some time just after the opening bell. In the case of a limit-on-close order, the trader's order is filled at the trader's price or better at some point just after the opening bell. In both cases, the order is not necessarily executed at the opening price, just at some price during the opening range.

Limit- or market-on-close (MOC) order.   For the sake of simplicity, rather than place an order at a limit price or at the market, some traders use market-on-close or limit-on-close orders to exit existing positions or execute new positions sometime during the trading day's closing period (typically within the last minute of trading). In the case of a market-on-close order, the trader's order is filled at the best available price at some time just prior to the closing bell. In the case of a limit-on-close order, the trader's order is filled at the trader's price or better at some point just prior to the closing bell. In both cases, the order is not necessarily executed at the closing price, just at some price during the closing range.

Fill-or-kill (FOK) order.   A fill-or-kill (FOK) is used when a trader wishes to make a single bid or offer to the trading floor for a specific quantity at a specific price. If the order, or a portion of the order, is not executed immediately upon being presented to the trading floor, then it is canceled. A FOK order can be filled in whole or in part, but can only be offered once. FOK orders can vary from exchange to exchange as to how many times the order must be presented to the floor (for example, some exchanges require that a FOK order be presented three times as opposed to one), so a trader might want to familiarize him- or herself with how the procedure is handled.

Cancel (CXL).   Very simply, a cancel order is used to eliminate a prior order that has not yet been executed. A canceled order must be communicated by a trader to the broker and such an order is not executed or confirmed until the floor broker reports back that the trader is out of the trade. Understand that once an order has been filled, it *cannot* be canceled.

Good-til-canceled (GTC) order.   A good-til-canceled order is simply an item that a trader can add to another type of order, such as a limit order or a stop order, to allow the order to extend beyond the current trading day. With a GTC order, the broker will attempt to execute the trade until the trade is filled. A GTC order will exist until the trade is filled, the order is canceled, or if the order has been standing for a long period of time without being executed (the period depends upon the exchange, but is usually many months). Not all exchanges accept GTC orders, so it is important to determine whether they do so before the order is placed. For those exchanges that do not accept GTC orders, the trade must be entered by the customer each day as a day order.

Spread order.   A spread order is used to simultaneously buy and sell two instruments. Spread orders are quoted as the price difference between the two instruments. Spread orders can be placed at the market or at a spread limit price. When enacting a buy spread order, thereby creating a debit on the trade, a trader wants to pay the lowest possible cost for the transaction (when offsetting the trade, the trader looks for the spread between the instruments' premiums to widen, or move further apart, so he or she can profit); and when enacting a sell spread order, thereby creating a credit on the trade, a trader wants to receive the greatest possible payment for the transaction (when offsetting the trade, the trader looks for the spread between the instruments' premiums to narrow, or move closer together, so he or she can profit).

Our preference is to place limit orders, and if for some reason the order is unfilled, then we seek other trading alternatives that may exist. One thing is for certain in this business: there is never an end to the trading possibilities and if an opportunity is missed or overlooked, there is always another which can serve as a replacement.

READING AN OPTION PRICE TABLE

Many major newspapers and trading publications today provide option-pricing tables so traders can track and follow the activity of certain listed options on a day-to-day basis. While the organization of these price tables may differ slightly for stock options, they all usually contain the security that the option covers, the prior day's closing price of the underlying asset, the varying strike prices and expiration months, the prior day's volume and closing prices for each call option, and the prior day's volume and closing prices for each put option. Other option listings, such as those for indices, also include items such as the net price change of the option from the previous day's closing price and the open interest of the call or put option.

Figure 3.1 illustrates a typical stock option listing taken from the *Wall Street Journal.* As you can see, the stock option information is separated into columns. The first column lists the stock to which the option applies and, below that level,

FIGURE 3.1   Sample stock option price listing much like the one you would find in your local newspaper.

Option	Strike	Exp.	—Call— Vol.	Last	—Put— Vol.	Last
Amazon	110	Feb	922	24 ½	377	11
123	120	Feb	1251	19 ½	467	16
123	120	Apr	1134	23 ¾	344	19
123	130	Feb	867	14 ¼	171	13 3/8
123	140	Feb	947	11	61	25 5/8
AmOnline	130	Feb	148	17 ¾	748	7 1/8
140 ¾	135	Feb	373	14 5/8	487	9
140 ¾	140	Feb	3670	12 ½	1665	11 ¼
140 ¾	140	Mar	475	17 ½	127	16
140 ¾	140	Apr	764	21 7/8	19	18 7/8
140 ¾	145	Feb	1983	10 ¼	205	14 ¾
140 ¾	150	Feb	3691	8 3/8	298	16 ¾
140 ¾	150	Apr	693	17 1/8	6	24

the prior day's closing price for the stock; the second and third columns represent the option strike prices and expiration months available to be traded, respectively; the fourth and fifth columns apply to call options and show the volume for each contract—the total number of contracts that traded for each particular option—and the last, or closing price, for that call option, respectively; and the sixth and seventh columns apply to put options and show the volume for each contract—the total number of contracts that traded for each particular option—and the last, or closing price, for that put option, respectively. Columns that do not have a value and are represented by ". . . ." mean that particular option did not trade that day. Option listings for index options or futures options are basically presented in the same manner as stock options but with a few slight differences, such as also including an option's net change and open interest. Figure 3.2 provides an example of an index option price listing and Fig. 3.3 shows a futures option price listing, both hypothetical examples much like those one would find in one's local newspaper.

SELECTING AN OPTION
Given the wide assortment of possible option expirations and strike prices, which is the preferable option contract selection for a trader? This answer is not black and white and varies depending upon the goals of the trader. For those option traders who believe that the trend of an underlying security has been or soon will be established for some time to come, they may wish to hold the option until it approaches expiration and a significant profit is captured. These individuals are referred to as *position traders*. Other traders are not concerned with long-term projections in the

FIGURE 3.2   Sample index option price listing much like the one you would find in your local newspaper.

Strike		Vol.	Last	Net Chg.	Open Int.
S & P 100 INDEX (OEX)					
Feb	600 c	96	26 ¾	- 2 ¾	5,347
Feb	600 p	4,003	14 ½	+ 1	8,120
Mar	600 c	2	38 ½	- 6 ¾	2,143
Mar	600 p	106	24	+ 2 ¼	1,526
Feb	605 c	292	23 1/8	- 2 7/8	3,749
Feb	605 p	712	16 3/8	+ 7/8	3,746
Mar	605 c	2	36 1/8	- 4 7/8	211
Mar	605 p	2	22 ½	- 2 5/8	18
Feb	610 c	3,289	20	- 3	11,865
Feb	610 p	4,955	18	- 1 ½	11,153
Mar	610 c	8	31 ¼	- 5 ¾	2,934
Mar	610 p	114	25 7/8	- 2 7/8	2,204

underlying security and are only interested in what will occur on a particular trading day. These individuals are referred to as *day traders*. Position traders and day traders have two very different approaches and attitudes when selecting the appropriate option contract to trade. Most position traders typically choose an expiration month and a strike price that matches their price target and the time frame in which they believe that target will be reached. Day traders, on the other hand, are not concerned with which expiration month or strike price they should choose, all they are concerned with is being on the right side of the market in the option that will bring them the greatest return.

When day trading options, various time and price considerations are not as important as they would be to a long-term option trader. Since option positions are held for such a short period of time, the impact of time decay is negligible when day trading and does not really work for or against the trader (unless it is the day of option expiration or one or two trading days before expiration, where time premium typically erodes more rapidly). Although our opinion is by no means absolute, we suggest that when one wishes to day trade options or intends to hold an option position for no more than one to two trading days, that one trade the nearby (closest expiration month) option contract which is at- or slightly in-the-money, when the underlying security has, or is just about to, exceed the exercise price. As we discussed earlier, as the price of the underlying security trades through the exercise price and proceeds to move in-the-money, the time value initially contracts and then begins to move almost one for one in lockstep with the price of the

FIGURE 3.3   Sample futures option price listing much like the one you would find in your local newspaper.

INTEREST RATE

T-BONDS (CBT)
$100,000; points and 64ths of 100%

Strike	Calls-Settle			Puts-Settle		
Price	Feb	Mar	Jun	Feb	Mar	Jun
125	2-44	3-11	....	0-01	0-24	....
126	1-45	2-27	3-33	0-01	0-40	2-08
127	0-48	1-49	....	0-01	0-64	....
128	0-03	1-16	2-33	0-22	1-26	3-06
129	0-01	0-53	....	1-19	2-01	....
130	0-01	0-34	1-46	2-19	2-46	4-18

Est. vol. 250,000;
Thur vol.   104,623 calls; 114,682 puts
Op. Int. Thur   596,880 calls; 636,920 puts

CURRENCY

JAPANESE YEN (CME)
12,500,000 yen; cents per 100 yen

Strike	Calls-Settle			Puts-Settle		
Price	Feb	Mar	Apr	Feb	Mar	Apr
8700	1.54	2.40	....	0.78	1.64	....
8750	1.26	2.13	....	1.00	1.87	....
8800	1.03	1.88	....	1.27	2.12	....
8850	0.85	1.67	....	1.59	2.41	....
8900	0.70	1.48	....	1.94	2.71	....
8950	0.57	1.31	....	2.31	3.04	....

Est. vol. 3,395   Thur 1,810 calls 5,547 puts
Op. Int. Thur 32,349 calls 49,102 puts

underlying security. Because the impact of time premium is generally minimal, day trading an at-the-money or slightly in-the-money option is essentially the same as trading the underlying asset, only for much less money, with a greater profit potential, and with a defined level of risk.

Another factor that must be considered when deciding which option contract to day trade is option liquidity. Typically, the nearby, closest to at-the-money option is the most actively traded option and has the greatest volume and open interest. This liquidity is important, not only when entering the trade, but also when exiting the trade as well, especially for a day trader. Inactive, light-volume, and low-liquidity markets are difficult to trade and large concessions must be made by the trader to obtain market positions, since the spread between bid and ask in these situations is typically wide and the increment within which a trader is able to transact is small. We cannot stress enough the significance of market liquidity to a day trader in the selection of option trading candidates. A familiarity with the recent volume and open interest for a particular option is crucial in determining the size of the commitment a trader should make to a specific option market.

HOW MUCH TO BUY

Perhaps the best advice we can provide to beginning traders is to manage your trades. This is especially true when trading options. One of the biggest problems option traders face is that they allow their emotions to dictate when they make their purchases and do so with reckless abandon. Since they are accustomed to paying so much more for other assets, they typically spend a comparable amount of money on options, leveraging their positions to the maximum, and hoping for the sizable price "pop" which will catapult their profits into orbit. However, this is the worst mistake an option buyer can make. If these large positions are not timed accurately, a trader can lose a large amount of money. Most people justify their option position size by rationalizing that they would have spent the same amount as they had on the underlying security, but now they are controlling more of the underlying security. What they don't always realize is that options do not retain their value like these other assets, because the passage of time will always have a negative effect upon the option. That is why options cannot be considered *investments;* they are simply *trades.*

Our suggestion in determining how much of an option to purchase is this: a prudent option trader will limit his or her exposure to any particular trade. The prerequisite for proper money management is different for a day trader versus a trader who holds the option position overnight or longer. While it is not our role to determine a trader's exposure to a market, we feel it is crucial to address this matter, as we have seen a number of traders execute imprudent option trades and money management. A good rule of thumb is that a day trader should not risk more than 2 percent of his or her portfolio in any one trade, and a position trader should not risk any more than 4 percent of his or her portfolio in any one trade. If traders prefer to exceed these prescribed limits, we recommend that the traders protect their positions with offsetting option trades and definitely with stop losses.

WHEN NOT TO BUY AN OPTION

It is also important to consider the time or the date at which one should enter the option market. While these option-buying suggestions are presented in the context of day trading options, they apply equally as well to option position trading.

- When day trading, a trader must give the market adequate time to perform. Consequently, eliminate day trading within the final hour of trading. If one is position trading options, this suggestion should not be a concern.

- Avoid trading in an illiquid option market.

- Avoid purchasing call options just prior to a stock going ex-dividend. Avoid buying or selling options based upon anticipated news (buyouts in particular). Besides bordering on unethical trading, the information received is more likely to be rumor than correct.

- Avoid purchasing options well after the market has established a defined trend—this is especially true when day trading, as any option premium advantage will have dissipated.

- Avoid purchasing way out-of-the-money options when day trading, as any favorable price movement will have a negligible effect upon premium.

- Avoid purchasing call options when the underlying security is up for the day versus the prior day's close, unless one intends to take a trend-following stance. (See Option Rules, Chap. 4).

- Avoid purchasing put options when the underlying security is down for the day versus the prior day's close, unless one intends to take a trend-following stance. (See Option Rules, Chap. 4).

- Be careful when holding long option positions beyond Friday's trading day's close unless one is option position trading. Many option theoreticians recalculate their volatility, delta, and time decay numbers once a week, usually after the close of trading on Fridays or over the weekend. The resulting adjustments in these values most often have a negative effect on the value of the long option, which may be acceptable when holding an option over an extended period of time but is detrimental when day trading.

WHY TRADE OPTIONS?

With the tremendous growth that has occurred in the option markets over the years, it should come as no surprise that options provide an excellent trading opportunity. As you have probably been able to gather thus far, buying options responsibly can provide a greater level of security to traders, allowing them to rest easy during the day and sleep better at night. Options give traders more time to think about their positions without worrying about how much they could potentially lose. As one family friend puts it, buying options enables the trader to leave the computer screen and hit golf balls. If traders were to take positions in the actual security, or sell options, they must closely monitor their positions and only watch others hit golf balls on ESPN.

If you have any other questions concerning option basics, mechanics, or other specifics, refer to any of the option literature listed at the end of this book, or contact your broker or any of the option exchanges listed in the appendix.

II

OPTION TECHNIQUES AND INDICATORS

C H A P T E R

4

TOOLS AND TECHNIQUES

FOLLOWING THE MARKETS *for many years has enabled us to make many trading observations regarding options and securities. One of the most noteworthy is the concept of buying weakness and selling strength. Timing the price zones where this can be performed is the foundation of our work and enables a trader or an investor to anticipate trends rather than strictly follow them. To assist one in identifying these low-risk opportunity zones, we suggest that one also incorporate a series of trading rules we have developed. These rules and observations are especially important when looking to day trade options.*

If you are trading as a hobby or on a part-time basis, then pause for a moment and deliberate how difficult your full-time job can be at times and think about the ways in which it can be made simpler. More than likely, others before you have been similarly challenged to create shortcuts, and most if not all quantum leaps in job improvements for your particular field of employment have been developed. Any upgrades in technology are few and far between and your knowledge is probably shared by all others performing similar tasks.

Now who says that trading is any less difficult or complex? The media has projected an image of wealth and luxury with trading. Certainly, there are extremely wealthy traders, but don't you think if it were as simple as many believe it to be that more traders would be successful? Trading is difficult.

However, whereas most professions are mature and thoroughly researched, trading is a fertile field for objective market-timing indicators. Only within recent years has it become acceptable to research the dynamics of the marketplace. Previously, not only were the technology and the software lacking, but also the legitimacy of pursuing such a research path was questioned by university professors and well-known investors alike. Now the brightest minds in the world are developing code to break the market and, although unsuccessful, are making progress. Prior to the advent of computers, intelligence was not necessarily an advantage or even a factor in trading success since a trader's emotions tended to interfere with prudent and thoughtful decision making. Technology has removed the element of emotionalism and enabled the process to become more objective and mechanical. We're not implying we have the Holy Grail by any means, but we have enjoyed a distinct advantage over other analysts by virtue of having observed and researched the markets for close to 35 years, collectively. Consequently, we have had the opportunity to develop a group of original techniques which have proven to be sensitive to identifying significant market reversal points.

BUYING WEAKNESS AND SELLING STRENGTH

As individuals, we are all products of our environment. Our feelings, attitudes, and actions are often influenced by a series of external events and conditions. A rush to buy winter wear typically occurs only after the first freeze or snowstorm arrives, just as the need to purchase umbrellas usually arises once the weather changes to rain. Most often, we are ill-prepared to adapt to the immediate future should it differ from what we are accustomed to. Simply put, we are creatures of habit—we wait for a change to make a change. Traders often react similarly, extrapolating current market trends of strength or weakness well into the future without properly establishing contingencies should an unexpected change in (market) conditions arise. They tend to exaggerate these trends because they possess a biased predisposition to the market due to either overall market sentiment or the fact that they are personally involved in a trade and are subconsciously promoting their own positions.

It is not difficult to understand why a trader might prefer to be a trend follower. Uncertainty in any aspect of life is difficult to deal with. To overcome this uncertainty, most people rely upon experts to explain the likely ramifications of an event or, failing to seek out just such an experienced individual, concede to the will of the masses, finding solace in conformity. There is a decided level of comfort and security in either allowing another to make a decision for us or by acceding to the influence of a group. In each instance, the burden of responsibility for making a mistake is removed from oneself, since the decision was ultimately determined by others. This attitude may be acceptable in life but to practice similarly in the market is financial suicide.

Approval and acceptance are essential to interacting harmoniously with others. To constantly oppose widely held opinions or decisions and to force one's beliefs upon a group is an invitation to exclusion. In today's society it is important to be socially correct and not be disruptive—flow with the crowd mentality, if you will. Conducting one's trading activities similarly may be easy psychologically but the implications to one's portfolio could prove financially disastrous. There is a common trading adage that states "The trend is a trader's friend." Our experience suggests that, for the sake of completeness, this expression should be qualified with an addendum that reads "Unless the trend is about to end," because that is the single worst time to enter into a trade in the direction of the prevailing trend. However, it is the single best point in time to enter into a trade against the overall trend. The price level just prior to that inflection point where price reverses its trend is the ideal time to enter the option market, for example, because it allows the trader to participate in the inception of a new trend. Unfortunately, this price reversal point is much easier to reference than it is to identify. Not only must traders acquire the expertise and the tools necessary to locate these low-risk opportunities, but they must also possess the courage to defy the dominant psychology of the market at that time, which is to extend the existing trend. Consequently, our goal is to share with you various methods we created to help identify these critical market turning points for securities, as well as their respective derivative products, such as options. Not only do these indicators provide a trader with insight as to how to anticipate price reversal points but also with a detailed list of conditions that generally exist at those turning points, all of which enable a trader to make this difficult process more objective and less emotional.

Market highs and lows differ in frequency and duration, depending upon the time frame one applies. For the most part, short-term highs and lows may not have much of an impact upon the overall market picture or trend. Obviously, at major turning points, short-term price bottoms and tops will coincide with and evolve into long-term price bottoms and tops, since longer-period market price moves are comprised of a series of shorter-period market price moves. Personally, our trading efforts are most often devoted to these short time frames. This enables us to participate in many short-lived price moves, and, at the same time, market conditions justifying, also allows us to extend our holding period for a longer period of time. Since any market turning point could extend into a significant bottom or top, we encourage day traders to hold their trading positions longer on occasion. However, because short-term signals may only be effective for a short period of time, we advocate protecting market positions at all times with stop losses. Because markets move in a series of price waves over various time periods, it is important for a trader to prudently place a stop loss and to do it consistent with the time interval which meets his or her trading preference and style.

Price never moves straight up or straight down, even when price moves are news-driven. There are rare instances when each trade over a short period of time will be consecutively higher or lower, but these moves will eventually be punctuated with price reactions until the price surge finally dissipates and trading normality resumes. Typically, price moves unfold in a series of waves. Traders' collective interpretation of the impact of any news developments upon a market determine the direction and the intensity of these waves. Since the market is a discounting mechanism, as soon as news is released, traders evaluate and process the perceived impact that it may have upon a security. The convergence of all these traders' expectations is reflected in one figure—price. Ultimately, the critical determinant of price movement is the degree of buying and selling pressure.

One important aspect of price movement which is often overlooked by overzealous traders is the fact that, over time, the intensity of both buying and selling diminishes. The reason is that as more and more traders commit their funds to the market, the reservoir of similarly disposed traders diminishes in size. Our research indicates that markets form bottoms, not because there is a group of smart buyers who are driving prices upward; rather, figuratively speaking, the last seller has sold and by default price moves sideways or higher. Conversely, markets form tops, not because there are smart sellers who are forcing prices downward, rather, figuratively speaking, the last buyer has bought; therefore, price moves sideways or lower. To illustrate this observation, consider the fact that as price moves higher, more and more trend followers enter the market. Usually, fundamental research becomes more positive, convincing the fundamentalists to enter the market as well. As the news continues to be favorable, more and more investors enter the market. At the same time, traders who were negatively disposed toward the market reverse their positions from sellers to buyers. Ultimately, the buyers exhaust themselves and the buying and selling pressure arrive at a standoff. Once the last buyer has bought, price declines. Keep in mind that the reverse scenario holds true in cases where a market's price is declining. These same principles can be applied to market activity on a time scale as short as one minute and consisting of a series of price ticks to much longer periods of time.

With these market-timing principles in mind, our research has uncovered certain market behavior and tendencies which occur near market tops and bottoms. For instance, we have found that a general skepticism is often associated with market lows. In this case, if price has declined for a period of time and the news continues to be bleak but price actually rallies, this event suggests that there is an apparent absence of sellers required to perpetuate the decline. Traders' prayers, hopes, or promises will do nothing to force price lower; only additional selling can accomplish that goal. Similarly, as a market rallies, news and analyst recommendations reflect this bullish market outlook. Ultimately, all the potential buyers have bought into the position and, despite additional favorable news, it is insufficient to sustain the rally unless a renewed source of buying develops. Again, prayers or promises will not move the market higher; only additional buying is capable of doing that. Our observations indicate that market bottoms are accompanied by negative news, just as market tops are usually formed with the release of positive news. Furthermore, when a market is incapable of rallying despite good news, it is often indicative of an imminent retreat in buying and a potential downside price reversal. Conversely, when a market is unable to decline despite negative news, it is often a sign that there is a decrease in selling pressure and a potential upside reversal is pending. At major market turns, the news is often so extreme that the sellers and buyers collectively exhaust themselves and the market is susceptible to establishing a meaningful reversal in trend. Since markets typically exaggerate advances and declines, opportunities arise for alert traders who are prepared for these price reversals. The challenge for a trader is to differentiate between the real and the perceived low- and high-risk opportunity zones.

The interaction between supply and demand determines price. Market expectations and news create occasional price imbalances and present traders with opportunities to profit. Fear and greed swing the price pendulum in any market. Fundamental information, such as earnings forecasts, new product introduction, crop reports, government policies, money supply, interest rates, and a host of other variables, are important factors influencing valuation. However, market sentiment and traders' perceptions have a dramatic impact and are oftentimes responsible for exaggerating and extending price movements. The impact of nonfundamental contributing factors, such as stop losses, margin calls, and so forth, cannot be measured but their influence is also significant.

Stock market specialists and option market makers play an important role in the marketplace. They supply liquidity to a market by providing supply when a market rallies and by providing demand when a market declines. Their method of trading is to operate against the prevailing market trend. Obviously, doing so is not always profitable—occasionally, markets will perpetuate a trend longer than expected. But, most often, retracements and market reactions allow those traders to offset their trades and continuously reset them. With proper discipline and money management, these professional traders are able to produce consistent profitable returns. We have known only one specialist firm to go bankrupt in the past 40 years, and most adequately capitalized, disciplined market makers have been able to withstand any drawdowns. This is not only a tribute to their trading expertise but also a recognition and testimony to their unique trading style. We believe that to trade options and other securities successfully, a trader must emulate their (countertrend) trading philosophy. For example, an option trader must abandon any false impression that trading decisions must be supported by other traders and the media because, very likely, they will not. Traders using our prescribed methods must be resigned to the fact that they must operate against the prevailing market trend and the overall trading environment and ignore external input or confirmation. The trading strategy is described as contra-trend and such traders are certainly market mavericks.

Forecasting precision is our goal but not at the expense of common sense or logic. We rely upon proprietary techniques that we have developed over the past 27 years and which have statistically withstood the rigors of time and countless data samples. By and large, these methods were designed to anticipate tops and bottoms, not confirm them. After all, knowing a high or low after it occurs is meaningless—but that is what most trend followers unwittingly do. Occasionally, our indicators may be premature, our price objectives may be overshot, or our calculated price reversal levels may be slightly off the mark, but the outcome should generally be correct. Sadly, nothing is or will be perfect when following the markets. But by mechanizing these market-timing approaches, traders can minimize ambivalence and ambiguity, two factors that ultimately destroy traders' confidence as well as their trading accounts.

OPTION PURCHASING RULES

It's human nature to want to buy a market when the media and brokers are positive, or bullish, and likewise to sell a market when they are negative, or bearish. This response is reflexive and characteristic of most inexperienced traders. However, by dissecting the dynamics of the market, it becomes apparent why the antithesis of this response would be more profitable, especially when day trading. With the majority of markets today, price fluctuates rapidly, leaving little time to enter at important price reversals. Oftentimes, a high or low is established and quickly followed by a price vacuum, as floor traders and other traders scramble to quickly reverse their positions. If one were to enter at this point, that individual would likely suffer considerable price slippage and experience terrible order fills, particularly if one were day trading. That is why we prefer to buy before a market low is recorded and price is still declining and why we prefer to sell before a market high is made and price is still advancing. If the crowd is buying, we are looking for a place to sell, and vice versa, if the majority is selling, we are looking for a place to buy. This way, we can enter the market and, oftentimes, actually enjoy positive slippage, realizing better fills than if we were attempting to participate in the market's trend. Therefore we realize a greater profit potential for our trades by participating in a larger portion of a market move. This practice is similar to the role played by both market makers and floor specialists. Someone must assume the opposite side of a transaction, as difficult as it may be at the time, both psychologically and emotionally.

We are not encouraging you to ignore fundamental analysis or common sense. After all, it is foolish to immediately take a trading stance against the direction of a news announcement, crop report, or earnings release—doing so is akin to stepping in front of an express train or catching a falling dagger. However, we are suggesting that traders view these announcements as opportunities to anticipate and identify key areas of price exhaustion, particularly when day trading. And because these important news releases are often followed by sharp price retracements, anticipating trend reversals can create sizable trading profits.

Our recommended practice of buying into market weakness and selling into market strength is an important trading lesson we learned early in our careers. This approach is applicable to all markets and is particularly valuable once a market's volatility, or intraday price movement, increases. More often than not, news serves as a catalyst causing a security's price volatility to increase. The increased public interest and participation in the market is reflected in the expansion of volume and wider price swings in the underlying asset. If the underlying security undergoes a transformation in its trading profile, a similar change becomes apparent in any related option activity since the accompanying option premium will expand to adjust to the increased volatility. Generally, if the news or market's perception of the news is tilted toward the positive, the premium attached to the calls is greater than that assigned to the puts. Conversely, all other factors being equal, if the outlook or traders' expectations are perceived negative, then the put premium is greater than that of the call premium. Regardless, the impact of news upon a security reverberates and resonates throughout its respective derivative markets as well.

Again, to reiterate, markets usually record trend reversals at a bottom when the last seller, figuratively speaking, has sold and at a top when the last buyer, figuratively speaking, has bought. Also, contrary to popular belief, the release of negative news generally coincides with and exhausts the downside of a market just as the release of positive news coincides with and exhausts the upside of a market. Obviously, as price declines, the ultimate low draws closer in terms of both time and price; and as price advances, the eventual high draws closer in both respects as well. Sooner or later, a down close signals the final low of a decline as does an up close signal the final high of a rally. By applying this concept to option price activity, the initial rule for trading is formulated. In other words, by requiring that the closing price of an option be down versus the prior period's closing price for a low-risk call buying opportunity and by requiring that the closing price of an option be down versus the prior period's closing price for a low-risk put buying opportunity, a distinct trading advantage can be established. One could also require that not only the option adhere to this trading qualifier, but also that the underlying security conform similarly by closing down for a call and up for a put. Additional layers of requirements can also be introduced to further filter short-term trades. By applying these concepts to both long-term and short-term trading, investors can realize greater trading success.

To take advantage of these observations we have outlined, we have devised a set of rules to determine the opportune environment in which to buy call and put stock options. Similar rules can be applied to futures options but since the homogeneity among contracts is lacking in this market, the prescription must be altered somewhat. Ideally, each of these trading rules should be aligned before entry into a market occurs; however, in the real world this requirement may be less restrictive. These rules stand well on their own and help prevent one's emotions from running rampant in the market, but the addition of other indicators, such as TD Percent Factor (TD % F) and the interrelationship between call and put volume and open interest, can be utilized to further fine-tune a trader's entry.

RULES FOR BUYING CALLS AND PUTS

Rule No. 1: Buy calls when the overall market is down; buy puts when the overall market is up.   By and large, when the stock market rallies, most stocks rally, and when the stock market declines, most stocks perform likewise. The extent of this movement can easily be measured by observing stock indices. We recommend using the advance/decline index as a proxy for the overall market. However, if this is unavailable, one could also use the net price change of a comprehensive market average, such as the Standard & Poor's 500, New York Stock Exchange Composite, NASDAQ, or Dow Jones Average. For the overall market to rally, the majority of individual stocks must rally, too. Sure there are days in which the market is rallying even though the number of advancing issues is less than the declining issues but this cannot last long if the stock market is to mount a sustainable advance. Similarly, on the downside, the market cannot undergo an extended decline unless the number of declining stocks outnumber the advancing stocks.

When the overall market trades lower, call option premiums typically decrease. Therefore, by requiring the market index to be down for the day at the time a call is purchased, the prospects for a decline in a call's premium are enhanced. Similarly, when the overall market trades higher, put option premiums typically decrease. Therefore, by requiring the advance/decline market index to be up for the day at the time a put is purchased, the prospects for a decline in a put's premium are enhanced similarly. Since most stocks rise and fall with the general market—with the possible exception of gold stocks—this provides a measure of much-needed discipline and helps prevent emotional, uncontrolled option buying.

Rule No. 2: Buy calls when the industry group is down; buy puts when the industry group is up.   Just as most stocks move in phase with the market, most industry group components move in sync with their counterparts within their specific industry as well. Therefore, when one stock within an industry group is down, chances are the others are down as well. It's the exception when one component of an industry advances while all the other members decline, or vice versa, especially over an extended period of time. For example, situations can arise where a buyout occurs and the accumulation of one company's stock causes it to outperform the others within the industry group. However, announcements such as these typically cause the other stocks within the same industry group to participate in the movement since the market's perception is that all companies within the group are likely acquisition candidates and their stocks are "in play," so to speak.

Rule No. 3: Buy calls when the underlying security is down; buy puts when the underlying security is up.   In order to time the purchase of calls, we look for the price of the underlying security to be down relative to the previous trading day's close. If the stock's current market price is less than the previous day's close, most traders extrapolate that the down trend will continue. It is also possible to relate the stock's current price with its opening price level to make this rule more stringent. Either relationship, that is, current price versus yesterday's close or current price versus the current day's open, can be applied or a combination of the two can be used to insure that the composite outlook for the market is perceived bearish by most traders.

In order to time the purchase of puts, we look for the price of the underlying security to be up relative to the previous trading day's close. If the stock's current market price is greater than the previous day's close, most traders extrapolate that the up trend will continue. It is also possible to relate the stock's current price with its opening price level to make this rule more stringent. Either relationship, that is, current price versus yesterday's close or current price versus the current day's open, can be applied or a combination of the two can be used to insure that the composite outlook for the market is perceived bullish by most traders.

Rule No. 4: Buy calls when the option is down; buy puts when the option is down.   Just as the previous series of rules required that specific relationships be fulfilled, so too must this prerequisite be met. In fact, of all rules listed, this requirement is singularly the most important. The option's price, be it a call or a put, must be less than the previous day's close. As an additional requirement, it may also be less than the current day's opening price level as well. Obviously, if an option's price is inevitably going to rally, it is smarter to buy as low as possible. Further, if the call or the put unexpectedly continues to decline to zero, then the loss incurred is nevertheless less than if one had chased the price upside and purchased the option when it was trading above the previous day's close.

The combination of the preceding rules serves to remove a degree of emotionalism from operating in the options markets and instills a level of discipline in the trading process. We can't tell you how long it took to acquire and apply these important rules to our trading regimen. Obviously, the risk always exists that despite the fact that all the previously described rules may be met, option prices may continue to decline, and as a result purchasing the call options or the put options will translate into a losing proposition. That's a concern that can only be diminished by introducing a series of sentiment measures or various market-timing indicators to confirm option buying at a particular point in time. The integration of these rules together with market sentiment information comparing put and call volume and the information regarding various indicators presented in the other chapters within this book enhance the timing and selection results further by concentrating upon ideal candidates which are low-risk opportunities based upon all four requirements.

We have included as an alternative to the closing price bar comparisons, the comparison of the current trading bar's close versus the current trading bar's open, as well as the current trading day's close versus the prior trading day's close. We believe the media and data-reporting services have unknowingly performed a dis-service to traders by publishing daily price change in terms of the current trading day's close versus the prior trading day's close. Our work throughout the years has shown that the activity from the current trading day's open to the current trading day's close is more valuable to a trader. Why do we believe this is the case? What occurred yesterday in the market is history and what happens today is current and relevant. After yesterday's close a news announcement could have been released which affects the market and therefore prices. By inserting the current trading day's open as a proxy for the prior trading day's close, we can process and accom-modate this information. The price movement above the opening suggests buying or accumulation and the price movement below the opening indicates selling or distribution. Now if the market had closed yesterday at 97 and closed today at 100 (up 3), the assumption might be that accumulation or buying had taken place from one close to another. However, if the market had opened this morning at 103, after a perceived positive news announcement overnight, and then proceeded to trade lower and close at 100, the accumulation/distribution picture would appear quite different. Instead of price closing up 3 points from one close to another, it closed down 3 points from its open. The perception to the part-time market watcher was that the market strength was exhibited, whereas market weakness was the true price movement. We refer to this particular pattern and its counterpart at a market low where current day's close is below the prior trading day's close but the same trad-ing day's close is above its open as *TD Camouflage.* Not only is this pattern preva-lent at the turning points for underlying securities, but it also appears, to a lesser extent, with the related options. Obviously, this method is not suitable for day trad-ing options or their underlying securities since one must await the close for confir-mation of internal, hidden weakness or strength. The technique can be used for short-term trading but it does require a few qualifiers to enhance its predictive abil-ities. A further discussion of TD Camouflage appears elsewhere in the book.

OUR INTRODUCTION TO OPTIONS

We believe the methodology we present in this book will supply you with the ammunition to buy options successfully. By citing one example in particular, you can appreciate the importance of market timing. In the late 1970s through 1980s we had a successful institutional consulting service. In this service, we would often share the results of a sensitive volume price change model we created to identify possible stock buyout candidates, the results of which were excellent. Occasionally, the buyout indications were so pronounced that we would inform our clients that an expected buyout was to be announced. Oftentimes, they would ask us about the timing of this expected takeover since they wanted to take advantage of the leverage conveyed by purchasing options. We discouraged the purchase of options only because it was often difficult to time the entry for this indicator accurately; despite the fact we were convinced of some positive news, we had no definitive means of confirming a low-risk option purchasing opportunity since our option-timing tools were still in the development stages. In any event, we had just been successful in alerting our clients to a series of successful buyouts, specifically Chenetron, Kennecott, Cutler Hammer, Monroe Auto, Pizza Hut, Babcock and Wilcox, and Budd Company, and many of these clients were satisfied with the results and willing to trade the findings. A relatively new institutional client was amazed by this string of accomplishments and frequently asked about the next buyout candidate. After a period of time, our model indicated to us that Cities Service was a prospective candidate—this occurred in April of 1982. Unknown to us, this client purchased a large number of shares of stock in this company but invested much more, relatively speaking, in options. Much later, after the transaction was completed, we learned that the options were the June expiration. Throughout this period of time, the director of this fund would often inquire about the timing of the impending buyout. We cautioned him that our accumulation/distribution work was accurate but incapable of pinpointing the specific week, let alone the exact day.

Coincidentally, the third Friday of June 1982, we were on the floor of the CBOE and just minutes after the close, indicating the expiration of the June call options, lo and behold, on the news monitor was the official announcement of the buyout of Cities Service. Accompanying us on the floor was an individual who was aware of our buyout prediction on the stock. He congratulated us and remarked, "Look at all the option 'chumps' who watched the June option series expire, only to hear the announcement after the close." Although we were frustrated by this revelation, for our client's sake, it made a lot of sense. Other companies made similar announcements subsequent to the nearby option expiration, we believe in an effort to frustrate and discourage illegal option insider trading. We admonished our client that this experience was the very reason we recommended trading the underlying security as opposed to the option. Subsequently, the exchange introduced Saturday settlements, which only added insult to financial injury for our client. The events of this and similar situations served as the catalyst in conducting additional work to develop most of our current option-timing techniques.

INDICATORS

Any system or set of indicators that can consistently identify low-risk trading opportunities that exist in the option markets will undoubtedly have a great impact upon the way options are viewed and traded. The most dramatic effect will be noted by the purchasers of options. Most traders are convinced the only way to make money trading options is to write options, not to purchase options. The biggest enemy of any trader who purchases an option is the time value of premium. It always appears that the premium's time value decays far more quickly than the option buyer would like. And as option traders know, the option decays quickly when the market fails to move in-the-money in a relatively short period of time, either moving further and further out-of-the-money or remaining dormant for a long period of time.

However, if traders were to time their market entries and only take trades at those times in which the market was vulnerable to price reversals, they would be able to reduce the negative impact of time decay to a tolerable, possibly minimal, level. This is particularly the case if one is trading options intraday or trading an option with an expiration far into the future; in each of these cases, a few bars of adverse movement will not have a consequential effect upon the overall status of the option. In fact, purchasers of options may be able to make the time value work to their advantage rather than to the option writer's favor. The primary reason is that the value of time is a somewhat arbitrary and subjective figure. If the underlying market were to experience a dramatic move, the time premium could conceivably experience a percentage increase that is exponentially greater than its initial value. Therefore, with effective market-timing techniques, time decay may in fact have no effect whatsoever and work on the side of the option holder as opposed to the option writer.

One of the biggest problems that the average trader has is timing his or her entry point. While traders may have opinions about a certain market or have heard a news announcement that influences them to enter a market, the question remains, when is the best time to enter? Even if one is able to select a day to enter, one must still pick the time of the day to enter. Most often, the average trader enters the market with a market order once he or she decides on a particular security, or the trader will pick an arbitrary price level at which to enter the market. These entry points may be fine, but there is usually no justification for or significance attached to the selection of these levels for one's entry—they are simply arbitrary prices. In a sense, these individuals are trading blindly; and while this subjective buying and selling (or call and put buying) may work for a short period of time, eventually one's luck will run out. By introducing indicators that can be applied effectively not only to daily price charts but to minute and hourly charts as well, such as TD Sequential and TD Combo, among others, traders can coordinate their buying or selling efforts with points of anticipated market strength or weakness. These indicators should greatly improve traders' market-timing abilities not only in timing the purchase of securities but also related options, allowing the traders to control their risk more efficiently.

The market-timing techniques in the chapters that follow have been the culmination of approximately 30 years of work. Approximately half of the indicators that we discuss are new indicators, with some applying directly to the option contract, such as TD % F and TD Dollar-Weighted Options, and the rest applying to the underlying asset which can, in turn, be utilized to trade the related option. While you may recognize some of these indicators from some of our earlier work, the descriptions that follow will be different in that new aspects, new qualifiers, and new settings will be introduced and emphasized, often allowing one to trade the indicator results differently; these descriptions are presented with option trading in mind; and the indicators are described in a much simpler and less-intimidating manner than before.

Even though many of these indicators were created to identify potential reversal points in the underlying stock and commodities markets, the results can be utilized to perfect one's entry in a security's option as well. These techniques work on a variety of levels; consequently, not only will you be able to apply these indicators to trade in the traditional long-term manner we have described in our previously published books and articles, but you will also be able to use them on shorter time periods, providing an excellent opportunity to day trade options and the underlying assets. While we both strongly believe in the effectiveness of these indicators, it is important that traders apply these indicators in the proper context. For example, it is counterproductive to permit an option's premium to erode, stubbornly holding a one-minute or a five-minute indicator-driven, low-risk trading position which fails to respond as expected. Also, just as option trading is not for everyone, neither is day trading. Of all investment strategies or stances one can take, day trading is definitely one of the most difficult to master. However, at the very least, these indicators, when applied on a short-term basis, should provide a trading edge in identifying reasonable entry points and exit points for the trader, so as to enable a trader to maximize profits.

5

OPTION INDICATORS: TD % F AND TD DOLLAR-WEIGHTED OPTIONS

ONE OF THE BIGGEST *complaints we have with many of the option trading strategies is that they are complicated, mathematically derived formulas designed to sell or write options. Not only does this limit option traders' rewards but it also leaves them vulnerable to an enormous level of risk. We have always felt that this approach is lop-sided, and any technique that would work in favor of the option buyer, containing one's risk while unleashing one's reward, would certainly be welcomed in the option-trading community. We believe that the indicators that follow, TD % F and TD Dollar-Weighted Options, are novel trading approaches to buying calls and puts, capable of anticipating not only option price movement, but also movement in the underlying asset. While these option trading indicators are certainly not the antidote to all of the ailments of an option buyer, they are incredibly simple ways to increase the potential for an option day trader's success.*

Economics 101 teaches that price moves higher when demand is greater than supply and price moves lower when supply is greater than demand. This ongoing battle between securities buyers and sellers is constantly being waged every minute and second of the trading day. Collectively, these intraday trading battles make up the overall daily trading war. This interaction can best be described in the context of a motion picture. At the completion of trading, an extensive collection of price frames are combined to create the complete daily trading picture. Rarely does the market close precisely on its high or low. These price extremes are often recorded intraday, lost amidst the flurry of price ticks (trades). Unless one examines each and every price transaction, a trader is oblivious to the time at which the daily high and the daily low are formed. In fact, given the daily reporting practices of the financial media, one can only speculate as to the daily trading sequence of a market, regardless of the proximity of these levels to one another. For example, an opening price near the daily high or the daily low does not necessarily mean the two were recorded approximately the same time of day, just as a closing price near the daily high or the daily low does not necessarily mean the two were recorded at the end of the day. Market volatility prevents one from drawing such conclusions. In any case, a full-time day trader's awareness to intraday trading nuances and price activity is particularly keen, as is the trader's sensitivity to other market factors, such as volume, bid and ask spreads, and so forth. Our assumption is that most of you are not provided the luxury of devoting your full time and attention to day trading. Consequently, we have limited our discussion of trading techniques to those which can be applied using the daily data commonly reported in financial papers or on quote machines. Although these techniques can all be programmed, they are sufficiently easy that they can be calculated with only basic math required.

Market expectations play an important role in creating supply and demand. In other words, fear and greed swing the price pendulum in any market. Fundamental information, such as earnings forecasts, new product introductions, crop reports, government policies, money supply, interest rates, and a host of other factors, contribute to expectations and determine price levels. Market sentiment and traders' perceptions play an important role as well, and are responsible oftentimes for exaggerating and extending price movements beyond realistic levels. The trading opportunities arise whenever these price extremes are exceeded and the traders' market-timing tools are sufficiently sensitive to identify these pending price reversals.

Various indicators have proven to be helpful in identifying those terminal inflection price levels where traders exhaust their selling campaigns and buyers initiate their buying, and vice versa. Usually, the termination of these price moves are accompanied by volatile price moves over a short period of time. In other words, one last lunge upside or downside occurs. Conventional methods of technical analysis have tried to identify these low-risk trend-reversal opportunity zones. However, these approaches are primarily subjective and oftentimes reflect the interpreter's emotions rather than a defined methodical process. We have chosen to rely upon objective research to develop a stable of proprietary indicators to identify these potential market turning points which produce exceptional trading opportunities. Throughout the years, these indicators have achieved a high rate of empirical success both within and across several different markets. As with all predictive approaches, however, there are no guarantees. But by installing a rigid and comprehensive series of parameters which have proven to produce reliable results in the past, traders can establish a distinct advantage over the methodology practiced by their trading peers.

It's amazing to observe the behavior of an apprentice option trader. The pattern of trading such an individual exhibits is reminiscent of our old next-door neighbor. Totally immersed in this trader's psyche was the belief that his option trading profits would grow faster than he could count. Excited and fantasizing about the imminent wealth he was to acquire, he initially traded with reckless abandon following every "whisper" buyout situation or rumored news event. As time progressed and his losses accrued, our disappointed and disenchanted option-trading neighbor finally abandoned following his emotions and withdrew from trading altogether, cursing his first trade in what he believed to be a "rigged" market. Our hope is to short-circuit your replay of this course of events and protect you from becoming another market fatality statistic like him. By following the list of option trading rules previously described, the risk of having the news and one's emotions dictate and influence one's trading style is eliminated. And once indicators TD % Factor (TD % F) and TD Dollar-Weighted Options are introduced, objectivity replaces subjectivity and further enhances the potential of trading profits. Unlike the bulk of the indicators presented in this book, these two are unique in that they are both applied directly to the option's price activity, as opposed to the activity of the underlying security, which provides insight into market sentiment and enables a trader to trade options without becoming completely dependent upon the activity of the underlying asset.

TD % F

One of the most significant option-related discoveries we made occurred quite by accident and its application has far surpassed the positive results achieved solely by applying the option rules described in the previous chapter. TD % F has added dimensions of precision and objectivity to the option-selection process. Whereas most traders justify the purchase of an option based upon their interpretation of the prospects for the underlying security and then in turn applying this forecast to the option, TD % F relies entirely upon the price activity of the option itself to measure the attractiveness of the option and totally ignores the price activity of the underlying security. In other words, in this instance, it's possible that the "tail could wag the dog" and the outlook for an underlying security can be forecast based upon the activity of the option. Not only can this indicator be applied to time the purchase of the option, but also to anticipate price reversals of the underlying stock. In this case, a stock trader could draw conclusions regarding the near-term outlook of a stock by applying TD % F to the option.

We developed TD % F as a result of evaluating a multitude of both profitable and unprofitable option trades throughout the years. The construction and description of TD % F are simple and straightforward. Neither confusing formulas nor complex mathematical models are required to perform the necessary calculations to arrive at trading conclusions. To demonstrate the simplicity and ease of its use, we taught the necessary conditions to the youngest member of our family, 11-year-old Dominic. He was able to master the process within minutes. We are confident that you will likewise be just as proficient as he in as short a period of time.

Like the majority of our market-timing indicators, TD % F is designed to buy into weakness and to sell into strength. However, since the indicator is applied directly to derivative securities, such as options, the timing of entries enables traders to leverage their trades to the maximum. As described earlier, it also provides an indication as to when the underlying security is susceptible to a potential price reversal.

The sum total of all traders' expectations regarding a security or its derivative securities is reflected in its price activity. Occasionally, these expectations can be skewed, creating price distortions and trading opportunities in the market. But with the application of various trading models designed to take advantage of these dislocations, price quickly reverts back into balance. TD % F operates in a similar manner. It attempts to identify and take advantage of severe short-term price disequilibrium or imbalance. Market psychology is responsible for short-term price moves and a quantifiable method for measuring human nature and price behavior is TD % F. How do these inefficiencies or trading anomalies become apparent to traders as opportunities? As with most discoveries or inventions, their creation is oftentimes accidental and not premeditated. Most traders review the prospects for an underlying security, research various options to select the one best suited to their trading needs, and then rely upon their expectation of this security's price activity to formulate their forecasts for the option. Similarly, most often TD Sequential, TD Combo, TD Lines, TD FibRange, TDST, TD Stop, and TD Retracements are applied to the underlying security to identify possible market reversals and trading opportunities, and then, in turn, this information is applied to the option, as are the TD Rules for option trading, all of which are used to time option entry. TD % F works in reverse. If TD % F indicates that the option appears to be vulnerable to a price reversal, then the trading assumption is that the underlying stock should respond in kind. For that reason, TD % F is a meaningful and original contribution to the library of analytical techniques on two trading levels, the option and the underlying security.

The key elements required to calculate and apply TD % F are an option's daily high, daily low, and daily close, as well as the previous trading day's close. Whereas other indicators may rely upon the underlying securities' price activity and interrelationships, TD % F concentrates solely upon the option's price profile. By multiplying the previous trading day's call option closing price level by 45 and 52 percent and then by subtracting that value from that same trading day's call option closing price, a price objective buy range for calls is established for the current trading day (an alternative method which merely requires multiplication and no subtraction is to multiply the previous trading day's call option closing price level by 48 and 55 percent to arrive at the call buy range zone for today). Conversely, by multiplying the previous trading day's call option closing price level by 90 and 104 percent and then by adding that value to the previous trading day's call option closing price, a price objective exit range zone for calls is established for the current day (another method which merely requires multiplication and no addition is to multiply the previous trading day's call option closing price level by 190 and 204 percent to arrive at the price objective exit range zone for calls for that trading day). In order to purchase the call option, TD % F requires that the market not open below 55 percent of the prior trading day's closing price; it must open greater than that level and then trade to that level to permit entry.

An identical exercise for puts can be conducted to arrive at ideal entry and exit price objective levels as well. By multiplying the previous trading day's put option closing price level by 45 and 52 percent and then by subtracting that value from that same trading day's put option closing price, a price objective buy range for puts is established for the current trading day (an alternative method which merely requires multiplication and no subtraction is to multiply the previous trading day's put option closing price level by 48 and 55 percent to arrive at the put buy range zone for today). Conversely, by multiplying the previous trading day's put option closing price level by 90 and 104 percent and then by adding that value to the previous trading day's put option closing price, a price objective exit range zone for puts is established for the current day (another method which merely requires multiplication and no addition is to multiply the previous trading day's put option closing price level by 190 and 204 percent to arrive at the price objective exit range zone for puts for that trading day). In order to purchase the put option, TD % F requires that the market not open below 55 percent of the prior trading day's closing price; it must open greater than that level and then trade to that level to permit entry.

It is likely that the price objective buy range for calls will often coincide with the price objective exit zone for puts and vice versa since, by definition, if a call declines in price, then the put should rally—the two are inversely related. The calculated buy price range, whether it be for calls or puts, provides a benchmark for downside option price risk for that particular trading day. Typically, TD % F is applied to the most active option contract which is usually the nearby expiration with the closest strike price and the largest volume and open interest. Because some options are inactive and may not trade daily, it is important to make certain that the closing price displayed is in fact the previous trading day's closing price and not a closing price from any prior trading day.

For the purpose of illustration, we contacted Steve Moore and Nick Colley at Moore Research to request some recent random option data which we in turn applied to TD % F. They provided daily high, low, and close data for the soybean (July '98) call option contracts with the closest expiration and nearest strike (exercise) to the underlying security price. For analytical purposes, we prefer to focus upon the most active option contracts as measured by daily call (or put) volume and open interest. Typically, the nearest strike price option has the most volume and open interest. In the following table, we identified with an asterisk (*) the day the most-active option strike price changed from 650 to 625 and that trading day coincided with the increase in volume and open interest as well.

Soybean (July '98) Call

Date	Close	Strike Price	High	Low	Close
1. 05/18/98	644.00	650	14.00	9.04	12.00
2. 05/19/98	632.00	650	10.04	6.06 (50.5%)	7.00
3. 05/20/98	634.50	650	7.04	5.06	7.04
4. 05/26/98	623.50	625*	12.02	9.00	9.03
5. 05/27/98	617.25	625	10.02	6.00	6.06
6. 05/28/98	618.75	625	9.00	7.00	7.00
7. 05/29/98	619.00	625	13.00	7.00	7.06
8. 06/01/98	619.25	625	8.00	5.00	7.06
9. 06/02/98	621.50	625	9.00	6.06	8.04
10. 06/03/98	619.00	625	9.00	6.00	6.06
11. 06/04/98	618.75	625	6.04	5.00	6.00
12. 06/05/98	616.25	625	6.00	3.06 (51.0%)	4.05
13. 06/08/98	611.25	625	3.06	2.04 (50.4%)	2.07
14. 06/09/98	609.00	625	3.00	1.06 (51.2%)	2.02
15. 06/10/98	613.50	625	3.00	2.00	3.00
16. 06/11/98	608.75	625	3.02	2.00	2.00
17. 06/12/98	613.75	625	3.00	1.04 (52.0%)	2.07
18. 06/15/98	608.75	625	1.06	.06**	.06
19. 06/16/98	617.00	625	3.02	.05	2.02

*The day the most-active option strike price changed from 650 to 625.
** The open was less than 55 percent (51 percent) of the previous day's close, therefore no trade.

A quick comparison of closing prices and subsequent trading days' lows and highs demonstrates how TD % F can be applied successfully. In each instance in which there is a percentage value in parentheses next to a low price in the low column—a total of five occurrences—the option low was contained within a price range defined as 48 to 55 percent of the previous option day's close. For example, the low for trading day no. 2 is 49.5 percent less than the close of trading day no. 1—in other words, 50.5 percent of trading day no. 1's close. This value is contained within the guidelines of 45 to 52 percent which TD % F requires be multiplied by the prior trading day's closing price and then subtracted from that same closing value; or, as a mathematical shortcut method, the value is simply calculated by multiplying 48 to 55 percent of the prior trading day's closing price. The close of trading day no. 11 and the following trading day's low (trading day no. 12), the close of trading day no. 12 and the following trading day's low (trading day no. 13), the close of trading day no. 13 and the following trading day's low (trading day no. 14), and the close of trading day no. 16 and the following trading day's low (trading day no. 17) are likewise examples in which price held 48 to 55 percent of the previous trading day's close.

Had a trader bought the call option when the low price was between 48 to 55 percent of day no. 17's close (no less than 1.03), a stop loss below 48 percent of the prior trading day's close would have produced a small loss. However, since there is no opening price level reported, it is possible that the market may have opened below the 55 percent low-threshold level and as a result there would have been no call option purchase since TD % F requires that the market not open below 55 percent of the prior trading day's close which it would have done. Consequently, without the opening price value, it is impossible to conclude whether the call would have been purchased or not. By reviewing the opening price of the underlying July soybean contract chart, one may conclude that the high for the call option occurred after the opening since that is what occurred for the underlying market which opened at 610.00, made a subsequent high at 612.00, and a close at 608.75. Therefore the call option would not have opened above 55 percent of the prior trading day's close and would not have been purchased.

The reverse of a price decline of 48 to 55 percent in the value of the call option from its prior trading day's closing price to the current trading day's low occurred on trading day no. 19. In this instance, the succeeding trading day's high was much in excess of 100 percent—over 50 times greater. This relationship complements the one described previously since, instead of multiplying 48 to 55 percent of the prior trading day's close to estimate a support level for low-risk buying, TD % F can be applied in reverse to arrive at potential resistance levels for low-risk exiting or selling since markets often stall and reverse at 100 percent of the previous trading day's close added to that close or, in other words, 200 percent times the prior trading day's close. We have found that it is best to avoid purchasing a call or a put option if the low of the current trading day is less than 48 percent of the prior trading day's close, as additional downside price movement should occur, just as it is best to avoid exiting or selling a call or a put option when price exceeds 208 percent of the prior trading day's close, as additional upside price movement should be attained that same trading day. Furthermore, because it is not uncommon for call and put markets to complement one another, when a call option records a price move between 190 and 204 percent of the prior trading day's close, it is important to monitor the put activity to observe how the market behaves once it declines 48 to 55 percent of its prior trading day's close. Conversely, when a put option records a price move between 190 and 204 percent of the prior trading day's close, it is important to monitor the call activity to observe how the market behaves once it declines 48 to 55 percent of its prior trading day's close.

We recall a stock put option trade we identified on September 11, 1995. Micron (MU) had enjoyed a phenomenal price rise from 15¼ on October 4, 1994, to a high of 94⅝ on September 11, 1995, almost one year later. At that time, a daily TD Combo low-risk sell indication was given by inserting open for day no. 13 of countdown instead of close and by ignoring recycling (see TD Combo). The nearby exercise or strike price for the puts was 95 and September 1995 was the nearby expiration. The stock closed at 89⅞ on September 8. At the same time, the closing price of the put on September 8 was 6⅜. On September 11, the stock recorded its closing high and the put option traded as low as 3¼. On that same trading day, we placed our purchase orders for the put between 48 and 55 percent of the prior trading day's close which was at 3⅛ and 3½. Price declined to 3¼ bid and 3⅜ offer but, as so often happens, the market did not decline to the bid; rather, it held the offering price on the downside. The put never once traded below 3⅜. Within five trading days, the stock declined from 94¾ to 88½, and within seven additional trading days, the stock further declined to 72⅞, down almost 22 points from its high a couple of weeks earlier. Had the option been trading at that time, the put position would have been worth at least 22⅛ and that includes no time premium.

Buying puts at the high of a secular (long-term trend) market move would have been avoided by all trend followers. But as price continues to rally, ultimately the peak of a price move grows closer in terms of time and price. We had no idea that TD Combo had identified any top other than possibly an interim price peak for Micron. The fact that TD % F had spoken loud and clear, that purchasing the put options was a low-risk opportunity, was sufficient evidence to us of an imminent trend change. Had we wanted to hold the position or roll it over into another put option expiration series further into the future, we could have participated in the decline to a further degree. However, day trading or holding the position for a few trading days was sufficiently profitable. Also, we could have exited the position daily and bought puts every additional time TD % F indicated the reduction in trading risk to doing so. It all depends upon the outlook a trader prefers to assume.

The concept of TD % F is simple to describe and easy to calculate, but was fairly difficult and costly to conceive. Many years ago when option trading was still in its infancy, we aggressively traded in the options market. On a number of occasions our exposure was greater than we had hoped and, consequently, we needed to place stop losses. Initially, our stops were too tight, which resulted in our exiting our option positions prematurely and just prior to major market moves. We experimented with a number of different stop-loss methods, attempting to remove our subjectivity and replace it with a mechanistic approach. We knew options were a risky market and we were determined not to lose any more than one-half of our investment on any one trade. Therefore, we applied a stop loss based upon a decline of 50 percent from the prior trading day's close. We were surprised with the results. What occurred most often was that an option's price would gravitate toward our stop-loss level but would reverse just prior to a 50 percent retracement of the previous trading day's closing price. Typically, price would decline to a point just prior to our being stopped out of the trade, whereupon the option would then commence its rally. Our arbitrary 50 percent stop-loss level proved to be a prudent decision. In addition, those instances in which we were stopped out of our position, the market price not only continued to decline further that trading day, but it also oftentimes failed to recover to the stop-loss level before the expiration of the option. The price declines that held above the stop-loss levels proved to be exceptional low-risk opportunities to purchase call options and put options.

It became quickly apparent to us that the dynamics of the market were such that once the low for an option approached, but did not exceed, 48 to 50 percent of the prior trading day's closing price, the option would usually rally. We experimented with a series of percentages between 50 and 60 percent of the prior trading day's option close and we also tested numerous stop-loss levels. The percentages presented in the preceding soybean example appeared to work the best. At the same time, we realized that once the option price declines below 48 percent of the prior trading day's close, apparently, the weight of the intraday price breakdown becomes so severe that price is unable to recover that trading day. To express this in another context, the option's price decline produces an extreme oversold condition which equates with a renewed selling, rather than a buying opportunity, due to its intensity.

Our research and observations indicate that an option price decline can readily tolerate an intraday decline of up to 48 to 55 percent of the option's previous trading day's close. However, declines which exceeded this threshold of intraday weakness have a debilitating effect upon the price of the option, as well as the underlying security. One might describe intraday option price declines from the prior trading day's close of less than 48 to 55 percent as minor injuries, scrapes, broken bones, all of which are easily recoverable; whereas declines of any greater amount would be something akin to a heart attack or a severed vertebra and consequently, irreparable. It would take a miracle for an individual to walk again after suffering paralysis and similarly it would require the option to record a one-day rally from its previous trading day's close of over 104 percent to demonstrate its ability to recover.

While we believe that TD % F is a revolutionary method to identify option trading candidates, we are aware it is not infallible, by any stretch of the imagination. Rather, TD % F is another tool an option trader can use to anticipate potential price reversals and changes in market trends. In fact, other percentages may work better than the set we propose here and we invite you to experiment to develop others. The critical consideration is the fact that the concept appears to have validity and is applicable to option trading, particularly on a day trading level, provided the option price declines occur sufficiently early in the trading day to justify entering the trade and capitalizing upon the reversal in trend.

Although it was difficult to acquire reliable option data, the CQG bar charts that follow nicely illustrate TD % F. Figures 5.1, 5.2, and 5.3 plot the price activity of three commodity options, Silver March 1999 575 Call, Japanese Yen March 1999 94.00 Call, and Copper March 1999 72.00 Call, respectively. As you can see, from the prior trading day's close, any move that is 48 to 55 percent of the previous trading day's close, downside, is identified on the chart with the intraday low and the prior trading day's closing price; and any move that is 190 to 204 percent of the previous trading day's close, upside, is identified on the chart with the intraday high and the prior trading day's closing price. Note how price has a tendency to reverse at these price levels intraday, if not for a series of trading days. Keep in mind that in order to qualify as a TD % F low risk buy, the opening price level must be above 55 percent of the prior trading day's close and the subsequent low that same trading day must not decline to 47 percent or less than the prior trading day's close—at that level, the trade should be stopped out at a small loss. Conversely, on the upside, the opening percentage gain over the prior trading day's close should not exceed 190 percent of the prior trading day's close or no exiting or selling of the option should occur.

We prefer reviewing the actual option price bar charts, instead of strictly the data, to develop enhancements to our techniques. TD % F should work equally well with other types of options. Due to the problems in collecting accurate data, we are unable to present any stock option chart examples. Hopefully, chart availability will increase as the ranks of option day traders increase in size. At the time this technique was developed in the mid-1970s, we subscribed to the William O'Neill stock option service which displayed daily option price activity. We were able to confirm our suppositions regarding TD % F and option trading with those charts. Unfortunately, they are no longer available. However, a situation that recently occurred illustrates the application of TD % F to the stock option market nicely.

A few days prior to the completion of this book, a good friend, who coincidentally happened to be a large hedge fund manager, mentioned that he had observed a tendency for the technology stocks to rally the last two days prior to option expiration. He informed us that he had taken advantage of this trading pattern by investing $25,000 in Dell Computer January 80 Call options. After a few minutes, conversation had moved to our involvement with this book. We described to him TD % F and he inquired about his prospects for trading success in applying this indicator to the option market. He indicated the prior trading day's call option close was 1⅜; we asked where the low had traded that morning and he said it had just occurred, at a price of ⅝. We quickly calculated the current value at the low to be 45 percent of the prior trading day's close—a sign that further downward movement was very likely. Upon realizing this, we advised him to get out of the trade immediately. He hung up the phone and proceeded to exit his option position; luckily, he was able to escape

FIGURE 5.1 This daily price chart applies TD % F to the Silver March 1999 575 Call option. In this chart, C represents the closing price and L represents the low price of the following trading day. As you can see, in the two instances which appear where TD % F identified low-risk option buying opportunities, the market's closing price was followed by a decline of almost 50 percent of the prior day's close. In each example, the option buying opportunity would have proved profitable.

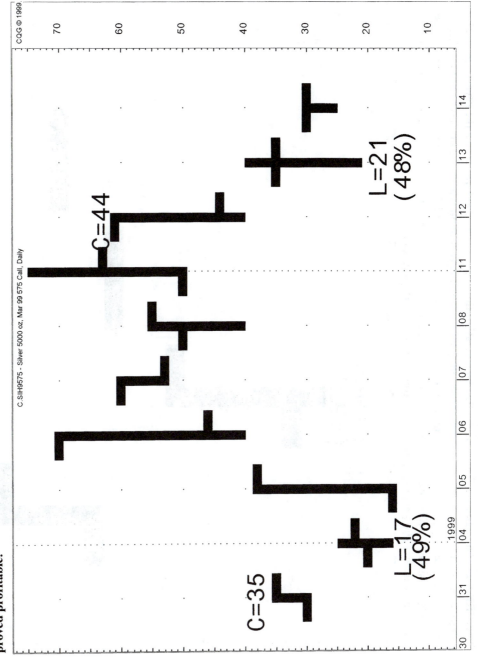

FIGURE 5.2 The Japanese Yen March 1999 94.00 Call option daily price chart illustrates the reverse scenario, where a low-risk TD % F option buying opportunity was profitable to a point where the low-risk option exiting opportunity was triggered. In this example, *C* represents the closing price and *H* represents the high price of the following trading day. The day after entering the trade following the low-risk option buying opportunity, the market rallied almost 200 percent higher, indicating a low-risk exit opportunity.

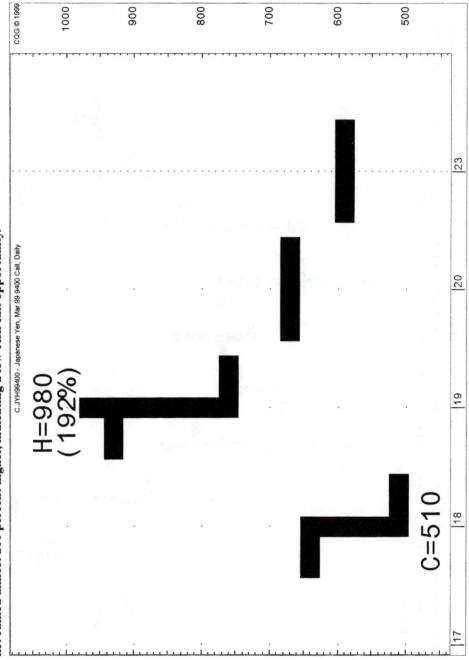

C.JYH99400 - Japanese Yen, Mar 99 9400 Call, Daily

H=980
(192%)

C=510

CQG © 1999

FIGURE 5.3 In this daily price chart of the Copper March 1999 72.00 Call option, three examples of TD % F are presented over a period of two weeks. Again, *C* represents the closing prices and *L* represents the low price the following trading day. In each example, the option market recorded a daily low that was 50 percent of the prior day's closing price, each time presenting a low-risk option buying opportunity. By day trading these option positions and holding each of these trades into the close, a trader would have realized a sizable profit, without ever taking a loss.

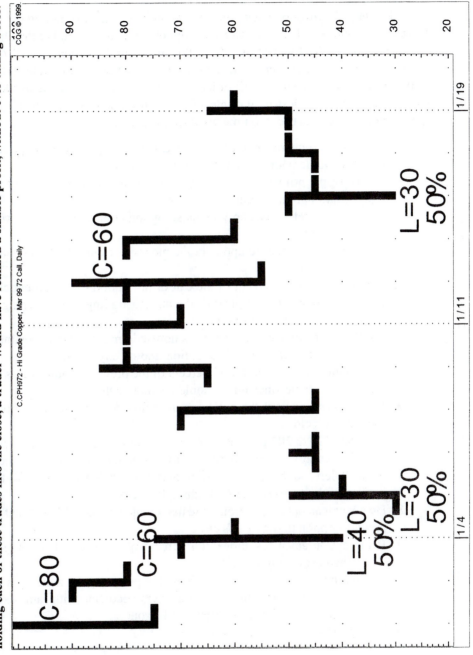

C.CPH972 - Hi Grade Copper, Mar 99 72 Call, Daily

CQG © 1999

the trade relatively unscathed, with only a ⅛-point loss. The next trading day, while the stock was almost able to rally to 80, his option never traded higher than his exit price level and expired worthless. The following expiration month's call option, however, held above a 50 percent decline of the prior trading day's close and the market was able to rally sharply off of its lows. He informed us that he had learned a good but frightening lesson and intended to apply this technique to his future option trades, as well as use it to time his stock purchases.

1. Identify the most recent trading day's call or put option closing price
   a. Concentrate upon the nearby expiration options
      (1) Apply primarily to those options which have three or fewer weeks until option expiration
          (a.) Preferably apply to those options that are within a week of expiration
          (b.) Concentrate upon "in the money" or close to "in the money" options
2. Calculate 48 to 55 percent of the call or put option's most recent closing price (yesterday's close) prior to the current trading day's opening price level to establish low-risk entry level
3. Install "alert" so that a day trader is notified once price declines intraday 48 to 55 percent of the previous option trading day's close
4. If the option declines below 47 percent of the previous trading day's close, then exit the trade since price should decline further
5. Do not take a trade if the option opens below 55 percent of the previous trading day's close
6. Calculate 190 to 204 percent of the call or put option's most recent closing price (yesterday's close) prior to the current trading day's opening price level
7. Install "alert" so that one is notified once price rallies intraday 190 to 204 percent of the previous option trading day's close
8. Do not exit an option position if the market opens above 190 percent of the previous option trading day's close
9. If the option advances above 204 percent of the previous trading day's close, then expect higher prices
   a. Coordinate this rally into the 190 to 204 percent price zone for a put or call to coincide with the reciprocal event occurring with same exercise price and expiration counterpart call or put
10. The option's closing price must be at least ¾.

TD DOLLAR-WEIGHTED OPTIONS

Initially, when listed options began trading on the Chicago Board of Options Exchange (CBOE), only calls were traded. Soon after, puts for the same securities were introduced as well. From that time forward, all new option issues included both puts and calls. In addition the exchange reported official trading statistics daily, which made it easier to analyze the market and to create sentiment indicators designed to predict market movement.

Many years prior to the trading of listed options, in the over-the-counter market, an unknown analyst created a put/call ratio indicator which was intended to measure market sentiment based upon the number of puts and calls traded daily. This volume ratio was calculated and the number plotted at the conclusion of each trading day. Although its application was logical, there existed many problems in properly accounting for the volume of the various puts and calls and numerous expirations. The data collection capabilities just didn't exist in the over-the-counter market and volume and other statistical information was regarded as specious. An old friend of ours described the method of obtaining this questionable data and the value of this information in creating option forecast models as *gigo*—garbage in and garbage out. That was the general attitude toward any information and data compiled and processed prior to the inception of listed option trading.

The release and publication of listed option information, however, changed this impression forever. Sure there were occasional errors, but that was to be expected what with the high volume of trades recorded daily. Many corrections were made but the increase in the number of options traded was enormous and some data escaped detection and correction. Despite the fact that occasionally daily intraday highs and lows are erroneously reported or attributed to the wrong option contract, or expiration or volume is late to be reported, if at all, among other problems, the daily composite statistics are generally reliable. It is important that the total volume or number of transactions be accurate for purposes of measuring market sentiment. Furthermore, it is important that open interest, which is the number of option contracts created for future delivery, be correct as well for the same reasons cited.

Unfortunately, some of the techniques we rely upon for intraday option trading require intraday open, high, low, close, and volume information which is impossible to retrieve consistently and accurately from data vendors or the various exchanges. Calculating option information similarly intraday is a different story altogether. Other than a few exchanges and interim business news updates which occasionally report these statistics intraday, there is no other source for this information during trading hours other than a quote machine. In the case of a quote machine, the figures must be compiled correctly from individual statistical information. Fortunately, we have been surrounded by sophisticated data reporting services throughout the years and we have been able to observe the interaction between various statistical information intraday. Once again, to reproduce this data is impossible due to the fact that the data vendors neither support nor provide historical intraday option data to subscribers and the little which is available is suspect as well. Consequently, for purposes of this discussion, you will have to rely upon our observations and experience in dealing with these techniques, particularly with TD Dollar-Weighted Put and Call and TD % F.

As mentioned earlier, it is not uncommon for a trader to calculate the daily put and call ratio to determine the level of bullishness or bearishness existing in the market at any one point in time. This is performed by comparing the volumes of puts and calls—specifically, dividing the put volume by the call volume. Volume is defined as the total number of option contracts traded during a specific period of time. The concept of relating put volume activity to call volume activity arises from the fact they are inversely related. If a majority of traders are buying calls and expecting the market to rally, then they have already placed their money where their minds are and the likely market direction is down rather than up. Conversely, if the majority of traders are buying puts and expecting the market to decline then they have already voted with their money and the market's direction is more likely up than down. This is consistent with the principles we have shared with you throughout this book, specifically, trend exhaustion and trend reversals. The only problems we have with this approach is the fact that the call and put volume may not measure sentiment properly unless it includes an adjustment for the price of the options, as well as a proper method of accounting for the option volume activity.

DOLLAR-WEIGHTED PUT/CALL RATIO

Is it possible that apples and apples and oranges and oranges may not be the same? What do we mean by this expression? First of all, whereas the call volume for a particular day will report how many call option contracts have traded and the put volume for a particular day will report how many put option contracts have traded, the volume statistics may not be comparable. For instance, a total of 1000 puts and 100 calls would represent a ratio of puts to calls of 10:1 based upon the conventional method of sentiment measurement. However, what if the 1000 puts were valued at $1 apiece and the 100 calls were valued at $10 apiece? Then the dollar-weighted value of the puts would be exactly equal to the dollar-weighted value of the calls, and the revised dollar-weighted put to call ratio would be 1.00 instead of 10:1. This minor dollar-weighted adjustment should be made to account for the varying costs of the options and to make the comparisons consistent with one another. In other words, by accounting for the dollar value of the options, by multiplying the put volume by the put price and the call volume by the call price, a valid comparison of dollars invested can be calculated; and then by dividing the put activity by the call activity, a measure of market sentiment can be derived.

Not only do we refer to the end-of-day dollar-weighted put/call ratio but we also calculate the intraday dollar-weighted put/call ratio to fine-tune our entries—in fact, we prefer the intraday measure over the end of day calculation. We identify the nearby expiration month and strike price, for both puts and calls, and make the relevant comparison. When the dollar-weighted put volume is at least two times larger than the dollar-weighted call volume on an intraday basis, meaning the dollar-weighted put/call ratio is 2.00 or greater, the call option becomes more attractive, and a low-risk call-buying opportunity presents itself. Conversely, when the dollar-weighted call volume is at least two times larger than the dollar-weighted put volume on an intraday basis, meaning the dollar-weighted put/call ratio is 0.50 or less, the put becomes more attractive, and a low-risk put-buying opportunity presents itself. These ratios identify where market sentiment resides, either oversold or overbought.

$$\text{Market Sentiment} = \frac{\text{Put Volume} \times \text{Put Market Price}}{\text{Call Volume} \times \text{Call Market Price}}$$

Therefore, if the dollar-weighted put/call ratio is greater than 2.00 on an intraday basis, then the market is defined as being oversold and traders should use an additional indicator to time their call-purchasing entry points; if the dollar-weighted put/call ratio is less than 0.50 on an intraday basis, then the market is defined as being overbought and traders should use an additional indicator to time their put-purchasing entry points; any value in between is defined as being a neutral reading. These ratios can be reduced to 1.25 for put options and 0.75 for call options when comparing the two on a daily closing basis.

DOLLAR-WEIGHTED PUT/CALL RATIO AS A PERCENT OF OPEN INTEREST

A more complete perspective of market sentiment can be acquired on an intraday basis by calculating volume as a percentage of open interest for both puts and calls. This process is similar to dollar-weighting the volume of puts and calls, and can likewise be applied on a daily basis or anytime throughout the day, but now we are introducing another variable: open interest. *Open interest* is defined as the number of option contracts that have been entered into or initiated and not yet liquidated and offset. To obtain this enhanced sentiment measure, one must first arrive at a put volume/open interest ratio and a call volume/open interest ratio. To calculate the put ratio, the put volume is divided by the put open interest; and to calculate the call ratio, the call volume is divided by the call open interest. These ratios are then dollar-weighted to properly consider their true value—the put ratio is multiplied by the current put market price to obtain its dollar-weighted value, and the call ratio is multiplied by the current call market price to obtain its dollar-weighted value. Once these final dollar-weighted volume/open interest values are calculated, the put value is divided by the call value to present an indication of market interest. If this fraction on an intraday basis is greater than or equal to 2.00, meaning the put volume as a percentage of open interest is at least two times larger than the call volume as a percentage of open interest, then traders are more bearish than bullish, and the market should rally—this occurs for the same reasons we mentioned earlier; specifically, because traders aren't expecting the market to move higher. On the other hand, if this fraction on an intraday basis is less than or equal to 0.50, meaning the call volume as a percentage of open interest is at least two times larger than the put volume as a percentage of open interest, then traders are more bullish than bearish, and the market should decline—this occurs for the same reasons we mentioned earlier; specifically, because traders aren't expecting the market to move lower. These ratios can be reduced to 1.20 for put options and to 0.80 for call options when making a dollar-weighted put/call comparison as a percentage of open interest on a daily basis.

$$\text{Dollar-Weighted Put Ratio as \% OI} = \frac{\text{Put Volume}}{\text{Put Open Interest}} \times \text{Put Market Price}$$

$$\text{Dollar-Weighted Call Ratio as \% OI} = \frac{\text{Call Volume}}{\text{Call Open Interest}} \times \text{Call Market Price}$$

$$\text{Market Sentiment} = \frac{\text{Dollar-Weighted Put Ratio as \% OI}}{\text{Dollar-Weighted Call Ratio as \% OI}}$$

Therefore, if the dollar-weighted put/call ratio as a percentage of open interest is greater than 2.00 on an intraday basis, then the market is described as being oversold and traders should use an additional indicator to time their call-purchasing entry points; if the dollar-weighted put/call ratio as a percentage of open interest is less than 0.50 on an intraday basis, then the market is described as being overbought and traders should use an additional indicator to time their put-purchasing entry points; any value in between is defined as being neutral.

To summarize, if the call volume as a percentage of its total open interest is extremely high and its counterpart put volume as a percentage of open interest is extremely low, the market is vulnerable to a downside reversal. Conversely, if the call volume as a percentage of open interest becomes extremely low and its counterpart put volume as a percentage of open interest gets extremely high, the market is likely to reverse upside. Now if a trader were to dollar-weight these comparisons by multiplying each ratio by its put and call dollar value—for the put comparison and the call comparison—a more meaningful number is expressed. Rather than conduct these mathematical exercises at the close of trading, a trader should be aware of other option traders' expectations throughout the trading day. This vigilance assures option trades executed are in harmony with overall market sentiment. As you can see, these calculations serve as a final filter to confirm the timing of various low-risk option trading opportunities.

DOLLAR-WEIGHTED PUT/CALL OPTION ENTRY POINT

TD Dollar-Weighted Options is a sentiment indicator, and because it does not provide a definitive entry point, per se, we typically apply the indicator on a daily and an intraday basis and then await entry confirmation with other market-timing indicators, such as TD % F or any of the other indicators presented throughout the book. Since it accounts for differences in price for a call option and a put option, this dollar-weighted put/call ratio is more representative of market expectations than the traditional means used by most option traders.

The real value of a sentiment indicator accrues to the option traders who are able to integrate dollar-weighted option trading intraday with other short-term indicators to perfect their timing. Typically, when the call volume exceeds the put volume, the market is expected to decline and, conversely, when the put volume exceeds the call volume, the market is expected to advance, resourceful traders can quickly meld the two and confirm their option trading decisions. Specifically, by dollar-weighting put and call volume intraday and reviewing the statistical information prior to placing a day trade, and then using this information with other market-timing indicators, one's timing should improve. For example, at a suspected trend reversal price level for the underlying security, if the option trading volume is tilted in the direction of a disqualified breakout, it further indicates that the majority of traders are expecting a breakout, and that it should fail. Therefore, more money can be invested in the trade than if the option activity failed to support the other indicator.

As the composition of market participants changes over time, the dollar-weighted put/call ratios representing whether a market is oversold, overbought, or neutral, occasionally need to be altered to better reflect trading sentiment. The important consideration is not so much the specific values, but rather the concept. We invite you to test alternate readings which may give an even more accurate indication of overbought and oversold conditions, and therefore a more accurate measure of the overall market environment.

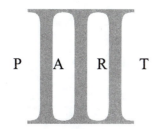

UNDERLYING
INDICATORS

C H A P T E R **6**

ANTICIPATING THE TREND: TD SEQUENTIAL, TD COMBO, AND TD SETUP TREND

OF ALL THE INDICATORS *we have created, TD Sequential, TD Combo, and TDST are certainly the most versatile. Their utility and accuracy in identifying long-term low-risk price reversal zones have withstood the test of time and the evolution of many markets. With the advent of computer technology, we have been able to take these indicators a step further to uncover a host of trading abilities and applications previously unimaginable. Much to our surprise, not only have these indicators demonstrated that they are effective low-risk, long-term trading methods, but also that securities and their related options can be applied intraday with remarkable precision.*

Markets that have recorded yearly or all-time price highs within the last few weeks can be traded with the long-term upside trend since that is the path of least resistance. Think of this trading opportunity as a rare experience, since at an all-time price high no one who has ever bought this market has endured a loss, and therefore there is limited overhead supply from disenchanted buyers; any pullback presents a trader with a buying opportunity within a reactionary mode. Conversely, at an all-time or yearly market low, no one who has purchased the market is enjoying a profit and consequently any rally should be viewed as a selling opportunity. Similarly, when the overall market or index is at a yearly price low and simultaneously a specific market is demonstrating strength by trading at its high for the year, a clear message is being sent that should the market reverse higher, the strong market

107

should be a distinct leader and outperform others. Likewise, when the overall market or index is at a yearly price high and simultaneously a specific market is demonstrating weakness by trading at its low for the year, this is a clear indication that once the overall market reverses lower, the individual weak market should underperform the overall market and possibly become a casualty of the economy.

The situations cited in the previous paragraph are ideal opportunities for traders involved in trading the trends of underlying securities over an extended period of time, but not as proxies or options representing these markets on a day-trading basis. Sooner or later, however, the trend will exhaust itself and price will reverse. Once a trader purchases an option contract the trading game of "beat the clock" commences. In many instances, the market will do what the trader wants it to do. However, the important question is, will it do it within the lifetime of the option contract? Because timing is so critical in determining when to purchase an option contract, it is extremely important that purchase be deferred until the market is prepared to reverse its trend. It is senseless to buy an option and then wait weeks for the market to move because time premium evaporates so quickly. Conversely, it serves no purpose to purchase an option after the underlying market has already recorded a price reversal, the new trend has been established, and the momentum is accelerating. The obvious change in trend has more than likely attracted numerous buyers who are aware of the change and their aggressiveness should significantly increase the value of an option's premium beyond any intrinsic value.

Because the timing of the purchase of the option contract is so important, it is necessary to apply market timing indicators which will identify to traders ideal low-risk and low-premium entry points. One such indicator designed to accomplish this is TD Sequential. We developed TD Sequential and TD Combo over 25 years ago as a method of identifying when a market has reached a point of trend exhaustion. TD Sequential and TD Combo are price anticipatory indicators designed to buy into price weakness and to sell into price strength. These indicators' greatest features include their objectivity, as well as the fact that their calculations and results are mechanical and reproducible. Another advantage is that they can both be applied to any market without the necessity of optimizing its parameters—there is no need to implement different settings for different markets. The parameters are universally set and applied regardless of whether the investor trades stocks, futures, indices, or foreign markets. One of the other features of TD Sequential and TD Combo is that they have both withstood the test of time very well. Whether the environment was a bull market, a bear market, or a trading range market, these two indicators have performed effectively throughout the years. Finally, TD Sequential and TD Combo have been proven to work well over several different time periods, from monthly and weekly charts all the way down to the lowest common time denominator, one-minute charts. Their versatility enables a trader to either day trade or position trade with both consistency and accuracy. In theory, a series of market perspectives from months and weeks could be coordinated with similar readings all the way down to a five- and one-minute basis. Nevertheless, calculating a daily TD Sequential or a TD Combo reading and then combining it with the one-minute activity is reasonable and easily accomplished. In fact, as a floor trader on the Chicago Board of Trade, T.J. successfully applied these indicators to the financial futures on a one-minute price activity basis to identify potential low-risk short-term price reversal levels. Similarly, day trading options works very well when utilizing TD Sequential and TD Combo, particularly in more active, volatile, and liquid markets.

Before you decide to quit your job and curse out your boss—thinking these indicators will deliver an obscene amount of profits—keep in mind that TD Sequential and TD Combo are indicators, not systems per se and are by no means the Holy Grail of trading or the perfect market timing tools. We'll tell you right now, they are not going to anticipate market turning points every time, nor will they be correct every time. In fact a long-standing, light-hearted criticism expressed by both authors has been the fact that TD Sequential has successfully predicted "10 out of the last 7 market price reversals" implying that 3 were likely premature and consequently wrong. Despite this perceived shortcoming, we believe no other indicators are capable of anticipating market tops and bottoms as consistently as TD Sequential and TD Combo have over the past 25 years. The distinct advantage of these related trading tools is that they are designed to sell unemotionally into market strength and buy into market weakness regardless of news, fundamental outlook, or any other factor unrelated to market dynamics. Provided a trader applies uniform parameter settings for the indicators over all markets and time periods, practices sound money management, and is capable of controlling his or her emotions, then these indicators should become an important trading companion, greatly contributing to a trader's success.

A large portion of any trader's success is attributable to his or her method of money management. Controlling one's losses and allowing one's profits to run is a lesson which is easy to teach but unusually difficult to learn and practice. Most books devoted to trading fail to emphasize the importance of riding at least a portion of a market trend. Option trading using TD Sequential and TD Combo provides an objective and mechanical dimension to trading which complements sound money management principles. The advantage of option trading with TD Sequential and TD Combo is that a position can be taken for far less money, or a much larger position can be taken with the same initial capital outlay. In addition, since the maximum loss of a long option is simply the initial cost of the position, the option acts as an inherent stop loss. Because these losses are predetermined by the trader at the time the long option position is initiated, price drawdowns in the underlying asset are not as threatening. Therefore, oftentimes options provide more leeway, and consequently more comfort, to traders than owning the underlying asset—the trader can hold an option position for a longer period of time without worrying about the financial impact of an adverse price move, since the trader's risk is defined at the time the option is purchased. If entry is premature, and price continues to move against the option position, a trader need not worry about exiting the position due to accruing losses and missing out on the desired price move, since the option conveys its trading rights for a specified time period with a defined risk level, regardless of the price of the underlying security. Selecting the time frame in which to apply these two indicators is left totally to the trader's discretion. However, if a trader prefers to hold positions for periods longer than a couple of trading days, then daily low-risk TD Sequential and TD Combo opportunities should be monitored. If a trader desires to be actively trading intraday, then it is prudent for him or her to follow one-minute TD Sequential and TD Combo activity. This choice is up to the trader, but operating intraday should be performed within the context of the bigger picture—by requiring intraday (one-minute) TD Sequential or TD Combo entries to conform to the daily indications, the results will often provide the reinforcement a trader needs to participate with the market's flow. Regardless of his or her preferred operating time horizon, an option buyer has the ability to time option market entries effectively and anticipate expansions in a call's premium off a market low and expansions in a put's premium off a market high by applying TD Sequential and TD Combo.

TD Sequential and TD Combo can be utilized to anticipate not only price reversals in the underlying stock, but also reversals in options as well. Although not always possible and definitely not required, these indicators can be applied to the option trading activity much like they are to the underlying security. In the past, we have relied upon the activity of the underlying security to dictate the TD Sequential low-risk entries or the TD Combo low-risk entries and then, in turn, we have applied the results to the option market. This was more a matter of option chart availability and convenience rather than choice. Due to the fact that the option charts are more readily available today, when trading options we occasionally look for both to confirm, or at least if one chart passes our qualifications' test, the other chart should produce similar indications since the option follows the activity of the underlying security. If one were to apply TD Sequential or TD Combo directly to an option, we suggest it be utilized on the more liquid and actively traded expirations and strike prices.

TD SEQUENTIAL

TD Sequential is made up of three phases: the Setup phase, the Intersection phase, and the Countdown phase. Each phase begins upon the completion of the previous phase. Of the three phases, Setup and Countdown are the most important in determining when a market has reached a point of exhaustion and is prone to a market reversal. Each phase is important in and of itself, but when utilized together until completion, it becomes even more so.

Please note that the numbered counts and the rules necessary to arrive at these counts are the recommended settings that we use. However, these settings are not absolute. TD Sequential is simply an indicator template, providing the structure from which to arrive at consistent and objective market-timing conclusions. While we recommend the settings that follow, as they have been applied successfully for approximately 27 years, we are not certain that these are necessarily the best selections possible. One may find that different comparisons and settings prove to be more profitable. Therefore, we encourage traders to experiment with different possibilities of TD Sequential, either with Setup, Intersection, Countdown, or any of its components.

Setup

The first phase of TD Sequential is called the Setup phase. A *Setup* is a comparison of closes—specifically, the close of the current price bar to the close four price bars earlier. If one is observing a daily bar chart, then one compares the close of the current day to the close four days earlier; if one is observing a one-minute bar chart, then one compares the close of the current minute to the close four minutes earlier. This closing comparison determines whether the market has recorded a buy Setup series or a sell Setup series. A *completed buy Setup* is defined as a series of nine consecutive price bars where the close of each price bar is less than the close four price bars earlier. Conversely, a *completed sell Setup* is defined as a series of nine consecutive price bars where the close of each price bar is greater than the close four price bars earlier. Therefore, a buy Setup will occur in a declining market and a sell Setup will occur in an advancing market. In each case, once the minimum Setup count of nine has been achieved, the Setup is complete. Setups can extend beyond this minimum requirement, which becomes important when addressing parameter settings, as well as other indicators such as TD Setup Trend (TDST), but nine is all that is necessary to proceed to the next phase of TD Sequential.

To reiterate, in order to complete a buy Setup, there must be at least nine consecutive price bars where the close of each bar is less than the close four price bars earlier. For example, a 1 count of a buy Setup series will be recorded if the close of the first price bar of the series is less than the close four price bars earlier. On the following price bar, a 2 appears for a buy Setup if the close of the new current price bar is less than the close four price bars earlier. At the close of the next price bar this comparison is made once again, and if this close is less than the close four bars earlier, a 3 count for a buy Setup will be formed. This process is repeated continuously. Once at least nine consecutive closes closing less than the closes four price bars earlier have been recorded, the buy Setup is completed. When a completed buy Setup has been formed, the first phase of TD Sequential is concluded—the trader can now proceed to the Intersection phase and then on to the buy Countdown phase. Each count of a buy Setup is numbered 1 through 9 beneath the price bar to which it refers. If, before a completed buy Setup count of nine is achieved, the market records a close that is greater than the close four price bars earlier (a sell Setup count) or if the market records a close that is equal to the close four price bars earlier (a neutral reading), then the buy Setup is canceled and the Setup phase must begin anew. Figure 6.1 displays a completed buy Setup phase.

Again, in order to complete a sell Setup, there must be at least nine consecutive price bars where the close of each bar is greater than the close four price bars earlier. For example, a 1 count of a sell Setup series will be recorded if the close of the first price bar of the series is greater than the close four price bars earlier. On the following price bar, a 2 appears for a sell Setup if the close of the new current price bar is greater than the close four price bars earlier. At the close of the next price bar, this comparison is made once again, and if this close is greater than the close four bars earlier, a 3 count for a sell Setup will be formed. This process is repeated continuously. Once at least nine consecutive closes closing greater than the closes four price bars earlier have been recorded, the sell Setup is completed. When a completed sell Setup has been formed, the first phase of TD Sequential is concluded—the trader can now proceed to the Intersection phase and then on to the sell Countdown phase. Each count of a sell Setup is numbered 1 through 9 above the bar to which it refers. If, before a completed sell Setup count of nine is recorded, the market registers a close which is less than the close four price bars earlier (a buy Setup count) or if the market records a close that is equal to the close four price bars earlier (a neutral reading), then the sell Setup is canceled and the Setup phase must begin anew. Figure 6.1 displays a completed sell Setup phase.

Now that we've presented how to complete a Setup series, let's identify how we determine where a Setup begins. One commonly asked question regarding the Setup phase is how one determines where a 1 count should begin. The first count of a Setup is confirmed when a price flip occurs. A *price flip* is simply a change in the direction of the Setup, from a buy Setup (or unchanged comparison) to a sell Setup or from a sell Setup (or unchanged comparison) to a buy Setup. For example, if today's close is greater than the close four days earlier, then a sell Setup count is recorded. However, if the following day's close is less than the close four days earlier, the market has gone from a sell Setup count to a buy Setup count. Since the market has changed its Setup series from the sell direction to the buy direction, a price flip has occurred. This price flip initializes the buy Setup and a number 1 appears coincident with the current price bar—this 1 count is numbered beneath the current price bar to indicate that it is the first bar of the buy Setup. If the following trading day's close is greater than the close four days earlier, then the market has experienced another price flip, changing its sentiment from a buy Setup to a sell Setup. This price flip marks the 1 count of the price bar and initializes the sell Setup—the 1 is numbered above the current price bar to indicate that it is the first bar of the sell Setup. And if the day succeeding this second price flip records a close that is equal to the close four days earlier, then the sell

FIGURE 6.1 An example of a completed buy Setup and a completed sell Setup are presented in this chart. In these examples, both the buy Setup phase and the sell Setup phase were initiated by price flips.

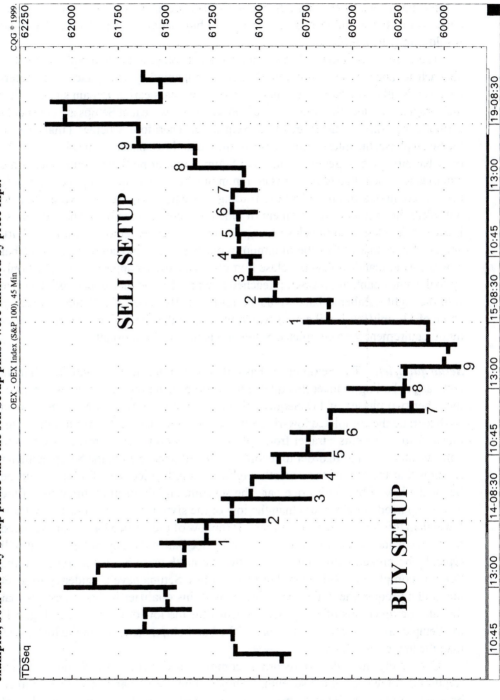

Setup count is erased at 1, and the market's bias becomes neutral. In this case, the current price bar would record neither a 1 of a buy Setup nor a 1 of a sell Setup—it would simply be left blank.

There are a few things to keep in mind when it comes to the Setup phase. First of all, each advance in the current price bar is accompanied by an advance in the reference bar. Neither the current bar nor the close four bars earlier remain static, rather they progress, as does the price comparison. Also, be aware that Setups are constantly forming, regardless of the stage of TD Sequential. Therefore, whether a market is in the Setup phase, the Intersection phase, or the Countdown phase, at the close of every price bar either a buy Setup count, a sell Setup count, or no Setup count (closes are equal) is recorded. In addition, it is common practice to record on a price chart only the nine count of a completed Setup. Trading convention requires that Setups that do not fulfill the minimum requirement of nine consecutive price bars where the close is greater than/less than the close four price bars earlier be removed from the chart, and any Setup that fulfills the minimum requirement of nine consecutive price bar closes greater than/less than the close four price bars earlier appear on the chart only up to the nine count. So, if a Setup reached a series of 8 and then experienced a price flip, the eight numbered bars would be removed. However, if a Setup recorded a count of 11, only the 1 to 9 counts would remain on the chart, since that is the minimum requirement for a completed Setup and is the most important.

Setup qualifier.   The Setup phase has only one requirement, or qualifier, that we emphasize. Failing to meet this qualifier has no bearing on the commencement of the other two phases of TD Sequential. This qualifier only applies to those who wish to trade the completed low-risk Setup indications. Using it when trading completed Setups prevents a trader from entering the market prematurely and serves to enhance one's timing. In order to record a completed buy Setup, the Setup qualifier requires that the low of the seventh, eighth, or ninth price bar of a buy Setup be below the low of the sixth price bar. The seventh, eighth, or ninth price bar of the buy Setup need not close less than the low of the sixth price bar, it must only trade lower than this level sometime intrabar. If the low of the 6 price bar is not exceeded to the downside by the low of the 7, 8, or 9 price bar of the buy Setup, then it will typically be broken within three days after the ninth price bar is recorded and the Setup is completed. Aside from the fact that buy Setups have a tendency to meet this trading requirement, the reasoning behind this qualifier is that it ensures that the later Setup counts of a buy Setup occur near the low of the move. In Fig. 6.1, the Setup qualifier is met on the 7 bar of the buy Setup phase, where the low is less than the low of the 6 bar.

Conversely, in order to record a complete sell Setup, the Setup qualifier requires that the high of the seventh, eighth, or ninth price bar of a sell Setup must be above the high of the sixth price bar. The seventh, eighth, or ninth price bar of the sell Setup need not close greater than the high of the sixth price bar, it must only trade higher than this level sometime intrabar. If the high of the 6 price bar is not exceeded to the upside by the high of the 7, 8, or 9 price bar of the sell Setup, then it will typically be broken within three days after the ninth price bar is recorded and the Setup is completed. Aside from the fact that sell Setups have a tendency to meet this trading requirement, the reasoning behind this qualifier is that it ensures that the later Setup counts of a sell Setup occur near the high of the move. In Fig. 6.1, the Setup qualifier is met on the 8 bar of the sell Setup phase, where the high is greater than the high of the 6 bar.

In either instance, if this qualifier is not met, the Intersection phase and the Countdown phase are unaffected, meaning they are neither postponed nor canceled. It only suggests that it may be premature to expect the market to record a trend reversal or retracement, if one elects to trade Setups. Again, this qualifier is presented strictly for those who wish to trade the Setups of TD Sequential, as the market has a reliable tendency to exhibit reversals or consolidations at these times.

Trading with setups.   Setups are very powerful price patterns in and of themselves. Because the rules required to complete a Setup are relatively strict and require the formation of an extended price move, most often upon completion it coincides with some form of price exhaustion where the market is prone to a price reversal. What we have found is that within four bars following the 9 count, the market should experience some sort of price reversal or at least a price consolidation. If the market doesn't respond by reversing its trend or consolidating its movement within this time, chances are it will resume its original price movement. While this price reaction, when it does occur, may not reverse the prevailing market trend, it does offer an excellent opportunity to capitalize on a price reversal or consolidation, particularly with options on a short-term basis. When taken together with other indicators, particularly TD Setup Trend, one can get an indication as to whether a price reversal following a completed Setup will lead to a reversal of the overall trend.

There are a few things that we suggest to those who wish to trade options using TD Sequential Setups. First of all, a trader should not purchase options with strike prices that are far from the prevailing market, expecting the market to move to that price. Again, a completed Setup does not necessarily indicate a change in the direction of the overall trend, but it does suggest that a price correction should ensue. By incorporating indicators such as TDST or TD Lines, one can establish a better determination of whether a Setup will be followed by a price "hiccup" or will develop into a sizable change in trend. Also, we feel it is crucial to time one's entry into the market. To do so, we look for additional signals in smaller time frames, either an additional completed Setup phase, a completed Countdown phase, or another indicator reading. In other words, we look to synchronize long-term results with short-term results. For instance, if we were trading options using a Setup signal on a 30-minute chart, we would then look at the 15-minute, the 10-minute, the 5-minute, and the 1-minute charts for confirmation of that signal. This would help perfect our entry price for the option. In addition, trading a Setup should be coordinated with the other market-timing indicators presented in this book, on both comparable and shorter time frames, such as qualified and disqualified TD Lines, TD REI and TD POQ, TD Relative Retracements, TD % F, and the option rules.

(Setup) size matters.   One misperception that many TD Sequential practitioners have is that once a Setup records nine consecutive price bars where the close is greater than the close four price bars earlier, or nine consecutive price bars where the close is less than the close four price bars earlier, the counting process ceases. In reality, a Setup can continue indefinitely (at least, in theory). A Setup continues to count until a price flip occurs, where the market changes its closing relationship from a buy Setup to either a sell Setup or a neutral reading, or where the market changes its closing relationship from a sell Setup to either a buy Setup or a neutral reading. This is illustrated in Fig. 6.2. A Setup's size becomes especially important when considering a phenomenon known as recycling.

Recycling is a trading nuisance that has arisen in the markets within the past 10 years. When TD Sequential was first created, it was not uncommon for a market to move directly from the completion of the Setup phase to the completion of the Countdown phase and then experience a significant price reversal. Today, however, recycling prolongs the extent of a market move and masks the indications of a possible price reversal. This tendency, especially in the stock and stock option market, has resulted from more widespread market participation—specifically, due to the larger number of individuals and funds who trade the markets today, buying and selling can continue relentlessly, often exaggerating price moves and resetting TD Sequential's evaluation of the market. TD Sequential is still effective today, regardless of the market or the time frame to which it is applied, but recycling makes a chart's interpretation of the market's status slightly more complicated.

Recycling refers to instances where a market has recorded two or more consecutive buy Setups, or two or more consecutive sell Setups. In other words, recycling occurs when a buy Setup is followed by another buy Setup, before recording a sell Setup; or when a sell Setup is followed by another sell Setup before recording a buy Setup. This occurrence can be seen in Fig. 6.3. The regeneration of the price trend is responsible for this trading phenomenon, which results when the forces of supply or demand reassert themselves. When a Setup recycles, it indicates that a renewed interest and intensity has occurred in the market, causing a continuation of the market trend. Another way to look at recycling is that new information comes into the market, prompting additional buying and selling, and resulting in a perpetuation of a directional price move.

FIGURE 6.2 This chart illustrates how a Setup can continue beyond the minimum series of 9. As you can see, the sell Setup reached a count of 17 before a price flip was recorded, and the buy Setup reached a count of 13 before a price flip was recorded.

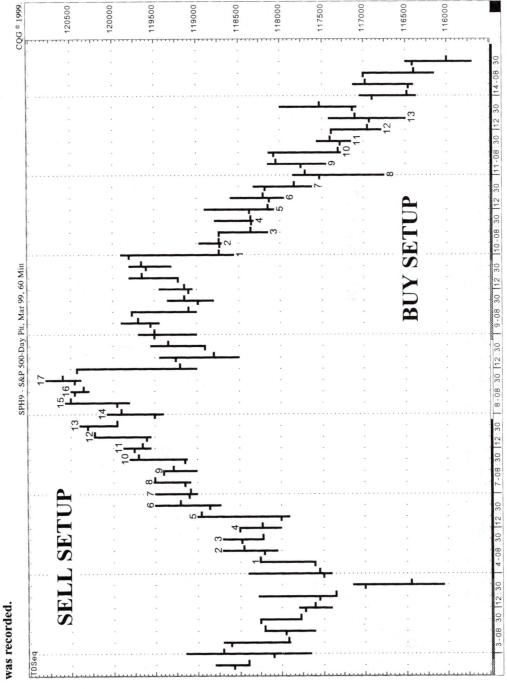

117

FIGURE 6.3 In some cases, Setups will recycle. In this example, multiple recycles were recorded. In each case, the Countdown phase had commenced but since it was unable to run to completion, the counts were removed from the chart. Recycling works in the same manner for both buy and sell Setups.

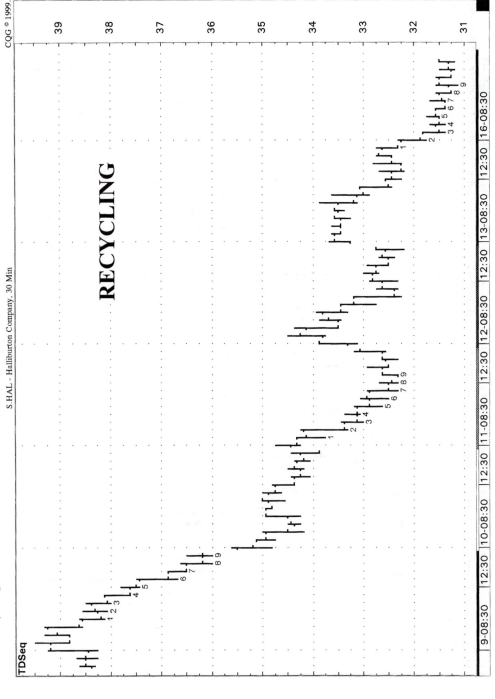

The biggest problem that recycling presents is determining which Setup should be used to commence the Countdown phase. This problem can be resolved by introducing a group of settings and rules that enable a trader to choose one Setup over another. There are many possible ways we have devised to classify a Setup recycling; however, we only utilize two of these ways regularly. The first setting, "before, on, or after," is a more conservative trading setting, while the second setting, "ignore the smaller true high/true low," is more liberal and typically applied if we desire more frequent trading activity. The first type of Setup recycling that we suggest is identified as "before, on, or after" and is far and away the easiest to implement. "Before, on, or after" simply states that if a Setup is followed by a subsequent Setup that is completed before, on, or after the completion of the previous Setup's resulting Countdown phase, then the recent Setup replaces the prior Setup. Therefore, if two consecutive buy Setups are recorded, then the recent Setup becomes more important, erasing any buy Countdown series that resulted from the previous buy Setup and marking the point at which the new buy Countdown phase can begin. Conversely, if two consecutive sell Setups are recorded, then the recent Setup becomes active, erasing any sell Countdown series that appeared from the previous sell Setup and marking the point at which the new sell Countdown phase begins. The implementation of this recycle setting is rather simple—any new Setup that forms becomes the designated Setup phase. The reasoning is that the previous Setup becomes a part of market history and is no longer a factor in determining the commencement of Countdown. This price series was completed using prevailing market information at that time. Because the new Setup processes current market information, conditions, and overall market sentiment, this Setup takes precedence over others.*

The second type of Setup recycling setting that we advocate is referred to as "ignore smaller true high/true low," or "ignore smaller THL," and is slightly more complicated than the conventional recycling parameter just described. This setting allows the trader to utilize either the current Setup or a previous Setup phase to commence Countdown, whichever is larger in size. In the case of the previous recycling setting—before, on, or after—any time a new Setup is completed, that Setup becomes active and proceeds to the Countdown phase. When this new Setup forms, any previous Setup count is nullified, thereby erasing any resulting Countdown series. This can be especially frustrating when the Countdown phase has almost run to completion, as a trader must begin anew and await the completion of another full Countdown phase. However, by electing to ignore the smaller-sized, recycled Setups, one can retain a previous Setup's Countdown series and continue

---

* This Setup regeneration is similar to instances in which a Setup is succeeded by—and therefore canceled by—a reverse Setup series in the opposite direction. In this case as well, the overall sentiment has changed (which is represented in the change from one Setup direction to another) due to current market information.

with the phase. Since this recycle setting does not cancel, or recycle, as many Setups, more low-risk trading opportunities are created.

When comparing the sizes of two Setups, one is relating the price ranges of the two Setups, from the lowest true low to the highest true high, and whichever Setup is larger becomes the active Setup. When making this comparison, it is important that one relate the full Setup ranges to one another, not just the nine price bars of each Setup—in other words, one must consider any count that exceeds the minimum Setup requirement of nine. Since a Setup continues to count until a price flip occurs, where the market changes its closing relationship from a buy Setup to either a sell Setup or a neutral reading, or where the market changes its closing relationship from a sell Setup to either a buy Setup or a neutral reading, the true range of either Setup could be larger than simply the range of the 1 bar through the 9 bar.

However, there is one exception to the selection of the larger Setup when utilizing "ignore smaller THL." If the larger Setup is more than a particular percentage greater than the smaller Setup, then the larger Setup is ignored. The factor that we use is 161.8 percent. The reasoning behind this qualifier is that if a Setup is more than 1.618 times greater than the previous Setup, then its range, or size, is exaggerated, causing the Countdown phase to also become exaggerated. Therefore, we require that a trader ignore a larger Setup, in terms of a true high and true low difference, if that Setup is more than 1.618 times greater than a smaller Setup.

With our trading style, we choose to alternate between using "before, on, or after" and "ignore the smaller true high/true low," depending upon how long the Countdown phase had proceeded and the overall market environment. We suggest that you look at both settings when trading with TD Sequential, as both will prove to be helpful in identifying low-risk trading opportunities.

Setup Cancellations

There are four ways in which a Setup can be canceled. The first relates to contratrend moves and the comparisons of individual price bar highs, lows, and closes to the lows, highs, and closes of the overall Setup; the second deals with Setup reversals; the third relates to recycling, a topic we mentioned earlier; and the last applies to a Setup that is contained within a previous Setup. In each of these cases, the resulting effect it has is either to deactivate the Setup (thereby resetting it and preventing it from proceeding to the next phase of TD Sequential), but retain the complete numbered Setup count on the price chart; or to erase the Setup series altogether. Which of the previous two outcomes will occur depends upon the type of Setup cancellation that occurs.

Contratrend moves. The first Setup cancellation refers to the extent to which price experiences a contratrend move prior to the completion of either the Setup phase or the Countdown phase. This cancellation applies to the current Setup period, meaning if any of the following selected rules are met, then the recent Setup is disregarded. It also provides a bit more leeway than the other cancellations, as a trader must choose from any one of six execution settings. These cancellation events are simply reversed for buy Setups and for sell Setups.

It is up to the trader to decide which of the following six alternatives will cancel an active buy Setup. They are all straightforward:

1.   If an intrabar high exceeds the highest close of the entire buy Setup period to the upside, then the active buy Setup (or buy Countdown) is canceled.

2.   If an intrabar high exceeds the highest high of the entire buy Setup period to the upside, then the active buy Setup (or buy Countdown) is canceled.

3.   If a close exceeds the highest close of the entire buy Setup period to the upside, then the active buy Setup (or buy Countdown) is canceled.

4.   If a close exceeds the highest high of the entire buy Setup period to the upside, then the active buy Setup (or buy Countdown) is canceled.

5.   If a close exceeds the highest true high of the entire buy Setup period to the upside (a *true high* is the highest high of the buy Setup period or the close the day prior to that highest high, whichever is greater), then the active buy Setup (or buy Countdown) is canceled.

6.   If a low exceeds the highest true high of the entire buy Setup period to the upside (a true high is the highest high of the buy Setup period or the close the day prior to that highest high, whichever is greater), then the active buy Setup (or buy Countdown) is canceled.

The most conservative buy Setup cancellation (in the sense that the Setup is disregarded so as not to take a perceived false Setup indication) is the first condition and the most liberal buy Setup cancellation (in the sense that the Setup is not disregarded so quickly) is the sixth condition. Personally, we use the sixth buy Setup cancellation, so we are less likely to cancel a Setup prematurely. However, in all of these cases, if price were able to advance to these levels, a significant price move would have already had to occur. Therefore, we'd be skeptical of the value and the practicality of the Setup or the Countdown reading at that point and would probably defer entry until a new Setup phase has been formed.

In the reverse case, it is up to the trader to decide which of the following six alternatives will cancel an active sell Setup. Again, they are all straightforward:

1.   If an intrabar low exceeds the lowest close of the entire sell Setup period to the downside, then the active sell Setup (or sell Countdown) is canceled.

2.   If an intrabar low exceeds the lowest low of the entire sell Setup period to the downside, then the active sell Setup (or sell Countdown) is canceled.

3.   If a close exceeds the lowest close of the entire sell Setup period to the downside, then the active sell Setup (or sell Countdown) is canceled.

4.   If a close exceeds the lowest low of the entire sell Setup period to the downside, then the active sell Setup (or sell Countdown) is canceled.

5.   If a close exceeds the lowest true low of the entire sell Setup period to the
downside (a *true low* is the lowest low of the sell Setup period or the close
the day prior to that lowest low, whichever is less), then the active sell Setup
(or sell Countdown) is canceled.

6.   If a high exceeds the lowest true low of the entire sell Setup period to the
downside (a true low is the lowest low of the buy Setup period or the close
the day prior to that lowest low, whichever is less), then the active sell Setup
(or buy Countdown) is canceled.

The most conservative sell Setup cancellation (in the sense that the Setup is
disregarded so as not to take a perceived false Setup indication) is the first condition and the most liberal sell Setup cancellation (in the sense that the Setup is not
disregarded so quickly) is the sixth condition. Personally, we use the sixth sell
Setup cancellation, so we are less likely to cancel a Setup prematurely. However, in
all of these cases, if price were able to decline to these levels, a significant price
move would have already had to occur. Therefore, we'd be skeptical of the value
and the practicality of the Setup or the Countdown reading at that point and would
probably defer entry until a new Setup phase has been formed.

When we discuss TD Setup Trend later in this chapter, you will be able to see
how both sets of these cancellations and the TDST line work together.

Reverse setups.   The second Setup cancellation is a reverse Setup, or a price flip,
prior to the completion of a current Setup. If a reverse Setup forms, then the previous Setup is canceled. For example, if a buy Setup is currently active (ongoing) and
a price flip occurs prior to that Setup's completion, meaning a series of fewer than
nine consecutive closes that are less than the closes four price bars earlier is interrupted by a close that is greater than the close four price bars earlier, then a reverse
Setup has developed and the previously active buy Setup is canceled. The new sell
Setup becomes the current and more important Setup. Conversely, if a sell Setup is
currently active and a price flip occurs prior to that Setup's completion, indicating
a series of fewer than nine consecutive closes which are greater than the closes four
price bars earlier is interrupted by a close that is less than the close four price bars
earlier, then a reverse Setup has occurred and the sell Setup is canceled. The new
buy Setup becomes the current and more important Setup.

The justification for a Setup cancellation upon recording a reverse Setup is
fairly obvious—specifically, new market information has been processed, and this
information takes precedence over prior market information. However, our work
with Reverse Setups is not complete, as we have found many instances where

retaining a Setup (and its respective Countdown series) that was canceled by a contradictory Setup produced excellent results, as well.

Setup recycling.   The third Setup cancellation occurs if a Setup recycles. Because we covered this topic previously in more detail, we will simply reiterate some of the more important points. Recycling occurs when a market has recorded two or more consecutive buy Setups or two or more consecutive sell Setups. This phenomenon typically appears when new market information or news has been introduced to the market, perpetuating price moves and causing the market's trend to become more positive after a sell Setup, or more negative after a buy Setup.

Whether a recycling will cancel a recent Setup or a previous Setup depends upon the execution setting selected by the trader. If the "before, on, or after" setting is chosen, then a recycling will cause the previous Setup (and any Countdown series resulting from that Setup) to be canceled. In this case, the Countdown phase will begin counting after the more recent Setup. If the "ignore the smaller true high/true low" setting is selected, then recycling will cause the previous Setup to be canceled if it is smaller in size than the more recent Setup, thereby canceling any Countdown series resulting from the previous Setup; or will cause the current Setup to be canceled if it is smaller in size than the original Setup, thereby maintaining the Countdown series from the previous Setup. Which setting one should select depends upon one's trading style and trading time frame. If a trader would like a smaller number of trading indications, he or she can select the more conservative "before, on, or after"; if a trader would like a greater number of trading opportunities, he or she can select the more liberal "ignore smaller THL."

Setup contained within the previous setup.   The final Setup cancellation occurs when a Setup recycles and the closing range of the more recent completed Setup is contained *within* the range of the previous completed Setup. In order for this cancellation to apply, the market must record two consecutive Setups without being interrupted by a reverse Setup in between the two. If the extreme high close and the extreme low close of the recently completed buy Setup phase are contained within the extreme high and the extreme low of the previously completed buy Setup, then the current Setup is ignored, and the previous buy Setup is dominant and its Countdown phase remains intact. Conversely, if the extreme high close and the extreme low close of the recently completed sell Setup phase are contained within the extreme high and the extreme low of the previously completed sell Setup, then the current Setup is ignored, and the previous sell Setup is dominant and its Countdown phase remains intact.

When comparing the two Setups, it is important that one compares the more recent Setup's closes to the previous Setup's price range—in other words, one must consider any count that exceeds the minimum Setup requirement of nine. As we mentioned earlier, a Setup series continues to count until a price flip occurs, where the market changes its closing relationship from a buy Setup to either a sell Setup or a neutral reading, or where the market changes its closing relationship from a sell Setup to either a buy Setup or a neutral reading. Since a completed Setup does not end until a price flip occurs, the true range of either Setup could be larger than simply the range of the 1 bar through the 9 bar. Therefore, when comparing the two Setups for this cancellation, one must examine the full Setup ranges, including the price bars that extend beyond the 9 count.

Setup Summary

In summary, whether examining a daily bar chart or a one-minute bar chart, to calculate a Setup one must compare the close of the current price bar to the close four price bars earlier. A buy Setup is initiated with a price flip, where a price bar's close that is greater than the close four price bars earlier is immediately succeeded (on the next price bar) by a close that is less than the close four price bars earlier. A completed buy Setup is formed when the market has recorded at least nine consecutive price bars where the close is less than the close four price bars earlier. If the market records a completed buy Setup before a price flip occurs, then the Setup count from 1 through 9 remains on the price chart. Once this completed buy Setup has been formed, the first phase of TD Sequential is concluded—the trader can now move on to the Intersection phase and then on to the buy Countdown phase. However, if, before the completion of this minimum buy Setup requirement, the market records a close that is greater than the close four price bars earlier or a close that is equal to the close four price bars earlier, then a price flip has occurred, the buy Setup numbers are canceled and erased from the price chart, and Setup counting must begin anew. A buy Setup's count can also be erased if any of the other three Setup cancellations occur. If an intrabar price high or price close exceeds to the upside the highest high or highest true high of the buy Setup, if the buy Setup recycles itself, or if the true range of a recent buy Setup is contained within the true range of a previous buy Setup, then the completed buy Setup remains on the price chart, but the most recent Setup phase is, or one of the two most recent buy Setup phases are, nullified and therefore cannot proceed to the buy Countdown phase.

If one wished to trade these completed buy Setups, one could do so by applying the Setup qualifier. This qualifier states that the low of the seventh, eighth, or ninth price bar of a buy Setup must be less than the low of the sixth price bar to permit the purchase of the asset or the purchase of the call option.

Conversely, a sell Setup is initiated with a price flip, where a price bar's close that is less than the close four price bars earlier is immediately succeeded (on the next price bar) by a close that is greater than the close four price bars earlier. A completed sell Setup is formed when the market has recorded at least nine consecutive price bars where the close is greater than the close four price bars earlier. If the market records a complete sell Setup before a price flip occurs, then the Setup count from 1 through 9 remains on the price chart. Once this completed sell Setup has been formed, the first phase of TD Sequential is concluded—the trader can now move on to the Intersection phase and then on to the sell Countdown phase. However, if, before the completion of this minimum sell Setup requirement, the market records a close that is less than the close four price bars earlier or a close that is equal to the close four price bars earlier, then a price flip has occurred, the sell Setup numbers are canceled and erased from the price chart, and Setup counting must begin anew. A sell Setup's count can also be erased if any of the other three Setup cancellations occur. If an intrabar price low or price close exceeds to the downside of the lowest low or lowest true low of the sell Setup, if the sell Setup recycles itself, or if the true range of a recent sell Setup is contained within the true range of a previous sell Setup, then the completed sell Setup remains on the price chart, but the recent Setup phase is, or one of the two most recent sell Setup phases are, nullified and therefore cannot proceed to the sell Countdown phase.

If one wished to trade these completed sell Setups, one could do so by applying the Setup qualifier. This qualifier states that the high of the seventh, eighth, or ninth price bar of a sell Setup must be greater than the high of the sixth price bar to permit the sale of the asset or the purchase of the put option.

Intersection

Of the three phases that comprise TD Sequential, Intersection is the least important. Intersection only applies to stocks and stock options and has no application to futures or indices. Intersection was introduced to TD Sequential to prevent premature market entry by determining whether a market's price was sufficiently weak or sufficiently strong to continue to move in the direction of the outstanding trend, thereby disregarding any Setup or Countdown indication. Specifically, it was designed to prevent a trader from purchasing the stock or the call options of a company which was going bankrupt, or conversely from selling the stock or buying the put options of a company which may be acquired. As you can probably guess, because these situations occur infrequently in today's financial markets, this phase has only limited application to TD Sequential.

Intersection requires certain Setup price bars to overlap one another. When a company is going bankrupt, or a highly negative news announcement is released, oftentimes price will decline rapidly, leaving a series of price gaps in the market. As price support fails to enter the market, traders liquidate existing positions, causing further price erosion. If buying doesn't come into the market, then the stock will continue this unpleasant decline. Intersection ensures that price activity consolidates, or at least overlaps, for a certain period of time before TD Sequential is able to advance to the third phase. Therefore, in order to begin the buy Countdown phase, Intersection requires that the high of price bar 8 of a buy Setup, or the first subsequent bar thereafter, be greater than or equal to the low three or more trading bars earlier, all the way back to the 1 bar of the buy Setup. If Intersection occurs on price bar 8 or price bar 9 of the buy Setup, then buy Countdown for TD Sequential can commence on the 9 bar. If Intersection occurs after the completion of the buy Setup phase, then buy Countdown for TD Sequential can commence on the bar the Intersection rule is fulfilled.

The reverse case applies in the same manner. Again, Intersection requires certain price bars to overlap one another. When a stock is being acquired, or bought out, or a highly positive news announcement is released, oftentimes price will advance sharply, leaving a series of price gaps in the market. As price resistance fails to enter the market, traders purchase the asset, hoping to realize some of these dramatic price gains, causing further market distortion. If selling doesn't enter the market, then the stock will continue this steep advance. Intersection ensures that price activity consolidates, or at least overlaps, for a certain period of time before TD Sequential is able to proceed to the third phase. Therefore, in order to begin the sell Countdown phase, Intersection requires that the low of price bar 8 of a sell Setup, or the first subsequent bar thereafter, be less than or equal to the high three or more trading bars earlier, dating all the way back to the 1 bar of the sell Setup. If Intersection occurs on price bar 8 or price bar 9 of the sell Setup, then sell Countdown for TD Sequential can commence on the 9 bar. If Intersection occurs after the completion of the sell Setup phase, then sell Countdown for TD Sequential can commence on the bar the Intersection rule is fulfilled.

Because the Intersection phase is a slightly dated aspect of TD Sequential, and because company bankruptcies and buyouts don't occur as often as they did when this condition was developed, we only occasionally look for the rule to be met. However, the other side of the coin is that since these actions don't occur as often today, the market rarely exhibits the type of drastic price moves just mentioned. In fact, because of this, Intersection often happens implicitly. So, although we may choose not to use Intersection, it doesn't mean that the rule for Intersection was not met—most likely, it was. In any case, it is only applied to individual stocks, not indices, financial futures, commodities, and currencies since these markets cannot be bought out or go bankrupt.

Once the Intersection phase (or the Setup phase, if one is disregarding Intersection) is completed, a trader can proceed to the final and most important phase of TD Sequential: Countdown.

Countdown

Once the Setup phase is complete, a trader can proceed to the Countdown phase. While the Setup phase is more voluminous in terms of subtopics than the Countdown phase, the latter phase is far more powerful. Whereas the Setup phase is a comparison of closes—specifically, the close of the current price bar to the close four price bars earlier—the Countdown phase is a comparison of closes and highs and lows—specifically, the close of the current price bar to the high or low two price bars earlier. If one is observing a daily bar chart, then one compares the close of the current day to the high or low two days earlier; if one is observing a one-minute bar chart, then one compares the close of the current minute to the high or low two minutes earlier. Countdowns can be identified as buy Countdowns or sell Countdowns, depending upon the direction of the previous phases. A complete buy Setup, once fulfilling Intersection, proceeds to buy Countdown; and a complete sell Setup, once fulfilling Intersection, proceeds to sell Countdown. A completed buy Countdown is defined as a series of 13 price bars where the close of each price bar is less than or equal to the low two price bars earlier. Unlike completed buy Setups, the 13 price bars of a completed buy Countdown need not be consecutive. Also, the earliest point at which the buy Countdown series can begin is on the 9 bar of the buy Setup. If the ninth price bar of the Setup phase also meets the requirements of the buy Countdown, then a 1 count of Countdown is recorded beneath the 9 count of Setup. Conversely, a completed sell Countdown is defined as a series of 13 price bars where the close of each price bar is greater than or equal to the high two price bars earlier. Unlike completed sell Setups, the 13 price bars of a completed sell Countdown need not be consecutive. Also, the earliest point at which the sell Countdown series can begin is on the 9 bar of the sell Setup. If the ninth price bar of the Setup phase also meets the requirements of the sell Countdown, then a 1 count of Countdown is recorded above the 9 count of Setup. In each case, once this Countdown series of 13 has been achieved, TD Sequential is complete.

In order to complete a buy Countdown, TD Sequential must first complete and then proceed from a buy Setup. As you will recall, a buy Setup is initiated after a price flip from a sell Setup count has occurred, where a close that is greater than the close four price bars earlier is followed by a close that is less than the close four price bars earlier, and must then record at least nine consecutive price bars where the close of each bar is less than the close four price bars earlier. Once this buy Setup is completed, and Intersection is checked, TD Sequential advances to the Countdown phase. If the Countdown requirement is met on the first price bar on which it can begin, meaning that the close of the final bar of the Setup phase is less than or equal to the low two price bars earlier, then a 1 count of a buy Countdown is recorded below the 9 count of the buy Setup; if this requirement is not met, then the initial count of Countdown is deferred to the next price bar. If, on the following price bar, the close is less than or equal to the low two price bars earlier, then the next count in the Countdown series appears below the price bar; if this requirement is not met, then the subsequent count in the Countdown series is deferred to the next price bar. At the close of the next price bar this comparison is made once again, and if the close is less than or equal to the low two bars earlier, then the next count in the Countdown series is recorded beneath the price bar; and if this buy Countdown requirement is not met, then the subsequent count in the Countdown series is deferred to the following price bar. This process is repeated continuously until a total of 13 closes less than or equal to the lows two price bars earlier is recorded. Once this transpires, TD Sequential is completed, and the market is vulnerable to a significant price reversal—one oftentimes more powerful than that experienced after a buy Setup is completed. If, before a completed buy Countdown series of 13 is achieved, the market records a completed sell Setup or another completed buy Setup, then the existing Countdown is canceled and the Countdown phase must begin anew.* A completed buy Setup phase and a completed buy Countdown phase for TD Sequential are illustrated in Fig. 6.4. Notice how Countdown begins on the 9 bar of the buy Setup phase and the close of each Countdown price bar is less than or equal to the low two price bars earlier.

In order to complete a sell Countdown, TD Sequential must first complete and then proceed from a sell Setup. As you will recall, a sell Setup is initiated after a price flip from a buy Setup count has occurred, where a close that is less than the close four price bars earlier is followed by a close that is greater than the close four price bars earlier, and must then record at least nine consecutive price bars where the close of each bar is greater than the close four price bars earlier. Once this sell Setup is completed, and Intersection is checked, TD Sequential advances to the Countdown phase. If the Countdown requirement is met on the first price bar on which it can begin, meaning that the close of the final bar of the Setup phase is greater than or equal to the high two price bars earlier, then a 1 count of a sell Countdown is recorded above the 9 count of the sell Setup; if this requirement is not met, then the initial count of Countdown is deferred to the next price bar. If, on the following price bar, the close is greater than or equal to the high two price bars earlier, then the next count in the Countdown series appears above the price bar; if this requirement is not met, then the subsequent count in the Countdown series is deferred to the next price bar. At the close of the next price bar this comparison is made once again, and if the close is greater than or equal to the high two bars earlier, then the next count in the Countdown series is recorded above the price bar; and if this sell Countdown requirement is not met, then the subsequent count in the Countdown series is deferred to the following price bar. This process is repeated continuously until a total of 13 closes greater than or equal to the high two price bars earlier is recorded. Once this transpires, TD Sequential is completed, and the market is vulnerable to a significant price reversal—one oftentimes more powerful than that experienced after a sell Setup is completed. If, before a completed sell

---

* There are some exceptions to this rule, as we discussed earlier in the Setup section, such as if one used a recycle setting of "ignore smaller THL," but these decisions remain up to the trader. These exceptions should be applied coincident with one's trading style and financial situation.

FIGURE 6.4 This chart illustrates a completed buy Setup and, more importantly, a completed buy Countdown. The buy Countdown phase began on the 9 count of the buy Setup phase. The 13 price bars indicating the completion of the Countdown phase were not consecutive. Their completion marked a point of price exhaustion and a low-risk buying (call-buying) opportunity.

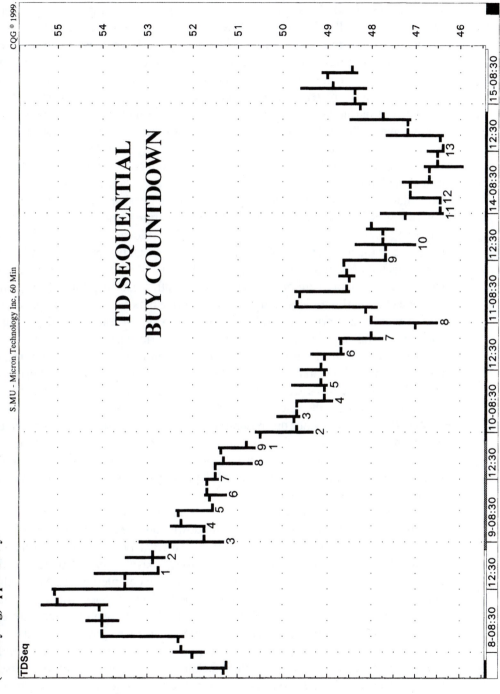

Countdown series of 13 is achieved, the market records a completed buy Setup or another completed sell Setup, then the existing Countdown is canceled and the Countdown phase must begin anew. A completed sell Setup phase and a completed sell Countdown phase for TD Sequential are illustrated in Fig. 6.5. Notice how Countdown begins on the 9 bar of the sell Setup phase and the close of each Countdown price bar is greater than or equal to the high two price bars earlier.

There is one additional change that can be made to the final price bar count of Countdown, called TD Termination Count. This setting can be introduced when a trader wishes to trade more aggressively, by allowing more leniency in the price level comparison of the thirteenth price bar of Countdown. Specifically, TD Termination Count states that all that is required to record the final price bar of a buy Countdown would be for the close, the open, or the intrabar low to be less than the low two price bars earlier. Conversely, TD Termination Count states that all that is required to record the final price bar of a sell Countdown would be for the close, the open, or the intrabar high to be greater than the high two price bars earlier. If a trader elected to be more aggressive with a low-risk Countdown indication, he or she could forego the requirement that the thirteenth close be greater than the high two price bars earlier or less than the low two price bars earlier, and simply require one of these other price values to do so—this way the trader could participate sometime intrabar, as opposed to the close of that price bar.

The completion of the Countdown phase oftentimes coincides with a major turning point in the market. Completed Countdowns are very powerful price patterns that indicate low-risk buying (call-purchasing) or selling (put-purchasing) opportunity. Because the rules required to generate a TD Sequential low-risk buying (call-buying) or selling (put-buying) opportunity are so stringent, from the first bar of the Setup phase to the last bar of the Countdown phase, and require an extended move consisting of at least 21 price bars, most often the completion of Countdown coincides with some form of price exhaustion where the market is prone to a major price reversal.

While we believe that Setup recycling is a nuisance in today's markets, we have recently found one instance where a Countdown and a recycled Setup can be utilized together to increase the likelihood of a market price reversal, particularly intraday. What we are looking for is a Countdown phase that is completed within a few price bars of another completed Setup. Since the completion of a Setup phase and the completion of the Countdown phase both identify zones where the market is vulnerable to a reversal of the existing trend, when the two coincide with each other, the low-risk entry opportunity becomes even more powerful. In the past, especially when position trading, we were reluctant to use these two phases together, as a Setup recycling generally meant the market would fail to reverse its trend. However, when the two phases occur at the same time, the Countdown phase and the Setup phase often work together to reverse the market. This works even

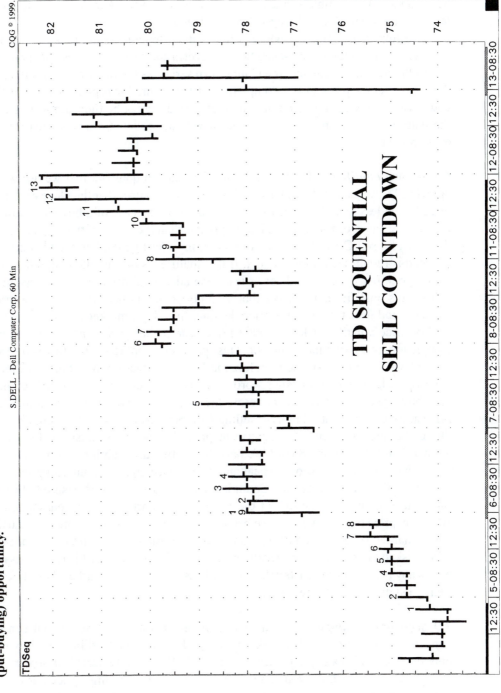

FIGURE 6.5 This chart illustrates a completed sell Setup and, more importantly, a completed sell Countdown. The sell Countdown phase began on the 9 bar of the sell Setup phase. The 13 price bars indicating the completion of the Countdown phase were not consecutive. Their completion marked a point of price exhaustion and a low-risk selling (put-buying) opportunity.

131

better on short-term time frames and was used successfully by T.J. to time entry levels on the floor of the Chicago Board of Trade.

Two important items for which a trader must remain on the lookout when it comes to the Countdown phase are Setup recycles and reversals. These phenomena pose a threat to the existence of a Countdown series, as the occurrence of either of these two Setups prior to the completion of the Countdown phase can reset the count. Before taking a position in a market, a trader must be thoroughly aware of the status of new Setup formations, since new Setup counts form with the close of every price bar.

Countdown qualifier.   There is only one Countdown qualifier that we use when applying TD Sequential to a market. This qualifier requires that the close of the 13 price bar be less than the close of the 8 price bar in the case of a buy Countdown, and that the close of the 13 price bar be greater than the close of the 8 price bar in the case of a sell Countdown. In either case, in order to complete the Countdown phase, this requirement must be met. If the qualifier is not fulfilled, then the thirteenth price bar is postponed for at least one additional price bar. The reasoning behind this qualifier is to ensure that a 13 count occurs near the high of a price advance, and near the low of a price decline. In today's markets, there is a great deal of price volatility, where market prices can make a price move prior to the completion of a particular indicator. This qualifier is implemented to ensure that Countdown's completion, and therefore market entry, does not occur after the market has made its move. In other words, this rule ensures that a low-risk buying (call-buying) opportunity occurs before the market has experienced a significant price advance, and that a low-risk selling (put-buying) opportunity occurs before the market has experienced a significant price decline. Why must the 13 bar be greater than/less than the 8 bar? We have found that the eighth bar of the Countdown phase is typically recorded near an interim price high or an interim price low. Therefore, the final count of the Countdown series can usually be ensured of coming in near the high or the low of the move by comparing it to the eighth count. Also, any price bar that would have been the thirteenth count had it met this qualifier is marked on a price chart with an asterisk. Some markets can record dozens of asterisked price bars before finally obtaining a TD Sequential 13. Regardless of how many price bars have asterisks, once a 13 is recorded, the market should experience a significant price reversal.

TD Sequential examples.   Figure 6.6 demonstrates how TD Sequential can be applied intraday to obtain low-risk buying (call-buying) and selling (put-buying) opportunities. This example presents a chart of a five-minute S&P 500 September 1998 futures contract. As you can see, a 13 comes in at the high price bar of the intraday move. One of the greatest advantages to this intraday trade is that it

FIGURE 6.6 Here, TD Sequential is applied to a five-minute S&P 500 chart. A TD Sequential 13, identifying a low-risk selling (put-buying) opportunity, was recorded at the high of the move and was followed by a decline of over 12.00 points.

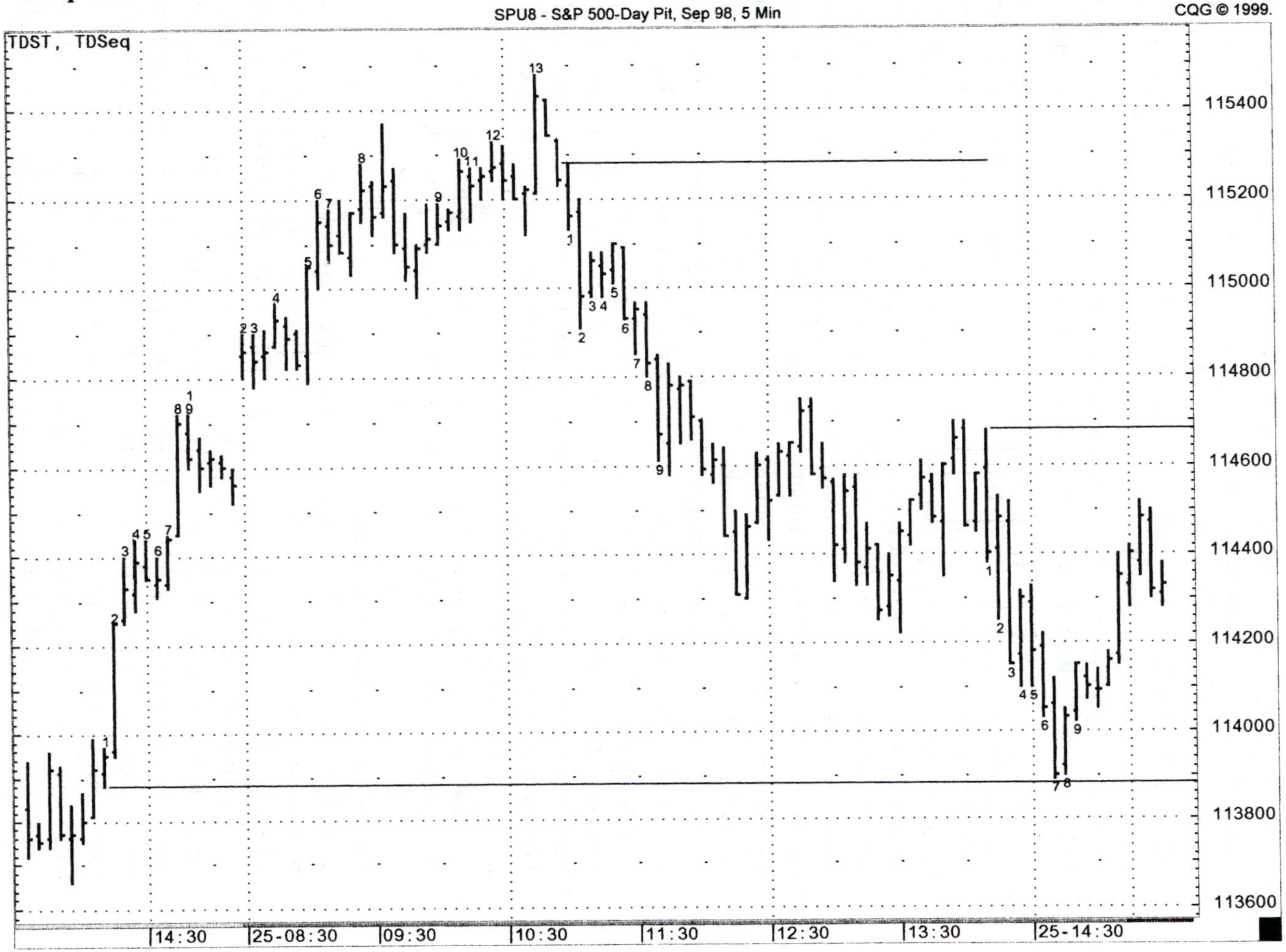

presents itself early in the trading day and then proceeds to decline over 10.00 points. This is an excellent opportunity to purchase puts, as premiums will be lower throughout the price advance. As you can see, price declined to the buy TDST (which is discussed later in the chapter) and held that level, indicating it might be a prudent time to exit the position.

Figure 6.7 presents a 30-minute chart of Lycos. Internet stocks have seen a great deal of volatility within the past year of trading and offer a tremendous amount of profit potential—which is perfect for trading options. In this example, you can see that a 13 comes in at the high near the end of November, and also at the low in early December. Because these contratrend indications are recorded when the market has mounted a substantial trending move, the option costs will be lower than what they would be after the inception of a new trend. This is a perfect example of how one can enter an intraday option position for a small cost and make it a profitable trade. Also, because these Sequential results came in on a larger time frame, it suggests that the indications are longer term in nature, and that one should consider extending the holding period beyond simply the current trading day, although exiting before the close would have also produced a good profit for the trader.

Figure 6.8 is a 45-minute chart of the CBOE Volatility Index (VIX) from late November 1998 to late December 1998. Over this time period, four 13 low-risk price reversals were recorded. As you can see, each indication was followed by a substantial price move. Again, this presents a great option trading opportunity, since option costs will be lower when a contratrend indication is presented. In addition, due to the larger time frame, we recommend that a trader seriously consider extending the holding period.

Additional TD Sequential examples ranging from one-minute charts to daily charts are presented in Figs. 6.9 through 6.24 and in other areas of the chapter as well.

New Countdown Setting for TD Sequential

As we highlighted earlier, the settings that we have recommend are by no means set in stone; they are dynamic and can be changed. We do not say this to confuse practitioners of TD Sequential, but to encourage others to test different settings in an effort to find better results. This indicator is simply meant to provide a foundation from which to build. Maybe a completed Setup phase should not be a count of 9; maybe a completed Countdown phase should not be a count of 13. Maybe these phases shouldn't be a comparison of closes and highs and lows, but rather midpoints. The settings that we utilize work well, but superior possibilities may exist. One alternative setting that we have found to be quite successful is identical to the standard TD Sequential rules and calculations, but involves a slight variation to the price-level comparison of the Countdown phase of TD Sequential.

As you will recall, in the traditional Countdown comparison setting, the market must record 13 price bars where the current price bar's close is greater than or

FIGURE 6.7 The 30-minute chart of Lycos illustrates a 30-minute TD sequential 13 low-risk sell occurred at the high. After finding support, the market proceeded to record a low-risk buy 13, which was followed by a price advance of 10 points.

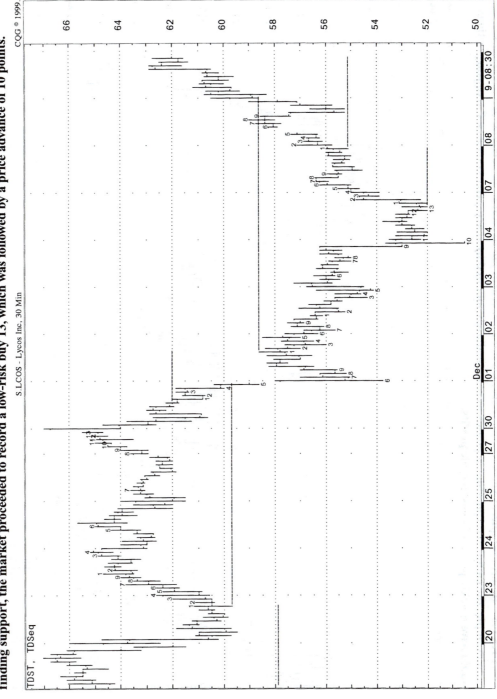

135

FIGURE 6.8   In this example, as you can readily see, 13s did an excellent job in indicating potential price reversals. In each example, the completed Countdown phases were immediately followed by sharp price reversals. Purchasing options would have quickly provided considerable profits.

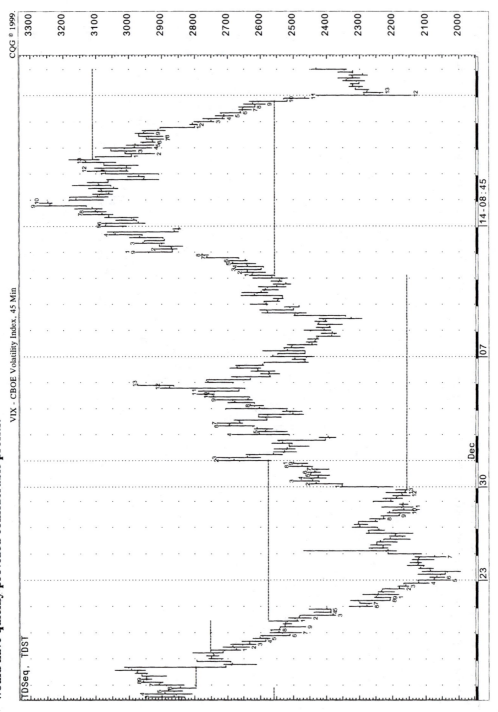

FIGURE 6.9 This chart demonstrates that TD Sequential and TDST work well even when applied on a one-minute basis. In this example, completed sell Countdowns indicated likely trend reversals and a decline in price. Both trades would have been profitable had the trader purchased put options.

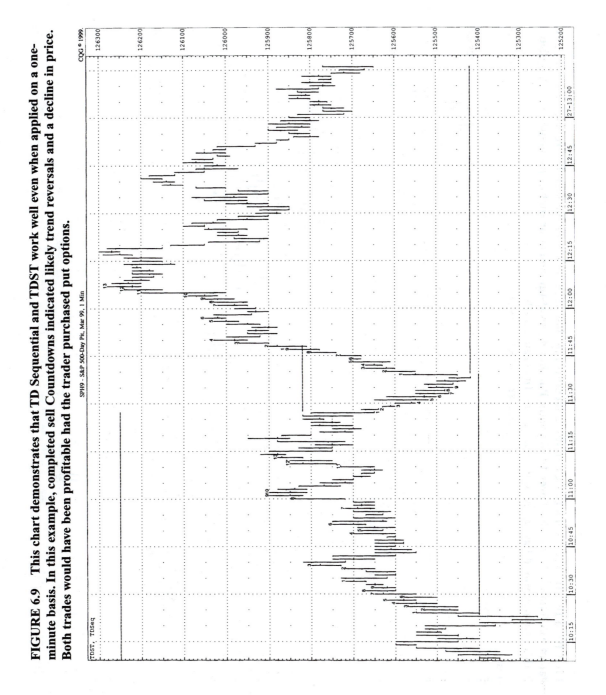

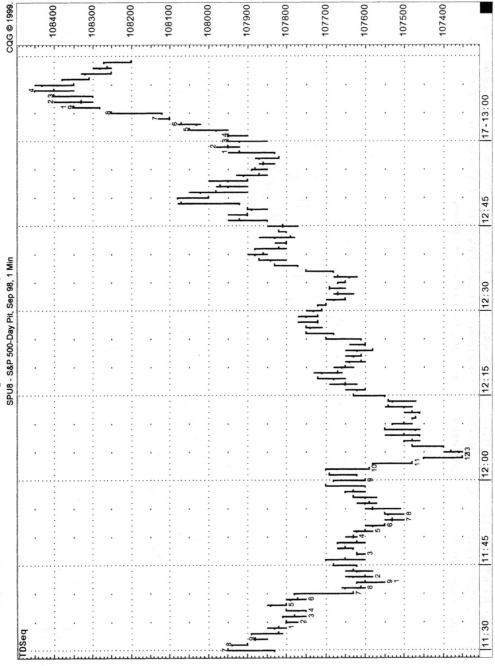

FIGURE 6.10 Here, a 13 of a buy Countdown identified the low of the move for the S&P future. This low-risk indication was followed by a rally of over 10.00 points. Purchasing an at-the-money or slightly in-the-money call option in this situation would have increased a trader's profits dramatically.

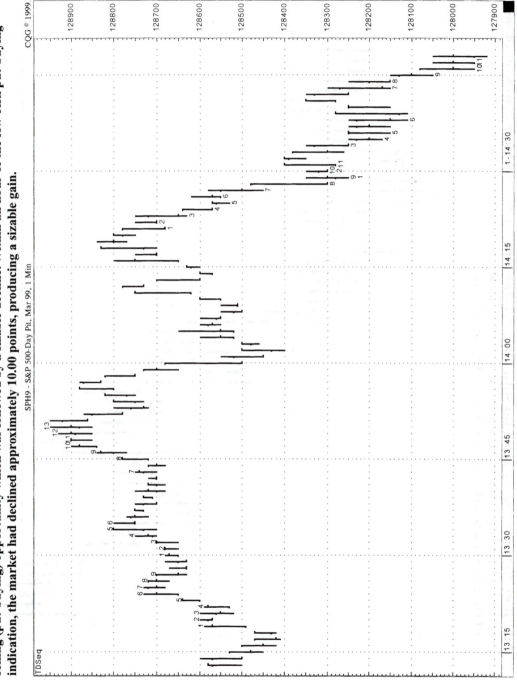

FIGURE 6.11 In this example on a one-minute S&P chart, the completed sell Countdown phase identified a low-risk selling (put-buying) opportunity which was followed by a sizable decline. Within an hour of the low-risk put-buying indication, the market had declined approximately 10.00 points, producing a sizable gain.

FIGURE 6.12 Note that the 13 low-risk sell (put-buying) opportunity on the eight-minute chart occurred into the rally, simultaneous with the highest closing price of the upside move. This indication was activated by a TD CLOPWIN. The two horizontal lines identify TDST price levels.

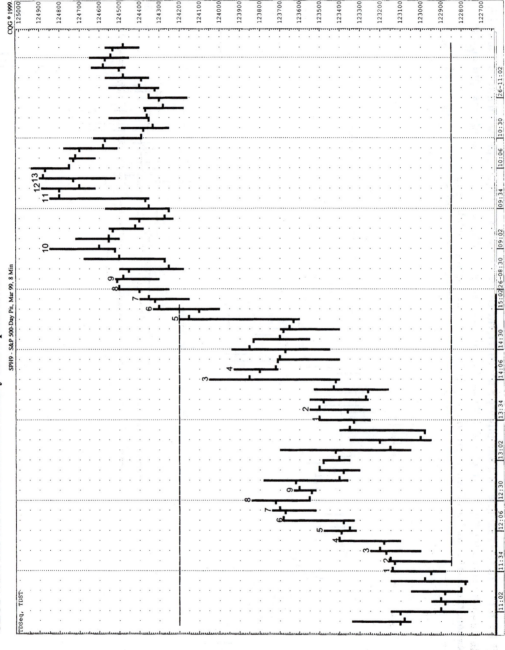

FIGURE 6.13 While the low-risk call-buying opportunity following a completed buy Countdown looks as if it is incorrect and unprofitable, it was actually quite accurate. When trading with TD Sequential or TD Combo, it is always important to apply one of the five entry techniques, whichever occurs first. The entry point in this example could have been timed even better by observing a shorter time frame.

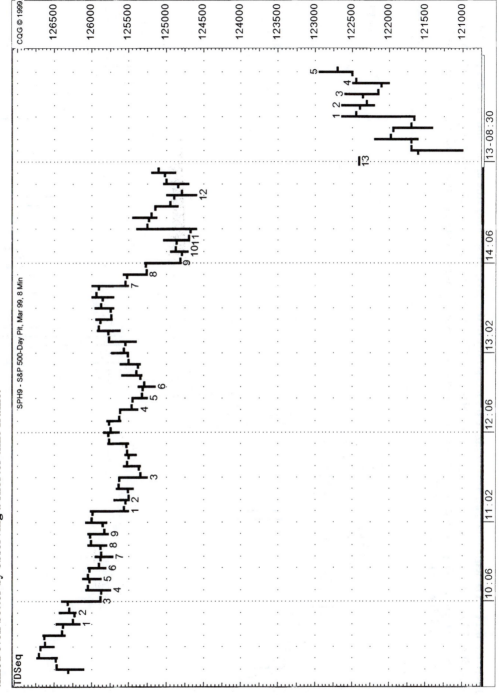

FIGURE 6.14 TD Sequential can also be applied successfully to the S&P all-sessions (the all-session includes pit trading as well as Globex trading). In this example, a completed TD Countdown phase coincided with major price reversals. Also note how the sell TDST provided market support because price was not able to close less than, and then open less and trade one tick lower than, the TDST line.

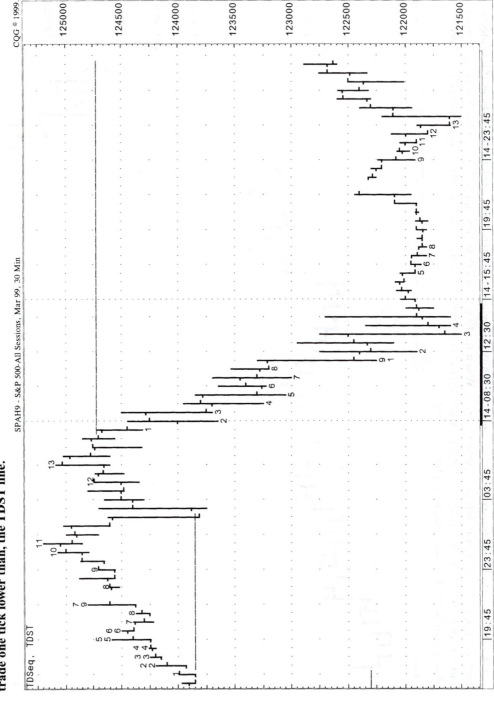

SPAH9 - S&P 500-All Sessions, Mar 99, 30 Min

CQG © 1999.

FIGURE 6.15 Notice that prior to the formation of the 13 of the sell Countdown, three price bars are labeled with an asterisk. This means that the price bar would have recorded a 13 count were it not for the Countdown qualifier. Also note the formation of the sell TDST line—the solid horizontal line—at the lowest price of the sell Setup series.

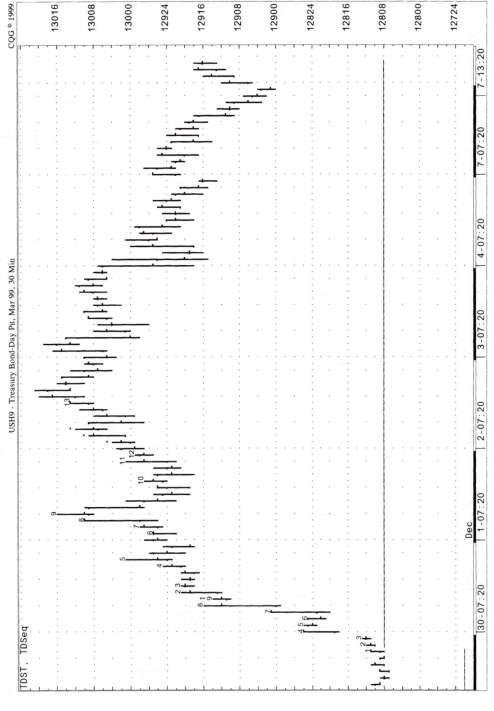

FIGURE 6.16 The TD Sequential low-risk put-buying indication was highlighted two bars after the 13 was recorded, when the close was less than that price bar's open.

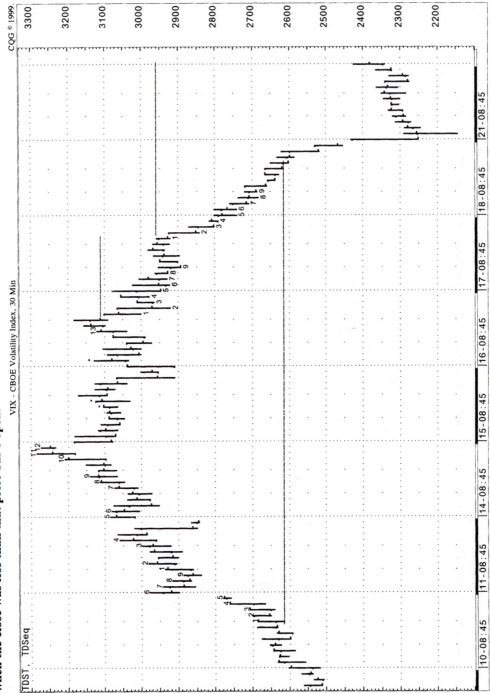

VIX - CBOE Volatility Index, 30 Min

CQG © 1999

FIGURE 6.17 Two low-risk 13 selling (put-buying) opportunities for Countdown were identified at the two high closes on the chart and each was followed by a dramatic price decline.

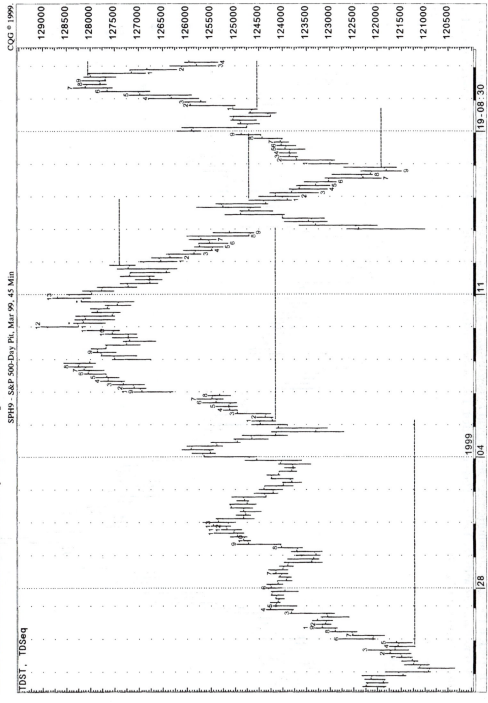

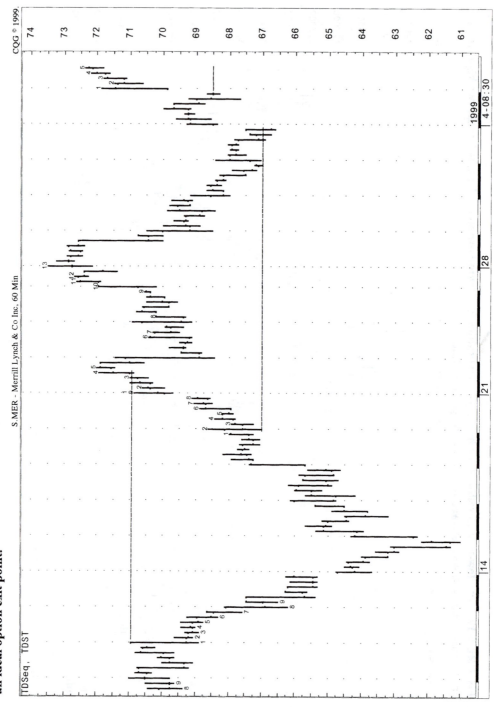

FIGURE 6.18 This 60-minute chart for Merrill Lynch displays a TD Sequential low-risk 13 sell (put-buying) opportunity simultaneous with the highest close recorded. The price decline was then halted at the sell TDST line, which provides an ideal option exit point.

FIGURE 6.19 A 13 low-risk buy Countdown was indicated prior to a strong market advance. Had an option trader held this position beyond the close of the trading period, his or her profits would have been much larger.

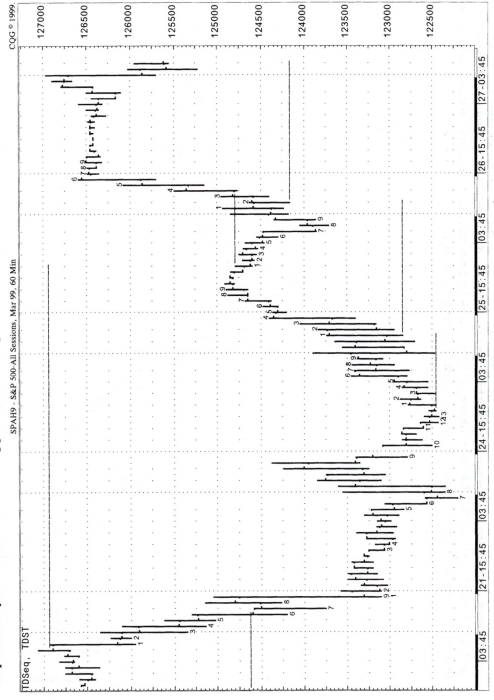

SPAH9 - S&P 500-All Sessions, Mar 99, 60 Min

CQG © 1999

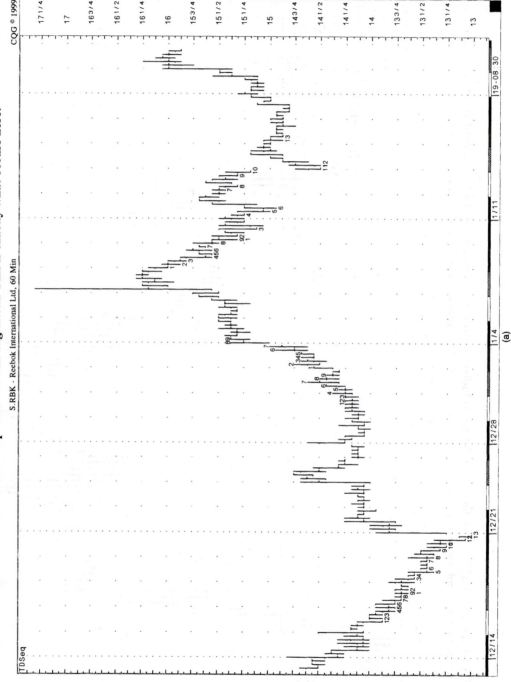

FIGURE 6.20 Chart A displays two completed low-risk buy Countdowns (marked with 13s) for Reebok (RBK) on a 60-minute basis. Each of these trades were followed by sharp market rallies and would have been profitable for an option trader. Chart B displays Reebok on a daily basis over the same period of time, although a more recent, liberal version of Countdown is applied. Ideally, traders would like to see a longer-term indication coincide with a shorter-term indication to time their entries better—a process we call *alignment*. This is exactly what occurs here.

(a)

148

FIGURE 6.20 (Continued)

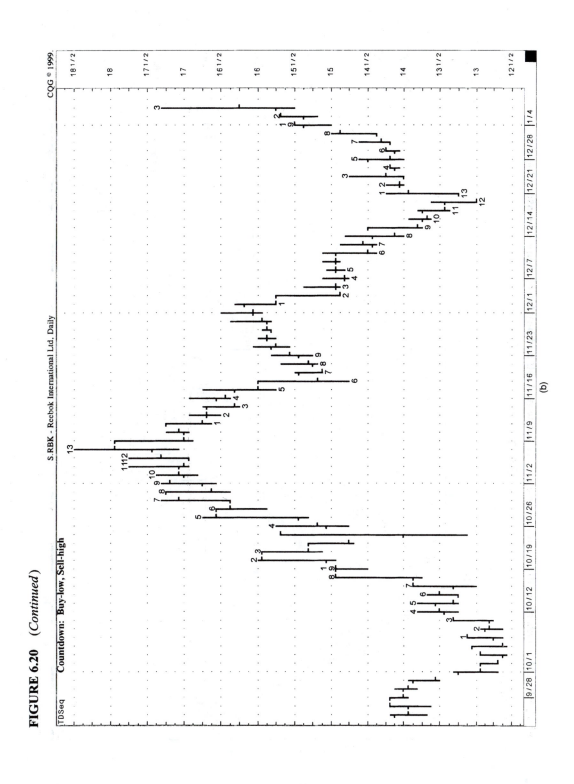

(b)

FIGURE 6.21 This chart illustrates a low-risk TD Sequential sell and buy for 60-minute Treasury bonds.

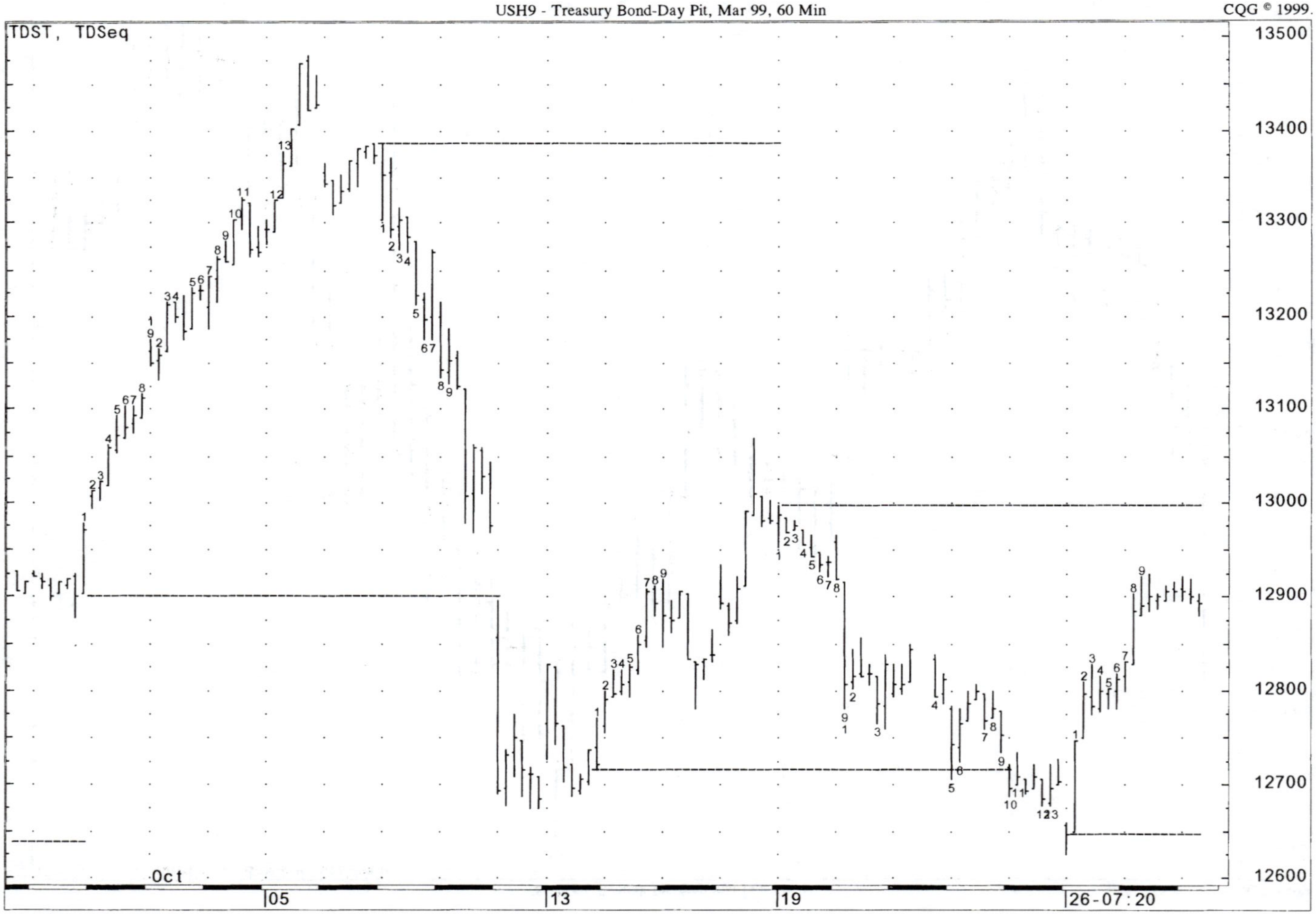

USH9 - Treasury Bond-Day Pit, Mar 99, 60 Min

CQG © 1999.

FIGURE 6.22   In the 60-minute chart of McGraw-Hill (MHP), TD Sequential records a low-risk buy 13 at the precise low close. Purchasing a call option at this time would have been profitable for the trader.

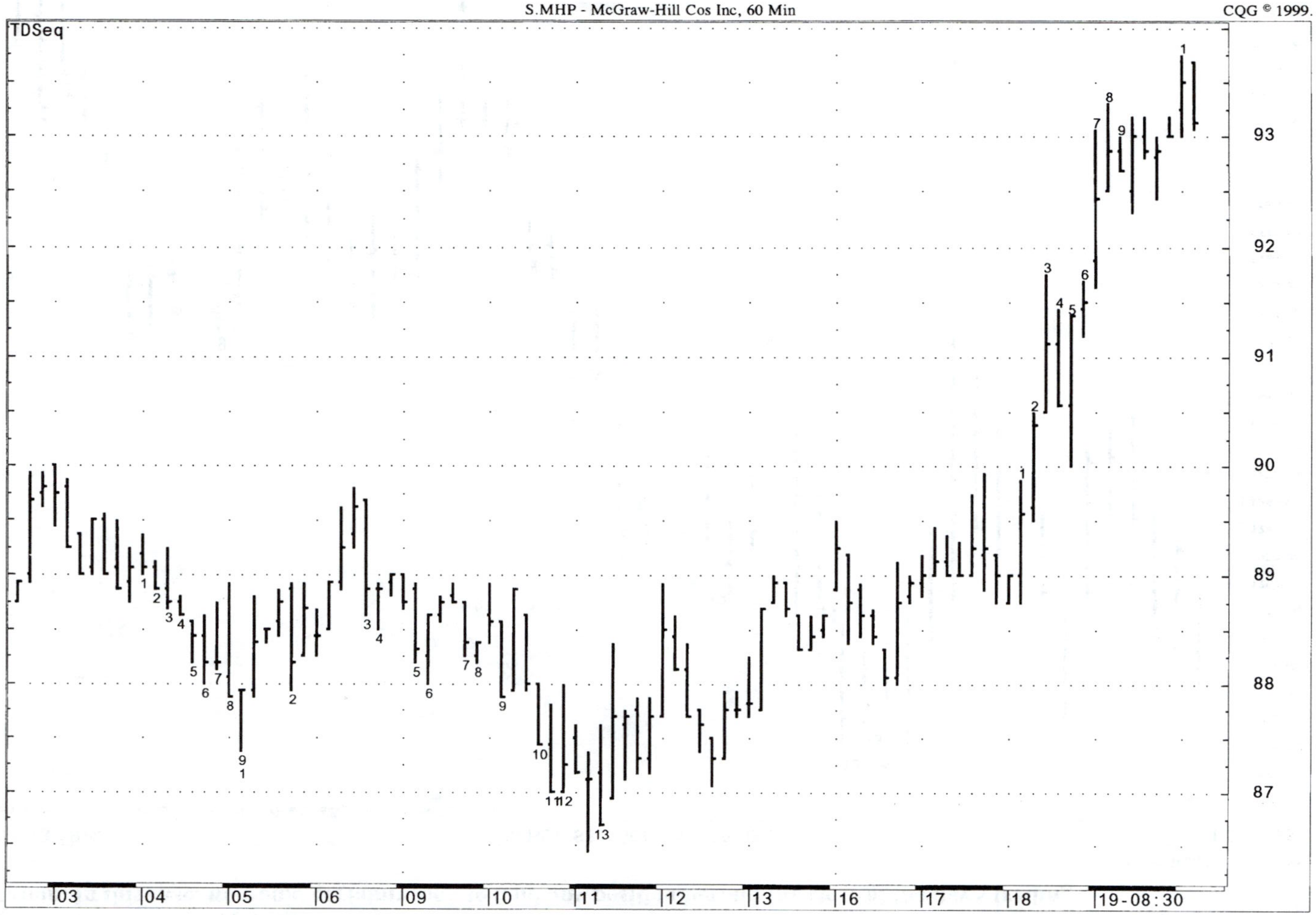

151

FIGURE 6.23 By applying TD Sequential to a daily chart of the S&P 500 March 1999 future, we have a longer-term indication. In this case, we would certainly look to hold any position beyond the close of the day's trading.

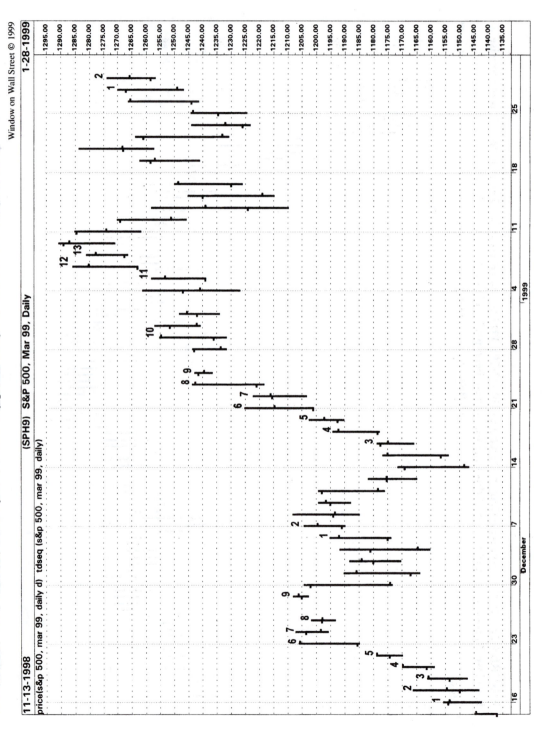

152

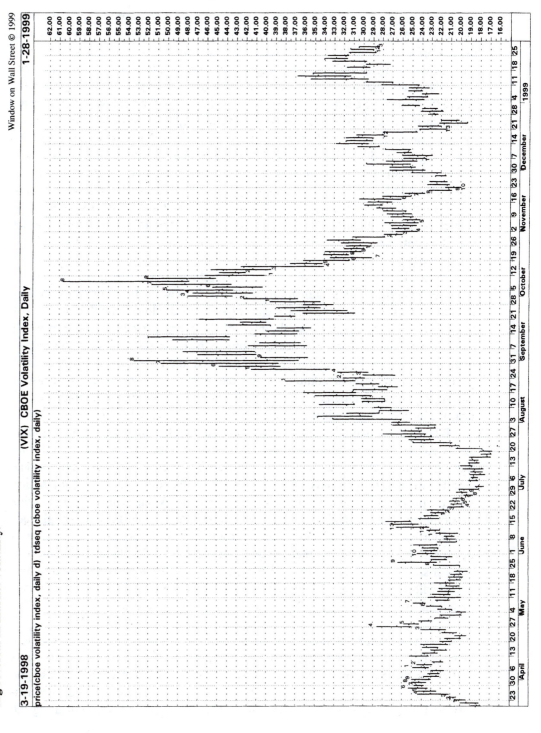

FIGURE 6.24 This chart of the daily CBOE Volatility Index (VIX) identifies both a TD Sequential low-risk sell (put-buying) and buy (call-buying) indication. Rather than an actual sell or a buy, these indications merely forecast an impending reversal in market volatility.

equal to the high two price bars earlier in the case of a sell Countdown, and where
the current price bar's close is less than or equal to the low two price bars earlier in
the case of a buy Countdown. However, the new Countdown setting does not compare closes to highs and lows, but highs and lows to highs and lows. This new
Countdown comparison setting states that the market must record 13 price bars
where the low of the current price bar is less than or equal to the low two price bars
earlier in the case of a buy Countdown, and the high of the current price bar is
greater than or equal to the high two price bars earlier in the case of a sell Countdown. Figure 6.25 displays a completed TD Sequential low-risk buying (call-
buying) indication with this new buy Countdown setting, and Fig. 6.26 displays a
completed TD Sequential low-risk selling (put-buying) indication with this new
sell Countdown setting. Since this comparison need not await the close of the current price bar to obtain a Countdown count, a trader is able to enter the market
sometime intrabar, which is especially helpful when the final count of Countdown
is achieved.

   Much like the standard Countdown phase, there is only one qualifier that we
use with this setting. This qualifier requires that the low of the 13 price bar be less
than the low of the 8 price bar in the case of a buy Countdown, and that the high of
the 13 price bar be greater than the high of the 8 price bar in the case of a sell
Countdown. In either case, in order to complete the Countdown phase, this requirement must be met. If the qualifier is not fulfilled, then the thirteenth price bar is
postponed for at least one additional price bar and the bar is marked with an asterisk. Again, the reasoning behind this qualifier is to ensure that a 13 count occurs
near the high of a price advance and near the low of a price decline.

   When TD Sequential is completed using this new Countdown setting, the market is vulnerable to a significant price reversal—oftentimes more powerful than
that experienced after a buy Setup is completed. This new setting can be utilized as
a replacement of the previous Countdown price-level comparison or in conjunction
with the previous Countdown price-level comparison. Along with TD Combo, this
new type of Countdown phase can be used with the traditional TD Sequential reading to further enhance one's entry point. If traders intend to utilize this new Countdown setting, we encourage them to do so together with the standard Countdown
comparison and with TD Combo. When these three Countdown phases are completed within a few price bars of each other, then the low-risk buying (call-buying)
or selling (put-buying) opportunities are much more powerful.

New TD Sequential Countdown setting examples.   Figure 6.27 is a 30-minute
chart of Pfizer. In this example, we are comparing the low to the low two price bars
earlier for the buy Countdown, as opposed to the traditional comparison of the
close to the low two price bars earlier. The low-risk buying (call-buying) opportunity occurs intraday when the market records a 13 of Countdown, indicating the

FIGURE 6.25 This chart displays a completed buy Countdown phase using the alternative setting, buy-low, sell-high, which requires that the low of each buy Countdown count must be less than or equal to the low two price bars earlier.

TD SEQUENTIAL
BUY COUNTDOWN
BUY-LOW SELL-HIGH

S.YHOO - Yahoo! Inc, 30 Min

CQG © 1999.

155

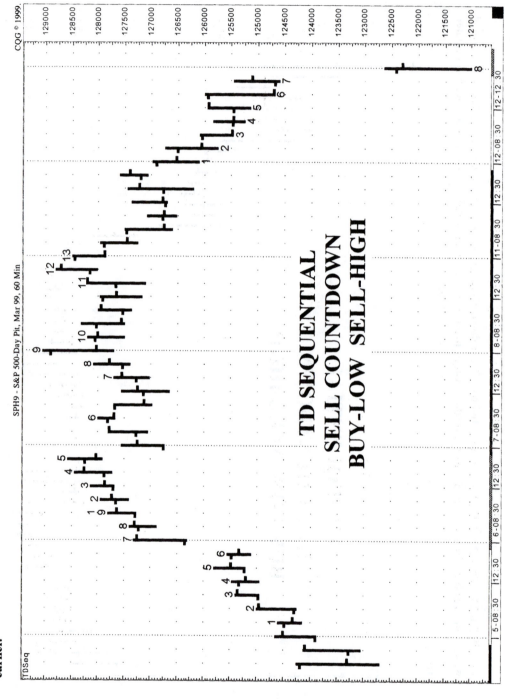

FIGURE 6.26 This chart displays a completed sell Countdown phase using the alternative setting, buy-low, sell-high, which requires that the high of each sell Countdown count must be greater than or equal to the high two price bars earlier.

FIGURE 6.27 The 30-minute chart of Pfizer (PFE) applies the alternative buy-low, sell-high setting for the Countdown phase. Note the chart identifies a low-risk 13 TD Sequential just before the steep rise upside.

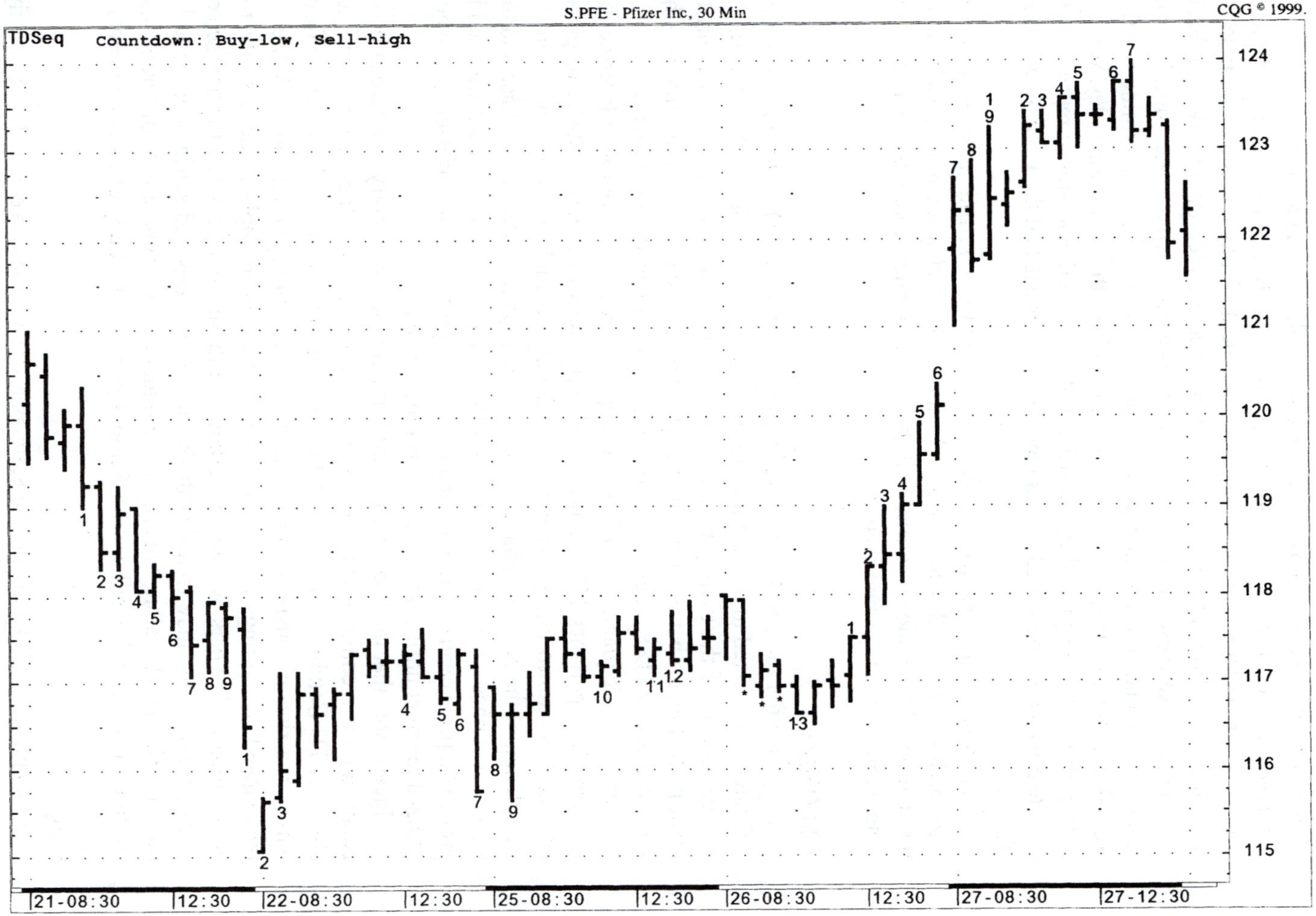

market is vulnerable to a substantial price reversal. As you can see, once the 13 is recorded midmorning on the 26th, price immediately commenced a significant price rally of over four points by the close. The next trading day price continued to trade higher, trading almost eight points higher before recording a price pullback. In examples like these, in which a 13 is recorded on such a large, intraday time frame, we evaluate our position prior to the close of trading to determine whether we will exit our day trade or carry it over until at least the next trading day. You will notice three asterisks preceding the 13 count of Countdown—these represent 30-minute price bars where a 13 would have been recorded, had the Countdown qualifier been met.

Additional examples using this new Countdown setting are presented in Figs. 6.28 through 6.32, while Figs. 6.33 and 6.34 are chart comparisons between the traditional Countdown setting and the new Countdown version over the same time frame and in the same security.

TD COMBO

A few years after the development and implementation of TD Sequential, a similar indicator was created to combat the possibility of overextending TD Sequential to a large portion of the trading public. This indicator was instituted in an effort to identify the highest bar of a price move. This related indicator operates in much the same manner as TD Sequential but the rules that applies are much stricter.

Unlike TD Sequential, which is made up of three phases (although Intersection is not really important), TD Combo is made up of only two phases: the Setup phase and the Countdown phase. As with TD Sequential, each phase begins upon the completion of the previous phase. Upon the completion of the Setup phase and the Countdown phase, the market has most often reached a point of exhaustion and is prone to a price reversal. Again, each phase is important in and of itself, but when utilized together until completion, it becomes even more so.

Please note that the numbered counts and the rules necessary to arrive at these counts are the recommended settings that we use. However, these settings are not absolute. TD Combo is simply an indicator template, providing the structure from which to arrive at consistent and objective market-timing conclusions. While we recommend the settings that follow, as they have been applied successfully for approximately 25 years, we are not certain that these are necessarily the best selections possible. One may find that different comparisons and settings prove to be more profitable. Therefore, we encourage traders to experiment with different possibilities of TD Combo, either with Setup, Countdown, or any of its components.

Setup

The first phase of TD Combo is the Setup phase. This phase is calculated in exactly the same manner as it is with TD Sequential. Again, the Setup phase for TD Combo

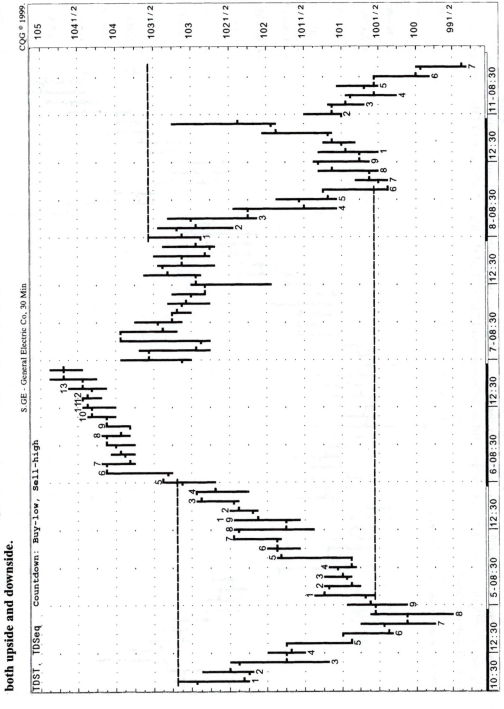

FIGURE 6.28 A low-risk TD Sequential sell (put-buying) indication 13 using the buy-low, sell-high Countdown setting is recorded at the 30-minute high of General Electric (GE). Also displayed are the TDST lines describing breakout levels both upside and downside.

FIGURE 6.29 Using buy-low, sell-high, a low-risk 13 sell indication on the 60-minute of the S&P 500 March 1999 futures contract was identified near the high of the move prior to a decline of almost 70.00 points. This chart is in Alignment with that of Fig. 6.17, where a traditional Countdown 13 identified the high closing price of the move on an S&P 45-minute chart.

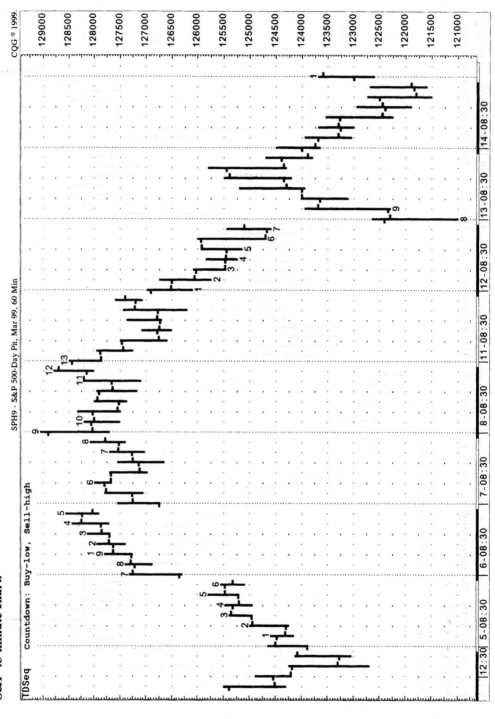

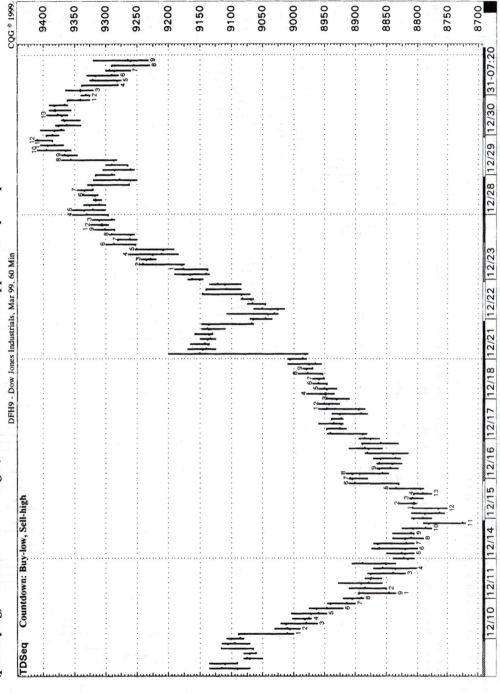

FIGURE 6.30 TD Sequential using the Countdown setting buy-low, sell-high presented a low-risk 13 buy (call-buying) indication just prior to a 600-point advance in the Dow Jones Futures contract. This was followed by a low-risk 13 sell (put-buying) indication near the highs, which resulted in a move of approximately 150 points.

161

FIGURE 6.31 This chart shows the versatility of TD Sequential by applying the buy-low, sell-high Countdown phase to a daily chart of Microsoft (MSFT). As you can see, a low-risk TD Sequential 13 buy indication occurred just prior to the price breakout and acceleration upside.

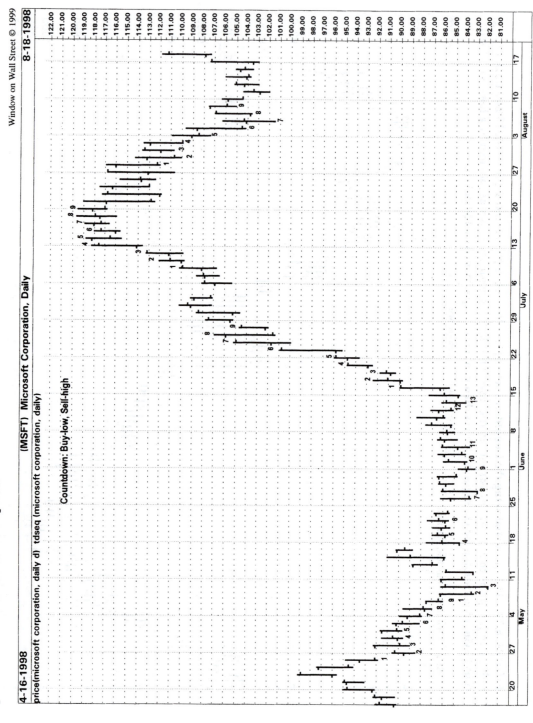

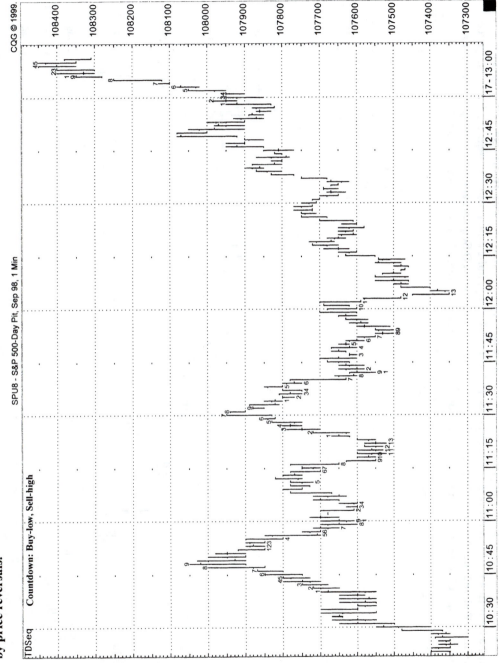

FIGURE 6.32 This chart demonstrates how the buy-low, sell-high setting can be applied successfully to liquid securities on a time frame as short as one minute. In this example, completed Setups and Countdowns were followed by price reversals.

163

FIGURE 6.33 This figure is actually two charts of the same time frame. Chart A shows JP Morgan (JPM) on a 60-minute basis, with a traditional Countdown low-risk 13 buy (call-buying) indication coming in near the low of the price move. Chart B shows the identical JPM price chart but in this instance the TD Sequential Countdown process compares the lows for a buy Countdown and the highs for a sell Countdown rather than the close versus the low.

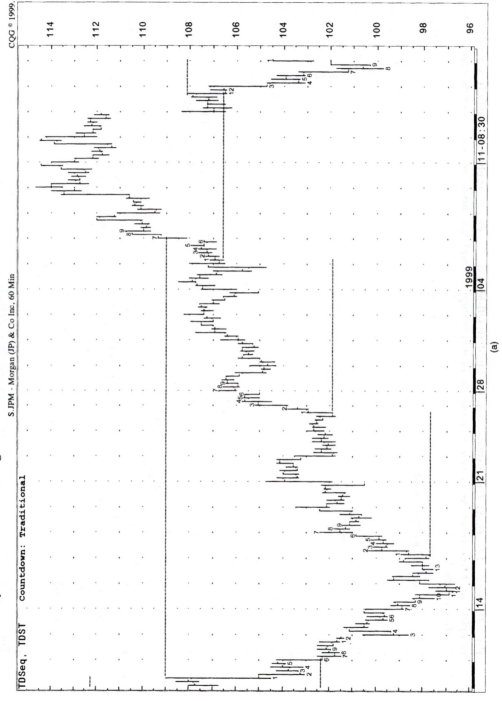

(a)

FIGURE 6.33 *(Continued)*

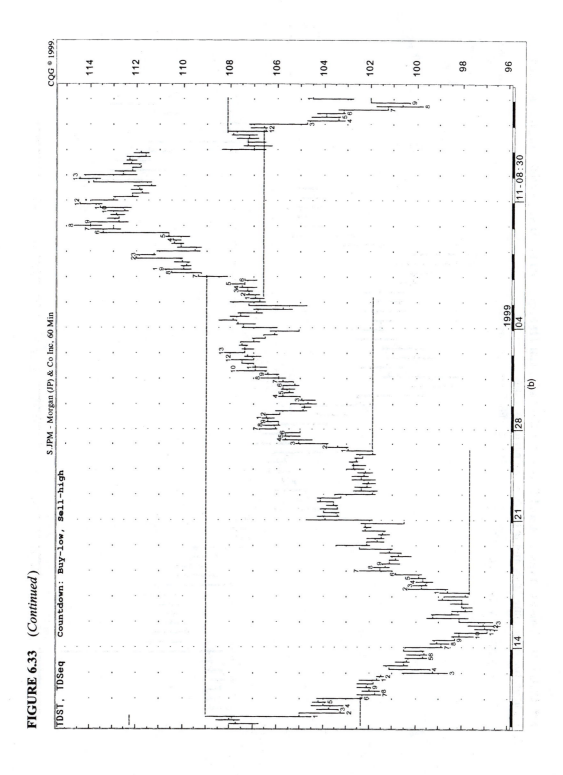

FIGURE 6.34 These two charts, A and B, compare the traditional TD Sequential to TD Sequential using buy-low, sell-high, on the same time basis and over the same period of time.

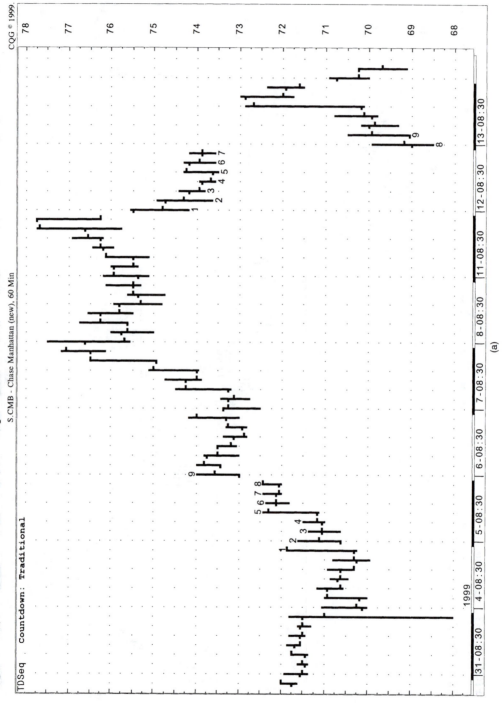

(a)

166

FIGURE 6.34 (*Continued*)

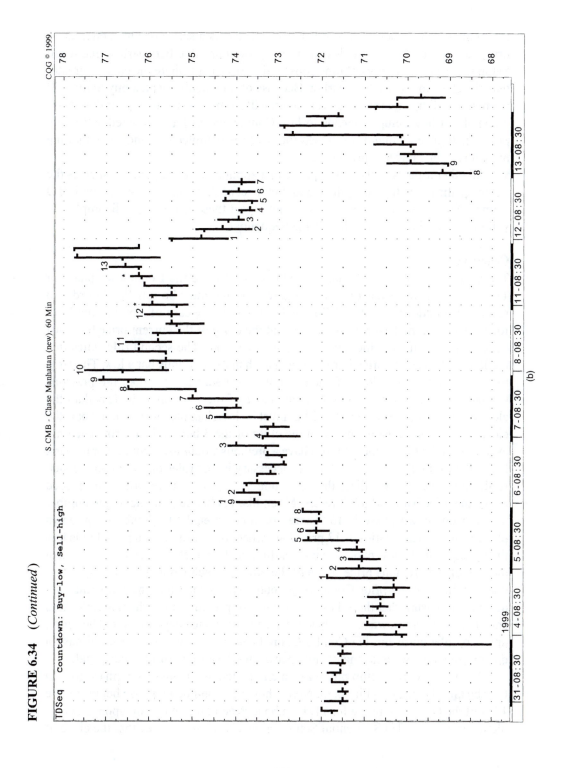

is a comparison of closes. A buy Setup is defined as a series of nine consecutive price bars where the close is less than the close four price bars earlier, and a sell Setup is defined as a series of nine consecutive price bars where the close is greater than the close four price bars earlier. Because of this requirement, a buy Setup will form in a declining market and a sell Setup will form in an advancing market. Also, a completed buy Setup proceeds to buy Countdown and a completed sell Setup proceeds to a sell Countdown. Once the Setup is completed, it indicates that the market is vulnerable to a price reversal.

All other aspects of the Setup phase that applied in TD Sequential, such as the Setup qualifier, Setup recycling, and Setup cancellations, also apply with TD Combo. For the sake of space, we will not repeat these items, we will simply ask you to refer to the Setup section of TD Sequential.

Countdown

The Countdown phase is the key to TD Combo. Unlike the Countdown phase of TD Sequential which has only one requirement that must be fulfilled in order to record a Countdown count, TD Combo has three. In the case of a buy Countdown for TD Combo, the first rule stipulates that the close of the current price bar must be less than or equal to the low two price bars earlier. The second rule states that the low of the current price bar must be less than the previous bar's low. The final rule requires that the close of each Countdown count be less than the previous Countdown count's close. Therefore, the close of the 2 bar must be less than the close of the 1 bar; the close of the 3 bar must be less than the close of the 2 bar; the close of the 4 bar must be less than the close of the 3 bar; and so forth. The only exception is the 1 bar which doesn't have a previous Countdown count. For the first bar of the Countdown phase, all that is necessary is that rules one and two are met. If all three rules are fulfilled, then a Countdown number is recorded and placed below the price bar to which it refers. Much like TD Sequential, the magic number for the Countdown phase is 13. Therefore, a completed TD Combo Countdown phase is defined as a series of 13 price bars where the close of each price bar is less than or equal to the low two price bars earlier, the low of each price bar is less than the low of the previous price bar, and the close of each Countdown count is less than the close of the prior Countdown count. The second and the third rules are designed to ensure that there is some downward pressure upon the market's price and that the Countdown series has not formed in a sideways market. Therefore, upon completion of the TD Combo Countdown phase, the market should have a downward slope, whereas that is not necessarily the case with TD Sequential.

A completed buy Setup phase and a completed buy Countdown phase for TD Combo are illustrated in Fig. 6.35. Notice how the Countdown phase begins on the 1 bar of the buy Setup phase for TD Combo instead of commencing upon the completion of 9 bar of TD Sequential Setup. In the chart, you can see that the close of

FIGURE 6.35 This chart displays a completed TD Combo low-risk buying (call-buying) indication. The asterisk represents a price bar that would have recorded a buy Countdown number for TD Sequential, but did not meet the rules for TD Combo. The buy Countdown phase for TD Combo is completed when a 13 is recorded.

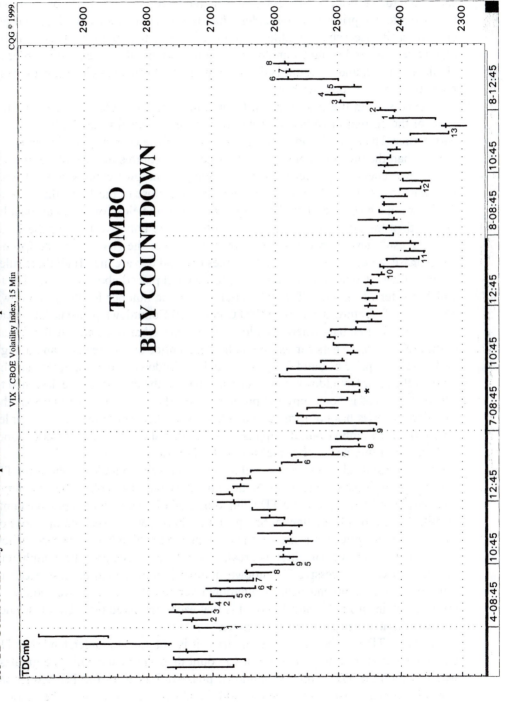

169

each Countdown price bar is less than or equal to the low two price bars earlier, each Countdown price bar's low is less than the previous price bar's low, and the close of each successive Countdown number is lower than the last. Keep in mind that we recommend using Countdown version 2, where all we require in order to obtain an 11, 12, and 13 count is that each numbered price bar close successively lower than the previous number.

Conversely, in the case of a sell Countdown, the first rule stipulates that the close of the current price bar must be greater than or equal to the high two price bars earlier. The second rule states that the high of the current price bar must be greater than the previous bar's high. The final rule requires that the close of each Countdown count be greater than the previous Countdown count's close. Therefore, the close of the 2 bar must be greater than the close of the 1 bar; the close of the 3 bar must be greater than the close of the 2 bar; the close of the 4 bar must be greater than the close of the 3 bar; and so forth. The only exception is the 1 bar which doesn't have a previous Countdown count. For the first bar of the Countdown phase, all that is necessary is that rules one and two are met. If all three rules are met, then a Countdown number is recorded and placed above the price bar to which it refers. Much like TD Sequential, the magic number for the Countdown phase is 13. Therefore, a completed TD Combo sell Countdown phase is defined as a series of 13 price bars where the close of each price bar is greater than or equal to the high two price bars earlier, the high of each price bar is greater than the high of the previous price bar, and the close of each Countdown count is greater than the close of the prior Countdown count. The second and the third rules are designed to ensure that there is some upward pressure upon the market's price and that the Countdown series has not formed in a sideways market. Therefore, upon completion of the TD Combo Countdown phase, the market should have an upward slope, whereas that is not necessarily the case with TD Sequential.

A completed sell Setup phase and a completed sell Countdown phase for TD Combo are illustrated in Fig. 6.36. Notice how the Countdown phase begins on the 3 bar of the sell Setup phase for TD Combo instead of commencing upon the completion of 9 bar of TD Sequential Setup. In the chart, you can see that the close of each Countdown price bar is greater than or equal to the high two price bars earlier, each Countdown price bar's high is greater than the previous price bar's high, and the close of each successive Countdown number is higher than the last. Keep in mind that we recommend using Countdown version 2, where all we require in order to obtain an 11, 12, and 13 count is that each numbered price bar close successively higher than the previous number.

Because TD Combo's rules are so strict, it is not hard to understand that TD Combo needs more time to develop a 13 count than TD Sequential. The greatest way in which the TD Combo Countdown phase differs from the TD Sequential Countdown phase, aside from the two additional counting rules, is in the point at

FIGURE 6.36 This chart displays a completed TD Combo low-risk selling (put-buying) indication. The sell Countdown phase begins its count on the third bar of the Setup phase, as this was the first price bar where each of the three rules for sell Countdown were met. The asterisk represents a price bar that would have recorded a sell Countdown number for TD Sequential, but did not meet the rules for TD Combo.

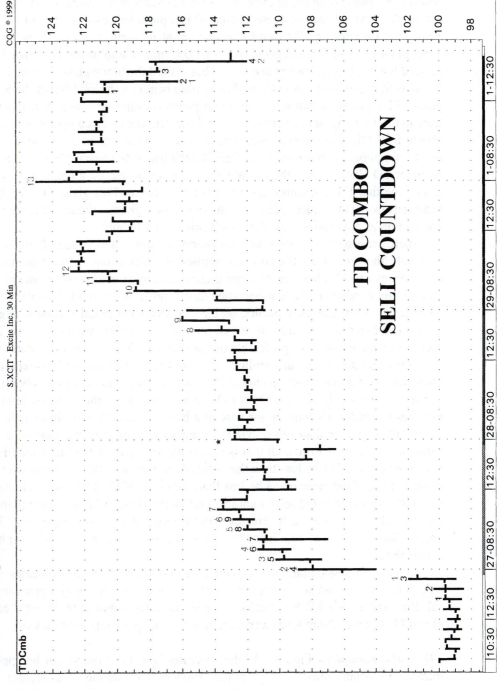

TD COMBO
SELL COUNTDOWN

which these phases can commence. Whereas TD Sequential can begin, at its earliest, on the 9 bar of the completed Setup phase, provided it meets the rule of TD Sequential Countdown, TD Combo can begin, at its earliest, on the 1 bar of the Setup phase, provided it meets the rules of TD Combo Countdown. However, keep in mind that the Countdown phase cannot begin until the Setup phase is completed. But how then can the Combo Countdown phase begin on the first bar of the Setup phase? The answer is that once the Setup phase is completed, one then must go back to the first day of the Setup phase and perform the three comparisons necessary to fulfill the Countdown requirements. For each bar that meets these requirements, a number is recorded. Therefore, if each bar of the Setup phase meets the rules for TD Combo, then the Countdown phase could record a count of 9 at the same time that TD Sequential has recorded its 1 count. This gives TD Combo a head start over TD Sequential to give the indicator a greater chance of running to completion as opposed to canceling itself prior to a 13 count.

There are also two versions of TD Combo: version 1 and version 2. Version 1 is simply the three Countdown rules applied to each count of the Countdown phase, from 1 to 13. However, because these rules are so strict, and as time passes and the trend exhausts itself it becomes more and more difficult to obtain a 13 count before a price reversal occurs, we have created an alternative version to generate more low-risk buy and sell or call-buying and put-buying indications. This second version is the more preferable of the two. TD Combo version 2 states that the three Countdown rules are applied to the market until a count of 10 is recorded. Once the Countdown phase reaches a 10 count, all that is necessary to obtain the last three counts (11, 12, and 13) is to have a closing price that is lower than the previous Countdown's count in the case of a buy Countdown, or to have a closing price that is greater than the previous Countdown's count in the case of a sell Countdown. In other words, all that is necessary for a completed buy Countdown is that the close of 11 be less than the close of 10, the close of 12 be less than the close of 11, and the close of 13 be less than the close of 12; conversely, all that is necessary for a completed sell Countdown is that the close of 11 be greater than the close of 10, the close of 12 be greater than the close of 11, and the close of 13 be greater than the close of 12. Once this 13 count is recorded, the Countdown phase is completed.

As with TD Sequential, the completion of TD Combo typically coincides with a point of price exhaustion, where the market is vulnerable to a major price reversal. However, unlike TD Sequential, because the rules required to obtain a completed TD Combo Countdown series are so strict, no qualifiers are necessary.

TD combo examples. Figure 6.37 demonstrates how TD Combo can be applied intraday to obtain low-risk buying (call-buying) and selling (put-buying) opportunities. This example presents a chart of the five-minute OEX Index (S&P 100).

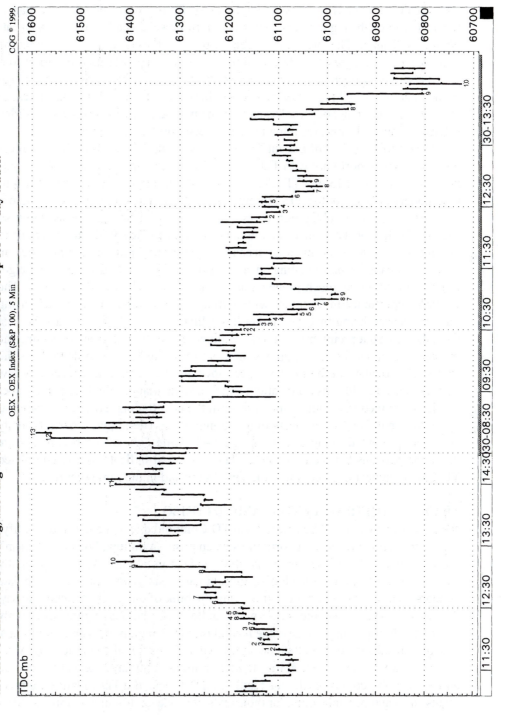

FIGURE 6.37 The five-minute chart of the OEX Index using TD Combo records a low-risk 13 selling (put-buying) opportunity at the exact high of the price rally. The advantage of the timing of this indication is that it occurred within the first 30 minutes of trading, allowing the trade much more time to develop for the day trader.

As you can see in the chart, the completion of TD Combo occurred when the market recorded a 13 on the highest closing price, thereby presenting a low-risk selling (put-buying) indication. The interesting aspect of this chart, aside from the fact that the trade was quite profitable, is that the low-risk put-buying indication occurred four price bars after the opening of the market, (only 20 minutes after the open) at the high of the trading day and proceeded to decline throughout the rest of the day. Because the low-risk entry point occurred so early in the trading day, the market was afforded sufficient time to decline, resulting in much greater profits on the trade.

The 60-minute chart of Lucent Technologies in Fig. 6.38 exhibited an excellent low-risk entry opportunity with TD Combo. In this example, the high of the market coincided with a 13 of a TD Combo low-risk selling opportunity. Most beginning traders choose not to sell such highs short (meaning selling the stock before one owns it with the obligation of buying it back at a later date), as doing so requires them to post a significant amount of margin and leaves them vulnerable to unlimited risk. However, in these scenarios, purchasing put options provides an excellent means of participating in a market decline, as traders are no longer required to put up as much money, nor do they face such considerable risk. The greatest opportunity in a market with activity such as this comes in purchasing puts, the reason being that the market has rallied so strongly for at least the past three days that put premiums will have declined. Because traders are expecting the market to continue its rally, purchasing a put once the 13 is recorded allows the trader to participate in the market price move and to do so at a surprisingly low cost. Because this low-risk indication came on such a large time frame, the trader would be inclined to remain in the trade until the next trading day at the very least.

Additional TD Combo examples ranging from one-minute charts to daily charts are presented in Figs. 6.39 through 6.44, while Figs. 6.45 through 6.54 are chart comparisons between completed TD Sequential indications and completed TD Combo indications over the same time frame and in the same security.

TRADING WITH TD SEQUENTIAL AND TD COMBO

We always knew that TD Sequential and TD Combo did an excellent job identifying potential price reversal opportunities when position trading; however, it wasn't until recently that we discovered that these indicators also worked exceptionally well on a short-term, intraday basis. Approximately six years ago, one of the data vendors approached us about programming the bulk of our work. Needless to say, the idea of having a computer perform the endless calculations required of us daily was certainly appealing. We gave the formulas to the programmers and for months, tested the results to confirm their accuracy. After all the initial computer bugs were corrected, we reveled in our ability to click a mouse and have the TD Sequential and TD Combo counts, oscillator readings, TD Lines, and TD Relative Retracements, among other indicators, for thousands of stocks and futures before us. After

FIGURE 6.38 Selling Lucent stock short at almost $120 per share upon receiving a low-risk 13 selling indication with TD Combo would have been expensive for a trader (with a large deposit required to cover the trade). By purchasing put options, the trader would have been able to participate in the move for much less money, and would have provided much greater returns.

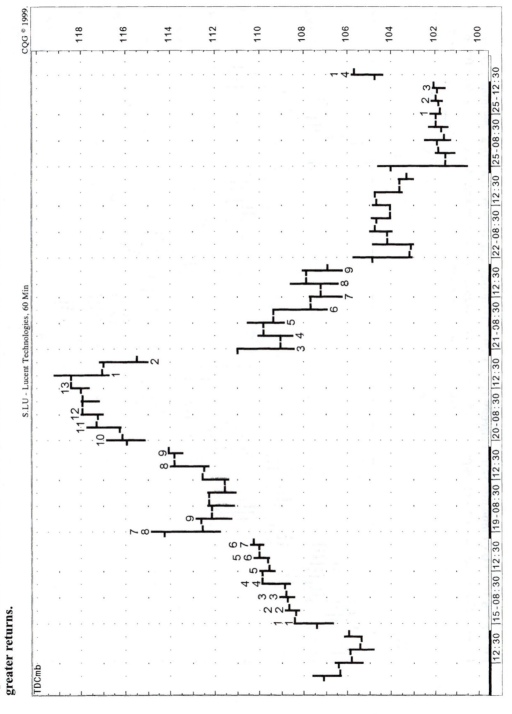

FIGURE 6.39 TD Combo also works effectively on a short-term basis, all the way down to a one-minute chart. A low-risk 13 buying (call-buying) opportunity is recorded two minutes before a bottom is made in the S&P future.

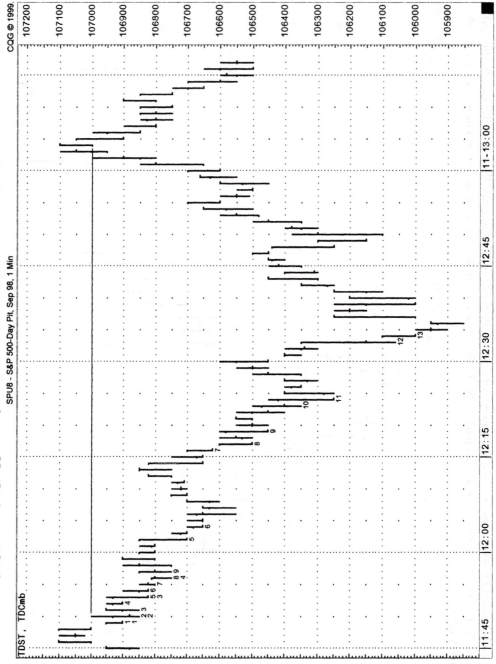

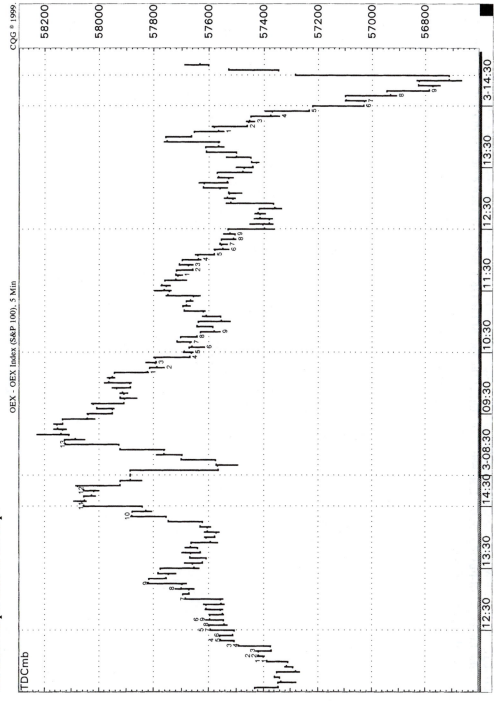

FIGURE 6.40 TD Combo recorded a completed sell Countdown phase two price bars prior to the high of the day in the OEX Index. The advantage to this put-buying opportunity was that it occurred early in the trading day, thereby allowing the trade ample time to develop.

177

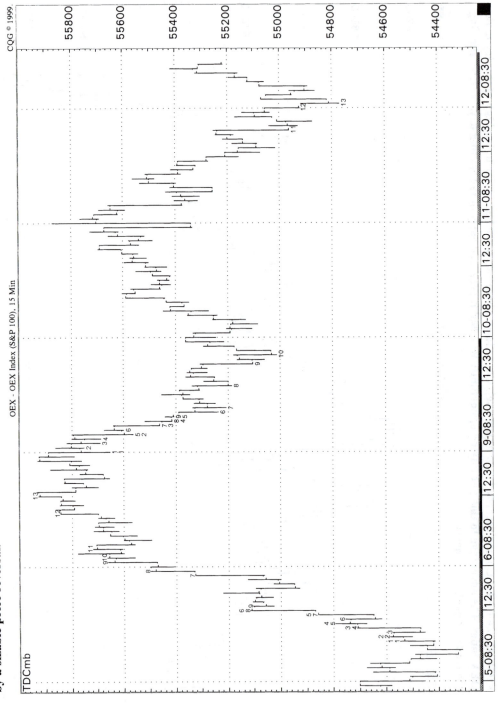

FIGURE 6.41 A low-risk TD Combo selling (put-buying) indication was recorded at the high, and a low-risk TD Combo buying (call-buying) indication was recorded at the low of the OEX Index. In each case, the market was followed by a sizable price reversal.

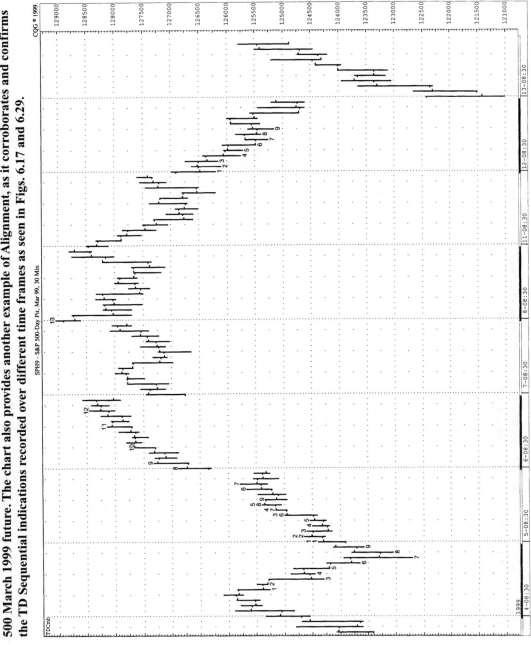

FIGURE 6.42 This example showcases the TD Combo low-risk sell at the precise high for the 30-minute S&P 500 March 1999 future. The chart also provides another example of Alignment, as it corroborates and confirms the TD Sequential indications recorded over different time frames as seen in Figs. 6.17 and 6.29.

179

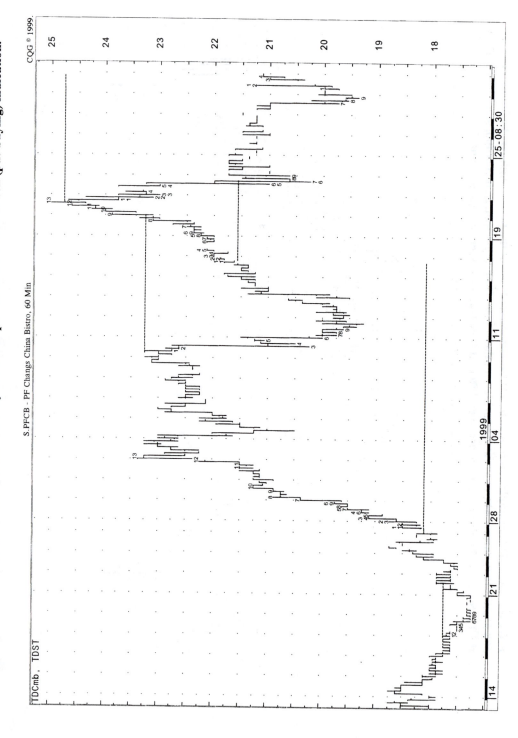

FIGURE 6.43 In this chart, two low-risk selling (put-buying) opportunities were presented. Note how the breakout through the horizontal buy TDST line preceded a rally to the completion of a low-risk 13 sell (put-buying) indication.

FIGURE 6.44 This daily chart of Amazon (AMZN) is used with TD Combo, which successfully identified the peak trading day. Due to the high cost of the stock and the large fund requirement necessary to sell this stock short, this indication presents an ideal put-buying opportunity.

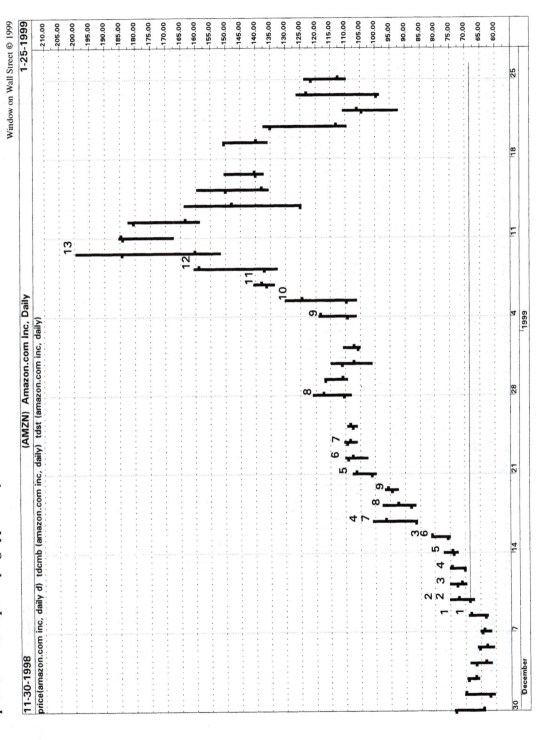

Window on Wall Street © 1999

FIGURE 6.45 Charts A and B compare the results of TD Sequential and TD Combo on the September 1998 S&P 500 futures contract on a one-minute basis over the same period of time. Both indicators gave low-risk selling (put-buying) indications near the high of the move, but TD Combo was more specific.

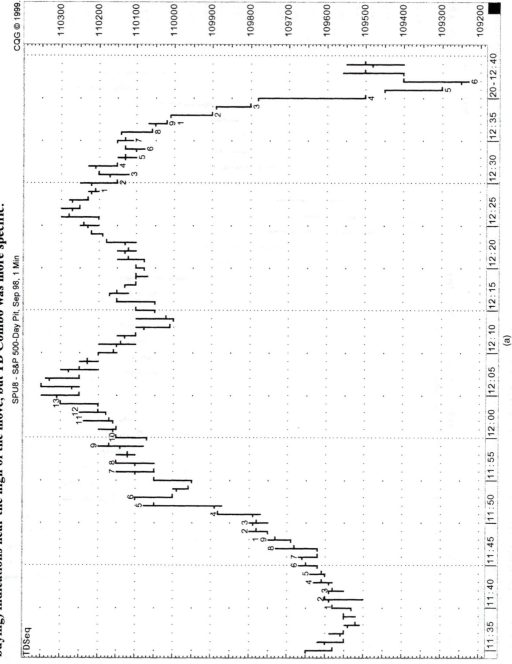

(a)

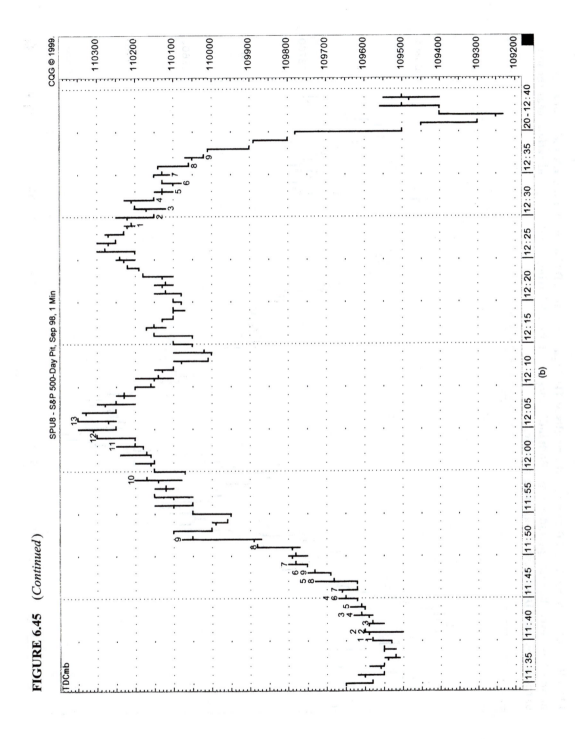

FIGURE 6.45 (*Continued*)

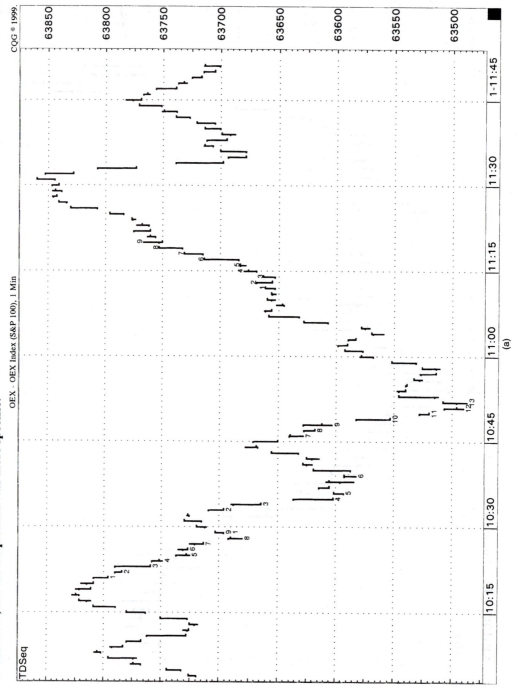

FIGURE 6.46 Charts A and B compare the results of TD Sequential and TD Combo on the OEX Index on a one-minute basis over the same period of time. Both indicators gave low-risk buying (call-buying) indications near the low of the move, but TD Sequential was more specific.

OEX - OEX Index (S&P 100), 1 Min

CQG © 1999.

(a)

FIGURE 6.46 (*Continued*)

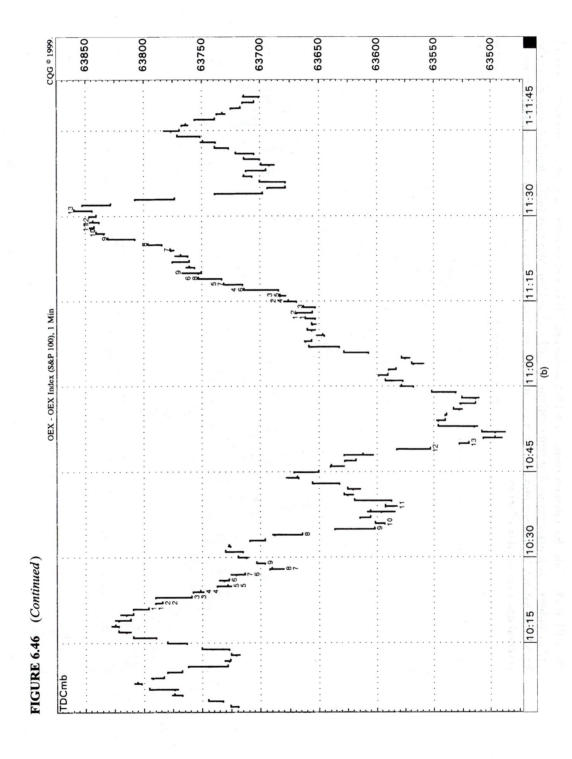

185

FIGURE 6.47 This chart demonstrates how TD Combo and TDST can be used together to determine when a 9 will be followed by a price reversal or will continue toward a 13 of Countdown. A conformed breakout above the TDST line usually indicates a move through countdown completion, whereas a failure to do so implies a price reversal upon completion of setup.

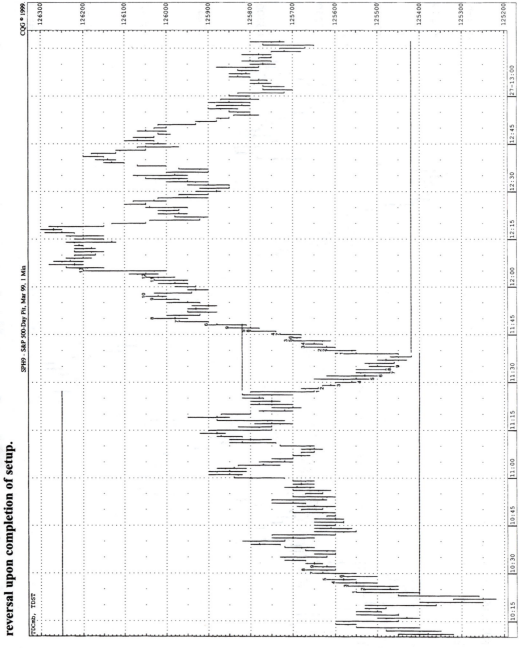

some time, we received a call from a longtime friend and fellow market enthusiast informing us of a startling revelation. It seemed that these indicators, particularly TD Combo and TD Sequential, were not limited in scope to daily price charts, as once thought. It turned out that these two indicators could be applied on intraday price charts with uncanny precision and accuracy. From hourly charts to one-minute charts, we were amazed to see how well 9s and 13s were followed by significant intraday price reversals. These completed Setups and Countdowns were not perfect, but they did do a great job of identifying short-term price movements.

Regardless of the market to which it was applied, TD Sequential and TD Combo consistently identified these low-risk opportunity zones, so much so that we did not have to rely solely on daily indicator readings, but could trade call and put options several times throughout the same trading day. This allowed us much more trading freedom. Over the years we have been able to integrate these short-term results with longer-term results to ameliorate our day trading success. At the very least, these intraday results should enable one to time one's option and security entries more effectively to maximize profit potential.

Now that we have established how a TD Sequential and a TD Combo low-risk opportunity is attained, let's look at the best way to day trade it. The most practical way to look at the completed TD Sequential and TD Combo Countdown phase is as identifying a price zone, anywhere within which the market could halt its current trend and mark the inception of an opposite trend. Typically, these completed phases are completed on or within a few bars of the market's high or low. Since these readings will not, and were not intended to, always occur at these high or low prices, it is important that one trade these indicators cautiously. Therefore, it is important that we address the issues of entry point, stop losses, and profit taking.

TD Sequential and TD Combo Entry

Since TD Sequential and TD Combo illustrate zones where the market is prone to a significant price reversal, when position trading with these indicators, entry price is crucial. Therefore, once a completed TD Sequential and TD Combo indication is achieved, we recommend any one of four low-risk indicator readings occur to justify entry. When trading on a greater time frame, we will typically utilize indicators such as TD Open, TD Trap, TD CLOP, or TD CLOPWIN in order to initiate a price reversal and to justify a low-risk entry. Because these four indicators, when used as a TD Sequential or TD Combo entry technique, do not apply to day trading, we will only provide a cursory explanation of each. These indicators have all been described in greater detail in our previous written work.

TD Open.   TD Open is designed to capitalize on the market's tendency to fill in price gaps. In its simplest form, a low-risk TD Open buying (call-buying) opportunity occurs when the current price bar's open is less than the prior price bar's low

FIGURE 6.48 Charts A and B are presented to demonstrate TD Sequential and TD Combo's versatility and effectiveness regardless of the time frame in which the indicators are used. In practice, TD Combo records a low-risk entry indication at the low or the high of a price move and TD Sequential further confirms that move by recording a low-risk indication at an interim high or low.

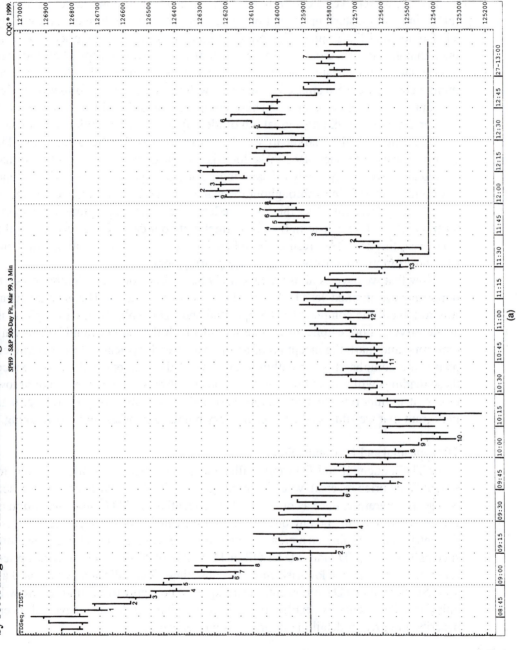

(a)

FIGURE 6.48 (*Continued*)

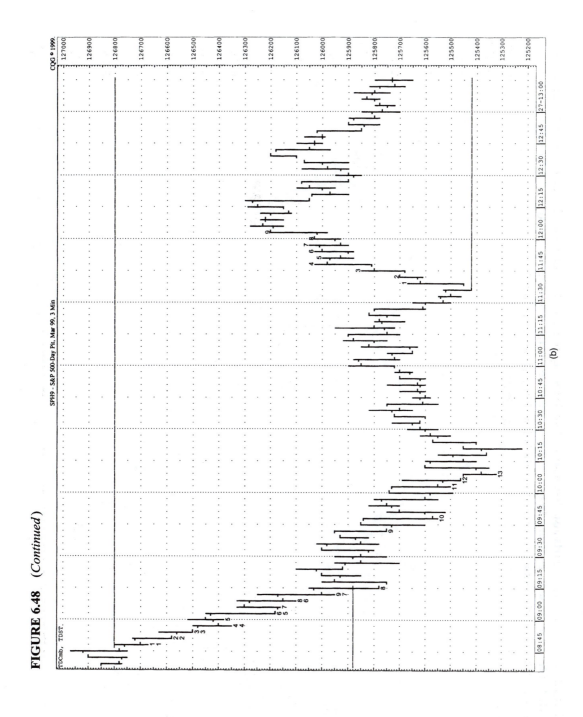

(b)

189

FIGURE 6.49 These two charts also demonstrate how TD Sequential and TD Combo work together over the same period of time for the same contract. In both Chart A and Chart B, the two indicators completed their buy Countdown phases with a 13 on the same price bar and were followed by a steady rally in price.

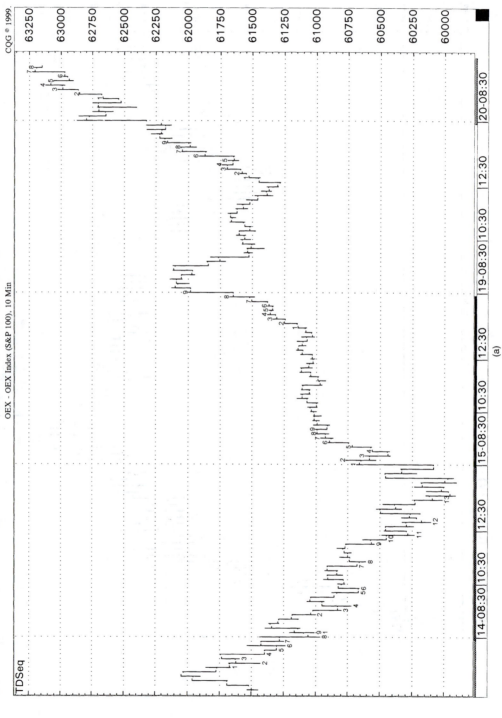

OEX – OEX Index (S&P 100), 10 Min

CQG © 1999.

(a)

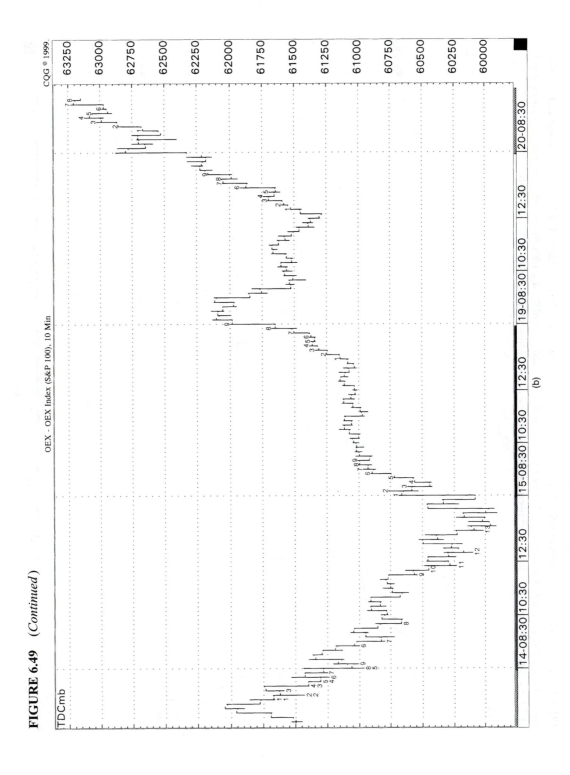

FIGURE 6.49 *(Continued)*

OEX - OEX Index (S&P 100), 10 Min

CQG © 1999.

(b)

191

FIGURE 6.50 These two charts utilize TD Sequential, TD Combo, and TDST on the OEX Index on a 10-minute basis. Over the course of a few trading days, TD Sequential and TD Combo identified a number of Setups, which formed a series of TDST lines. These TDST lines provided support and resistance when price traded to these levels.

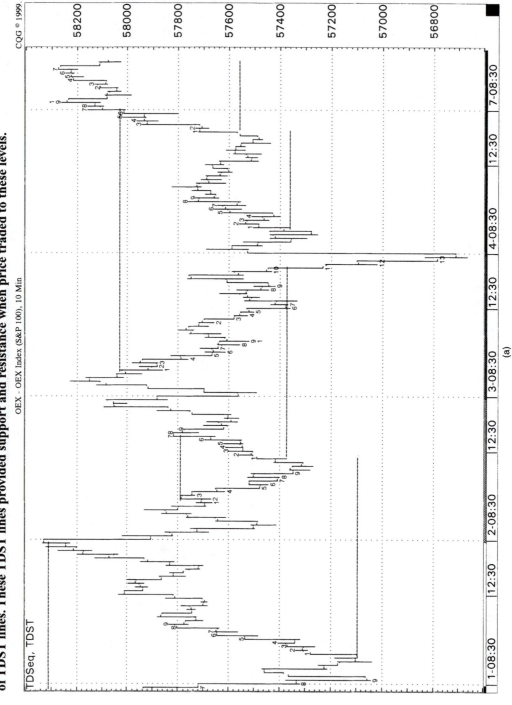

OEX - OEX Index (S&P 100), 10 Min

CQG © 1999.

(a)

FIGURE 6.50 (*Continued*)

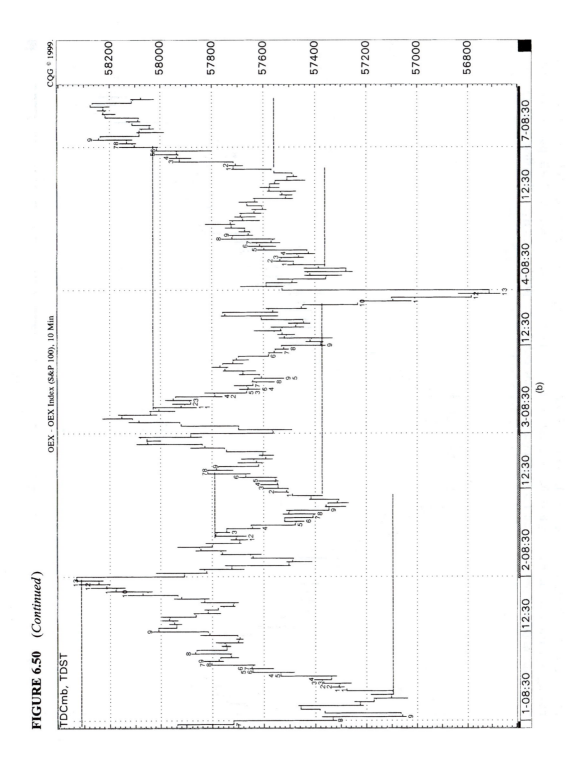

(b)

193

FIGURE 6.51 Charts A and B using TD Sequential and TD Combo, respectively, both completed low-risk selling (put-buying) opportunities near the high of the 15-minute S&P move. TD Combo gave a low-risk 13 sell (put-buying) indication on the high close price bar, and TD Sequential gave a low-risk 13 sell (put-buying) indication shortly afterward.

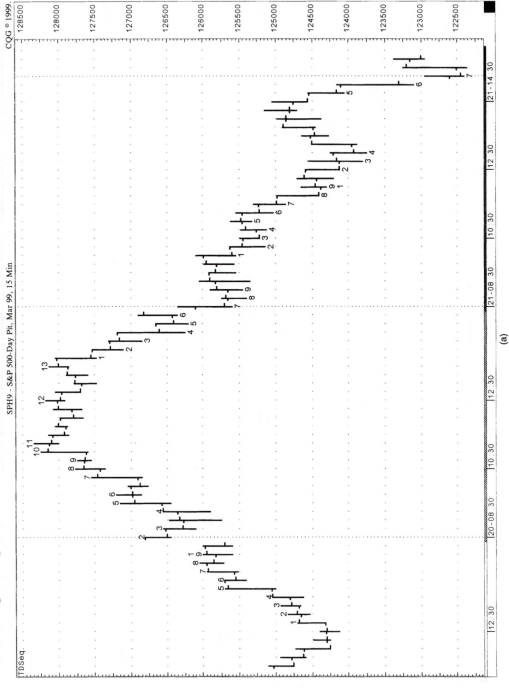

(a)

FIGURE 6.51 (*Continued*)

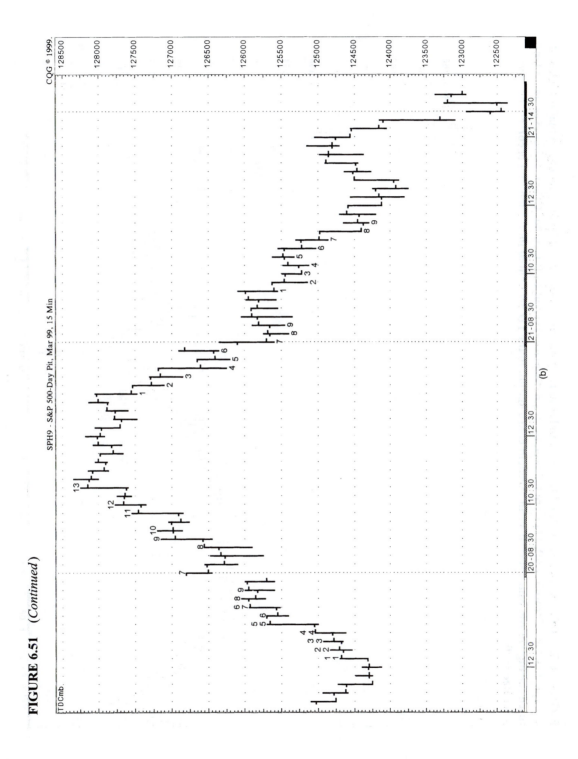

(b)

FIGURE 6.52 Of these two examples, TD Sequential (Chart A) was more effective in identifying both a major high and a major low for Microsoft. Both 13s were followed by dramatic price reversals. TD Combo (Chart B), however, only identified the high move, which served as an excellent confirmation to the TD Sequential indication that occurred only one price bar earlier.

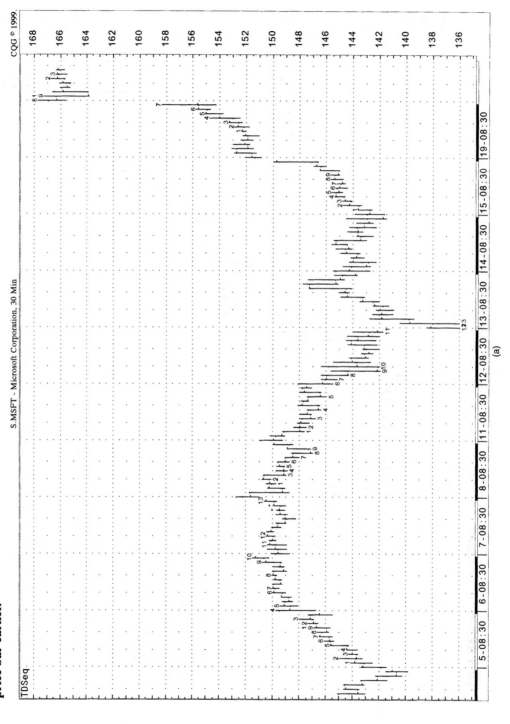

S.MSFT - Microsoft Corporation, 30 Min

CQG © 1999.

(a)

FIGURE 6.52 (Continued)

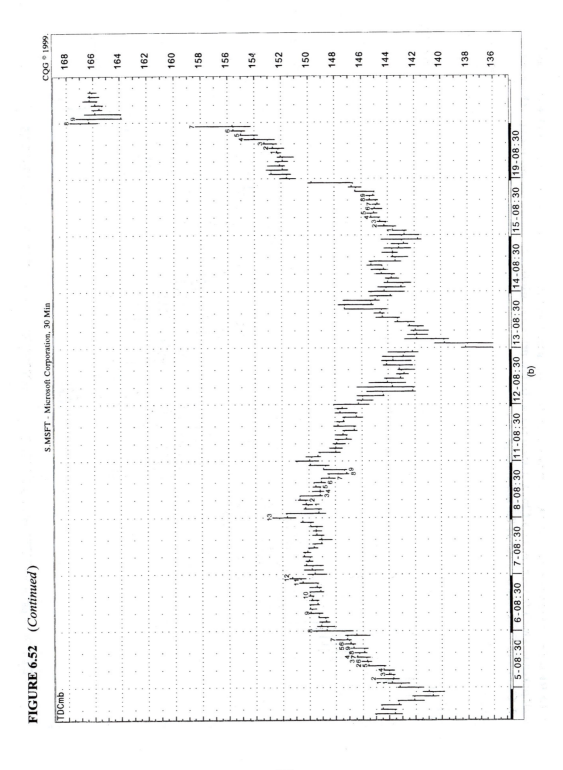

(b)

FIGURE 6.53 TD Sequential and TD Combo are applied to Charts A and B for Staples. Note that the 13 low-risk buy (call purchase) for TD Sequential in Chart A occurred at the low price bar, while the 13 low-risk buy (call purchase) for TD Combo in Chart B occurred at the low close price bar.

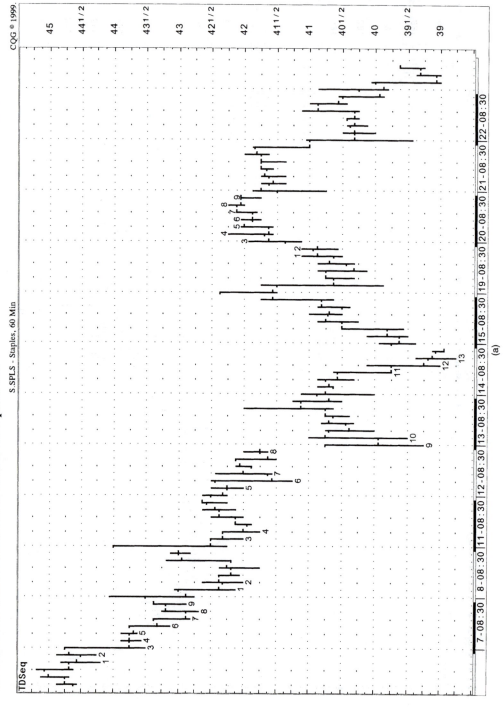

S.SPLS - Staples, 60 Min

CQG © 1999.

(a)

FIGURE 6.53 *(Continued)*

S.SPLS - Staples, 60 Min

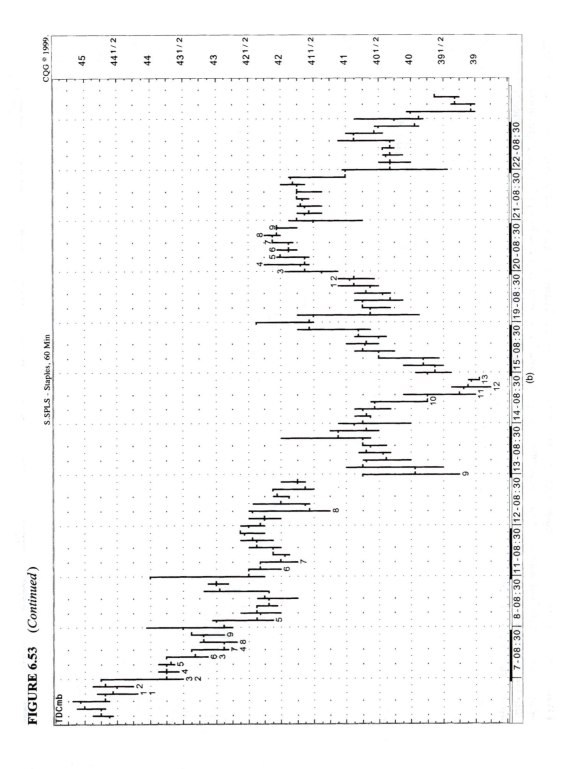

CQG © 1999.

(b)

199

FIGURE 6.54 In these two examples over the same period of time, TD Sequential gave two low-risk selling (put-buying) opportunities coincident with a 13 sell Countdown (Chart A), and TD Combo gave one low-risk selling (put-buying) opportunity coincident with a 13 sell Countdown (Chart B). In both instances, the market experienced a price reversal upon recording the 13 count.

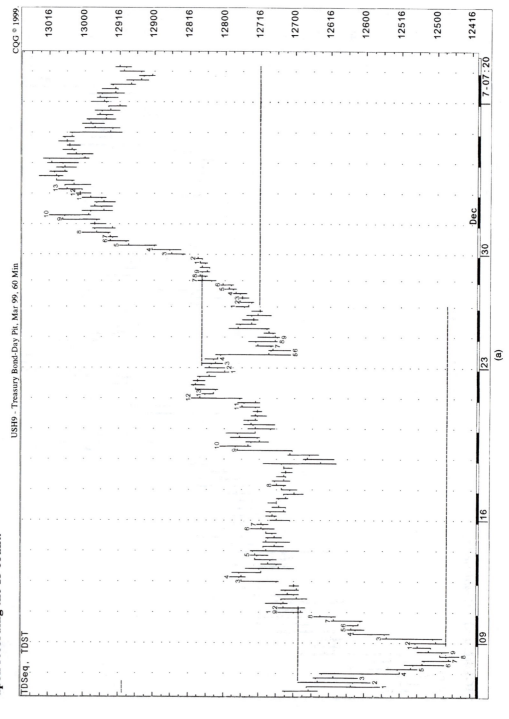

USH9 – Treasury Bond-Day Pit, Mar 99, 60 Min

CQG © 1999.

(a)

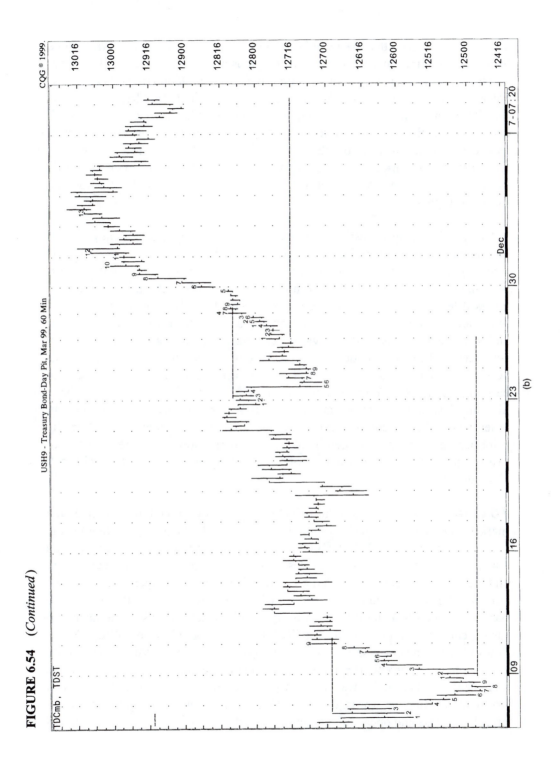

FIGURE 6.54 (*Continued*)

(b)

201

and then trades above that low by at least one tick. In other words, the current price bar's opening price must open below the previous price bar's range and then break into that range to the upside to justify entry upon the completion of the TD Sequential and TD Combo buy Countdown phase. Conversely, in its simplest form, a low-risk TD Open selling (put-buying) opportunity occurs when the current price bar's open is greater than the prior price bar's high and then trades below that high by at least one tick. In other words, the current price bar's opening price must open above the previous price bar's range and then break into that range to the downside to justify entry upon the completion of the TD Sequential and TD Combo sell Countdown phase.

TD Trap.   TD Trap is designed to capitalize on the market's tendency to gain momentum upon breaking out of the previous price bar's range. A low-risk TD Trap buying (call-buying) opportunity occurs when the current price bar's open is contained, or trapped, within the previous price bar's high and low and then trades at least one tick greater than the prior bar's high. In other words, the current price bar's opening price must be contained within the prior bar's price range and then break out above the previous price bar's high to justify entry upon the completion of the TD Sequential and TD Combo buy Countdown phase. Conversely, a low-risk TD Trap selling (put-buying) opportunity occurs when the current price bar's open is contained, or trapped, within the previous price bar's high and low and then trades at least one tick less than the prior bar's low. In other words, the current price bar's opening price must be contained within the prior bar's price range and then break out below the previous price bar's low to justify entry upon the completion of the TD Sequential and TD Combo sell Countdown phase.

TD CLOP.   TD CLOP is similar to TD Open and is designed to capitalize on a market's momentum upon exceeding the prior bar's close and open, either upside or downside. A low-risk TD CLOP buying (call-buying) opportunity occurs when the current price bar's open is less than the prior price bar's close and open, and then trades greater than both the previous bar's close and open by at least one tick. In other words, the current price bar's open must be below the prior price bar's close and open and then must exceed both of these levels to the upside to justify entry upon completion of a TD Sequential and TD Combo buy Countdown phase. Conversely, a low-risk TD CLOP selling (put-buying) opportunity occurs when the current price bar's open is greater than the prior price bar's close and open, and then trades less than both the previous bar's close and open by at least one tick. In other words, the current price bar's open must be above the prior price bar's close and open and then must exceed both of these levels to the downside to justify entry upon completion of a TD Sequential and TD Combo sell Countdown phase.

TD CLOPWIN.   TD CLOPWIN is the most complicated of the four entry indicators and is designed to anticipate the following day's price activity based upon a relationship between the current price bar's close and open and the previous price bar's close and open. A low-risk TD CLOPWIN buying (call-buying) opportunity occurs on the price bar following the current price bar, when the current price bar's open and close are contained within the previous price bar's open and close, and the current price bar's close is greater than the prior price bar's close. In other words, when the current bar's close and open are contained within the previous bar's close and open and this relationship is an up close, then the following bar should move higher—this would justify entry upon completion of a TD Sequential or TD Combo buy Countdown phase. Conversely, a low-risk TD CLOPWIN selling (put-buying) opportunity occurs on the price bar following the current price bar, when the current price bar's open and close are contained within the previous price bar's open and close, and the current price bar's close is less than the prior price bar's close. In other words, when the current bar's close and open are contained within the previous bar's close and open and this relationship is a down close, then the following bar should move lower—this would justify entry upon completion of a TD Sequential or TD Combo sell Countdown phase.

TD CLOP, TD CLOPWIN, TD Open, and TD Trap all appear in Fig. 6.55 of Cotton March 1999. The TD Open downside required an open above the prior trading day's high and then a subsequent decline below that high by at least one tick. The TD Open upside required an open below the prior trading day's low and then a subsequent advance above that low by at least one tick. The TD Trap downside displays an open above the prior trading day's low and then records a low below the prior trading day's low. The TD Trap upside displays an open below the prior trading day's high and then records a high above the prior trading day's high. The TD CLOP downside required an open above the prior trading day's close and open and then a decline below both the same trading day. The TD CLOP upside required an open below both the prior trading day's close and open and then an advance above both the close and the open. The TD CLOPWIN downside required a close and an open to be contained within the prior trading day's close and open, a down close relative to the prior trading day's close, and then on the following trading day, a low below the prior trading day's close. The TD CLOPWIN upside required a close and an open to be contained within the prior trading day's close and an open, an up close relative to the prior trading day's close, and then on the following trading day, a high above the prior day's close. This is a unique sit-

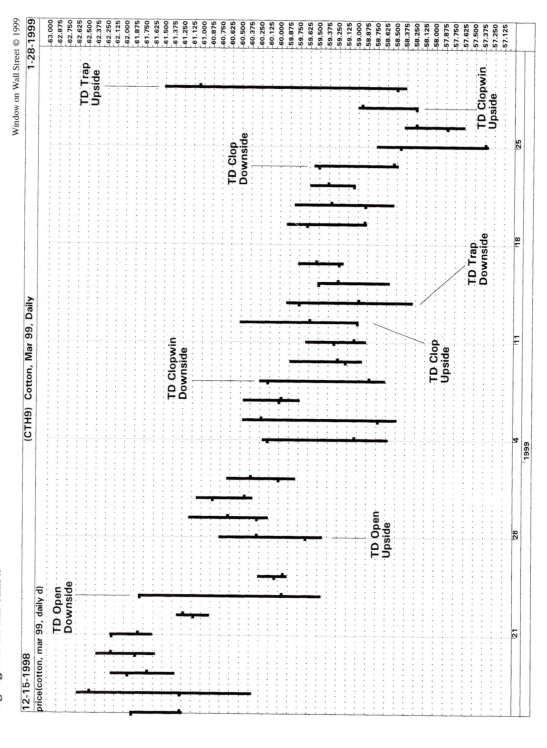

FIGURE 6.55 This chart documents each of the four entry indicators, both upside and downside—TD Open, TD Trap, TD CLOP, and TD CLOPWIN. The final entry technique is not an indicator so much as it is a rule, and is therefore not highlighted on this chart.

204

uation to have so many examples of these various short-term low-risk price pattern indications within such a short period of chart history. Also, keep in mind that some days exhibited more than one of these indicators in the same direction—on these trading days, the low-risk entry indications were much stronger than singular indicator readings. These situations, and their more effective results, are very common when applying these indicators to the markets. These four indicators are also extremely effective in and of themselves, and any low-risk upside indication in the underlying security could be utilized to purchase call options, and any low-risk downside indication in the underlying security could be utilized to purchase put options.

In addition to the occurrence of any of these four indicators, we could also use one other technique following a completed Countdown series to justify entry into a market. This fifth entry technique requires that a price bar's close following the 13 count of a buy Countdown must be greater than its open in order to obtain a low-risk buying (call-purchasing) opportunity; or that a price bar's close following the 13 count of a sell Countdown must be less than its open in order to obtain a low-risk selling (put-purchasing) opportunity. Any of these five indicators can be used to initiate one's entry into the market in the case of a long-term, specifically a daily, TD Sequential and TD Combo low-risk buying, selling, call-buying, or put-buying opportunity.

However, when day trading options or securities with TD Sequential and TD Combo, these entry techniques are less stringent. In these cases, we place the greatest emphasis upon the fifth entry indicator mentioned previously. What we will typically look for in the case of a shorter-term TD Sequential low-risk entry opportunity is for a price bar's close following the 13 count of a buy Countdown to be greater than that price bar's open; or for a price bar's close following the 13 count of a sell Countdown to be less than that price bar's open. This requirement indicates that the market's sentiment is slowly beginning to change and that price should commence its price reversal coincident with its completed TD Sequential and TD Combo Countdown phase.

Stop Loss Levels

The stop loss level that we choose to utilize with TD Sequential and TD Combo depends upon the timescale on which we are trading. When day trading options on a longer time frame, such as an hourly chart, or when position trading, our stop loss levels are more defined. What we are looking for in the case of a TD Sequential or TD Combo stop level is the extreme price high or price low over the duration of the Countdown phase. In the case of a stop loss for a buy Countdown, we first identify the lowest price bar of the Countdown phase. Once this bar is identified, we calculate the true range of this price bar—the price bar's low subtracted from the price bar's high or the previous price bar's close, whichever is greater—and subtract this value from the low of that price bar. In other words, the true range of the price bar is subtracted from that price bar's low price. This establishes a support line and our stop loss level. However, this stop loss level must be penetrated to the downside on a closing basis and then must follow through the next price bar by opening below this level, in order to justify exiting the position. This breakout indicates that the market is not able to support the downward pressure and that price should continue to decline. Conversely, in the case of a stop loss for a sell Countdown, we first identify the highest price bar of the Countdown phase. Once this bar is identified, we calculate the true range of this price bar—the price bar's high minus the price bar's low or the previous price bar's close, whichever is lower—and add this value to the high of that price bar. In other words, the true range of the price bar is added to that price bar's high price. This establishes a resistance line and our stop loss level. However, this stop loss level must be penetrated to the upside on a closing basis and then must follow through the next price bar by opening above this level, in order to justify exiting the position. This breakout indicates that the market is not able to contain the upward pressure and that price should continue to rally.

On the other hand, when day trading options on a shorter-term basis, things are handled differently. Obviously, when trading on a one-minute basis, our stop level will be much tighter than when trading on a daily basis. When we are day trading options, we typically implement a stop loss that is representative of the most we would like to lose on the trade. However, if the cost of the option is lower than this loss threshold, a stop is oftentimes unnecessary. In addition, when day trading, we can also use stop loss levels close to points of market resistance and support, identified on price charts or calculated by the process just mentioned for position trading.

Taking Profits

Since TD Sequential and TD Combo are not systems and do not identify specific entry and exit points, knowing when to take profits with these indicators can be difficult. A large portion of this decision-making process is contingent upon the situation at hand and one's profit targets. What we recommend is that traders follow at least a portion of their TD Sequential or TD Combo positions with stop losses and profit targets and to stick to these levels rigidly, especially when day trading. Also, when we record an indicator reading with TD Sequential, TD Combo, TDST, TD Lines, TD REI, or TD Relative Retracements that is contrary to our TD Sequential or TD Combo position, we liquidate at least a portion of our position. This second method of profit taking is a little more difficult to perfect, but it can often increase one's profits realized on the trade.

TD SETUP TREND (TDST)

Both Setup and Countdown can be very powerful price reversal indicators. But how do we determine whether the market will stop at a Setup or continue to the completion of Countdown? This is determined by using TD Setup Trend. TDST is a very important indicator which has tremendous value, regardless of the time frame in which it is used. TDST gives an indication as to the direction and the strength of a trend which determines whether a market will reverse its price upon the completion of a Setup series or will proceed to a 13 count of a Countdown series. Whether it is used on a daily price chart or on a one-minute chart, TDST has an uncanny ability of identifying market support and resistance levels. We are not exactly sure how or why this indicator has performed as well as it has, but we are certainly not complaining.

As you can tell by its name, TDST is derived from a major component of TD Sequential and TD Combo: the buy Setup and the sell Setup. This successive relationship between the close and the close four price bars earlier establishes the environment for the market and determines whether a trader should be anticipating a low-risk buy or a low-risk sell. Specifically, if the market has recorded nine or more consecutive closes less than the closes four trading bars earlier, then a buy Setup is completed; and if the market has recorded nine or more consecutive closes greater than the closes four trading bars earlier, then a sell Setup is completed. In some instances, a complete Setup signals a minor price reaction followed by the resumption of the prior trend and the commencement of the Countdown phase, and in other instances, a complete Setup signals a sharper price reversal followed by the inception of a new market trend.

The distinction between a continuation of a price move through the Countdown phase after the completion of Setup and a price reversal upon completion of Setup is dependent upon the market's current price level relative to the prior TD Setup Trend line in the opposite direction. There are two types of TDST lines: those that arise from completed buy Setups, which we consider buy TDST lines, and those that arise from completed sell Setups, which we consider sell TDST lines. A buy TDST line is formed from the highest true high of the buy Setup phase—therefore, the highest high of the 1 count through the 9 count, or the close of the price bar just prior to the 1 count, whichever is greatest, establishes the TDST price level. This level provides a key area of resistance regardless of the time frame. A buy TDST is extended horizontally into the future and remains on the chart until price exceeds this level to the upside on a closing basis and on the following price bar's open, thereby indicating that a trend has been established to the upside, or until a subsequent buy Setup has formed, indicating that more current information has come into the market and that the new TDST line is more important. Conversely, a sell TDST line is formed from the lowest true low of the sell Setup phase—therefore, the lowest low of the 1 count through the 9 count, or the close of the price bar just prior to the 1 count, whichever is the lowest, establishes the TDST price level. This level provides a key area of support regardless of the time frame. A sell TDST line is extended horizontally into the future and remains on the chart until price exceeds this level to the downside on a closing basis and on the following price bar's open, thereby indicating that a trend has been established to the downside, or until a subsequent sell Setup has formed, indicating that more current information has come into the market and that the new TDST line is more important.

Figure 6.56 displays both a buy TDST line and a sell TDST line. Notice how the sell TDST is formed from the lowest true low of the sell Setup, which occurs at the low price of the 1 price bar of the Setup phase; and how the buy TDST is formed from the highest true high of the buy Setup, which occurs at the high price of the 2 price bar of the Setup phase. These lines are extended into the future until a new TDST line is formed or the until the TDST line is exceeded on a closing basis, the following price bar's opening price, and then follows through by trading at least one tick further in the direction of the breakout. These levels have an uncanny ability of repelling price. As you can see in this example, price exceeded the downside (sell) TDST line twice, but was unable to close below that level, indicating the trend was not necessarily established at that point in time.

The TD Setup Trend level indicates when the market has established a trend and should continue to gain momentum. If price is able to close above a buy TDST line and then open above that level on the following price bar and trade at least one tick higher, it suggests that the market is sufficiently strong and should continue its price advance until a completed sell Setup is recorded, if it hasn't been already, and that this sell Setup should proceed to a completed sell Countdown without a major price reversal. In other words, breaking out above a buy TDST line implies that the market should continue to rally until a 13 of a sell Countdown has formed, upon which the market should experience some sort of exhaustion and major price reversal. If the market were not able to exceed this buy TDST line to the upside on a closing and an opening basis (plus one additional price tick) then it suggests that the market is not yet strong enough to mount a sustainable trend upside, and that price should decline. Furthermore, if the market is able to hold this level while at the same time recording a completed sell Setup, then it states that the Setup will probably not proceed to the completion of the sell Countdown phase, or at least may not do so anytime soon, and should instead be followed by a significant price decline. Conversely, if price is able to close below a sell TDST line and then open below that level on the following price bar and trade at least one tick lower, then it suggests that the market is sufficiently weak and should continue its price decline until a completed buy Setup is recorded, if it hasn't been already, and that this buy Setup should proceed to a completed buy Countdown without a major price reversal. In other words, breaking out below a sell TDST line implies that the market should continue to decline until a 13 of a buy Countdown has formed, upon which the

FIGURE 6.56 This chart illustrates the construction of a sell TDST line and a buy TDST line. Price has a tendency to gravitate to these lines.

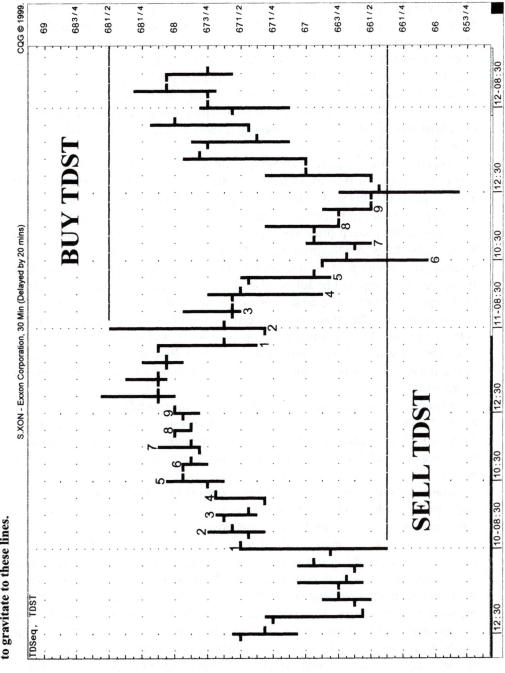

209

market should experience some sort of exhaustion and a major reversal in price. If the market were not able to exceed this sell TDST line to the downside on a closing and an opening basis (minus one additional price tick) then it suggests that the market is not yet weak enough to mount a sustainable downward trend, and that price should rally. Furthermore, if the market is able to hold this level while at the same time recording a completed buy Setup, then it states that the Setup will probably not proceed to the completion of the buy Countdown phase, or at least may not do so anytime soon, and should instead be followed by a significant price advance.

Therefore, if a completed sell Setup is unable to exceed the prior buy TDST line to the upside, or if a completed buy Setup is unable to exceed the prior sell TDST line to the downside, then it indicates that the market does not possess enough momentum to resume its trend and it is likely that the Setup phase will be followed by a sharp price reversal. On the other hand, if a completed sell Setup is able to exceed the prior buy TDST line to the upside on a closing basis, a subsequent opening basis, and then trade at least one tick higher, then it is likely that the Setup will be followed by a mild price reaction and a resumption of the upward price trend until a 13 of a sell Countdown is recorded. Conversely, if a completed buy Setup is able to exceed the prior buy TDST line to the downside on a closing basis, a subsequent opening basis, and then trade at least one tick lower, then it is likely that the Setup will be followed by a mild price reaction and a resumption of the downward price trend until a 13 of buy Countdown is recorded.

Figure 6.57 of Broadcom (BRCM) illustrates what typically occurs when price meets the TDST line and fails. It's uncanny how price will hold exactly at the TDST price level regardless of the price bar's time interval. In this case, price met resistance on a daily basis and commenced a short-term intraday decline of over 25 points.

Figure 6.58 of the daily January 1999 Soybean Oil identifies the TDST levels, both upside and downside. In October, price traded exactly to the sell TDST level, where price met support and then also immediately reversed its movement. At the end of November, the market rallied to the buy TDST level and immediately reversed its trend by the next trading day. Although price penetrated the buy TDST on a closing basis for one trading day, an upside breakout was not confirmed since the following trading day's open was not above the TDST line, indicating that the breakout was legitimate. This told traders that the market's trend was not yet defined and would not necessarily continue its advance at that time. As you can see, both of these daily indications contained the market's price movement and preempted a sizable price reversal, which would have been profitable had an option trader day traded the market or would have been even more profitable had the trader held his or her position. Figure 6.59 also provides an example of TDST lines.

FIGURE 6.57 The buy TDST identifies the highest true high and constructs a horizontal line into the future. In this case, price rallied precisely to this line and failed, declining over 12 points intraday.

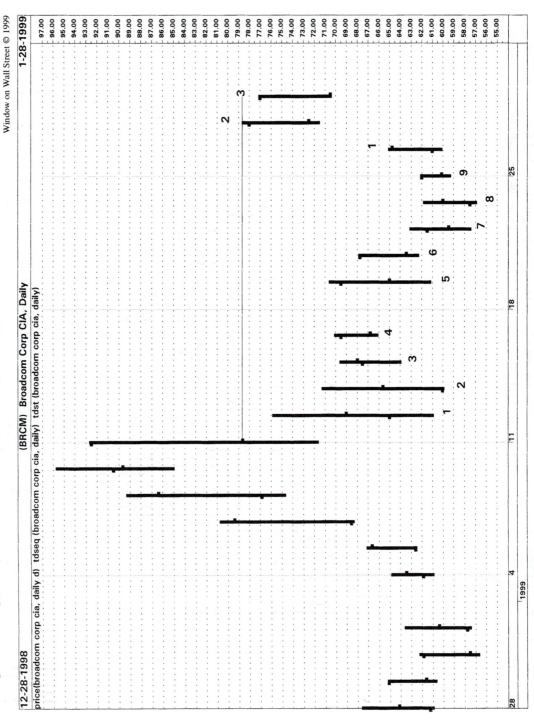

FIGURE 6.58 The sell TDST line contained each price decline and the market subsequently rallied intraday and over the next few days. At the high, price exceeded the buy TDST line on a closing basis one day, but opened the next day below this level. Consequently, the breakout was a failure.

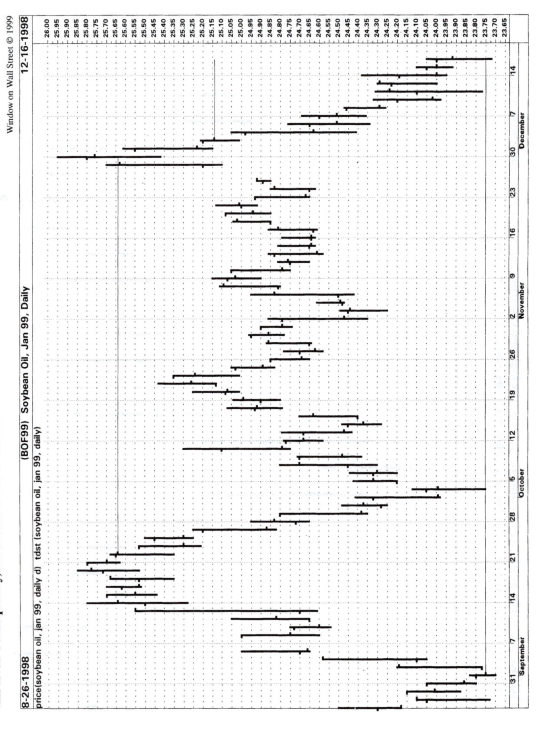

(BOF99) Soybean Oil, Jan 99, Daily

8-26-1998   12-16-1998

price(soybean oil, jan 99, daily d) tdst (soybean oil, jan 99, daily)

Window on Wall Street © 1999

FIGURE 6.59 Note that price was not able to exceed the sell TDST line on a closing basis, thereby indicating that the trend was not necessarily down at that time. This was correct, as the market rallied over 100 points during the next three trading days.

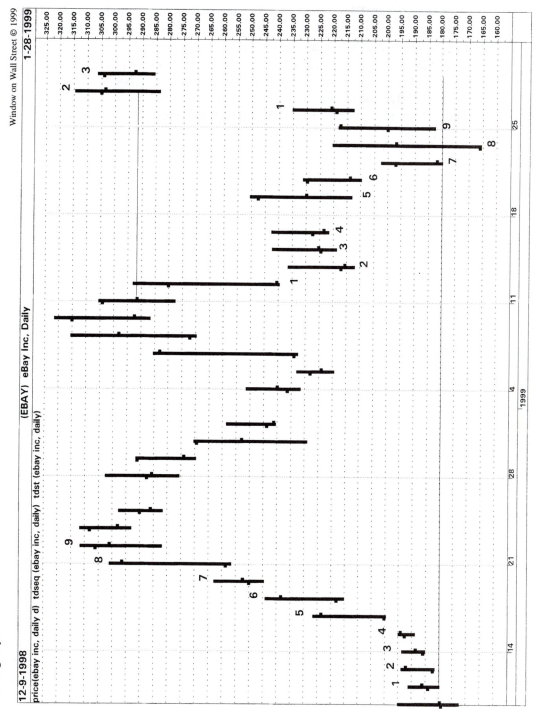

Window on Wall Street © 1999

Although TDST lines can be used by themselves, they have tremendous value when used in conjunction with TD Sequential and TD Combo. Regardless of the time frame to which TD Setup Trend is applied, this indicator is amazing in its ability to identify areas where price should be supported, where price should be contained, and where price momentum and trending markets should occur. TDST is also extremely versatile and can be utilized as a trend-following technique, a contratrend technique, or even as a legitimate stop loss level.

C   H   A   P   T   E   R

DISQUALIFIED BREAKOUTS: TD LINES AND TD RETRACEMENTS

*A*LMOST ALL TECHNICAL ANALYSTS *are familiar with trendlines and retracements. While the majority of these traders have used these indicators at some point in their careers, few have adopted a uniform application. Calculation of these levels are completely arbitrary and a function of one's mood and market disposition. We introduce mechanical processes which removes emotion and permits the construction of these levels consistently and accurately. More notably, we present a series of breakout qualifiers to these market-timing indicators, enabling a trader to determine whether a breakout is valid, and should be traded, or disqualified, and should be faded. We will also introduce two new indicators—TD Line Gap and TD Line Gap REBO—which will provide the reader with a new method of approaching and trading trendlines.*

QUALIFIED AND DISQUALIFIED TD LINES

Practically all traders are trend followers. It is not uncommon for these traders to draw trendlines to establish the probable trend of the market. Unfortunately, there exists no widely accepted method or industry standard for the construction of these trendlines. Consequently, five different traders may draw five completely different trendlines on the same price chart. To confront this inconsistency, we developed an objective means of drawing trendlines, called TD Lines. This trading methodology can be effectively applied to price activity across a variety of markets and various time frames. By applying TD Line breakouts to underlying securities, a trader can then extrapolate from these breakouts that the options for these securities will likely behave similarly. While this approach is a legitimate means of trading options in a trend-following fashion, we have developed rules and other indicators that are designed specifically for evaluating contratrend option trading opportunities.

One of the biggest problems with trendlines is that while they may be useful in establishing points of market price resistance and support when drawn properly, they are often constructed arbitrarily and therefore they are unreliable and difficult to reproduce. The selection of these lines is many times a function of a trader's bias, current trading position, or market outlook. We developed TD Lines to overcome these shortcomings and to introduce a degree of objectivity and consistency to trendline construction. In order to draw a trendline, one must connect two price points. For most traders, it is second nature to refer to the left-hand side of a chart to select a price point and then work their way to the right to connect to another more recent subjectively selected price point. It concerns us that this process is random and arbitrary. The price activity at the left-hand side of a chart is part of trading history. It makes more sense to rely upon more recent market activity for the selection of price points. Figuratively speaking, we do just that since TD Line price points (TD Points) are selected from the right side of the chart to the left side of the chart. We do not mean to imply that we draw our TD Lines from right to left, rather we simply review price activity from the right side of the chart to the left to identify TD Points and then to select the two most recent price reference points to draw our TD Line.

The first step in drawing a TD Line is to identify the two most recent TD Points. A *Level One TD Point Low* is a price low which is immediately preceded by one higher price bar low and immediately succeeded by one higher price bar low—in other words, it is a low that is surrounded by higher lows. Conversely, a Level One TD Point High is a price high which is immediately preceded by one lower price bar high and immediately succeeded by one lower price bar high—in other words, it is a high that is surrounded by lower highs. Once these objective points are identified, they can be connected to create a Level One TD Line. The distinction between Level One and higher-level TD Points and TD Lines is related to how many consecutive price bars immediately to the left and immediately to the right of the TD Point are required. For purposes of this discussion, we always refer to Level One which is the most basic.

A TD Demand Line is an upward-sloping trendline and a TD Supply Line is a downward-sloping trendline. To create a TD Demand Line, we connect the two most recent TD Point Lows. Because a TD Demand Line is upward-sloping, these TD Point Lows must be ascending, meaning the more recent TD Point Low is higher than the previous TD Point Low. Once a more recent TD Point Low is formed, a new TD Demand Line is drawn and becomes active. If the previous TD Demand Line was exceeded to the downside, the TD Line remains on the chart and a new TD Demand Line is added; if the previous line was not exceeded, the TD Demand Line is simply redrawn. To draw a TD Supply Line, we connect the two most recent TD Point Highs. Because a TD Supply Line is downward-sloping these TD Point Highs must be descending, meaning the more recent TD Point High is lower than the previous TD Point High. Once a more recent TD Point High is formed, a new TD Supply Line is drawn and becomes active. If the previous TD Supply Line was exceeded to the upside, the TD Line remains on the chart and a new TD Supply Line is added; if the previous line was not exceeded, the TD Supply Line is simply redrawn.

Figure 7.1 of Merck (MRK) illustrates both an up-sloping TD Demand Line and a down-sloping TD Supply Line. The two most recent TD Points at that time which were connected to construct these TD Lines are identified with asterisks (*). Figures 7.2, 7.3, and 7.4 are all qualified TD Line trades. In almost every case, a validated breakout above a TD Supply Line or a validated breakout below a TD Demand Line was followed by a continuation of the trend. The horizontal lines identified on the chart are a series of TD Line breakout projections, which we will discuss later in the chapter. While we could trade these qualified TD Line breakouts, and would do so if we were trading on a small time frame, we prefer to trade longer-term disqualified TD Line breakouts—by longer-term, we mean that we look for disqualified breakout trades primarily on daily price charts, although any large intraday time frame can be utilized.

Even beginning trendline traders can recite instances when they drew a trendline, witnessed a perceived price breakout, and entered a trade intraday only to see the breakout fail and price reverse. Naturally, a trader's emotions elevate once price breaks out above or below a trendline. Unfortunately, it is just those instances in which a trader is most convinced that a breakout is genuine and warrants intraday entry that they fail. Just like other traders, we suffered with this affliction of buying and selling failed breakouts. Consequently, many years ago we examined the trading activity prior to a valid intraday breakout versus an invalid intraday breakout. This exercise highlighted a list of four important breakout qualifiers, any one of which would validate intrabar entry.*

Like other trendline approaches, TD Lines are trend-following in nature. However, by introducing qualifiers, one has an innovative way of trading breakouts above or below these levels. TD Lines can be either qualified or disqualified. Qualified TD Lines are treated as any other type of trendline and any intrabar price breakout is valid, suggesting that price will continue to move in the direction of the breakout. On the other hand, if a disqualified TD Line breakout occurs, an intrabar price breakout in the direction of the trend is invalid. Instead of trading with the

---

* By *intrabar,* we mean that trading takes place at some point during that price bar's time interval, such as intraday or intraminute, and so forth.

FIGURE 7.1 The two most recent TD Points (identified by asterisks) are connected to create TD Lines. The ascending TD Line is called a TD Demand Line and connects consecutively higher TD Point Lows, and the descending TD Line is called a TD Supply Line and connects consecutively lower TD Point Highs.

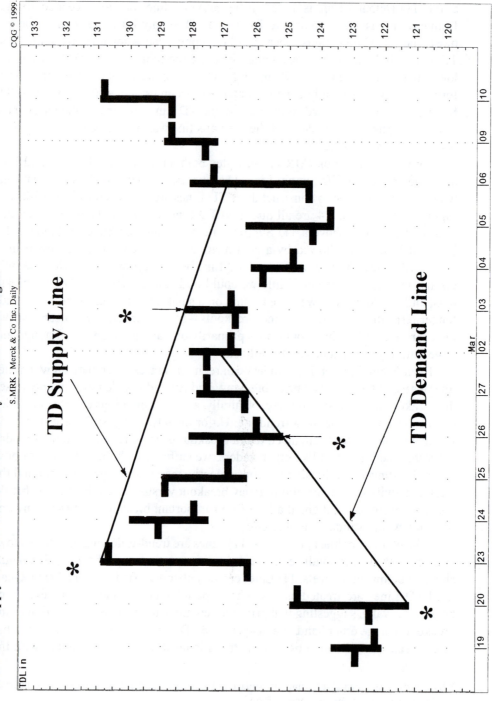

S.MRK - Merck & Co Inc, Daily

CQG © 1999.

218

FIGURE 7.2 This chart displays a series of qualified TD Line breakouts and each breakout is accompanied by price projections.

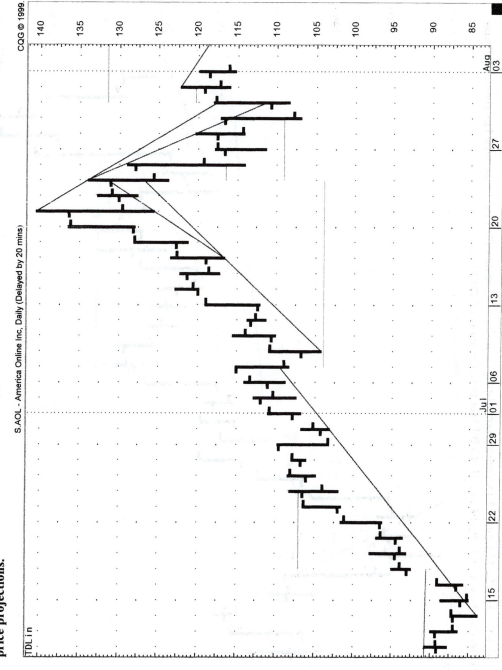

219

FIGURE 7.3 The 15-minute VIX Index chart displays a series of qualified TD Line breakouts. The shorter the time frame, the more we rely upon qualified TD Lines than disqualified TD Lines.

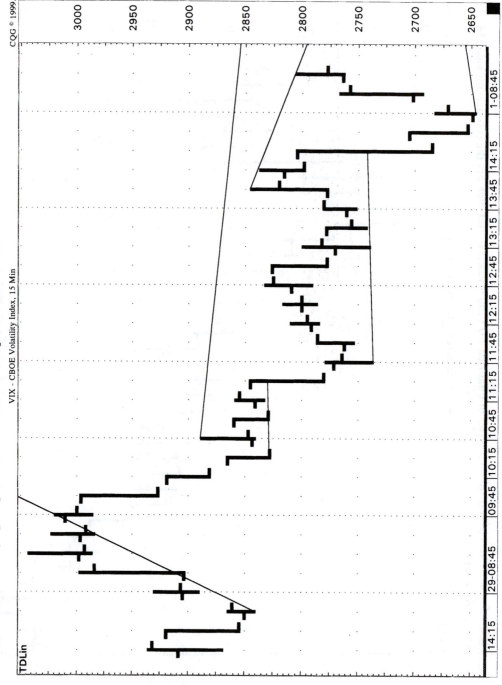

VIX - CBOE Volatility Index, 15 Min

CQG © 1999.

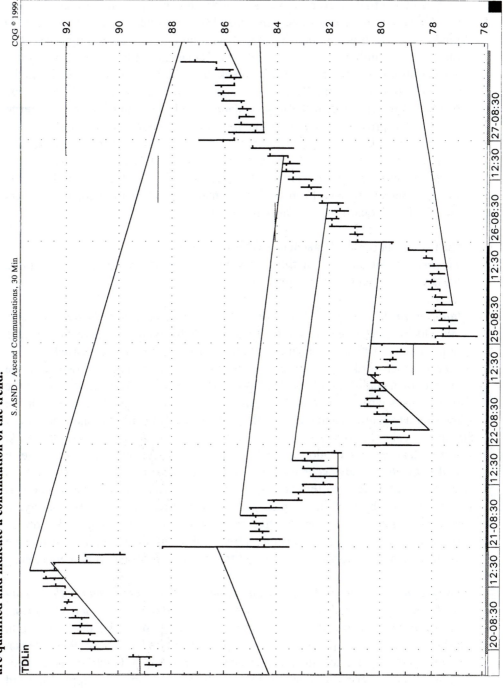

FIGURE 7.4   This chart also illustrates how TD Lines can be applied intraday. In this example, each of the TD Lines are qualified and indicate a continuation of the trend.

S.ASND - Ascend Communications, 30 Min

CQG © 1999

trend, this latter trading event provides a trader with an opportunity to fade the perceived breakout. In other words, rather than buy an intraday breakout above a TD Supply Line which is not qualified, one would sell the false breakout instead; and rather than sell an intraday breakout below a TD Demand Line which is not qualified, one would actually buy the false breakout. Whether a trader should take the breakout signal or fade that signal is determined by four qualifiers. Meeting any one of the following four qualifiers validates the TD Line and enables a trader to enter intrabar price breakouts in a trending market. If none of the qualifiers are met, however, then any intrabar price breakout is invalid and indicates that one should trade against the trend. The latter situation provides an ideal time to enter the option market in anticipation of a trend reversal. The first three qualifiers presented subsequently have been applied to markets successfully for many years while the fourth qualifier is of fairly recent vintage.

Qualifiers for an Upside Breakout of a TD Supply Line

The existence of any *one* of the following four qualifiers validates an intrabar upside breakout above a TD Supply Line:

Qualifier no. 1. *The price bar prior to an upside breakout must be a down close.* If the closing price one price bar before an upside breakout is a down close versus the prior price bar's close, then an intrabar upside breakout is qualified for purchase. In other words, if the close one price bar ago is less than the close two price bars ago, then qualifier no. 1 is met. Upon reflection, this makes sense, since if the previous bar's closing price is down, then traders' likely expectations are for the down trend to continue and therefore they will probably be initially skeptical of any intrabar breakout upside. As we have mentioned repeatedly throughout this book, most traders are trend followers and are not likely to acknowledge a change in trend until after it has occurred. Once a conventional trendline is broken, most traders typically defer to the closing price for confirmation that the breakout is legitimate, thereby forfeiting a good portion of the breakout move. By qualifying an intrabar breakout and then entering at the breakout price, as opposed to awaiting a market's close for confirmation, a trend-following trader is afforded an edge over trading peers who await the close of trading for confirmation of a breakout.

Qualifier no. 2. *The current price bar's open must be greater than both the current TD Supply Line and the previous price bar's close and must then trade at least one tick higher.* If qualifier no. 1 is not met and the price bar one prior to an upside breakout is an up close versus the previous price bar's close, then one can refer to qualifier no. 2 to validate an intrabar price breakout. Qualifier no. 2 states that if the current price bar's open is above both the declining TD Supply Line and the prior price bar's close, and the current price bar's high exceeds the current price bar's open upside by at least one price tick (smallest increment of trading in that market), then the trade is qualified and intrabar entry is justified. The price gap upside from the prior price bar's close above the TD Supply Line indicates that the balance between supply and demand has dramatically shifted in favor of demand since the close of the previous price bar. This is usually the result of an unexpected news announcement or development, the implications of which were not previously discounted in the price of the security.

Qualifier no. 3.   *The previous price bar's buying pressure must be less than the current price bar's TD Supply Line price level.*   If neither qualifier no. 1 nor qualifier no. 2 are fulfilled, then qualifier no. 3 can be applied. Qualifier no. 3 states that if the previous price bar's measure of demand—the difference between the previous price bar's close and its true low (that price bar's low or the previous price bar's close, whichever is less)—when added to that price bar's close is less than the current TD Supply Line, then a breakout above the TD Supply Line is qualified. An easy way to learn this qualifier is to first subtract the previous price bar's true low (either the previous bar's low or the close two bars earlier, whichever is lower) from the previous price bar's close. This will give the trader a numerical value that represents the previous bar's buying pressure. This value is then added to the previous price bar's close to obtain a measure of demand. This demand value is applied to the current price bar and compared to the TD Supply Line. If the demand value is less than the TD Supply Line, then any upside breakout above the TD Supply Line is qualified because price has not only exhibited more demand than the previous price bar's expression of demand but it has also exceeded the resistance upside offered by the TD Supply Line itself, thereby demonstrating market strength.

Qualifier no. 4.   *(This qualifier is new and optional.) The current price bar's open must be greater than both the previous two price bars' closes, and the current price bar's TD Supply Line must be greater than the previous price bar's high.*   If qualifiers 1, 2, and 3 are not fulfilled, one can look to qualifier no. 4. If the current price bar's open is above *both* the previous two price bar closes, and the current price bar's TD Supply Line value is greater than the previous price bar's high and the current price bar's high is above the current price bar's open, then a high above the TD Supply Line is qualified.

Qualifiers for a Downside Breakout of a TD Demand Line

The existence of any *one* of the following four qualifiers validates an intrabar downside breakout below a TD Demand Line.

Qualifier no. 1.   *The price bar prior to a downside breakout must be an up close.* If the closing price one price bar before a downside breakout is an up close versus the prior price bar's close, then an intrabar downside breakout is qualified for sale. In other words, if the close one price bar ago is greater than the close two price bars ago, then qualifier no. 1 is met. Upon reflection, this makes sense since if the previous bar's closing price is up, then traders' likely expectations are for the up trend to continue and therefore they will probably be initially skeptical of any intra-bar breakout downside. Again, as we have mentioned, most traders are trend fol-lowers and are not likely to acknowledge a change in trend until after it has occurred. Once a conventional trendline is broken, most traders typically defer to the closing price for confirmation that the breakout is legitimate, thereby forfeiting a good portion of the breakout move. By qualifying an intrabar breakout and then entering at the breakout price, as opposed to awaiting a market's close for confir-mation, a trend-following trader is afforded an edge over trading peers who await the close of trading for confirmation of a breakout.

Qualifier no. 2. *The current price bar's open must be less than both the current TD Demand Line and the previous price bar's close and must then trade at least one tick lower.* If qualifier no. 1 is not met and the price bar one prior to an intra-bar downside breakout is a down close versus the previous price bar's close, then one can refer to qualifier no. 2 to validate an intrabar breakout. Qualifier no. 2 states that if the current price bar's open is below both the ascending TD Demand Line and the prior price bar's close, and the current bar's low exceeds the current price bar's open downside by at least one price tick (smallest increment of trading in that market), then the trade is qualified and intraday entry is justified. The price gap downside from the prior price bar's close below the TD Demand Line indicates that the balance between supply and demand has dramatically shifted in favor of supply since the close of the previous price bar. This is usually the result of an unexpected news announcement or development, the implications of which were not previously discounted in the price of the security.

Qualifier no. 3. *The previous price bar's selling pressure must be greater than the current price bar's TD Demand Line price level.* If neither qualifier no. 1 nor qual-ifier no. 2 are fulfilled, then qualifier no. 3 can be applied. Qualifier no. 3 states that if the previous price bar's measure of supply—the difference between the previous price bar's true high (that price bar's high or the previous price bar's close, whichever is greater) and its close—when subtracted from that price bar's close is greater than the current TD Demand Line, then a breakout below the TD Demand Line is qualified. An easy way to learn this qualifier is to first subtract the previous price bar's close from its true high (either the previous bar's high or the close two bars earlier, whichever is greater). This will give the trader a numerical value that represents the previous bar's selling pressure. This value is then subtracted from the previous price bar's close to obtain a measure of supply. This supply value is applied to the current price bar and compared to the TD Demand Line. If this supply value is greater than the TD Line, then any downside breakout of the TD Demand Line is qualified because price has not only exhibited more supply than the previous price bar's expression of supply but it has also exceeded downside the support offered by the TD Demand Line itself, thereby demonstrating market weakness.

Qualifier no. 4. *(This qualifier is new and optional.) The current price bar's open must be less than both the previous two price bars' closes and the current price bar's TD Demand Line must be less than the previous price bar's low.*   If qualifiers 1, 2, and 3 are not fulfilled, one can look to qualifier no. 4. If the current price bar's open is below *both* the previous two price bar closes, and the current price bar's entry price is less than the previous price bar's low, and the current price bar's low is below the current price bar's open, then any intrabar breakout below the TD Demand Line is qualified.

The series of qualifiers for both TD Supply and TD Demand Line breakouts legitimize an intrabar breakout entry. These qualifiers allow traders to gain an edge over those who await a breakout confirmation on the close. However, for the purpose of option trading our recommended usage is to apply them to the underlying securities and to scenarios where none of the qualifiers are met. In these instances, trendlines no longer act as trend-following indicators. Since disqualified price breakouts are very likely to fail, one could sell an upside TD Line disqualified breakout (buy puts) or buy a downside TD Line disqualified breakout (buy calls). This reverse trading strategy is an effective method to day trade options, especially if the disqualified breakout occurs during the early trading hours. While a call option can be purchased by a trend follower once an underlying security records a qualified TD Line upside breakout, purchasing a put option in response to a disqualified TD Line upside breakout of an underlying security provides more potential. The primary reason is that a trader will be bucking the current trend; this implies that put premiums should contract as price advances and the put's price at that time will likely be down versus the prior price period's close. Conversely, while a put option can be purchased by a trend follower once an underlying security records a qualified TD Line downside breakout, purchasing a call option in reaction to a disqualified TD Line downside breakout of an underlying security provides more potential. The primary reason is because a trader will be bucking the current trend; this implies that call premiums should contract as price declines and the call's price at that time will likely be down versus the prior price period's close.

Although they can be applied to a chart of practically any time frame, the five examples selected to illustrate disqualified TD Lines are all of a daily nature. On the charts, disqualified TD Lines are represented by dotted lines, while qualified TD Lines are represented by solid lines. Price is expected to be repelled or reverse once the dotted lines are penetrated. Since these price levels are defined before trading begins, it is possible to place orders in anticipation of price reaching these levels. Since the charts and the TD Lines within apply to the underlying securities and not the options, the information provided on the charts must be reapplied to the options. The first chart of the S&P 500 September 1998 contract, Fig. 7.5, identifies two instances in which price intersects disqualified TD Lines; in each case, price reversed its trend for at least that trading day. Figure 7.6 illustrates the same type of response to penetrations of the Dow Jones December 1998 contract, and in each case the market reversed its movement at least by the close of trading that day. The chart of Merck (MRK) identifies two instances in which disqualified TD Line breakouts coincided with market price reversals (see Fig. 7.7). In the first example, the market declined after exceeding the disqualified TD Supply Line breakout level. In the next example, the market penetrated the disqualified TD Demand Line downside intraday and then proceeded to reverse its price movement, rallying over five points. Since none of the four TD Line qualifiers were met, both breakouts proved to be false, providing an excellent low-risk put-buying opportunity above the disqualified TD Supply Line breakout and an excellent call-buying opportunity following the downside breakout of the disqualified TD Demand Line. Figures 7.8 of Cisco, 7.9 of Corn, and 7.10 of Intel provide further examples of disqualified TD Lines and how they would apply to option trading.

Having so few disqualified TD Line trades is not unusual, but with the vast selection of stocks with related options available, many trading opportunities appear daily. If a trader chooses to trade more often, lower-level charts, such as hourly or 30-minute charts, can be surveyed as well for additional low-risk trading opportunities. However, we do not necessarily recommend trading disqualified TD Lines on any level other than a daily basis since the profit potential for these trades intraday is limited.

Calculating TD Line Breakout Price Objectives
Once a qualified TD Line breakout occurs either upside or downside, then trend-following traders can calculate price objectives. These price objectives are irrelevant when trading disqualified breakouts; they only apply when trading qualified TD Line breakouts. To arrive at an upside price objective after recording a qualified upside breakout of a TD Supply Line, one must first identify the lowest price beneath the TD Supply Line. Next, one must calculate the difference between that lowest price beneath the TD Supply Line and the TD Supply Line value immediately above that lowest price—in other words, on the same price bar (same date) as that lowest price. This difference is then added to the upside breakout price level (on the price bar that the TD Supply Line is exceeded) to arrive at an approximate upside price objective. Conversely, to arrive at a downside price objective after recording a qualified downside breakout of a TD Demand Line, the highest price value above the TD Demand Line must be identified. One must then calculate the

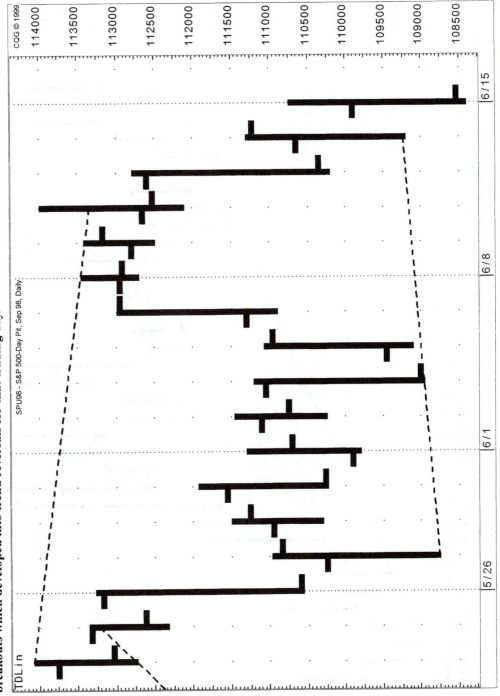

FIGURE 7.5 Within a trading range market, it is not uncommon to record both false breakouts upside and false breakouts downside. TD Line Qualifiers are often effective in distinguishing between real and bogus price breakouts. This chart of the daily S&P September 1998 futures contract displays two instances in which disqualified TD Lines identified false breakouts which developed into trend reversals for that trading day.

FIGURE 7.6 This chart of the daily Dow Jones Future December 1998 has two dotted (disqualified) TD Lines—the upper, a TD Supply Line, and the lower, a TD Demand Line. In both cases, false breakouts presented ideal trading opportunities for the trader prepared to operate against the trend.

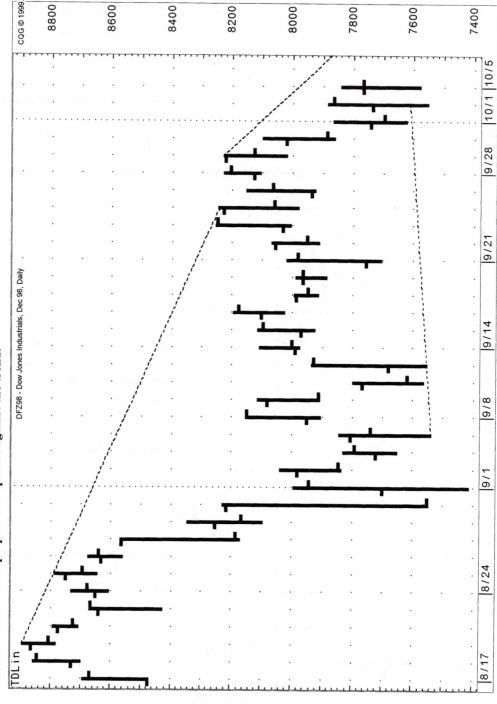

FIGURE 7.7 Two disqualified TD Lines for Merck (MRK) are presented in this example. In both instances, the market reversed trend coincident with the false (disqualified) breakouts.

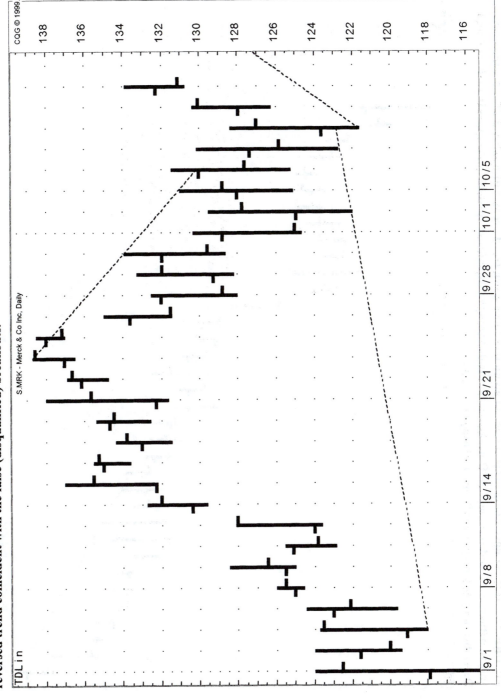

FIGURE 7.8 It is not uncommon to see a stock in an up trend or a down trend break a disqualified TD Line intraday, only to witness the trend resume. CSCO broke out downside through disqualified up-sloping TD Lines in early and mid-December, only to have price rally off of those price levels.

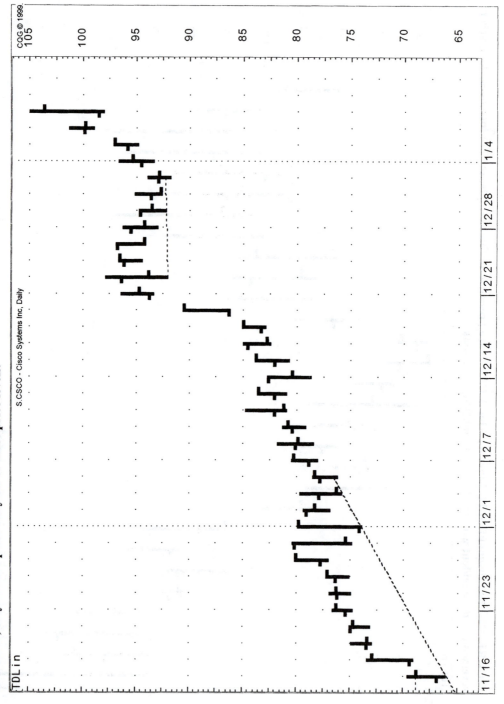

FIGURE 7.9 This chart is somewhat deceptive in that what appears to be one disqualified TD Supply Line is in fact two TD Supply Lines that happen to be superimposed upon one another. These disqualified lines are dotted to differentiate them from any solid, qualified TD Lines which may appear on the chart.

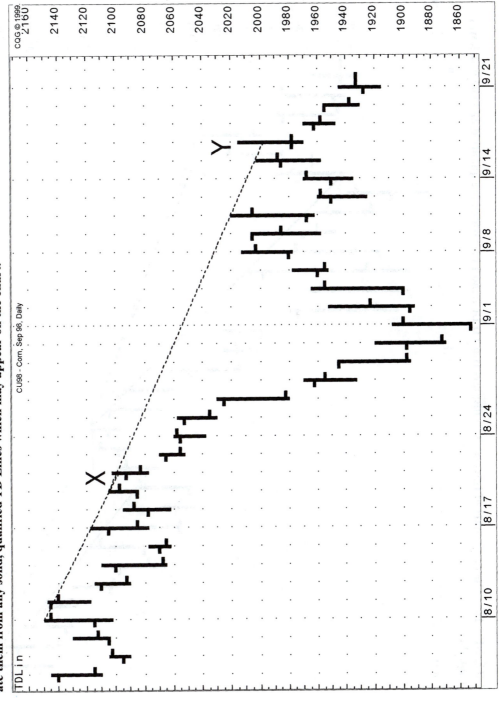

FIGURE 7.10 The daily chart of Intel (INTC) displays two TD Demand Lines which are qualified and one which was disqualified.

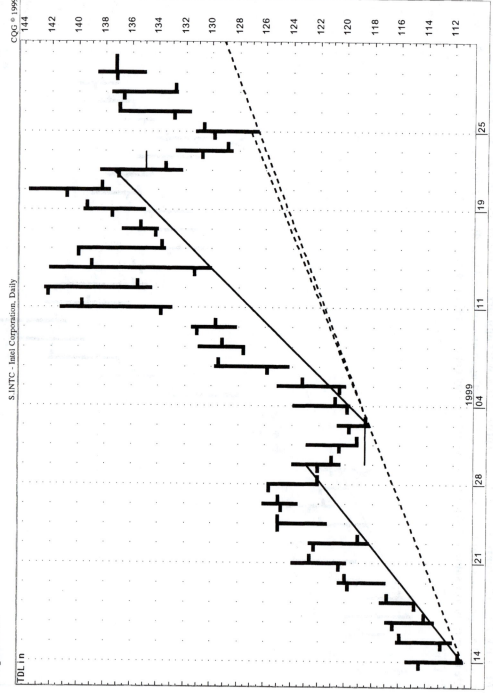

difference between the highest price above the TD Demand Line and the TD Demand Line value immediately below that highest price—in other words, on the same price bar (same date) as that highest price. This difference is then subtracted from the downside breakout price level (on the price bar that the TD Demand Line is exceeded) to arrive at an approximate downside price objective. Once these primary price objectives are reached, additional price objective levels can be calculated by multiplying the difference between the TD Supply Line and the low price or TD Demand Line and the high price by different percentages. A good selection is multiples of 100 percent, since the market has a tendency to advance or decline in incremental price bursts.

TD Line Cancellations

If one is day trading, then these cancellations can be ignored. However, if a trader is a trend follower, then any one or all of these cancellations or exits can be introduced. Three cancellations to an upside breakout above a TD Supply Line exist. If any of these cancellations occur, then the breakout above the TD Line is invalidated.

1. If the price bar immediately following an upside qualified breakout opens below the breakout price level, then exit the trade once the market opens.
2. If the price bar immediately following the breakout bar opens below the close of the breakout price bar and then closes below the breakout price level, then exit the trade.
3. If the price bar immediately following the breakout bar fails to exceed the high of the breakout price bar upside, then exit the trade.

Conversely, three cancellations to a downside breakout below a TD Demand Line exist. If any of these cancellations occur, then the breakout below the TD Line is invalidated.

1. If the price bar immediately following a downside qualified breakout opens above the breakout price level, then exit the trade once the market opens.
2. If the price bar immediately following the breakout bar opens above the close of the breakout price bar and then closes above the breakout price level, then exit the trade.
3. If the price bar immediately following the breakout bar fails to exceed the low of the breakout price bar downside, then exit the trade.

TD Line Summary

As you can see, TD Lines are constructed objectively and are a great aid to trend followers who wish to be alerted to potential low-risk intrabar price-breakout trading opportunities. By introducing the trading qualifiers we mentioned earlier, a trader can distinguish between valid and invalid trendline breakouts. Although not perfect, this filtering process enables a trader to enter an intraday breakout instead of awaiting the closing price to confirm the trade. A preferred use of the TD Line breakout qualifiers for option trading is to trade against the market's trend and only concentrate upon those breakouts which are disqualified. Once these trading opportunities are identified, a trader can select specific options related to the underlying security and further confirm the signals with the option-related rules and other indicators described throughout this book.

TD LINE GAP

TD Line Gap is a derivative of TD Lines which introduces a novel way of drawing trendlines. Just as it does with TD Lines, price activity has a way of respecting these trendlines. Their construction is simple and the interpretation is straightforward. In fact, the numerous qualifiers and conditions associated with TD Lines can be applied or ignored totally with TD Line Gap. This indicator has a special application to option trading, allowing a trader to enter the market just after the open and to remain in the trade throughout the trading day. It's a form of trend following, but the entry is sufficiently early to allow participation throughout the trading day.

TD Line Gap is an indicator which constructs a TD Line from a TD Point and a subsequent price gap or price lap. A *price gap* is described as a low which is above the previous price bar's high, or a high which is below the previous price bar's low. A *price lap,* on the other hand, is described as a low which is above the previous price bar's close but not greater than the previous price bar's high, or a high which is below the previous price bar's close but not less than the previous price bar's low. The construction of TD Line Gap first requires the identification of the most recent TD Point Low or TD Point High and the low or the high of the most recent price gap or price lap following the TD Point Low or TD Point High. In other words, to draw an upward-sloping TD Line Gap line, one must connect the most recent TD Point Low to the low of the most recent price gap upside or price lap upside. Conversely, to draw a downward-sloping TD Line Gap line, one must connect the most recent TD Point High to the high of the most recent price gap downside or price lap downside. For purposes of this discussion of TD Line Gaps, we treat price gaps and price laps similarly; however, they can be separated into two groups if a trader prefers, TD Lines with gaps and TD Lines with laps.

As with trendlines and TD Lines, once a breakout of a TD Line Gap line occurs, a low-risk buying (call-buying) or selling (put-buying) opportunity is presented. In the case of an upside breakout of a downward-sloping TD Line Gap line, the current price bar's open must be greater than the previous price bar's close to justify entry. Alternatively, if the current price bar opens above the descending TD Line Gap line and then trades at least one additional tick higher, a low-risk entry point is defined. In either of these cases, an upside TD Line Gap breakout presents a low-risk buying (call-buying) opportunity. Conversely, in the case of a downside breakout of an upward-sloping TD Line Gap line, the current price bar's open must be less than the previous price bar's close to justify entry. Alternatively, if the current price bar opens below the ascending TD Line Gap line and then trades at least one additional tick lower, a low-risk entry point is defined. In either of these cases, a downside TD Line Gap breakout presents a low-risk selling (put-buying) opportunity.

Figures 7.11 and 7.12 demonstrate the ease of TD Line Gap construction, as well as its interpretation. Figure 7.11 illustrates three TD Line Gap trades for the S&P March 1999 future. In each instance, entry at the opening upon exceeding the TD Line Gap produced large intraday profits. Each of these three trades worked on a closing basis, and even followed through the next trading day. By evaluating his or her position prior to the close, a day trader may have chosen to remain in the trade, thereby realizing a greater profit. Also, had a trader elected to day trade options rather than the future, larger intraday returns should have been realized due to the fact that options are highly leveraged. Figure 7.12 of Intel (INTC) displays three TD Line Gaps—two up-sloping (demand lines) and one down-sloping (supply line). In each instance, the opening price of the breakout price bar exceeded the TD Line Gap line in the direction of the breakout and then traded at least one tick further in the direction of the breakout, indicating a legitimate TD Line breakout. Each TD Line Gap low-risk entry level provided ideal option purchasing entry points and sizable profits, particularly the first and third occurrence. Had the more restrictive confirmation indicator TD Line Gap REBO (see following section) been installed, the entry levels would not have been as favorable, as a trader would need to await a breakout above or below both the TD Line Gap level and the TD REBO level. In these cases, if one were to use TD Line Gap REBO, an option trader would be forced to await a subsequent TD REBO indication rather than enter immediately following the opening price, since each TD Line Gap breakout occurred on the open.

TD LINE GAP REBO

Due to the high levels of market volatility over the recent years and the market's tendency of forming a series of consecutive price gaps, creating numerous TD Line Gaps, we have added an additional element to perfect low-risk entries for TD Line Gaps. We refer to these enhanced TD Line Gap indications as TD Line Gap REBO, since we combine the critical TD REBO component to the TD Line Gap indicator. TD REBO is an indicator that identifies upside and downside levels at which market price momentum occurs. TD REBO is calculated by taking a percentage of the previous price bar's true price range and adding that value to (for an upside move) or subtracted that value from (for a downside move) the current price bar's opening price. When price breaks out above the upper TD REBO level, it indicates that further price movement to the upside should continue; when price breaks down below the lower TD REBO level, it indicates that further movement to the downside should continue. For TD Line Gap REBO, we typically use a modest percentage

FIGURE 7.11   The S&P March 1999 futures contract displays three instances where TD Line Gap occurred. In each instance, price broke out at the opening and produced a profitable return for an option day trader.

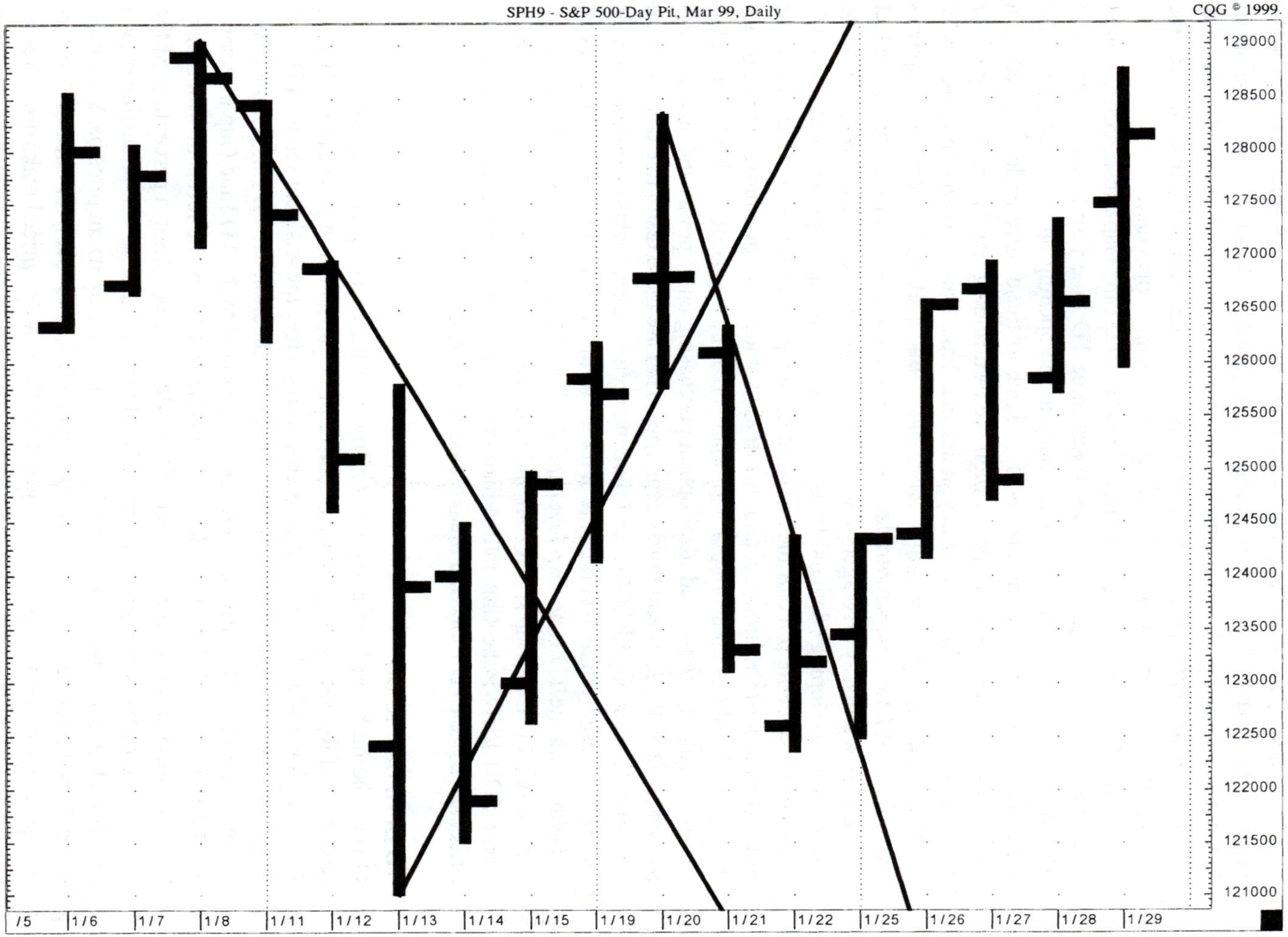

FIGURE 7.12 This chart illustrates three daily TD Line Gap trades for Intel. In each case, price exceeded the TD Line Gap line on or just after the open and was immediately followed by favorable price moves.

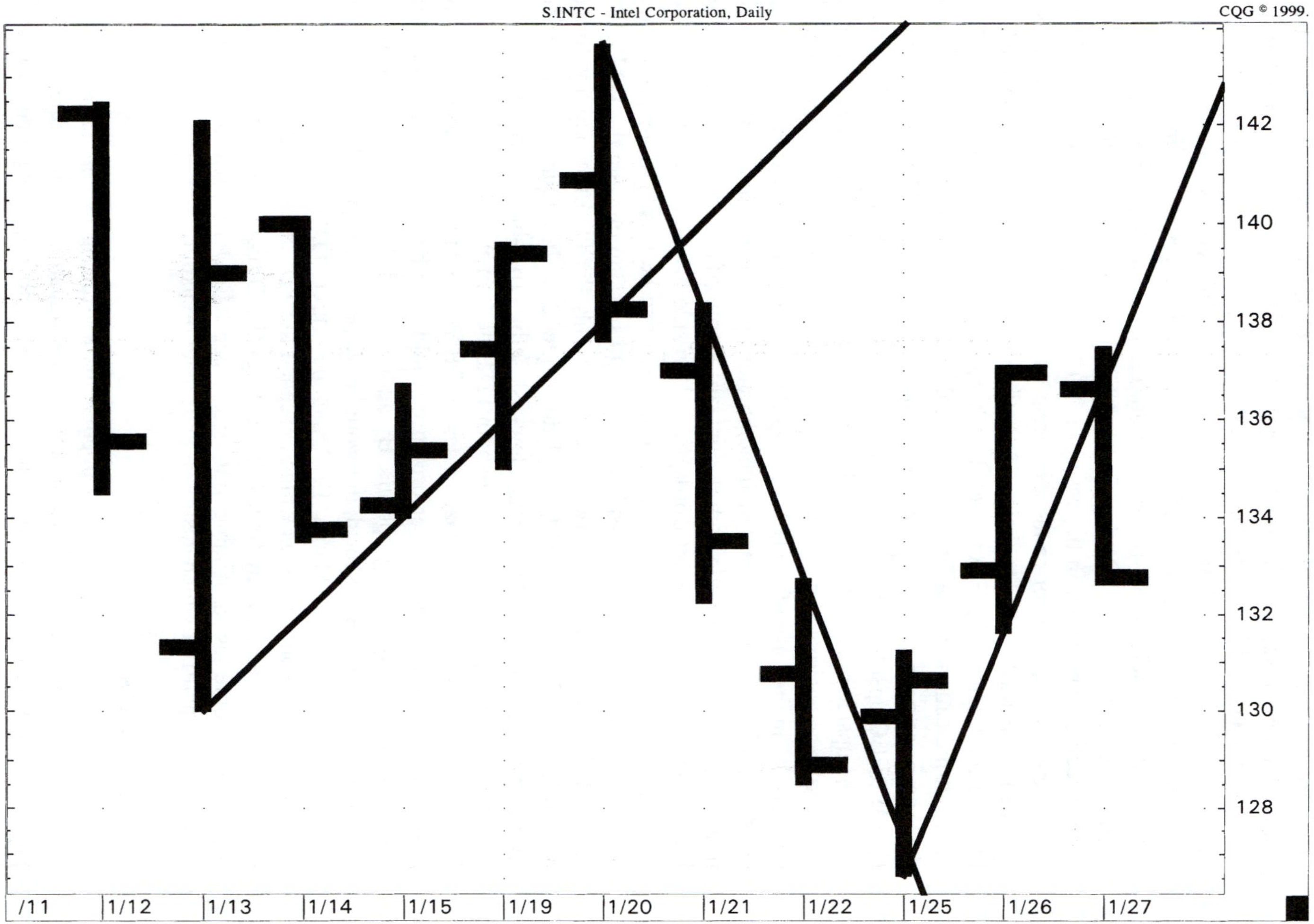

S.INTC - Intel Corporation, Daily

CQG © 1999.

factor for TD Line Gap REBO of 38.2 percent of the previous price bar's true range. Chapter 9 discusses TD REBO and TD REBO Reverse in greater detail.

TD Line Gap REBO combines these two momentum indicators to confirm a TD Line Gap breakout. While this method is trend-following in nature and therefore occasionally results in delayed market entries, it serves to confirm the breakout. In order to obtain a low-risk entry point for TD Line Gap REBO, the market must exceed not only the TD Line Gap level, but also the TD REBO level in the same direction. Therefore, in the case of a TD Line Gap REBO upside breakout, the current bar's opening price must be greater than the previous price bar's close, and then price must exceed to the upside both the downward-sloping TD Line Gap line and the higher TD REBO level. In other words, for an upside TD Line Gap breakout indication to be given, we require that not only the open be greater than the prior price bar's close, but that price advances above the TD Line Gap line and the TD REBO upside level as well. When price exceeds not only the TD Line Gap line to the upside but also the TD REBO level upside as well, it indicates that price momentum is positive and presents a low-risk buying (call-buying) opportunity. Conversely, in the case of a TD Line Gap REBO downside breakout, the current bar's opening price must be less than the previous price bar's close, and then price must exceed to the downside both the upward-sloping TD Line Gap line and the lower TD REBO level. In other words, for a downside TD Line Gap breakout indication to be given, we require that not only the open be less than the prior price bar's close, but that price declines below the TD Line Gap line and the TD REBO downside level as well. When price exceeds not only the TD Line Gap line to the downside but also the TD REBO level downside as well, it indicates that price momentum is negative and presents a low-risk selling (put-buying) opportunity.

The following charts demonstrate both TD Line Gap and TD Line Gap REBO. Figure 7.13 shows the TD Line Gap trades for EBAY. Note that significant intraday profits were achieved and the performance would have been further enhanced in each instance by day trading options. By adding the REBO filter, entries would once again not have been as ideal, but would have produced profits as well. Figure 7.14 of Treasury Bonds March 1999 includes three TD Line Gaps. In each instance, the breakout openings which exceeded the TD Line Gap lines were precursors to profitable intraday trades. By adding REBO requirements to the entry, the trades become less profitable, but safer, since REBO serves as an additional confirmation qualifier which ensures a legitimate breakout.

RETRACEMENTS
Next to trendlines, one of the most popular market-timing techniques is retracement analysis. Just like trendlines, however, its application can be subjective and purely arbitrary. Prior to our work with retracements, no objective process for trading usage had been established. Fortunately, when we were describing our ap-

proaches to our computer programmers, our descriptions and explanations needed to be clear and specific, forcing us to standardize the process of calculating retracements. We developed two unique retracement methods which were designed to calculate precise retracement levels for markets: TD Relative Retracement and TD Absolute Retracement. And just as they were with TD Lines, qualifiers were introduced to validate retracement entries prior to a price bar's close.

TD Relative Retracement

Once a price decline has occurred and it appears that a recent price low has been formed, a series of upside retracement price objectives can be calculated. Previously, retracement work stipulated that one subtract the recent price low from a prior market high and then multiply that difference by a series of specific ratios. However, difficulty and confusion arise as to which prior high should be selected to calculate these retracement levels. We wanted this selection process to be purely objective and consistent. Consequently, we devised the following procedure to identify these TD Relative Retracement levels upside. Once a market decline has transpired and it appears that a recent price low has been formed and will likely hold, we refer to the left-hand side of a price chart to the last time in which price traded at a lower low (not including the recent price low). This establishes the time frame in which we will work. Within this period, we then select the highest high in between these two price lows. As a result of this mechanical selection process, a trader is able to identify one and only one price high and ignore all other intermediate price highs. The next step is to calculate the difference between the highest price high and the recent price low. This difference is then multiplied by a series of Fibonacci ratios, the first two (and most important) being 38.2 and 61.8 percent, and the resulting values are then added to the recent price low to identify price objectives upside—the 0.382 level and the 0.618 level. One commonly held perception is that when price exceeds both of these levels to the upside, the next price objective level is a full 100 percent retracement of the price decline—in other words, the highest high. Our research indicates that this is not the case. We have found decisively that price usually rallies to the highest price bar's close, and not necessarily the highest price bar's high. This observation is an important contribution to the study of retracement analysis. We refer to this retracement level as the *magnet price,* since price gravitates to, or is drawn toward, that highest price bar's close once the 61.8 percent level is exceeded upside. Additional retracement levels are calculated in the same manner as the 38.2 percent level and the 61.8 percent level, and include multiplying the difference between the highest high and the lowest low by other Fibonacci-derived percentages, such as 138.2, 161.8, 223.6, 361.8, 461.8 percent, and so on. In each case, once a retracement level is exceeded to the upside, and the market further confirms this breakout by closing above this level and then following through on the next price

FIGURE 7.13 Chart A illustrates TD Line Gap breakouts for EBAY. Chart B applies TD REBO with a ratio of 38.2 percent of the previous price bar's true range added to or subtracted from the breakout price bar's opening price.

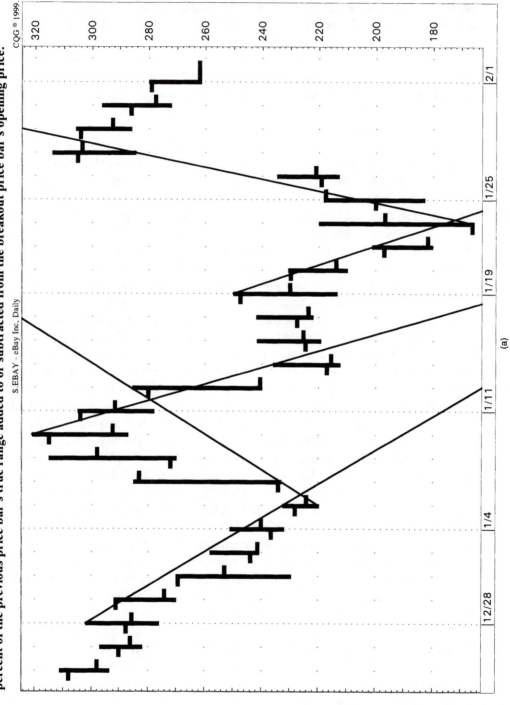

S.EBAY - eBay Inc, Daily

CQG © 1999.

(a)

FIGURE 7.13 (*Continued*)

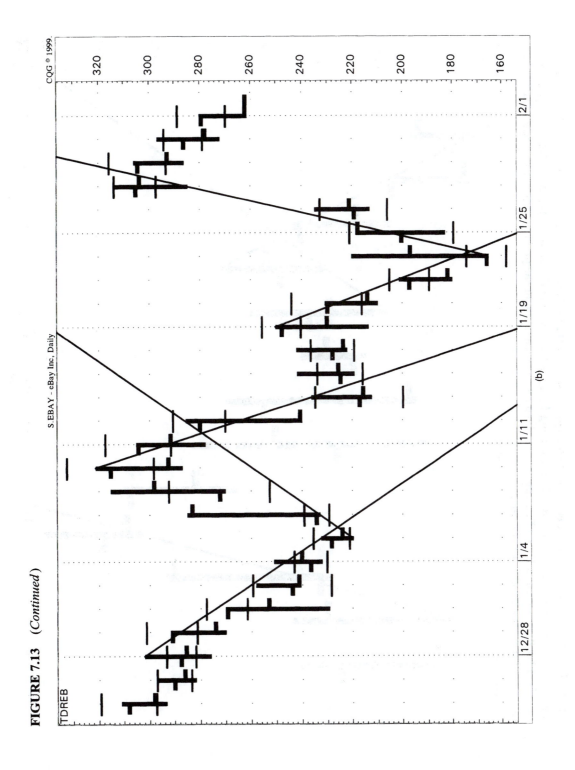

241

FIGURE 7.14 These charts also demonstrate the application of TD Line Gap and TD Line Gap REBO. Chart A displays the March 1999 U.S. Treasury Bond future using TD Line Gap. Breakouts can be confirmed with the help of TD Line Gap REBO, as seen in Chart B, using the standard 38.2 percent ratio of the previous day's true range added to or subtracted from the breakout bar's open.

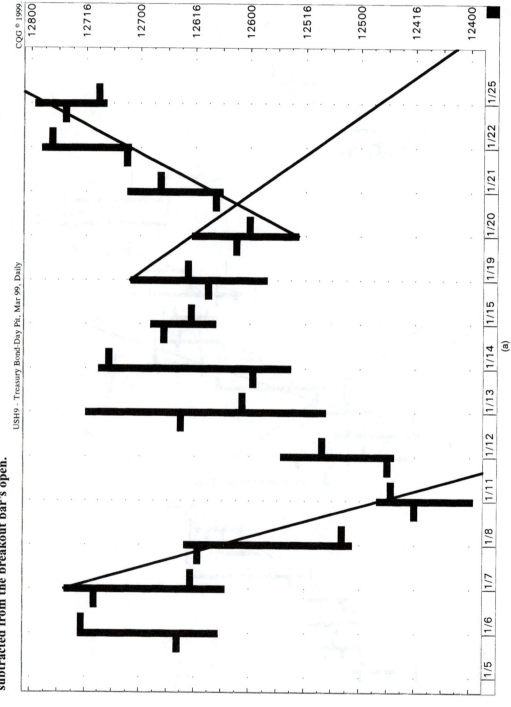

USH9 - Treasury Bond-Day Pit, Mar 99, Daily

CQG © 1999

(a)

FIGURE 7.14 (*Continued*)

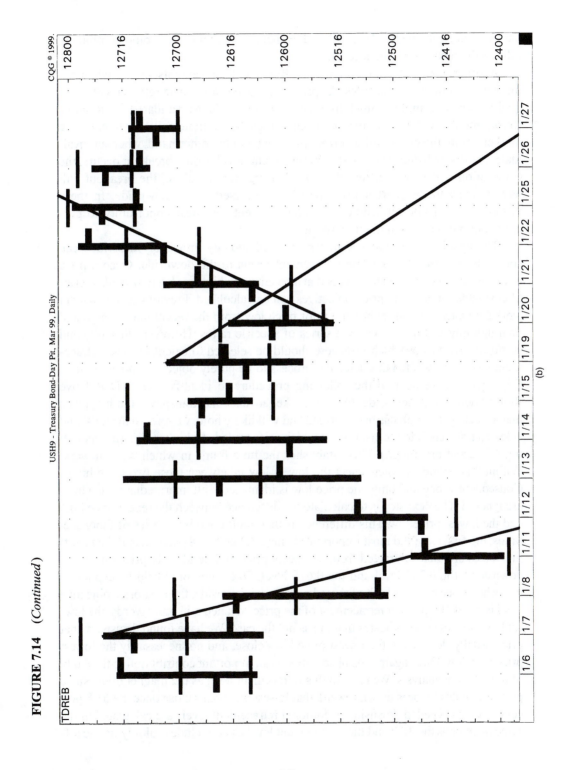

USH9 - Treasury Bond-Day Pit, Mar 99, Daily

CQG © 1999.

(b)

bar by opening above this level, it implies that the market price should continue to rally to the next retracement level.

Another novel introduction to TD Relative Retracements arises when we implement certain trading rules. As price approaches a specific retracement level, qualifiers can be applied, much like with TD Lines. When a validated TD Relative Retracement–level upside breakout occurs, it enables a trend follower to enter the market before the close of the current price bar. On the other hand, when an invalidated, or disqualified, TD Relative Retracement–level upside breakout occurs, the expectation is that by the time the price bar registers its close, the breakout will have failed and the market price will have reversed to the downside. In these instances, an upside retracement breakout presents an ideal opportunity to purchase put options or sell the underlying.

The upside TD Relative Retracement methodology previously described can simply be reversed to calculate retracement levels to the downside. Once a price advance has occurred and it appears that a recent price high has been formed, a series of downside retracement price objectives can be calculated. Previously, retracement work stipulated that one subtract a prior price low from the recent market high and then multiply that difference by a series of specific ratios. However, difficulty and confusion arise as to which prior low should be selected to calculate these retracement levels. We wanted this selection process to be purely objective and consistent. Consequently, we devised the following procedure to identify these TD Relative Retracement levels downside. Once a market advance has transpired and it appears that a recent price high has been formed and will likely hold, we refer to the left-hand side of a price chart to the last time in which price traded at a higher high (not including the recent price high). This establishes the time frame in which we will work. Within this period, we then select the lowest low inbetween these two price highs. Consequently, one and only one price low is identified—all intermediate price lows are ignored. The next step is to calculate the difference between the recent price high and the lowest price low. This difference is then multiplied by a series of Fibonacci ratios, the first two (and most important) being 38.2 and 61.8 percent, and the resulting values are then subtracted from the recent price high to identify price objectives downside—the 0.382 level and the 0.618 level. One commonly held perception is that when price exceeds both of these levels to the downside, the next price objective level is a full 100 percent retracement of the price advance—in other words, the lowest low. Our research indicates that this is not the case. We have found decisively that price usually declines to the lowest price bar's close, and not necessarily the lowest price bar's low. Once again, this observation is an important contribution to the study of retracement analysis. We refer to this retracement level as the magnet price, since price gravitates to, or is drawn toward, that lowest price bar's close once the 61.8 percent level is exceeded downside. Additional retracement levels are calculated in the same manner as the 38.2 and the 61.8 percent levels, and include multiplying the difference between the highest high and the lowest low by other Fibonacci-derived percentages, such as 138.2, 161.8, 223.6, 361.8, 461.8 percent, and so forth. In each case, once a retracement level is exceeded to the downside, and the market further confirms this breakout by closing below this level and then following through on the next price bar by opening below this level, it implies that the market price should continue to decline to the next retracement level.

Again, in each case, as price approaches a specific retracement level, qualifiers can be introduced, much like with TD Lines. When a validated TD Relative Retracement–level downside breakout occurs, it enables a trend follower to enter the market before the close of the current price bar. On the other hand, when an invalidated, or disqualified, TD Relative Retracement–level downside breakout occurs, the expectation is that by the time the price bar registers its close, the breakout will have failed and the market price will have reversed to the upside. In these instances, a downside retracement breakout presents an ideal opportunity to purchase call options or buy the underlying.

A variation of TD Relative Retracement, described as TD Double Retracement, requires that price retrace two retracement levels in one price bar to identify a potential price exhaustion level and low-risk price reversal opportunity. The discussion of TD Double Retracement appears in a subsequent section.

The qualifiers presented in the discussion on disqualified TD Lines can be applied similarly to TD Relative Retracements.

Qualifiers for an Upside Breakout of a TD Relative Retracement Level
The existence of any *one* of the following four qualifiers validates an intrabar upside breakout above a TD Relative Retracement level.

Qualifier no. 1. *The price bar prior to an upside breakout above a retracement level must be a down close.*   If the closing price one price bar before an upside breakout is a down close versus the prior price bar's close, then an intrabar upside breakout is qualified for purchase intraday. In other words, if the close one price bar ago is less than the close two price bars ago, then qualifier no. 1 is met. Upon reflection, this makes sense, since if the previous bar's closing price is down, then traders' likely expectations are for the downtrend to continue and therefore they will probably be initially skeptical of any intrabar breakout upside. As we have mentioned repeatedly throughout this book, most traders are trend followers and are not likely to acknowledge a change in trend until after it has occurred. Once a conventional retracement level is broken, most traders typically defer to the closing price for confirmation that the breakout is legitimate, thereby forfeiting a good portion of the breakout move. By qualifying an intrabar breakout and then entering at the breakout price, as opposed to awaiting a market's close for confirmation, a trend following trader is afforded an edge over trading peers.

Qualifier no. 2. *The current price bar's open must be greater than the current retracement level and must then trade at least one tick higher.* If qualifier no. 1 is not met and the price bar one prior to an upside breakout is an up close versus the previous price bar's close, then one can refer to qualifier no. 2 to validate an intrabar price breakout. Qualifier no. 2 states that if the current price bar's open is above the retracement level and the current price bar's high exceeds the current price bar's open upside by at least one price tick (smallest increment of trading in that market), then the trade is qualified and intrabar entry is justified. The price gap upside from the prior price bar's close above the retracement level indicates that the balance between supply and demand has dramatically shifted in favor of demand since the close of the previous price bar. This is usually the result of an unexpected news announcement or development, the implications of which were not previously discounted in the price of the security.

Qualifier no. 3. *The previous price bar's buying pressure must be less than the retracement level.* If neither qualifier no. 1 nor qualifier no. 2 are fulfilled, then qualifier no. 3 can be applied. Qualifier no. 3 states that if the previous price bar's measure of demand—the difference between the previous price bar's close and its true low (that price bar's low or the previous price bar's close, whichever is less)—when added to that price bar's close is less than the current retracement level, then a breakout above the retracement level is qualified. An easy way to learn this qualifier is to first subtract the previous price bar's true low (either the previous bar's low or the close two bars earlier, whichever is lower) from the previous price bar's close. This will give the trader a numerical value that represents the previous bar's buying pressure. This demand value is then added to the previous price bar's close to obtain a measure of demand. This value is applied to the current price bar and compared to the retracement level. If the demand value is less than the retracement level, then any upside breakout above the retracement level is qualified because price has not only exhibited more demand than the previous price bar's expression of demand but it has also exceeded the resistance upside offered by the retracement level itself, thereby demonstrating market strength.

Qualifier no. 4. *The current price bar's open must be greater than both the previous two price bars' closes and retracement level must be greater than the previous price bar's high.* If qualifiers 1, 2, and 3 are not fulfilled, one can look to qualifier no. 4. If the current price bar's open is above *both* the previous two price bar closes, and the current price bar's retracement-level value is greater than the previous price bar's high, and the current price bar's high is above the current price bar's open, then any high above the retracement level is qualified.

Qualifiers for a Downside Breakout of a TD Relative Retracement Level

The existence of any *one* of the following four qualifiers validates an intrabar downside breakout below a TD Relative Retracement level.

Qualifier no. 1.   *The price bar prior to a downside breakout below a retracement level must be an up close.*   If the closing price one price bar before a downside breakout is an up close versus the prior price bar's close, then an intrabar downside breakout is qualified for sale intraday. In other words, if the close one price bar ago is greater than the close two price bars ago, then qualifier no. 1 is met. Upon reflection, this makes sense, since if the previous bar's closing price is up, then traders' likely expectations are for the up trend to continue and therefore they will probably be initially skeptical of any intrabar breakout downside. Again, as we have mentioned, most traders are trend followers and are not likely to acknowledge a change in trend until after it has occurred. Once a conventional trendline is broken, most traders typically defer to the closing price for confirmation that the breakout is legitimate, thereby forfeiting a good portion of the breakout move. By qualifying an intraday breakout and then entering at the breakout price, a trend-following trader is afforded an edge over trading peers.

Qualifier no. 2.   *The current price bar's open must be less than the current retracement level and must then trade at least one tick lower.*   If qualifier no. 1 is not met and the price bar one prior to an intrabar downside breakout is a down close versus the previous price bar's close, then one can refer to qualifier no. 2 to validate an intrabar breakout. Qualifier no. 2 states that if the current price bar's open is below the retracement level and the current bar's low exceeds the current price bar's open downside by at least one price tick (smallest increment of trading in that market), then the trade is qualified and intraday entry is justified. The price gap downside from the prior price bar's close below the retracement level indicates that the balance between supply and demand has dramatically shifted in favor of supply since the close of the previous price bar. This is usually the result of an unexpected news announcement or development, the implications of which were not previously discounted in the price of the security.

Qualifier no. 3.   *The previous price bar's selling pressure must be greater than the retracement level.*   If neither qualifier no. 1 nor qualifier no. 2 are fulfilled, then qualifier no. 3 can be applied. Qualifier no. 3 states that if the previous price bar's measure of supply—the difference between the previous price bar's true high (that price bar's high or the previous price bar's close, whichever is greater) and its close—when subtracted from that price bar's close is greater than the current retracement level, then a breakout below the retracement level is qualified. An easy way to learn this qualifier is to first subtract the previous price bar's close from its true high (either the previous bar's high or the close two bars earlier, whichever is greater). This will give the trader a numerical value that represents the previous bar's selling pressure. This value is then subtracted from the previous price bar's close to obtain a measure of supply. This supply value is applied to the current price bar and compared to the retracement level. If this supply value is greater than the retracement level, then any downside breakout of the retracement level is qualified because price has not only exhibited more supply than the previous price bar's expression of supply but it has also exceeded downside the support offered by the retracement level itself, thereby demonstrating market weakness.

Qualifier no. 4. *The current price bar's open must be less than both the previous two price bars' closes and the retracement level must be less than the previous price bar's low.* If qualifiers 1, 2, and 3 are not fulfilled, one can look to qualifier no. 4. If the current price bar's open is below *both* the previous two price bar closes, and the current price bar's entry price is less than the previous price bar's low, and the current price bar's low is below the current price bar's open, then any intrabar breakout below the retracement level is qualified.

TD Relative Retracement Cancellations

If one is day trading, then these cancellations can be ignored. However, if a trader is a trend follower, then any one or all of these cancellations or exits can be introduced. Three cancellations to an upside breakout above a TD Retracement Level exist. If any of these cancellations occur, then the breakout above the TD Retracement Level is invalidated.

1. If the price bar immediately following an upside qualified breakout opens below the breakout price level, then exit the trade once the market opens.

2. If the price bar immediately following the breakout bar opens below the close of the breakout price bar and then closes below the breakout price level, then exit the trade.

3. If the price bar immediately following the breakout bar fails to exceed the high of the breakout bar upside, then exit the trade.

Conversely, three cancellations to a downside breakout below a TD Retracement Level exist. If any of these cancellations occur, then the breakout below the TD Retracement Level is invalidated.

1. If the price bar immediately following a downside qualified breakout opens above the breakout price level, then exit the trade once the market opens.

2.   If the price bar immediately following the breakout bar opens above the close of the breakout price bar and then closes above the breakout price level, then exit the trade.

3.   If the price bar immediately following the breakout bar fails to exceed the low of the breakout bar downside, then exit the trade.

Figure 7.15 of the 60-minute S&P 500 March 1999 identifies a series of TD Relative Retracement levels. Note that a TD Double Retracement is recorded in one 60-minute price interval which produced a small intrabar rally and also forewarned of the impending trend reversal for the market. The market stalled upon reaching the subsequent series of upside retracement levels; the magnet level was initially disqualified, and a few bars later, price was repelled, beginning a sizable intraday decline which persisted for two additional trading days. Likewise, on the downside, price regrouped upon penetrating the retracement levels downside, and the two levels that were initially disqualified caused price to rally even more sharply.

Figure 7.16 demonstrates how TD Relative Retracements can be applied intraday to obtain legitimate levels of support and resistance. The 20-minute Coffee March 1999 chart displays an initially disqualified upside 38.2 percent TD Relative Retracement level, as well as a disqualified 61.8 percent retracement level, both taken from the low around 10:15 on the fifth. In both cases, these disqualified levels caused price to reverse its movement. Also shown is a TD Double Retracement in one price bar—it's actually a triple retracement. These levels were all projected off of the high on the last 20-minute trading bar of the eighth and coincided with a sizable price trend reversal. Examining the chart, you will notice that the low-risk call-buying indication, corresponding with the low-risk buy indication in the Coffee futures market, occurred on the low price bar of the day within the first 20 minutes of trading following the 8:15 open. The next-day price made new highs and then, upon breaking out above the disqualified 0.618 retracement level, began its decline. This also provides a good example as to how these indicators can be used together to create definitive low-risk entry and exit points.

Figures 7.17 through 7.20 illustrate other examples of TD Relative Retracements, ranging from intraday charts to daily charts.

TD Double Retracement

Regardless whether a retracement breakout is described as qualified or disqualified, if two retracement levels are traversed within one price bar period, usually the market experiences a price reaction. Since price must travel a sizable distance to exceed these two retracement levels within one price bar, TD Double Retracement identifies potential levels of price exhaustion. It is important that subsequent to the recording of the opening price that the two retracement levels are exceeded. In other

FIGURE 7.15 The standard TD Relative Retracements are presented in this chart. As you can see, these levels coincided with market turning points.

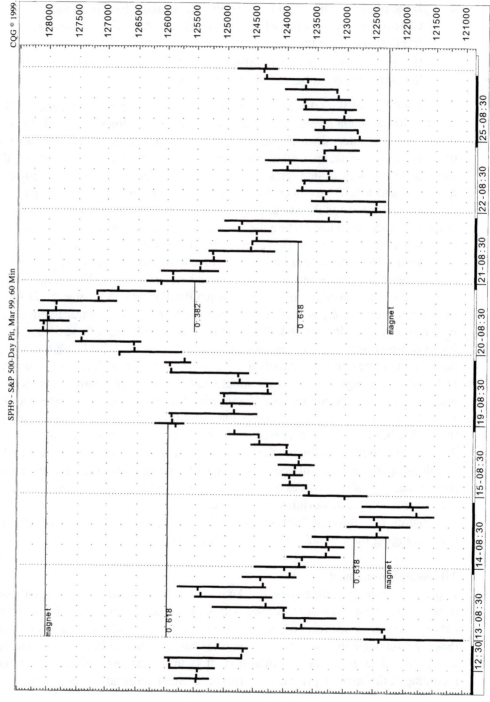

FIGURE 7.16 This chart shows how TD Relative Retracements can be applied to markets intraday. In this example, a triple retracement preceded a price reversal to the upside. The move upside was in turn contained by a disqualified 61.8 percent retracement level.

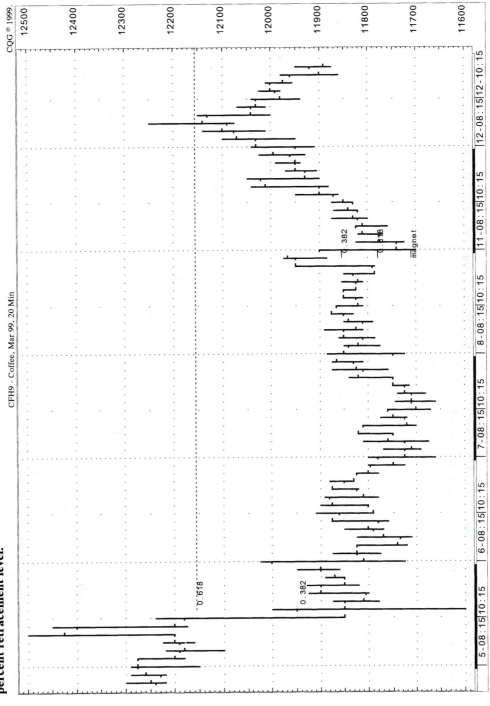

FIGURE 7.17 The 60-minute chart of Merck (MRK) identifies the 0.382 and the 0.618 TD Relative Retracement levels, both projected from the low coming in on December 15.

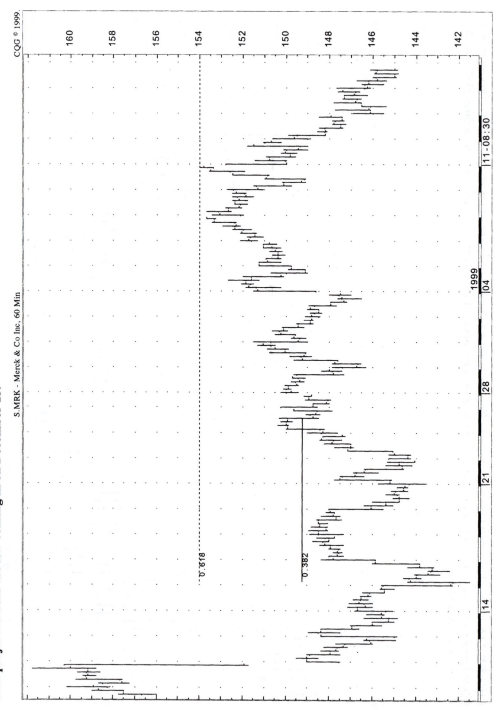

S.MRK - Merck & Co Inc. 60 Min

CQG © 1999.

FIGURE 7.18 In each of these examples, the price bar from which the TD Relative Retracements were calculated are identified with asterisks. In both cases, these retracements were disqualified because none of the four qualifiers were met.

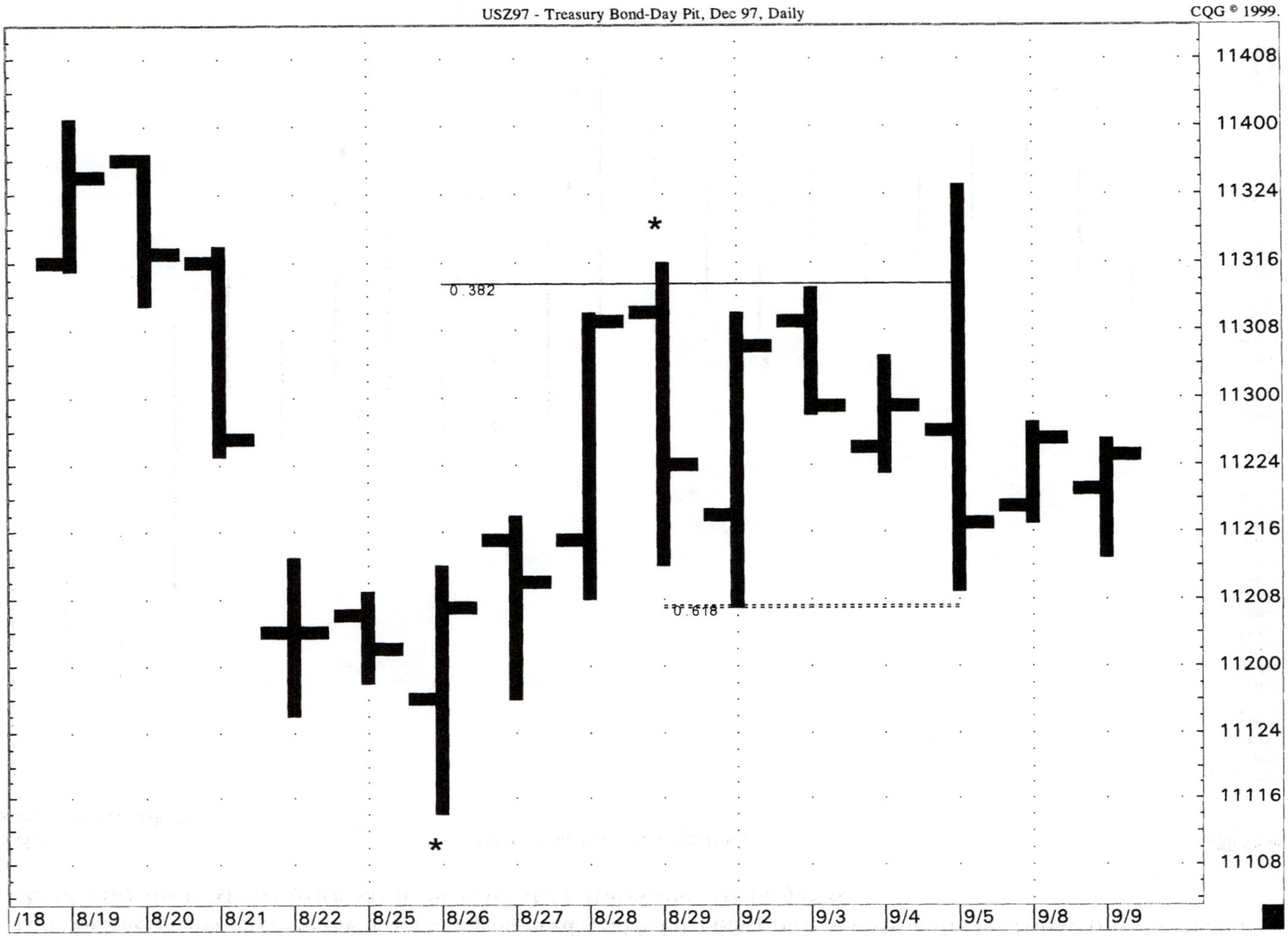

253

FIGURE 7.19 This chart illustrates several examples where TD Relative Retracements occurred. In some cases TD Double and Triple Retracements reversed the trend and produced sizable intraday profit opportunities for option traders. Again, asterisks identify the reference price bar from which the retracements are projected.

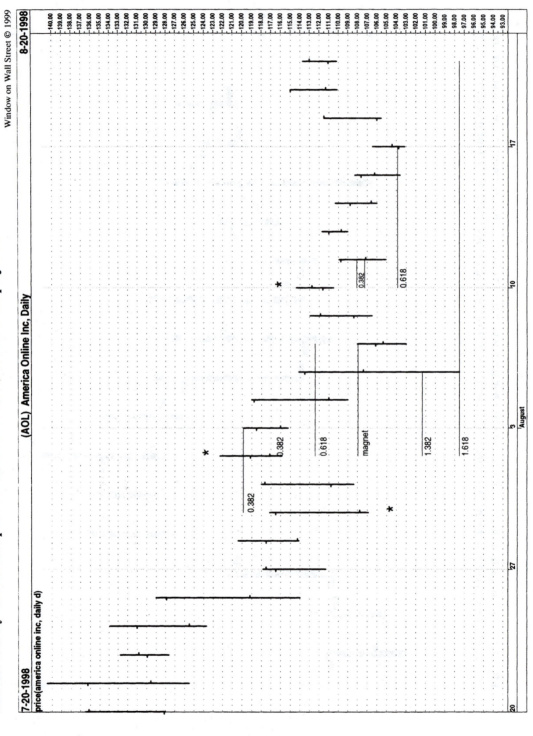

Window on Wall Street © 1999

254

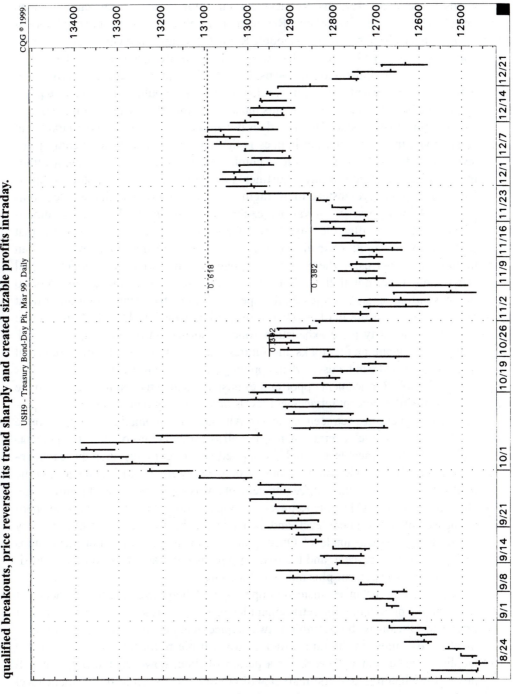

FIGURE 7.20 TD Relative Retracements show two disqualified and one qualified breakout. In the case of the two disqualified breakouts, price reversed its trend sharply and created sizable profits intraday.

words, to record a TD Double Retracement indication upside, the current bar's open must be less than two TD Relative Retracement levels and then must exceed both of them. Conversely, to record a TD Double Retracement indication downside, the current bar's open must be greater than two TD Relative Retracement levels and then must exceed both of them to the downside. Should the price opening exceed one or both of the retracement levels, this would not fulfill the double retracement requirement since both retracement breakouts must occur after the opening of the market.

An important consideration that does not affect individual security markets but does impact most cash market indices is the manner in which the opening price levels are established. For example, a number of exchanges use the previous trading day's closing price less any adjustments for dividend payouts or stock splits as the opening price level instead of averaging the opening price of all the index components. Another practice of various exchanges is to survey the various components of an index after the first 5 or 10 minutes of trading and then use that calculated value as its official opening price. Although the latter practice is an improvement over using the prior trading day's closing price as an opening-level proxy, many times not all the individual securities are open within the first 5 or 10 minutes of trading and, as a result, the opening is not a true representation of what has taken place in the market. Therefore, applying the TD Double Retracement indicator to identify price exhaustion zones is suspect in the case of some cash indices. The openings for stocks and futures indices, on the other hand, are actual market trades and can be used when applying TD Double Retracement.

TD Double Retracement opportunities upside require an opening below both the 38.2 and the 61.8 percent retracement levels or an opening below both the 61.8 percent and magnet price retracement levels. Although a combination of magnet price and 138.2 percent double retracements, as well as combinations of other 100 percent-plus double retracement levels could be applied, we prefer to rely upon those retracement levels that include combinations of only 38.2 percent, 61.8 percent, and the magnet price levels, as these three retracement levels are of the greatest significance. On the other hand, TD Double Retracement opportunities downside require an opening above both retracement levels and then a decline below both to establish a likely downside price exhaustion level. Once again a combination of the retracement ratios 38.2 percent, 61.8 percent, and the magnet price is preferable to, and more significant than, the 100 percent-plus ratio combinations.

In some rare instances, instead of opening and then traversing two retracement levels in one price bar, three retracement levels may be crossed in one retracement price bar. Obviously, by definition, two retracements occur before three retracements. Most often, in the rare instances when triple retracements occur, the TD Double Retracement will work for a period of time; however, the pressure will prove overwhelming and the market will continue to its triple retracement level where the move should be exhausted. Consequently, if a position were taken because two retracements had been exceeded, then additional trading can occur at the triple retracement level since that level should most definitely coincide with price exhaustion. A trader may elect to forego TD Double Retracements and concentrate upon only the triple retracement exhaustion price levels. This latter proposition occurs much less frequently than the TD Double Retracements but the degree of coincidence with market-exhaustion low-risk trading opportunities is enhanced considerably.

Figure 7.21 shows the trading activity of Digital River. Not only did a TD Double Retracement occur the day of the sharp move upside, but a third retracement was exceeded as well. Regardless, if a put option had been purchased above the second retracement level, by the close that trading day, price had declined sufficiently to produce a sizable profit. Note that the third retracement level over the same price period was only one point above the TD Double Retracement level.

Figure 7.22 displays the Natural Gas March 1999 futures contract. The 38.2 percent retracement level was preceded by a down close thereby qualifying the breakout upside for a low-risk intraday entry. However, the following trading day's breakouts above both the magnet and the 61.8 percent levels were disqualified since the previous trading day recorded a strong up close. Additionally, that same trading day recorded a TD Double Retracement. The fact that the market failed to reverse downside the day of the disqualified TD Double Retracement was a surprise but, as so often happens when an immediate response fails to appear, the next trading day the market opened lower and proceeded to decline below both retracement levels.

Absolute Retracements

While TD Relative Retracements can be utilized to obtain price objective levels upside or downside, they cannot be applied to those instances in which either the price of a security or a market is at a multimonth high—which has not been exceeded upside for over 12 months or a low which has not been exceeded downside for over 12 months—or an all-time low or high. In the case of a multimonth or all-time low, there exists no prior low which can be used as a reference price level to identify an intermediate high. Similarly, in the case of a multimonth or all-time high, there exists no prior high which can be used as a reference price level to identify an intermediate low. Without being able to relate a recent low to a prior low or a recent high to a prior high, TD Absolute Retracement is a viable alternative method. A high can be multiplied by 61.8 or 38.2 percent to arrive at downside price objectives. Conversely, a low can be multiplied by 138.2, 161.8, 223.6, 361.8, 461.8 percent, and so forth to arrive at likely upside retracement levels. Once again, the same qualifiers which can be utilized with TD Relative Retracements can be applied to TD Absolute Retracements as well.

TD Absolute Retracements are especially effective in predicting support levels for newly listed securities. It is not uncommon for recent public stock offerings and

FIGURE 7.21 This example illustrates TD Double Retracement (and TD Triple Retracement). Since the triple retracement level was within a point of the double retracement level, two profitable entry opportunities presented themselves for an option day trader (put buyer).

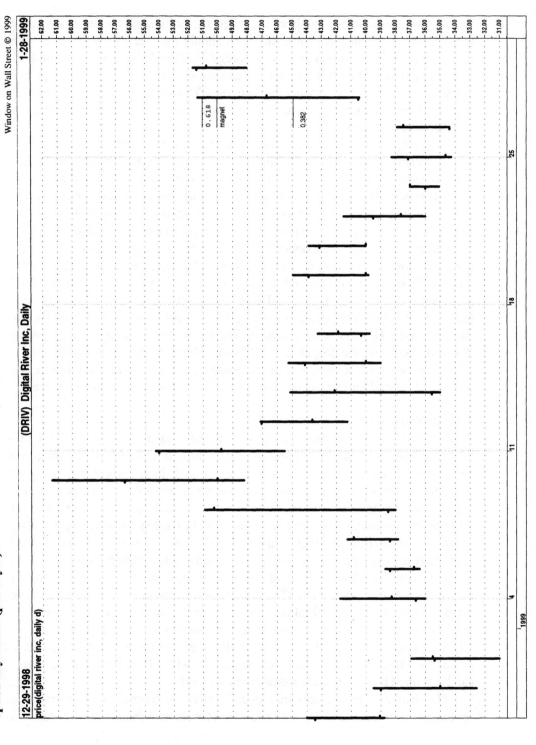

FIGURE 7.22 The response to exceeding the TD Double Retracement level in this example was deferred for a day. If a trader had restricted him- or herself to exiting at the close, the trade would have been slightly unprofitable; however, by postponing exit until the following day, it evolved into a profitable trade.

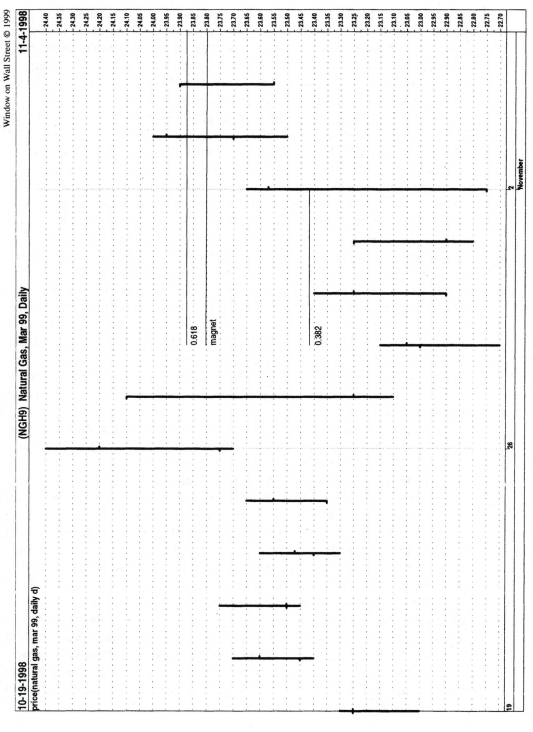

recently listed New York Stock Exchange securities to decline from their peak price levels 61.8 and 38.2 percent. This tendency is also apparent at the conclusion of bear market declines as well. Whenever a market records a multimonth or all-time price high and then commences a downside correction, TD Absolute Retracement can be used by multiplying the price peak itself by the ratios 61.8 and 38.2 percent to arrive at potential downside price support levels.

Figures 7.23 through 7.28 demonstrate how TD Absolute Retracements can identify price support and potential intraday price reversal levels. Figure 7.23 demonstrates how a trader can apply TD Absolute Retracement to a likely price reversal level. By multiplying the Egghead (EGGS) price peak of 40, recorded during the Internet craze, by 38.2 percent, TD Absolute Retracement identifies downside price support. The price objective low was hit almost precisely on the third trading day following the high and was succeeded by a sharp price rally over the next few days. Subsequently, this daily price low on December 3 provided a level from which to project a series of upside TD Relative Retracements. The initial 0.382 level upside was disqualified since it failed to meet any of the four qualifiers, and therefore price reversed. The magnet level was not disqualified, but it did cause price to reverse intraday due to a TD Double Retracement indication (although this is not indicated on the chart. The 0.382 level should be extended until a qualified breakout above that level is recorded; this would not have occurred until December 24, when price also rallied to the magnet level). Even though both retracement levels were qualified individually, as a result of the low-risk TD Double Retracement indication, a low-risk put-buying opportunity around the magnet level would have been presented.

Highly volatile stocks and recently released new issues often decline to their respective TD Absolute Retracements and then record bold and steep retracements. We randomly selected two Internet-related stocks, CMGI and Lycos, to demonstrate the movement off of these levels intraday into the close of trading. For example, CMGI (Fig. 7.24) rallied from below 96 to 131 at the close of trading upon breaking this TD Absolute Retracement level; while Lycos (Fig. 7.25) rallied from below 90 to 105 at the close of trading upon exceeding the TD Absolute Retracement level to the downside. Figure 7.26 applies TD Absolute Retracements to a daily price chart for Morgan Stanley Dean Witter (MWD) in order to time entry intraday. In this example, the market declined below 42½ and then rebounded sharply intraday. Figure 7.27, MindSpring, and Fig. 7.28, Cyberian Outpost, also illustrate the effectiveness of TD Absolute Retracements. In almost all of these examples, a trader's profit would have increased had he or she held the position beyond the current price bar's close. With an indicator as powerful as TD Absolute Retracements, traders should always evaluate their trading positions and stance prior to that trading day's close to determine whether to remain in the trade.

FIGURE 7.23 By multiplying the Egghead price peak of 40 by 38.2 percent, TD Absolute Retracement identifies downside price support.

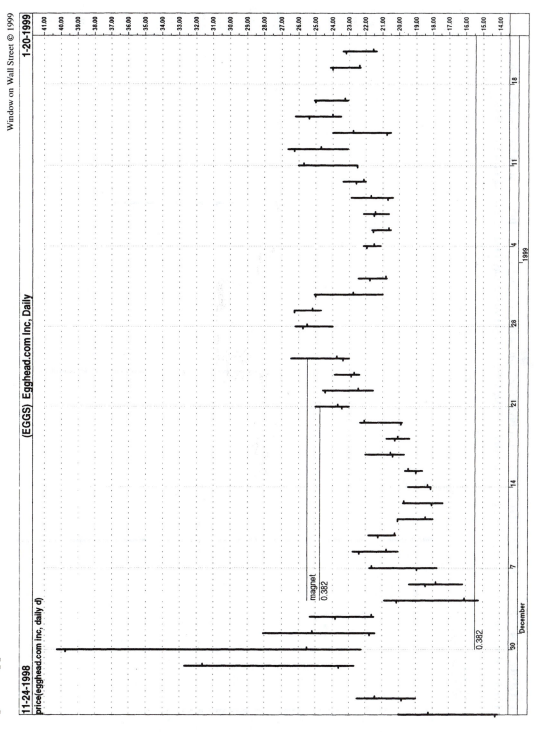

FIGURE 7.24 This chart of CMGI (CMGI) displays what commonly happens when price trades for the first time to the TD Absolute Retracement Level. In this case, price rallied the same trading day over 35 points into the close.

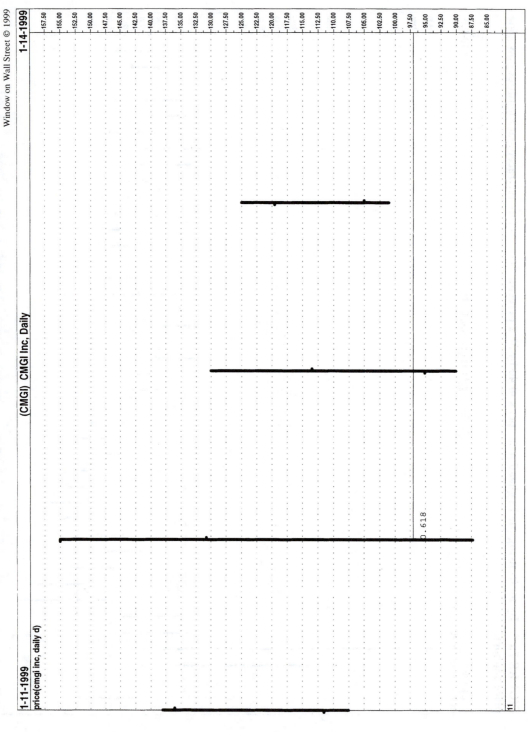

FIGURE 7.25 Lycos (LCOS) illustrates a common occurrence for stocks recently listed on the exchange, recently public, or highly volatile stocks to record sharp declines and to find price support at the TD Absolute Retracement Levels. Although it may not appear to be a major rally off the 61.8 percent TD Absolute Retracement Level the day of penetration, the rally from the retracement level to the close was over 14 points.

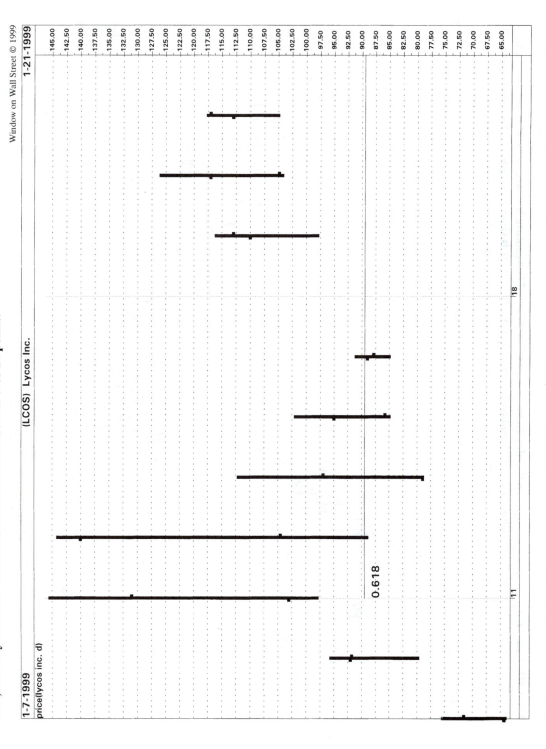

Window on Wall Street © 1999

FIGURE 7.26 Chart A presents Morgan Stanley Dean Witter (MWD) and TD Absolute Retracement. It is not uncommon to have major trend reversals coincide with TD Absolute Retracement levels. Chart B shows a magnification of the low of Chart A, and how price recorded a reversal the exact day of the penetration of the TD Absolute Retracement level.

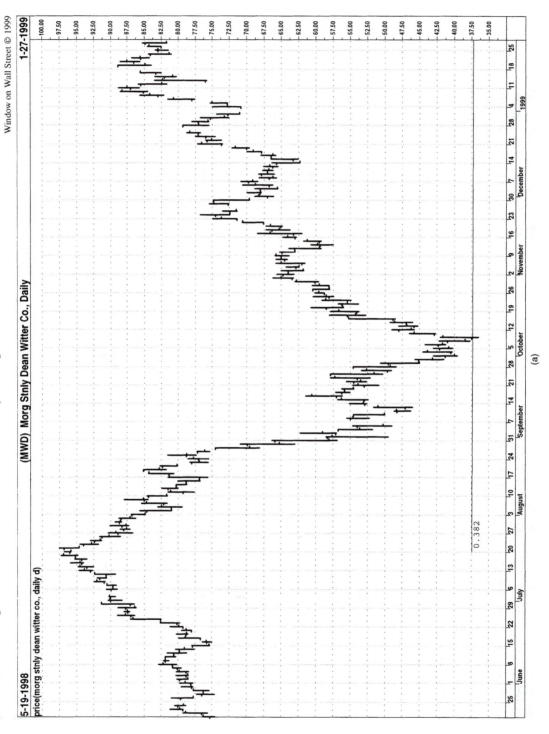

FIGURE 7.26 (*Continued*)

(b)

FIGURE 7.27 MindSpring (MSPG) illustrates how price slightly exceeded the retracement level at the opening of trading but then immediately rallied the same trading day over 33 percent (25+ points). This would have been a great trading opportunity for an option trader.

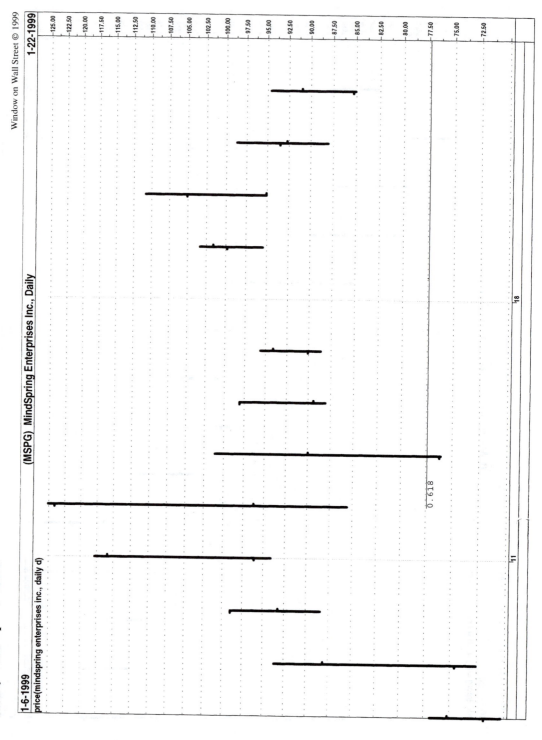

FIGURE 7.28 This chart of Cyberian Outpost (COOL) once again demonstrates the ability of TD Absolute Retracement to predict levels of price support. In this case, the market recorded its low and closed at the retracement level. The next trading day, it rallied over 15 percent, and in the ensuing four trading days rallied an additional 50 percent plus.

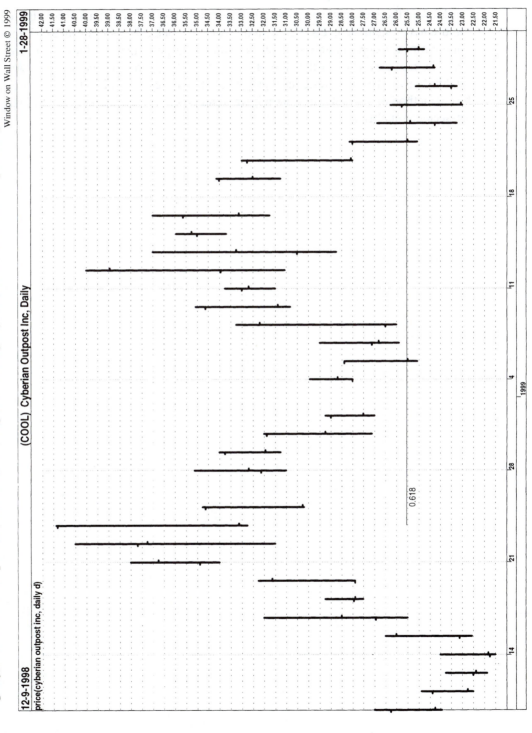

Window on Wall Street © 1999

Each of these examples demonstrated instances in which the market held these important retracement levels. These highly volatile stocks also provide an excellent opportunity for option trading, as an individual can participate in these lucrative yet risky markets while at the same time effectively containing one's losses. An established trend accelerates once these retracement lines are violated, but our preferred method of operation is to anticipate trend reversals with the help of the four retracement qualifiers.

PERFECTING
AN OSCILLATOR:
TD REI AND TD POQ

MANY MARKET FOLLOWERS *identify overbought and oversold trading zones with the help of market-timing oscillators. Here, we
discuss and address some of the problems associated with many
of the widely accepted, exponentially calculated market-timing
oscillators. We suggest utilizing an oscillator that is arithmetically calculated, capable of removing many of the distortions inherent in these
exponentially derived oscillators. In addition to introducing one such oscillator,
named TD Range Expansion Index (TD REI), we also present an important qualifying indicator, TD Price Oscillator Qualifier (TD POQ), which assists in the timing and the confirmation of one's entry.*

MARKET-TIMING OSCILLATORS

Most traders are familiar with a set of market-timing indicators that are described
as oscillators. Their goal is to identify trading opportunities which may exist whenever the oscillator indicates a market is overbought or oversold.* Those who use
oscillators typically relate market price activity to oscillator behavior over compa-

---

* For those of you unfamiliar with the terms *overbought* and *oversold*, essentially an oversold oscillator reading will be recorded when selling has persisted over an extended period of time and price
has been declining, and an overbought oscillator reading will be recorded when buying has persisted
over an extended period of time and price has been advancing.

rable time periods. The relationship between successive price and successive indicator movement over the same time period is important to some traders who rely upon divergence analysis. They believe that if the two movements diverge for any period of time, this disparity will be resolved in favor of the indicator. In other words, the movement of the oscillator should precede and therefore predict price movement. For example, if over a period of time, price has recorded two successively lower price lows and, over the identical period of time, the oscillator has failed to record a succession of two lower lows, then a positive divergence exists and the expectation of these traders is for price to rally. Conversely, if price has recorded two successively higher highs and the oscillator fails to confirm a succession of two higher highs, then a negative divergence exists and the expected outcome is for price to decline.

Despite the widespread acceptance of divergence analysis among traders, we are convinced that the tendency for price activity and oscillator activity to diverge at possible market turning points is merely a coincidence and to attribute it to divergence analysis is incorrect. We believe divergence analysis has many shortcomings: (1) a series of more than two successive price/oscillator divergences can often occur and consequently produce a series of premature, false price reversal signals; (2) a series of price/oscillator divergences can occur over an extended period of time thus reducing the effectiveness of this tool; and (3) a single overbought or oversold oscillator reading can occur without any secondary movement into this oversold/overbought zone, thereby preventing any divergence analysis.

We believe duration analysis, or the amount of time in which an oscillator resides in overbought or oversold indicator zones, is a more important determinant of market conditions and price reversals than divergence analysis. Our research indicates if the period of overbought or oversold lasts six or more price bars, then it is considered to be a severe or extreme reading. *Severe* readings imply that the market still has a great deal of momentum left and traders best not expect a price reversal at that time. In fact, if a trader were inclined to do anything, it should be to participate in the prevailing flow of the market. On the other hand, if the overbought or oversold period is limited to five or fewer price bars, then the duration is described as a *mild* reading. Generally, whenever a mild recording exists, the market experiences a price reversal. If an extreme oscillator reading is recorded, however, then a trader must await a subsequent mild reading to indicate a likely price reversal and justify entry. We feel this is the reason many traders who apply divergence analysis have some degree of success—usually an extreme reading is first recorded and is then followed by a mild secondary reading. It's more than pure coincidence but it has to do with frequency, or amount of time spent in overbought or oversold, rather than divergence.

Although the preceding comments are applicable to almost all market-timing oscillators, we are partial to using them with the ones we have developed. Many other widely followed oscillators are exponentially calculated and, consequently, have a tendency to create faulty readings. Also, the calculations for these oscillators require closing price comparisons from one price bar to the next. Because of this requirement, unscheduled market closings due to electrical failures or bad weather or unexpected news or political events such as assassinations or earthquakes can all skew closing price levels, thereby distorting the overall oscillator reading, not only for that trading session but for future sessions as well. Due to the inherent problems associated with these conventional exponential indicators, the oscillators we have developed are arithmetically calculated which have the advantage of removing any aberrant price data. In addition, we prefer to compare price levels other than consecutive price bar closes to remove the distortions caused by news which may affect consecutive price bar comparisons. For example, our TD REI indicator compares the highs and lows of alternating price bars.

TD RANGE EXPANSION INDEX (TD REI)

TD REI is a mathematically derived oscillator. Calculating TD REI manually is a tedious process since it requires the identification of reference prices, price comparisons, and qualifiers, as well as a series of mathematical steps. Fortunately, with the advent of computers this task has become simplified, and a long list of securities can be calculated and reviewed in a matter of minutes. Therefore, if you intend to use this oscillator and you are prone to arithmetic miscalculations or want to review many securities at one time, we suggest that you program the formula and rely upon the computer output for your results. The computation that follows is intended to give you an appreciation for the logic involved and the series of steps required to calculate a reading for TD REI. This way, TD REI will not simply be a black-box formula where practitioners blindly plug values in and obtain results. The five steps necessary to arrive at a (five-period) TD REI oscillator are as follows:

Step One.   Rather than comparing the current price bar to the previous price bar as is done in calculating most oscillators, step one in the calculation of TD REI requires that one compare the current price bar to the price bar two periods earlier. More specifically, the high of the current price bar is compared to the high two price bars earlier; similarly, the low of the current price bar is compared to the low two price bars earlier. By performing this alternating price bar comparison rather than a successive price bar comparison, the impact of news-driven price distortions is reduced and the appearance of a much smoother oscillator reading is apparent. It also increases the likelihood that a discernible price trend has been established. In this first step, one must subtract both the current bar's high from the high two bars earlier and the current bar's low from the low two bars earlier. These differences are then added together to create a summed value. Keep in mind that this summation can be either positive or negative, depending upon whether the current bar's high or low is greater than or less than the respective high or low two price bars earlier.

Step Two.   Step two determines whether step one should be performed or a zero should be assigned to the oscillator reading. It does so by applying comparison qualifiers. The rule states that either the current price bar's high must be greater than or equal to the low five or six price bars earlier *and* the current price bar's low must be less than or equal to the high five or six price bars earlier, or the high two price bars earlier must be greater than or equal to the close seven or eight price bars earlier *and* the low two price bars earlier must be less than or equal to the close seven or eight price bars earlier. If neither condition exists, then a value of zero is assigned to the oscillator sum for that price bar, and the high-to-high and the low-to-low price bar comparisons described in step one are ignored. This adjustment reduces the likelihood that TD REI will record a premature overbought or oversold reading when markets are advancing or declining both rapidly and steeply.

Step Three.   Step three adds the positive and the negative values from step one (if any) and the zero values from step two (if any) for each of five consecutive price bars and that value becomes the numerator. Next, the absolute value of the summed differences from step one (meaning the summation, whether positive or negative, is treated as a positive value for each of the most recent five price bars) becomes the denominator. In other words, the numerator can be positive, negative, or zero, and the denominator can only be positive. Once the numerator is divided by the denominator, a positive or a negative ratio appears. This value is then multiplied by 100 to create a percentage.

Step Four.   Step four establishes an indicator band. Usually, a five-period TD REI fluctuates between −45 and +45, with the former level defining oversold and the latter defining overbought.

Step Five.   Step five requires an analysis of price behavior once the TD REI has recorded an oversold or an overbought reading. In order to record a mild oscillator reading, TD REI must not spend more than five consecutive price bars in either the overbought or the oversold zone. Coincident and subsequent to a mild oscillator reading, oscillator conditions are ripe for a potential price reversal provided that a trigger mechanism, such as TD POQ (see the following section), generates and confirms a low-risk entry. Recording more than five consecutive price bars in the oversold or the overbought zone creates a severe or an extreme oscillator reading which suggests that the market's momentum is sufficiently intense to perpetuate its current movement, either upside or downside. Until the oscillator moves back into the neutral zone and then records a subsequent mild oversold or overbought reading, the prevailing market trend should continue. A countertrend entry may be indicated once a mild oscillator reading is recorded, provided TD POQ confirms, but it would be canceled if the duration of this move consumes more than five consecutive price bars.

Figure 8.1 of the 30-minute Johnson & Johnson chart demonstrates those situations where the TD REI has recorded extreme overbought and extreme oversold conditions. These readings are marked with a 6 next to the TD REI oscillator, which indicates that the market has recorded at least six price bars in the overbought or the oversold region. We mentioned that these extremities were not determined by divergences, but by duration. In the cases where the market for Johnson & Johnson was extremely oversold, and the TD REI has remained below −45 for a period of more than five price bars, one can see how it was best to avoid purchasing the security or a call option at that time, as further downward price movement occurred. Similarly, in the case where the market is extremely overbought, and the TD REI has remained above 45 for a period of more than five price bars, one can observe how it was advantageous to avoid selling the security or purchasing a put option at that time, as further upward price movement occurred.

TD PRICE OSCILLATOR QUALIFIER (TD POQ)

Most traders view an oversold market as a low-risk buying (call-buying) opportunity and an overbought market as a low-risk selling (put-buying) opportunity. As we described previously, they fail to make the distinction between degrees of overbought or oversold. By overlooking the critical difference between mild and severe or extreme overbought and oversold readings, they are operating at a distinct trading disadvantage. Even after they acquire the knowledge to distinguish between the two types of oscillator readings, however, traders must apply a device or trigger mechanism which signals that the price prerequisites have been fulfilled to confirm a low-risk entry opportunity. We rely upon TD Price Oscillator Qualifier (TD POQ) to perform this function for us.

Once TD REI has established an overbought or an oversold environment, TD POQ must be applied to the coincident price action in order to receive entry confirmation. This indicator is critical to the qualification and disqualification of an

FIGURE 8.1 If an oscillator remains in overbought or oversold for an extended period of time, it implies that the indicator reading is severe or extreme. Trend reversals usually coincide with mild overbought or oversold readings. In the case of extreme readings, a trader would be wise to defer anticipating a reversal.

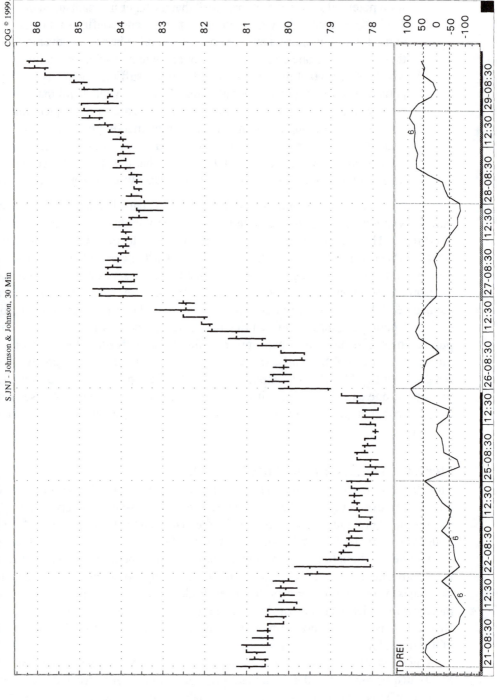

oscillator trade, especially as it relates to day trading options. TD POQ requires that once TD REI has registered a mild reading, meaning the indicator has moved into an oversold condition or an overbought condition for a period of five or fewer price bars, a specific price pattern must develop to perfect market entry. There are four possible qualified TD POQ scenarios that can occur. The type and the strength of the indication is determined by the current price bar's opening price relative to the previous price bar's high or low and/or the high or low two price bars earlier. Scenarios 1 and 2 are the more preferable of the four qualified TD POQ confirmations and are more powerful than scenarios 3 and 4.

Scenario no. 1: qualified TD POQ upside breakout—buy calls.   In the case of anticipating an upside move from an oversold condition, price must first record a close that is greater than the previous price bar's close. This up close price bar must be immediately followed by an opening price level that is less than or equal to the previous bar's high (the up-closing price bar's high). This lower upside opening after recording an up close indicates a degree of bullish skepticism off a market low. The low-risk entry point for the underlying security or the option would occur when the current bar's high exceeds the previous bar's high to the upside (the up close price bar's high). In other words, following a mild oversold reading where the oscillator has remained in the oversold zone for no more than five price bars, the close of the previous price bar must be greater than the close two price bars earlier; the current price bar's opening price must then open below the previous bar's high and then trade at least one tick greater than that high to present a low-risk buying (call-buying) opportunity. This scenario is illustrated in Fig. 8.2.

Scenario no. 2: qualified TD POQ downside breakout—buy puts.   In the case of anticipating a downside move from an overbought condition, price must first record a close that is less than the previous price bar's close. The price bar's opening price level immediately following this down close price bar must be greater than or equal to the previous bar's low (the down close price bar's low). This higher-downside opening after recording a down close indicates a degree of bearish skepticism off a market high. The low-risk entry point for the underlying security or the option would occur when the current bar's low exceeds the previous bar's low to the downside (the down close price bar's low). In other words, following a mild overbought reading where the oscillator has remained in the overbought zone for no more than five price bars, the close of the previous price bar must be less than the close two price bars earlier; the current price bar's opening price must then open above the previous bar's low and then trade at least one tick less than that low to present a low-risk selling (put-buying) opportunity. This scenario is also illustrated in Fig. 8.2.

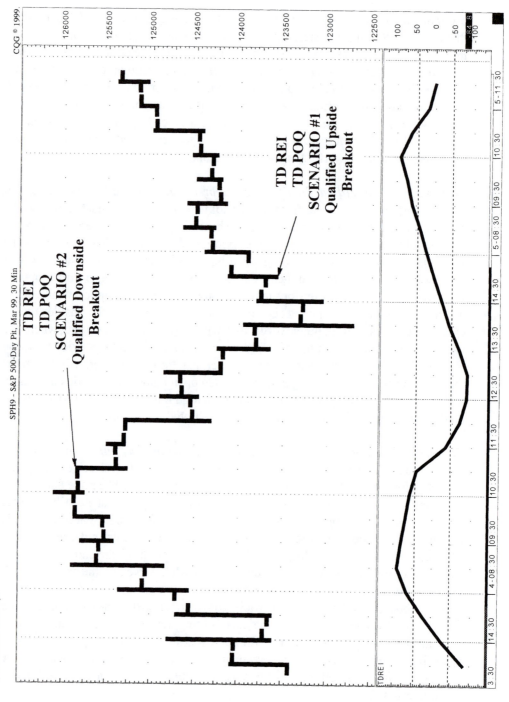

FIGURE 8.2 A qualified TD POQ breakout downside (scenario no. 2) and a qualified TD POQ breakout upside (scenario no. 1).

Scenario no. 3: qualified TD POQ upside breakout—buy calls.   In the case of an alternative upside TD POQ low-risk call-buying opportunity, the first step is met when, after recording an up close coincident with a mild TD REI oversold reading, the current price bar's open is greater than the previous price bar's high, but less than the high two price bars earlier. The final step requires that price break out above the high two price bars earlier and then close greater than the current price bar's open. Once these rules are met, a low-risk buying (call-buying) opportunity is presented. Whereas the first qualified TD POQ low-risk call-buying scenario permits the purchase of a call option at the time the TD POQ low-risk indication is given, the second, weaker scenario cannot be day traded because purchase of a call option occurs at the close of the current price bar's trading, or at the open of the following price bar. This scenario is illustrated in Fig. 8.3.

Scenario no. 4: qualified TD POQ downside breakout—buy puts.   In the case of an alternative downside TD POQ low-risk put-buying opportunity, the first step is met when, after recording a down close coincident with a mild TD REI overbought reading, the current price bar's open is less than the previous price bar's low, but greater than the low two price bars earlier. The final step requires that price break out below the low two price bars earlier and then close less than the current price bar's open. Once these rules are met, a low-risk selling (put-buying) opportunity is presented. Whereas the first qualified TD POQ low-risk put-buying scenario permits the purchase of a put option at the time the TD POQ low-risk indication is given, the second, weaker scenario cannot be day traded because purchase of a put option occurs at the close of the current price bar's trading, or at the open of the following price bar. This scenario is also illustrated in Fig. 8.3.

If one were a trend follower and wished to trade qualified TD POQ breakouts, any of these four possible scenarios would provide good, low-risk option-buying opportunities. As we mentioned earlier, of the four possibilities, recording an opening price that is less than the previous two highs in the case of an upside TD POQ breakout, or recording an opening price that is greater than the previous two lows in the case of a downside TD POQ breakout, are the more preferable scenarios, as their results are typically more powerful. While TD POQ applies to the underlying security, any low-risk indication would apply equally well to their respective options.

Figure 8.4 displays a market with the application of both TD REI and TD POQ. In this example, referring to the 10-Year U.S. Treasury Note March 1999 futures, the TD REI entry level is coordinated with a qualified or a disqualified TD POQ reading. In this example, low-risk qualified buying (call-buying) and selling (put-purchasing) opportunities occurred at the point marked X. As you can see, the TD

FIGURE 8.3 A qualified TD POQ breakout upside (scenario no. 3) and a qualified TD POQ breakout downside (scenario no. 4).

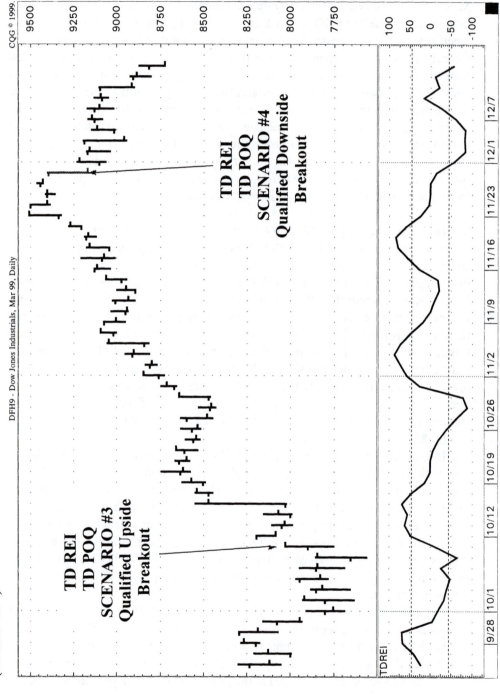

DFH9 - Dow Jones Industrials, Mar 99, Daily

CQG © 1999.

TD REI
TD POQ
SCENARIO #3
Qualified Upside
Breakout

TD REI
TD POQ
SCENARIO #4
Qualified Downside
Breakout

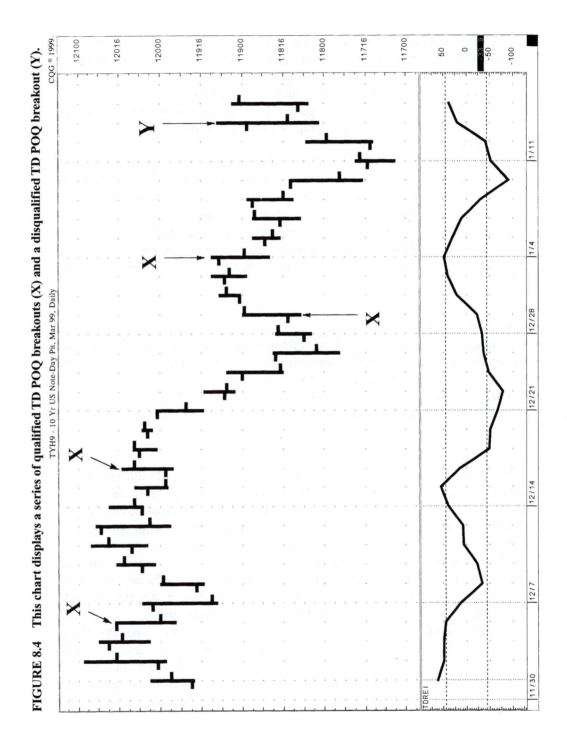

FIGURE 8.4 This chart displays a series of qualified TD POQ breakouts (X) and a disqualified TD POQ breakout (Y).

POQ breakouts occurred in the context of a mild overbought or a mild oversold market reading. However, these indications are trend-following in nature, so option premiums will have increased coincident with the respective price move prior to entry. A low-risk disqualified selling (put-purchasing) opportunity occurred at the point marked Y. Observe that the upside TD POQ breakout occurred coincident with a mild oversold condition reading and was preceded by an up close, thereby permitting entry.

Each of the four possible TD POQ breakout scenarios were qualified low-risk option-purchasing opportunities. These qualified entry techniques are all trend-following in nature. This is oftentimes a serious drawback when day trading options because option premiums would have expanded prior to entry to reflect this price advance or decline. Rather than trade these qualified TD POQ breakouts, a trader could instead trade disqualified or canceled TD POQ breakouts. Disqualified breakouts afford much greater option trading opportunities for a day trader.

Disqualified TD POQ Readings

A variation of the qualified, trend-following approaches previously described provides a unique option trading opportunity. If one preferred to trade against the prevailing trend, even intraday, and wished to trade options as opposed to the underlying security, then one could fade a qualified TD POQ reading, and instead trade a disqualified TD POQ indication. Two possible disqualified scenarios exist.

Disqualified TD POQ upside breakout—buy puts. If the REI indicator reading for the underlying security is currently, or most recently has been, rated mildly oversold, TD POQ requires for a disqualified low-risk selling (put-buying) opportunity that an up close must be immediately followed by an opening price that is above *both* of the previous two price bars' highs. In other words, to receive a low-risk put-buying opportunity, the first step states that the close of the previous price bar must be greater than the close two price bars earlier; the next step states that the current price bar's opening price must then open greater than both the high of the previous price bar *and* the high two price bars earlier. In these instances, the opening price has been exaggerated upside and the market will typically decline, most often filling in any price gaps. In these cases, entry is permitted at any time after the open—if one so chooses, entry could occur once a trader receives confirmation from another intraday indicator, such as a one-minute or a five-minute TD Sequential or TD Combo indication. This scenario is illustrated in Fig. 8.5.

FIGURE 8.5   This chart shows a disqualified TD POQ downside and upside reversal.

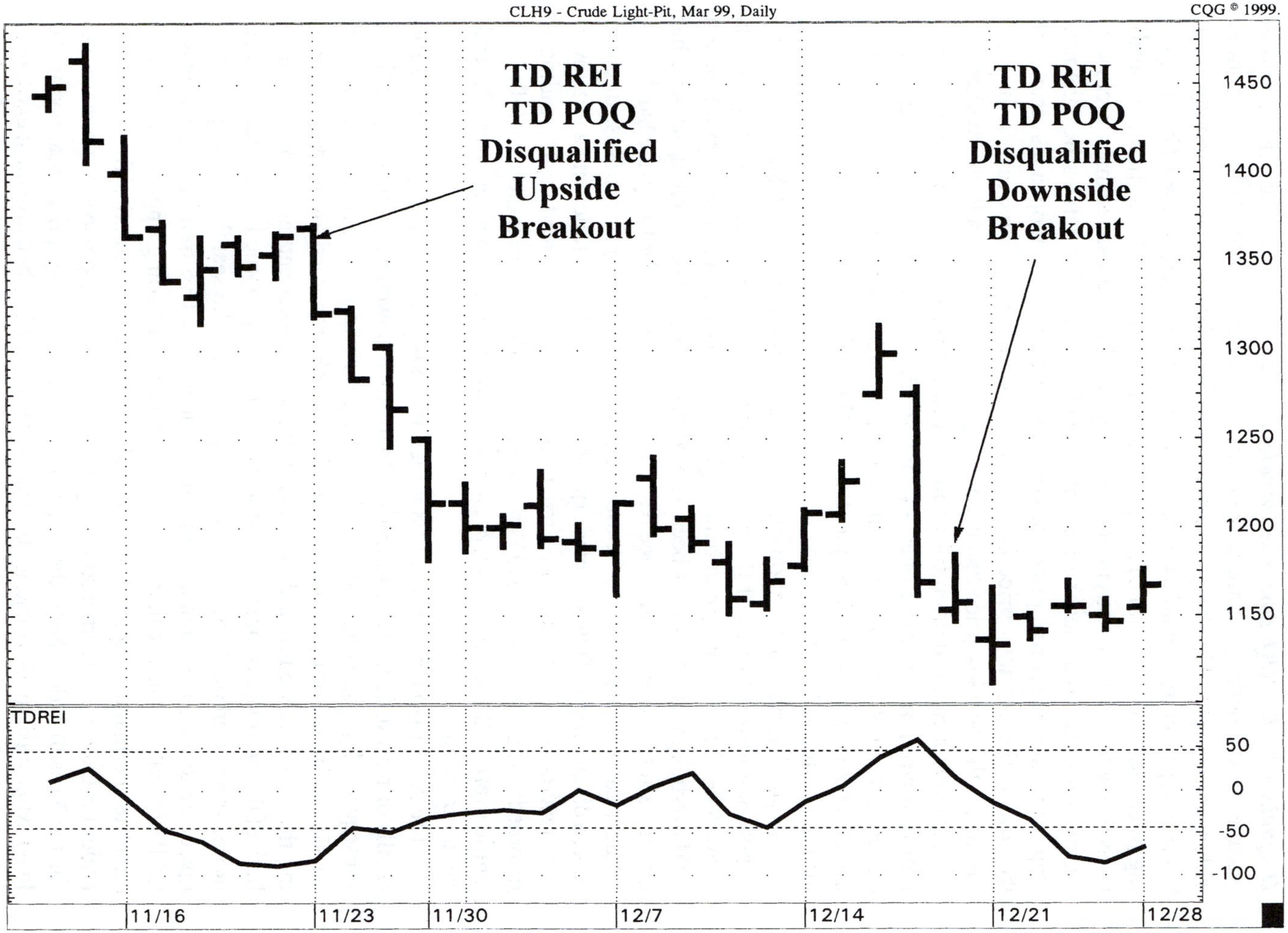

TD REI
TD POQ
Disqualified
Upside
Breakout

TD REI
TD POQ
Disqualified Downside
Breakout

CLH9 - Crude Light-Pit, Mar 99, Daily

CQG © 1999.

281

Disqualified TD POQ downside breakout—buy calls. If the REI indicator reading for the underlying security is currently, or most recently has been, rated mildly overbought, TD POQ requires for a disqualified low-risk buying (call-buying) opportunity that a down close must be immediately followed by an opening price that is below *both* of the previous two price bars' lows. In other words, to receive a low-risk call-buying opportunity, the first step states that the close of the previous price bar must be less than the close two price bars earlier; the next step states that the current price bar's opening price must then open less than both the low of the previous price bar *and* the low two price bars earlier. In these instances, the opening price has been exaggerated downside and the market will typically advance, most often filling in any price gaps. In these cases, entry is permitted at any time after the open—if one so chooses, entry could occur once a trader receives confirmation from another intraday indicator, such as a one-minute or a five-minute TD Sequential or TD Combo indication. This scenario is also illustrated in Fig. 8.5.

By purchasing a put option once a mild oversold condition has been determined, provided the open of the price bar directly after the up close price bar is above *both* the prior two price bars' highs, or by purchasing a call option once a mild overbought condition has been determined, provided the open of the price bar directly after the down close price bar is below *both* the prior two price bars' lows, a trader can take advantage of these overzealous, extreme price moves. In either case, a disqualified TD POQ upside (put-buying) indication following a mild oversold reading is active until the first price bar where an overbought reading is recorded; and a disqualified TD POQ downside (call-buying) indication following a mild overbought reading is active until the first price bar where an oversold reading is recorded.

The Xs on Figs. 8.6, 8.7, and 8.8 identify those instances where the TD REI oscillator recorded an oversold reading that was followed by an up close with the subsequent day's opening above both of the prior two trading days' (the up close days') true highs; or conversely, where the TD REI recorded an overbought reading that was followed by a down close with the subsequent day's opening below both of the prior two trading days' (the down close days') true lows. Once a market moves from overbought into oversold or vice versa, the search for a gap opening upside or downside terminates. Figure 8.6 identifies five trend reversals for the S&P 500, all of which can be translated into option trading opportunities subsequent to the market's open. Figure 8.7 shows three opportunities for option day trades for Excite, an Internet stock. Figure 8.8 shows three prospective turnarounds for the Russell Index. Note the importance of the opening price in applying TD POQ. Most *cash* markets cannot be traded using TD POQ because most exchanges report the prior trading day's close (with any adjustments for stock dividends or splits) as the cash index's opening price. In those cases where an opening price is

FIGURE 8.6 This example of the daily S&P 500 March 1999 Futures contract identifies with a series of Xs disqualified TD REI low-risk indications.

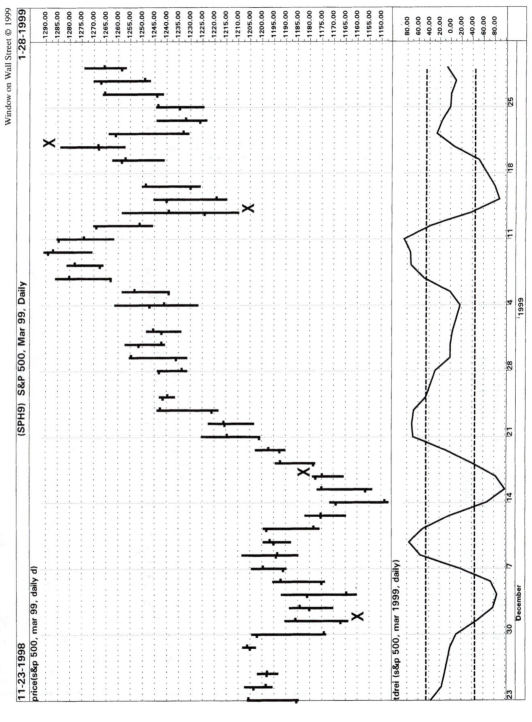

FIGURE 8.7 The daily chart of Excite (XCIT) identifies three times when TD REI produced pending indications of a potential trend-following entry which was disqualified by TD POQ. In each case, from the opening of trading, the market reversed trend. For an option day trader these were unique opportunities.

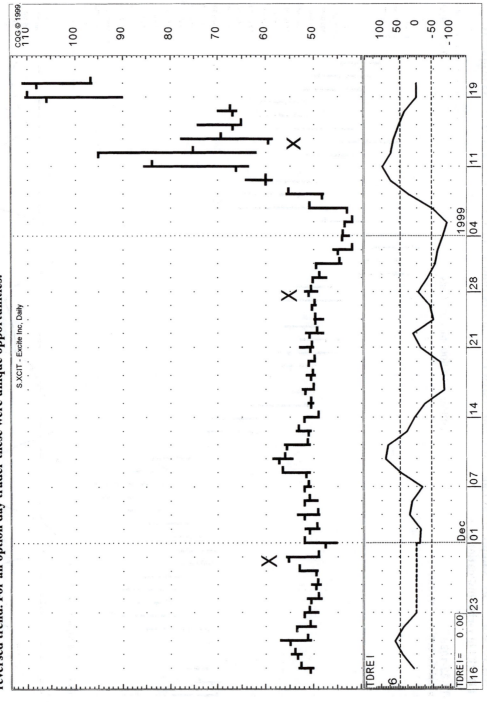

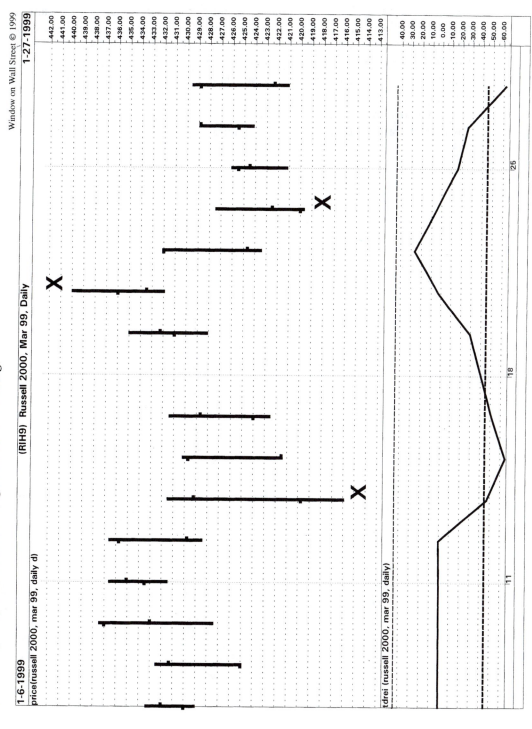

FIGURE 8.8 The daily Russell Index Futures March 1999 identifies TD POQ disqualified trades when applying TD REI. In each instance, at the opening of trading an alert trader could take advantage of this short-term false breakout by purchasing an option and then exiting at the close of trading.

calculated, there could still be a misrepresentation of a cash index. For example, most cash industry group indices use the openings of all market components that have opened at the time of the first opening reporting period, which is usually the first five or ten minutes of trading. If some of the industry components open later than the survey period, for any reason, their effect upon the opening price is ignored.

To insure a trader's chance of success, these option purchases should be coordinated with other trading techniques recommended throughout this book.

MOVING FORWARD IN REVERSE: TD FIB RANGE, TD EXIT ONE, TD REBO REVERSE, TD CAMOUFLAGE, AND TD RANGE PROJECTION

THE FIRST FOUR INDICATORS, *TD Fib Range, TD Exit One, TD REBO Reverse, and TD Camouflage, are of relatively recent vintage and are designed to capitalize on intraday price exhaustion. The fifth indicator, TD Range Projection, is intended to provide a trader with a means of effectively predicting the following trading day's price range. In the context of day trading options, these five indicators work well in establishing levels of impending price reversals. Because they are contratrend in nature and by design, they enable a trader to anticipate potential levels of support and resistance, in the option as well as the underlying security.*

TD FIB RANGE

As we indicated earlier, it's easy for a trader psychologically to jump upon an existing trend or participate with the majority of traders, but it's much more difficult to operate against the prevailing trend by anticipating likely trend reversal levels. To overcome this apprehension and accomplish this goal we researched what market characteristics preceded or coincided with possible market turning points. What we came up with was an indicator called TD Fib Range. TD Fib Range gets its name from utilizing a ratio that is Fibonacci-derived. *Fibonacci numbers* are a number series where each successive number in the series, when divided by its prior number in the series, yields 1.618, and each number in the series, when divided by the following number in the series, yields 0.618. TD Fib Range uses this Fibonacci ratio—1.618—to calculate expected price movement termination levels. In our research, we discovered that oftentimes when short-term market tops and bottoms occur, daily price range movements added to or subtracted from the previous trading day's close either exceeded (1) 1.618 times the previous trading day's true price range or (2) 1.618 times an average of the previous three trading days' true price range.* When price reached these TD Fib levels, the market had a tendency to exhaust itself. When the market trades outside of these points of exhaustion, an ideal low-risk call-buying opportunity in the case of a price decline below the lower TD Fib level, or an ideal low-risk put-buying opportunity in the case of a price advance above the upper TD Fib level is presented at the close of the price bar or the following price bar's open. Oftentimes, the market records these TD Fib Range moves in excess of 1.618 times the previous price bar's true range or 1.618 times the average of the previous three trading days' true price ranges added to or subtracted from the previous trading day's close coincident with a news announcement. News releases have the effect of causing a noticeable increase in volume, both in a security and its related option contract. Although this indicator is intended to be applied to the underlying security, the implications of a potentially exhaustive price move should be felt similarly by any related options. Consequently, we suggest monitoring the underlying security and once an indication of price exhaustion exists, then apply the conclusions to the option, as well as the underlying security. Furthermore, we strongly recommend TD Fib Range be used in conjunction with option-related trend exhaustion indicators, such as TD % F and intraday TD Dollar-Weighted Put-Call and Open Interest statistical information, to confirm short-term market tops and bottoms.

TD Fib Range can be perfected by including a series of qualifiers which will insure that the market is sufficiently short-term oversold downside or short-term overbought upside to exhaust a price move intraday or on the close. For example, one might require the current price bar's high to exceed upside 1.618 times the previous price bar's true range added to the previous close coincident with that same price bar's high exceeding both true highs three and four price bars earlier; or the current price bar's low to exceed downside 1.618 times the previous price bar's true range subtracted from the previous close coincident with that same price bar's low

---

* The *true* price range is the difference between a price bar's high or the prior price bar's close, whichever is greater, and the price bar's low or the prior price bar's close, whichever is less.

exceeding both true lows three and four price bars earlier. This rule would provide an indication that the market may be sufficiently overbought or oversold intraday to reverse prices at least for a short period of time. We experimented with a series of preconditions and arrived at the following additional qualifier. If the market exceeds upside 1.618 times the previous trading day's true price range, or 1.618 times the previous three trading days' average true price range, added to the prior trading day's close, then a low-risk sell entry (put purchase) occurs at the close of the current day. A secondary qualifier requires that the close of the current day must be greater than all prior four closes. Conversely, if the market exceeds downside 1.618 times the previous trading day's true price range, or the previous three trading days' average true price range, subtracted from the prior trading day's close, then a low-risk buy entry (call purchase) occurs at the close of the current day. Again, a secondary qualifier requires that the close of the current day must be less than all prior four closes. If any of the requirements are not fulfilled, a trader could expect the market to continue its move in the direction of the breakout and no action is to be taken. Although we don't necessarily recommend its application, one could use the failure of the high upside exceeding both the highs three and four price bars earlier for a low-risk sell (put purchase), or the failure of the low downside exceeding both the lows three and four price bars earlier for a low-risk buy (call purchase) as a trend confirmation indication. In any case, other qualifiers can be introduced and other daily range multipliers besides 1.618 can be substituted. It is important for an option trader, when applying this indicator to the underlying security, to confirm the results for the option as well by applying the option rules discussed earlier, as well as TD % F and TD Dollar-Weighted Put-Call and Open Interest.

TD Fib Range requires that a day trader enter at the close of trading or at the succeeding trading day's opening provided that the open is in the direction of the anticipated trade. Obviously, entry at the succeeding trading day's opening is more reasonable if one is an option day trader. The only requirement we recommend be introduced to perfect this day trade is that the open occur in the direction of the trade; that is, if a call option is to be purchased, then the open must be above the previous trading day's close, and if a put option is to be purchased, then the open must be below the previous trading day's close. This requirement is similar to the qualifier included with indicator TD REBO Reverse. Also, a day trader can elevate the TD Fib Range factor to 2.00 (double the previous day's true price range) instead of 1.618 to ensure that any entry that occurs on the TD Fib Range breakout bar is not premature.

Figure 9.1 (Coffee March 1999) identifies those occurrences in which TD Fib Range fulfills the preceding requirements. Specifically, to identify a potential low-risk sell opportunity (put purchase), 161.8 percent is multiplied by the previous trading day's true price range and then added to that day's close. The TD Fib Range

FIGURE 9.1 March Coffee 1999 displays four times in which TD REBO Reverse identified possible short-term price exhaustion levels.

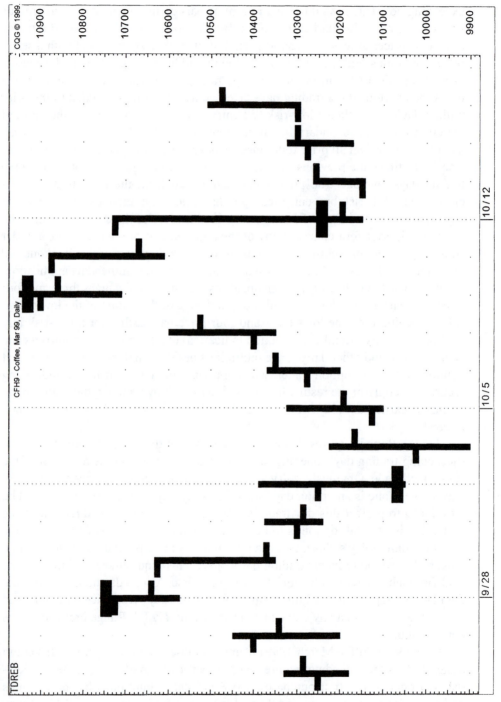

level is plotted on the chart but the low-risk selling opportunity (put purchase) exists not at that specific price level marked on the chart with a hash mark, but rather at that day's close. Note that this example does not include an average of the previous three trading days' true ranges as an alternative value. Conversely, to identify a low-risk buy opportunity (call purchase), 161.8 percent is multiplied by the previous trading day's true price range and then subtracted from that day's close. The TD Fib Range level is plotted on the chart but the low-risk buying opportunity (call purchase) exists not at that specific price level marked on the chart with a hash mark, but rather at that day's close. Note that this example does not include an average of the previous three trading days' true ranges as an alternative value.

Figure 9.2 (Dollar-Mark Cash) shows seven instances over an 11-week period in which TD Fib Range spoke. In every instance but one, the market responded the next trading day by following through in the direction of the low-risk indications and the lone instance in which it didn't respond the next trading day, it did soon afterward. Once again the placement of the rectangles on the chart is merely for purposes of illustration since the low-risk entry levels are defined at the close that trading day.

The settings for TD Fib Range are provided only for purposes of example. They can be changed or substituted with other qualifiers. The measurements are all applied to the underlying securities and the conclusions drawn are in turn applied to the related options. By applying the settings we proposed initially, the low-risk entries are limited to the close of the TD Fib Range breakout day or the following day's open if it opens in the direction of the breakout. Additionally, by expanding the factor to 2.00 from 1.618, the opportunity exists for intraday entry and day trading. When used independently or preferably in conjunction with other indicators described in this book, timing of option purchases, whether they be calls or puts, can be improved.

TD EXIT ONE

TD Exit One is an indicator that we originally developed to exit outstanding market positions. Today, however, we have found that this indicator is also effective in initiating market positions in options and their underlying securities. Very simply, there are three requirements for a TD Exit One low-risk buy (call purchase):

1. The market must record three consecutive down close price bars, where the close one price bar ago is less than the close two price bars ago, the close two price bars ago is less than the close three price bars ago, and the close three price bars ago is less than the close four price bars ago.

2. The current price bar's open must be greater than the close one price bar ago and the current price bar's low must trade less than the close one price bar ago.

3. The price range one price bar ago—chart high to chart low—must be greater than the true price range two price bars ago—true high to true low.

FIGURE 9.2 The Cash German Mark recorded four instances in which price exceeded the TD REBO Reverse momentum thresholds. In each case, the following trading day's opening provided an opportunity for a day trader to assume a position and enjoy the inception of a trend reversal.

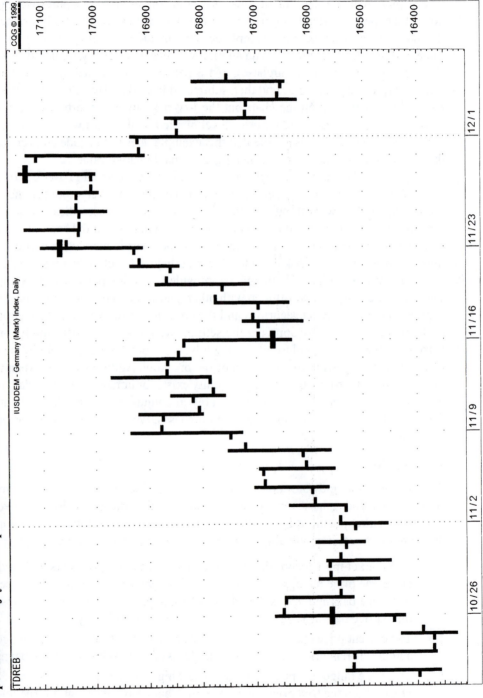

A low-risk buy (call-buying) entry occurs one tick less than the close one price bar ago; however, in some instances, the low-risk buy (call-buying) entry can also appear at the low one price bar ago. Consequently, a dual-entry possibility can exist depending upon one factor, referred to as TD Differential (downside). The distinction between the two entries arises from the comparison of the price difference between the low and the close of the previous price bar versus the low and the close two price bars ago. If the difference between the close one price bar ago and the low one price bar ago is greater than the difference between the close two price bars ago and the low two price bars ago, then the low-risk buy (call-buying) level is one tick below the previous price bar's close; and if the difference between the close one price bar ago and the low one price bar ago is less than the difference between the close two price bars ago and the low two price bars ago, then the low-risk buy (call-buying) level is one tick below the previous price bar's low. Now there will be instances when the market will fail to decline below either reference price level—the close one price bar ago or the low one price bar ago—and to avoid missing these trading opportunities, a trader should buy a partial position at the current price bar's open. At that time, it may be prudent to purchase one-third of the intended call option position at the opening and the balance once price declines below either reference level.

Conversely, there are three requirements for a TD Exit One low-risk sell (put purchase):

1. The market must record three consecutive up close price bars, where the close one price bar ago is greater than close two price bars ago, the close two price bars ago is greater than the close three price bars ago, and the close three price bars ago is greater than the close four price bars ago.

2. The current price bar's open must be less than the close one price bar ago and current price bar's high must trade greater than the close one ago.

3. The price range one price bar ago—chart high to chart low—must be greater than the true price range two price bars ago—true high to true low.

A low-risk sell (put-buying) entry exists one tick greater than the close one price bar ago; however, in some instances, the low-risk sell (put-buying) entry can also appear at the high one price bar ago. Consequently, a dual-entry possibility can exist depending upon one factor, referred to as TD Differential (upside). The distinction between the two entries arises from the comparison of the price difference between the high and the close of the previous price bar versus the high and the close two price bars earlier. If the difference between the high one price bar ago and the close one price bar ago is greater than the difference between the high two price bars ago and the close two price bars ago, then the low-risk sell (put-buying) level is one tick above the previous price bar's close; and if the difference between the high one price bar ago and the close one price bar ago is less than the difference between the high and the close two price bars ago versus the difference between the high and the close two price bars ago, then the low-risk sell (put-buying) level is one tick above the previous price bar's high. Now there will be instances when the market will fail to advance above either reference price level—the close one price bar ago or the high one price bar ago—and to avoid missing these trading opportunities, a trader should sell (purchase a put) at the current price bar's open. At that time, it may be prudent to purchase one-third of the intended put option position at the opening and the balance once price advances above either reference level.

Figure 9.3 (S&P 500 December 1998) displays various instances in which a series of down or up closes are punctuated with a price exhaustion move which develops into a price reversal. On the chart, price hash marks are used to indicate the low-risk buying (call-buying) opportunities. There are four instances over a relatively short period in which TD Exit One successfully identified trend exhaustion and price reversal levels. In each of these instances, the most recent of the series of down closes or up closes is exceeded intraday the next trading day, enabling a trader to enter the market. As you can see, only the second example—September 1—had its low-risk call-buying level below the prior trading day's low due to the failure of TD Differential. The other three had their low-risk call-buying entry levels a tick below their respective trading day's closes because of TD Differential.

Figure 9.4 applies TD Exit One to a daily Intel chart. TD Exit One is designed to identify potential price exhaustion zones. This chart displays two examples of this indicator for INTC. Once three consecutive up closes or down closes are recorded, the market is vulnerable to a price reversal. If three successively lower closes are recorded, the next price bar's opening price must be above the most recent (previous price bar's) close and that same price bar's low must be less than or equal to that close. Conversely, at a potential price exhaustion peak once three successively higher closes are recorded, the next price bar's opening price must be below the most recent (previous price bar's) close and that same price bar's high must be greater than or equal to that close. The first instance was a low-risk sell (put-buying) indication and the market recorded a sharp one day decline. In the second instance, the market recorded a low-risk buy (call-buying) indication but did not respond until the next trading day. The next day the market responded with a gap opening upside to establish market equilibrium which was suppressed the previous trading day. The latter example illustrates that even though a day trader may have suffered a loss, had the trader held the position overnight, it would have proved profitable. An indication that a day trade may be unprofitable exists whenever the trade occurs late in the trading day since time is an important factor. Our recommendation is that if day traders are determined to trade within the last two hours of trading, they should be prepared to extend their holding periods until the next trading day.

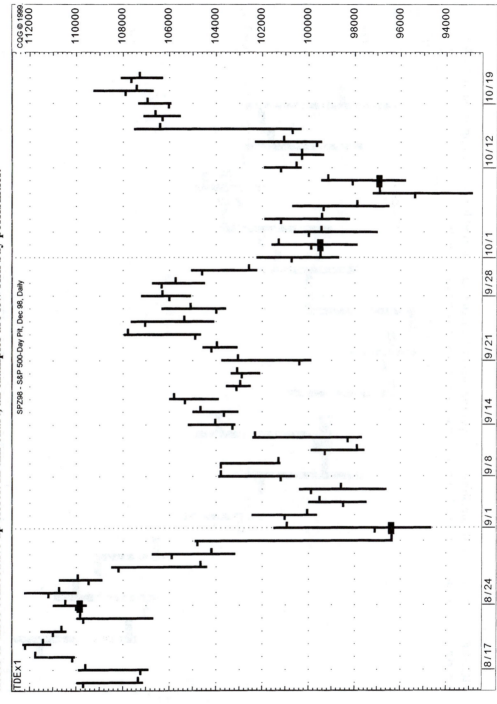

FIGURE 9.3 This is a chart of the December 1998 S&P 500. TD Exit One must be preceded by three consecutive down closes or three consecutive up closes. In this chart, all examples are low-risk buy possibilities.

FIGURE 9.4 This chart of Intel illustrates two examples of TD Exit One. The first is a day trading opportunity for a low-risk selling opportunity and the second presents a low-risk buying opportunity.

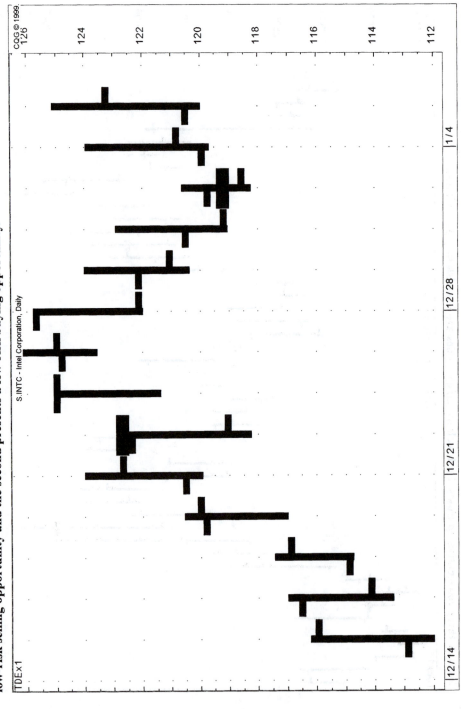

The December British Pound 1998 futures contract (Fig. 9.5) identifies an example of a TD Exit One low-risk buy. Three consecutive down closes were recorded and the open of the next trading day was above the prior day's close. Once the low traded less than or equal to the prior trading day's close, a low-risk call-buying opportunity occurred. Again, this indicator works well when applied to a daily chart and can be used to predict continued movement of the TD Exit indication. For that reason, we suggest one consider holding one's position longer than the close if other indicators confirm. Other qualifiers can be introduced to perfect trades. For example, the trading range of the most recent of the three consecutive down or up closes must be greater than the prior trading day's price range.

TD REBO REVERSE

Many trend-following traders enter the market based upon market momentum. We are no strangers to this market-timing approach, having developed numerous breakout and range expansion techniques during the 1970s to capitalize upon the inflationary trends existing in the markets and the economy during that period. In order to facilitate the research we conducted in this area, we created a market-timing template which we referred to as TD REBO to represent *Range Expansion BreakOut.* By having such a structure at our disposal, we were able to research and apply numerous variations of momentum-based indicators. At the time we worked with this indicator format, most traders focused their attention upon very basic analytical approaches, such as moving averages and trendline analysis, to anticipate price trends. However, over the years, traders have become increasingly aware of this momentum-trading approach to market timing and we would venture a reasonable guess that currently well over 50 percent of all Commodity Trading Advisors (CTAs) use a similar approach to managing their portfolios.

Just to reinforce our initial observations that by adding a percentage of a specified price value—previous trading bar's price range or series of price bars' price ranges—to the current opening price level is effective, we invite you to examine how often the current price bar's open is within a short distance from the current price bar's high or low. In other words, it is not uncommon to witness the opening price occur within 10- to 20% of the current trading day's high or low. The dilemma is determining what the current bar's price range is in advance. In order to accomplish that prediction, a trader can use the previous bar's price range as a proxy or an average of a series of price bars as a substitute. This process enables a trader to forecast a reasonable price range and then calculate a percentage of that range to establish possible low-risk buy or sell entry levels. This is one context in which to apply TD REBO as a trend follower. Another is to use the technique to anticipate possible reversal or trend exhaustion levels.

Without exception, those who apply techniques similar to TD REBO are trend followers, which was our original intention in creating TD REBO. However, we

FIGURE 9.5 The December 1998 British Pound exhausted its downside momentum at the TD Exit One low-risk entry level. At that price level, a trader was presented not only with a low-risk day trading possibility, but also a more profitable opportunity had the trader held the trade even longer.

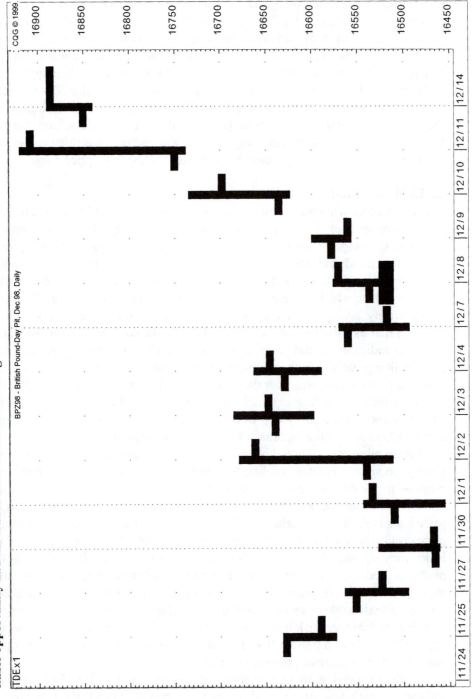

found that, in the case of anticipating trend reversals, TD REBO can perform effectively as well. The features of its construction enable an option buyer to take advantage of an anticipated change in direction of the underlying security. In those instances in which an opening price exceeds a series of consecutive closing price levels, either upside or downside, and, consequently, the accompanying entry price level is exaggerated above a series of consecutive daily price range extremes, rare opportunities arise for a short-term trader to operate against the trend, rather than to anticipate its likely continuation.

Statistical information we compiled a number of years ago indicated that markets operated within a trading range 76 to 82 percent of the time. Of the other 18 to 24 percent, markets trended higher 12 to 16 percent of the time and trended lower 6 to 8 percent of the time. The reason market moves last longer to the upside than to the downside has to do with the psychology of traders. Buying is a cumulative process—traders like a market, so as the market rallies, their margin (and profits) allows them to add to their positions and purchase more, and news reinforces their decisions; whereas selling is generally a single-minded decision—traders don't like the market, so they liquidate everything.

During periods of sideways market movement, a trend-following trader is always vigilant, awaiting a price breakout in which to participate. A consolidation phase requires one form of trading, while the breakout and subsequent trending phases require another. To differentiate between the valid and the invalid breakouts, we created TD REBO. We measured the typical or average thrust of the market over various time periods to determine a level which, when added to or subtracted from a subsequent trading day's open, would qualify as a breakout. This exercise included multiplying the previous price bar's true range by either 38.2 or 61.8 percent (or any other percentage with a reliable history of effectiveness) and then either adding this value to or subtracting it from the current price bar's opening to establish a low-risk entry. This exercise reduced the possibility of false breakouts and indicated market momentum. As you can imagine, a trending market is a perfect environment for TD REBO. On the other hand, within a trading-range market, oscillators, such as TD REI and qualifier TD POQ, which produce overbought and oversold readings and low-risk entry levels, are tradable indicators. Although TD REBO may not be suited for these trading-range markets, TD REBO hybrid TD REBO Reverse is effective in these environments and is also a valid indicator for option trading as well.

In order to apply TD REBO Reverse, we are looking for extreme conditions where the market activity can be labeled as oversold or overbought based upon the relative opening price level and entry price level versus a prior series of closes, a prior series of highs, and a prior series of lows, depending whether the anticipated move is up or down. The type of oversold or overbought condition required to initiate TD REBO Reverse is not defined by the position of an oscillator and its relationship to price activity. Rather, the type of oversold or overbought condition required to initiate TD REBO Reverse is determined by the relative relationship between a price period's open and entry price versus the prior three price periods' highs, lows, and closes. For example, in the case of a low-risk buy (call-buying) entry, if the current price bar's open is above the previous three price bars' closes and the entry price is above the prior three price bars' highs, then buying at a price level which is calculated by multiplying the greater of the two previous price bars' true ranges by a percentage—such as 61.8 or 38.2 percent—and adding that value to the current price bar's open would be too aggressive. Instead of buying the presumed breakout, as a trend follower might do, this would present a selling (put-buying) opportunity. In other words, if the current bar opens greater than the close of each of the three prior price bars, and the entry price is greater than the high of each of the three prior price bars, then one would fade the perceived REBO upside breakout. Conversely, for a low-risk sell (put-buying) entry, if the current price bar's open is below the previous three price bars' closes and the entry price is below the prior three price bars' lows, then selling (buying a put) at a price level which is calculated by multiplying the greater of the two previous price bars' true ranges by a percentage—such as 61.8 or 38.2 percent—and subtracting that value from the current price bar's open would be too aggressive. Instead of selling, or buying a put, upon the presumed breakout, as a trend follower might do, this would present a buying (call-buying) opportunity. In other words, if the current bar opens less than the close of each of the three prior price bars, and the entry price is less than the low of each of the three prior price bars, then one would fade the perceived REBO downside breakout.

Rather than add to or subtract from the current trading day's open, we originally used the previous trading day's close and used 161.8 percent as our multiplier instead of 38.2 and 61.8 percent. Figure 9.1 (Coffee March 1999) identifies the three instances in which the market exceeded the 161.8 percent TD REBO Reverse price levels and in each case they coincided with price exhaustion. We were satisfied with these and similar results but TD Fib Range better accomplished the goal of identifying potential trend reversals. Consequently, with TD REBO Reverse, we rely upon the opening price level as a reference and 161.8 percent as our multiplier. It is designed to identify those instances when the market has been strained intraday and is about to react.

Certainly, other qualifiers can be introduced as well to insure ideal disqualified entries and low-risk reversal candidates for option trading have been formed. We will highlight one. Due to the fact that TD REBO Reverse may not speak until the end of the trading day, we have developed a technique which gives us, as option day traders, the benefit of a full day's trading. Specifically, it requires that once the preceding prerequisites for TD REBO Reverse are fulfilled and price closes above the TD REBO Reverse level upside or closes below TD REBO Reverse level downside, the trader should await the next trading day's open. If the following day's opening is below the close on the price bar of the TD REBO Reverse upside exhaustion breakout, then a low-risk selling (put-buying) opportunity exists for that trading day; and, conversely, if the following day's opening is above the close of the TD REBO Reverse downside exhaustion breakout, then a low-risk buying (call-buying) opportunity exists for that trading day. In this example, nothing could be better for option day traders because they are able to initiate trading positions from the opening price level, provided it confirms the indication forecast the previous trading day. In other words, if the market is able to exceed the required percentage of the previous price bar's true price range or the previous series of price bars' true price range, then the market is vulnerable to a reversal in price, given all the prerequisites described previously, provided the next price bar's opening price level confirms.

Another version of TD REBO Reverse respects unfilled price gaps and improves the results further. There is a distinction between price gaps and price laps. Price gaps occur when the low of the current price bar is greater than the high of the previous price bar or the high of the current price bar is less than the previous price bar's low; while price laps occur when the low of the current price bar is above the prior price bar's close but less than the prior price bar's high, or the high of the current price bar is below the prior price bar's close but greater than the prior price bar's low. If the ingredients are there for a price reaction, particularly after a price gap, then we suggest awaiting the next trading day's opening price level to determine whether the open has broken out in the correct direction, and then purchasing options. This also allows a trader to take advantage of a full trading day.

Figure 9.6 is a daily IBM bar chart. This chart of IBM identifies the raw version of TD REBO Reverse without additional qualifiers. The price bars are marked on those days in which the high or low exceeded the TD REBO Reverse level. Had a trader awaited the next trading day's open to buy an option in order to insure that price would follow through, all the trades would have produced profits. By using the exhaustion TD REBO Reverse without this additional qualifier, other indicators would be required to confirm the trades.

In Fig. 9.7, the chart of March Cocoa 1999 identifies those days in which TD REBO Reverse indications were given and they were followed the succeeding day by an open in the direction of the reversal of trend. Options purchases could have been postponed until the next trading day's open and held the balance of the trading day for a series of profitable day trades.

TD REBO Reverse is most decidedly antitrend and often occurs at the completion of a short-term move when the trend typically exhausts itself. Other qualifiers can be introduced for option trading but the beauty of this indicator is its simplicity. Once again, if one is day trading options, then it is more prudent to enter the option market as early as possible in the trading day.

FIGURE 9.6 This TD REBO Reverse example of IBM stresses the enhanced opportunity for day trading success if a trader is willing to postpone entry until the day following the indicator breakout level, provided the open of that trading day confirms the price reversal.

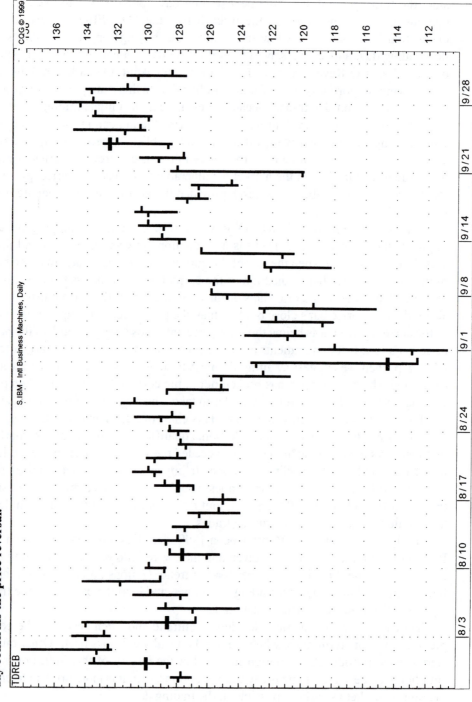

S.IBM - Intl Business Machines, Daily

CQG © 1999.

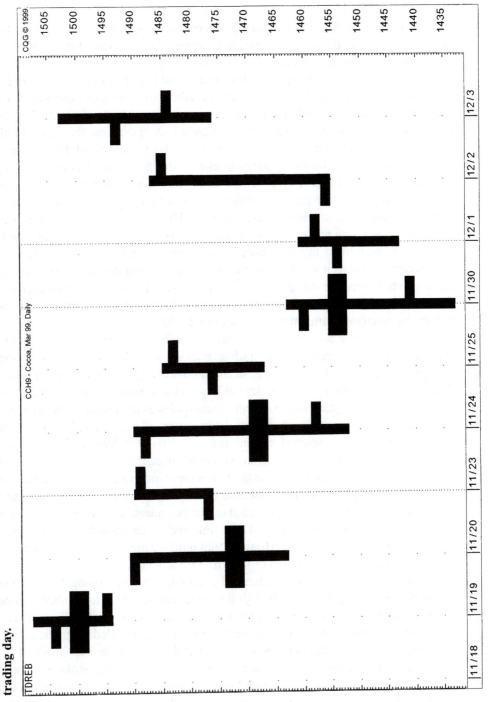

FIGURE 9.7 This chart of March 1999 Cocoa emphasizes the importance of deferring entry until the price bar succeeding the TD REBO Reverse indication on the chart. This enables a day trader to potentially participate in the entire trading day.

TD CAMOUFLAGE

Many beginning traders believe that a group of trading syndicates control the price activity of stocks. In fact, when we first entered this business there were many claims by market commentators that an elite group of traders, known as market specialists, were able to manipulate stock prices and that it was best to trade defensively in order to avoid their maneuverings. Although we were skeptical of this widespread notion, we could understand the reason most traders carried this concern; after all, since these specialists operated the posts on the floor of the exchanges, all trades had to pass through their hands to be executed. By definition, the specialists provided liquidity to the markets—during rallies, they provided supply and during declines, they provided demand. In other words, they operated against the trend. At that time, we were working with a large financial institution, where we would initiate large market positions. The greatest difficulty we encountered was in entering and exiting these sizable positions—we had to sacrifice far too much to be a trend follower. Since it was impossible for us to buy after lows were recorded, just as it was impossible to sell after the completion of market tops, we attempted to mimic the specialists' trading style in order to gain an edge over the trading public. Our trading attitude and outlook needed to change, and we became preoccupied with anticipating market trends.

In our formative market research years, the aura and mystique attached to the specialists were dominant in our trading background. Because of their trading style—buying weakness and selling strength—we always knew they were trading forces to reckon with. All limit orders to buy and sell were recorded in their trading books and it was their job to execute these trades as the market moved to these levels. Since we were a large financial institution who generated a significant amount of money in commissions, any time we arrived in New York our brokers would take us down on the floor so we could meet the various specialists and observe their trading. It was fascinating to see these individuals trade, and many of them were willing to share their specific trading styles. Surprisingly, it appeared that they were genuinely as concerned about large traders, such as ourselves, as we were of them. Friendships developed over time and we attempted to glean as much trading information as possible. However, not until we met one specialist in particular did we become aware of this group's true trading style.

A number of years ago, we attended a trading seminar hoping to learn new approaches to trading the markets. Upon introducing ourselves to another attendee sitting at our table, we were surprised to learn that he was a specialist. We were confused—why would a specialist be at a seminar when he controlled the trading activities in various stocks? Supposedly, this secret club in which he was involved was composed of the wealthiest and most devious denizens of the marketplace. What we learned was a true revelation. This individual was in search of answers as well. Admittedly, all market orders in various stocks passed through his hands, so he had an advantage in that he was aware of what the trading public was doing. The specialists were successful when trading short term, but established trends, particularly the unrelenting stock market decline in 1974, eventually took their toll upon these traders' accounts. He wanted to diversify his trading style to protect and insulate his company from risk. We shared trading techniques and it quickly became apparent that his role was strictly mechanical—all he was looking to do was to chip away one-eighth of a point of profit and earn a fixed fee for each transaction. He went into trading each day with no preconceived notions of the market—a clean trading slate, if you will—and then continuously operated against the trend of the day, content to make his money on a series of small, profitable trades. This was not what we envisioned a specialist doing. Trading propaganda had memorialized this group as the ultimate insiders. It turned out the only advantage they possessed was that they were responsible for establishing the opening price level by matching orders from buyers and sellers as they passed through their portals at the pit post on the floor of the exchange. By the time we became aware of this trading edge they had, we had already experimented with and concluded the importance of the market's open price level as a key trading reference.

We mentioned earlier the unintended hoax perpetrated upon the financial community by the financial media. Specifically, every time a price change is reported by a quote machine, a business news announcement, or similar events, the movement is expressed in terms of the previous day's closing price level versus the current price today. Early on in our careers, we learned quickly that yesterday's close was history and a more realistic measurement of price change was defined by price movement from the current price bar's open to the current price level. By relating the price change from the current price bar's open to close, rather than relying upon the price change from yesterday's close to today's close, the distortions caused by overnight news developments are avoided. When I shared this trading theory with the specialist, he agreed with our trading approach, particularly when applied to day trading, and he confirmed that we had uncovered one of the secrets of trading successfully. Despite the fact that this discovery was made close to 30 years ago, its basis permeates most of our trading techniques. In fact, one indicator that we have created relies upon the relationship of closing price and opening price, as well as the conventional relationship of closing price to closing price relied upon by most traders. This combination of price comparisons resolves itself more often than not in favor of the opening price to closing price relationship. Because its existence is not obvious, we describe it as TD Camouflage.

TD Camouflage requires that, at a suspected market low, the current price bar's low must be less than the previous price bar's low and the current price bar's close must be less than the previous price bar's close, but at the same time the current price bar's close must be greater than the current price bar's open. Conversely, at a suspected market high, the current price bar's high must be greater than the previous price bar's high and the current price bar's close must be greater than the previous price bar's close, but at the same time the current price bar's close must be less than the current price bar's open. In each instance, the critical price relationship and comparison exists between the current bar's open and close, whereas most traders concentrate upon the less important and relevant relationship between consecutive closes.

Now, if trading were this simple, the road to riches would be quick and worry-free. However, not all market reversals are accompanied by this important price pattern. Furthermore, there are times when TD Camouflage simply will not work. We have developed a couple of qualifiers to improve our chances for success. We invite you to experiment with and develop enhancements of your own to improve your trading performance with this indicator. Still, with any additional condition it does not preclude the possibility of a bad trade.

How do traders best apply TD Camouflage to day trade options? First of all, traders could execute their positions at the opening of the succeeding price bar following the formation of this price pattern. Should they be more inclined, traders could enter at the close the day the pattern is formed but then the trade would have to be held overnight. Since price has a tendency to gap at the opening the day after the pattern, it may be prudent to secure two trading positions—one at the conclusion of the pattern and the other at the next price bar's opening price level. By awaiting the next price bar's open, it helps avoid those trades in which the succeeding opening reverses the implications of that price pattern by opening below or above a low-risk buy (call purchase) or sell (put purchase) entry level, respectively. For example, if a possible low occurs and the next price bar's open is below the low of the pattern day or, conversely, the opening price following a suspected high is above the high of the pattern day, then the trades should be canceled. This price pattern is also important when day trading on time intervals smaller than daily price charts, such as 30-minute charts and hourly charts.

Figure 9.8 of the CBOE Volatility Index (VIX) identifies two TD Camouflage patterns—the first a low-risk buy and the second a low-risk sell. The low-risk buy indication in the underlying index would correspond with a low-risk call-buying opportunity, and the low-risk sell indication in the underlying index would correspond with a low-risk put-buying opportunity. Note the low-risk buy day recorded a close greater than the open, a close less than the previous trading day's close, and a low less than the prior trading day's low. Conversely, the low-risk sell day recorded a close less than the open, a close greater than the previous day's close, and a high greater than the previous trading day's high.

Figure 9.9 of the S&P 500 March 1999 displays numerous TD Camouflage low-risk indications. In order to present all of these indications over this time period and also make them visible, we identified them with Xs on the chart. In each instance where a low-risk buy in the underlying S&P index occurred, thereby translating into a low-risk call-purchasing opportunity, the low-risk buy day's low is less than the prior trading day's low, its close is less than the prior trading day's close, and its close

FIGURE 9.8 TD Camouflage is an important precursor to market trend reversals. This chart demonstrates the importance of the price relationship between open and close rather than close versus close.

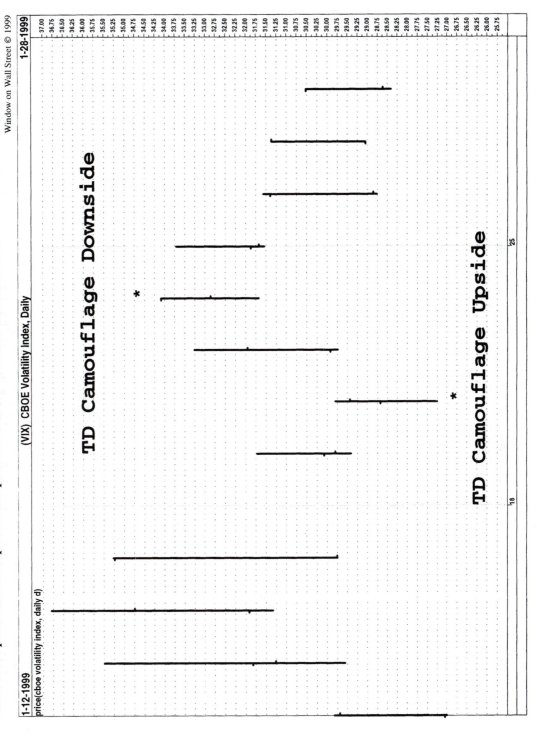

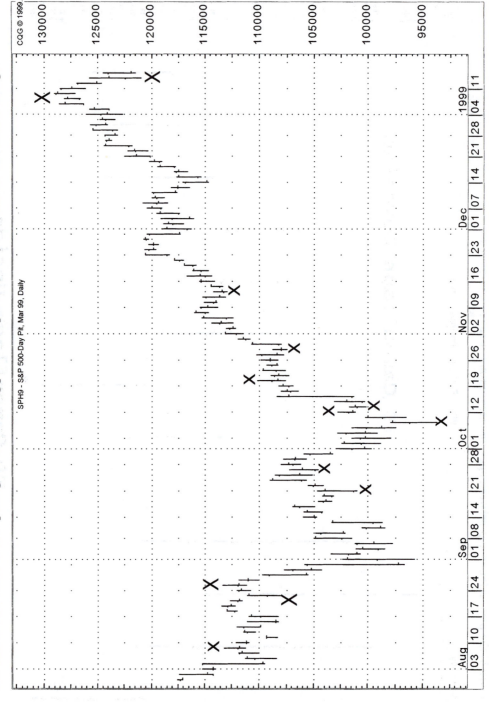

FIGURE 9.9 An entire series of TD Camouflage opportunities appear on this chart of the March 1999 S&P. The ideal low-risk entries occur at the openings of the following price bars provided they confirm the directional change.

is above the open. At the same time, in each instance where a low-risk sell in the underlying S&P index occurred, thereby translating into a low-risk put-purchasing opportunity, the low-risk sell day's high is greater than the prior trading day's high, its close is greater than the prior trading day's close, and its close is below the open.

Figure 9.10 illustrates various occurrences of TD Camouflage. See how deceptive one's eyes can be by focusing only upon the relationship between consecutive closing prices and ignoring, at the same time, the relationship of the close to that same trading day's open. It isn't enough to have an up close versus the previous trading day's close—it must be accompanied by a close above the open—likewise, it isn't sufficient to record a down close versus the previous trading day's close—it must be accompanied by a close above the open. The Xs on the chart reflect those instances in which both requirements were fulfilled.

TD RANGE PROJECTION

When Financial News Network (FNN) broadcast market coverage in the mid-1980s, we were invited to be daily commentators on the markets. The producers asked that the comments be directed to the overall markets in general, as well as specifically to forecast the projected high and low for both the U.S. Treasury Bond Futures and the S&P 500 Futures for that particular trading day. Fortunately, a number of years earlier, I had developed a formula designed to project the daily price ranges.

The components of TD Range Projection necessary to calculate the following trading day's price range were open, high, low, and close. Each price was weighted according to the relationship between the open and the close. For example, if the close was above the open, then the high was weighted two times and the low and close were weighted once; if the close was less than the open, then the low was weighted two times and the high and close were weighted once; and if the close and the open were equal, then the close was weighted two times and the high and low were weighted once. These formulas are as follows:

1. If the Current Price Bar's Close > Current Price Bar's Open, then
    - (Current High $\times$ 2) + Current Low + Current Close = X
    - $X/2$ – Current High = Projected Low
    - $X/2$ – Current Low = Projected High
2. If the Current Price Bar's Close < Current Price Bar's Open, then
    - Current High + (Current Low $\times$ 2) + Current Close = X
    - $X/2$ – Current High = Projected Low
    - $X/2$ – Current Low = Projected High
3. If the Current Price Bar's Close = Current Price Bar's Open, then
    - Current High + Current Low + (Current Close $\times$ 2) = X
    - $X/2$ – High = Projected Low
    - $X/2$ – Low = Projected High

FIGURE 9.10 The chart of March 1999 Soybeans display numerous instances of TD Camouflage. In this chart the open the following trading day was critical in filtering the trading possibilities for a day trader. Although not essential, it is important to have the open confirm the trend reversal.

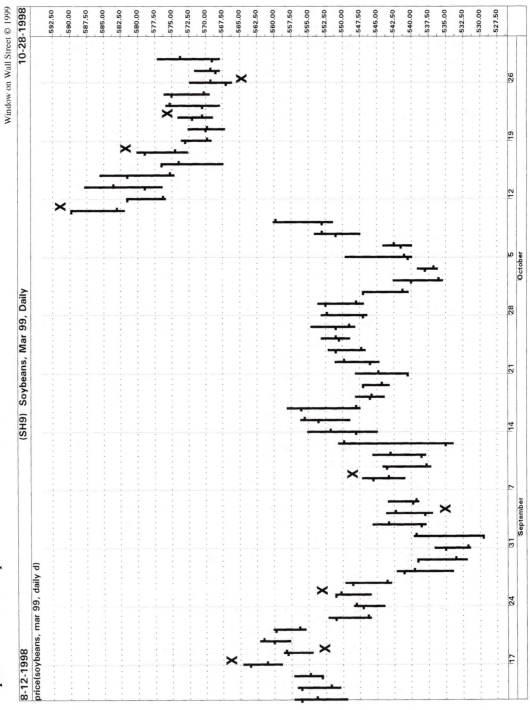

Window on Wall Street © 1999

The greatest advantage to TD Range Projections is that a trader can calculate them the day prior to their application. The projected high and low are used as benchmarks for the following trading day. Ideally, if tomorrow's open is within the projected high and the projected low, a trader can expect resistance at the projected high and support at the projected low. If the open occurs outside the projected range, meaning it occurs above the projected high or below the projected low, it qualifies as a possible price breakout, provided price follows through by at least one price tick in the direction of the breakout. In addition, if the opening price exceeds the projected high to the upside, then this level would now provide support and should be held on a closing basis; similarly, if the opening price exceeds the projected low to the downside, then this level would now provide resistance and should be held on a closing basis.

There are periods when the actual prices seem to conform well with the projected highs and projected lows. An option trader can use the projected range to confirm other indicators or to buy puts when the underlying security opens within its projected range and then exceeds upside the projected high or to buy calls when the underlying security opens within its projected range and then exceeds downside the projected low. Should the open occur outside the projected range, an option trader can trade with the trend breakout, but this practice would be described as trend following and the option premiums would more than likely have already expanded.

Figure 9.11 of the German Dax March 1999 Future presents the TD Daily Range Projection. The first and third trading days opened outside the confines of the projection, thereby implying a continuation of price moves in the direction of the respective breakouts. Of the nine trading days shown on the chart, only the fifth and the seventh failed to open within the projected ranges. Amazingly, the latter two projections hit the low and the high exactly, while most of the other projections effectively contained any movement outside of these two levels. In these cases where the opening price is contained within the projected price range, it indicated that any intraday price movement outside the range should have been corrected by the close, where price could have been expected to close within this range. In but one of these examples this occurred.

Figure 9.12 includes a daily chart of EBAY with a series of daily projected ranges. As you can see, breakouts outside the range projection have a tendency to continue to trade in the direction of the breakout. Most openings within the projected range tend to close within the projected range as well, thereby indicating that moves outside this range are simply aberrations and should return to the projected area by the time of the close. Figure 9.13 also displays EBAY on a daily chart but over a different set of dates. The previous comments apply equally to this chart as well.

Figure 9.14 presents a daily chart of U.S. Treasury Bonds accompanied by the daily range projections. Each example has an open contained within the projected price range, and movement outside this range is temporary and followed by a price reversal by the close of trading.

FIGURE 9.11 In this chart of the March 1999 German DAX, if the opening is between the projected high and low, any movement outside the band should equate with intraday low-risk selling or buying opportunities. An open outside the projected range indicates a possible trend breakout for the day in the direction of the open.

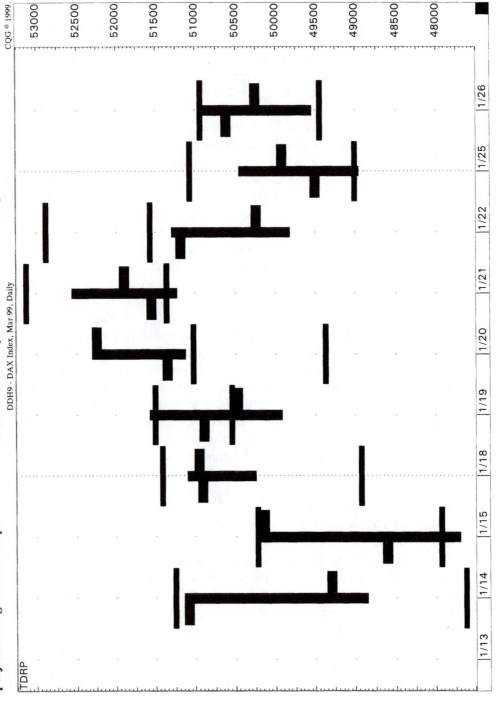

312

FIGURE 9.12 EBAY is a good example of how most openings within the TD Range Projections were usually followed by closes the same price bar within the band and how opening breakouts either upside or downside outside the projections usually continued in that direction through the close of that price bar.

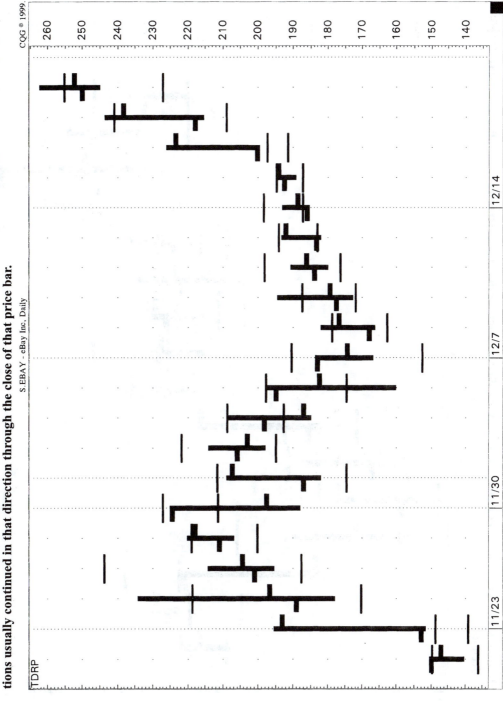

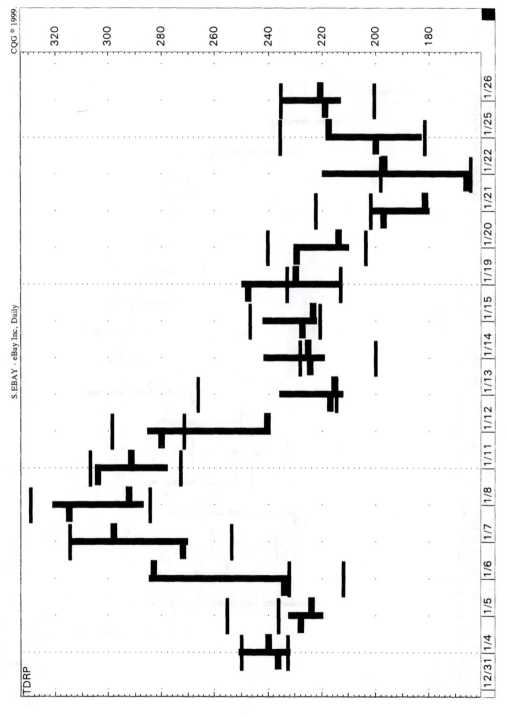

FIGURE 9.13 This is another chart of EBAY over a different time period demonstrating the application of TD Range Projections.

314

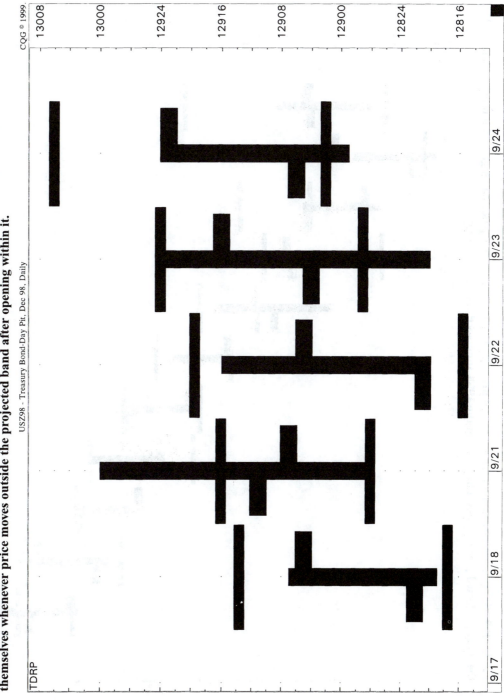

FIGURE 9.14 The December 1998 Treasury Bond gravitated to the daily range projections but failed to close outside the range for those instances in which price opened within the projected range. Intraday trading opportunities present themselves whenever price moves outside the projected band after opening within it.

315

FIGURE 9.15 It is not uncommon for the actual price to record its respective price bar high and low coincident with the daily projected price ranges. The chart of the 1998 June S&P was no exception.

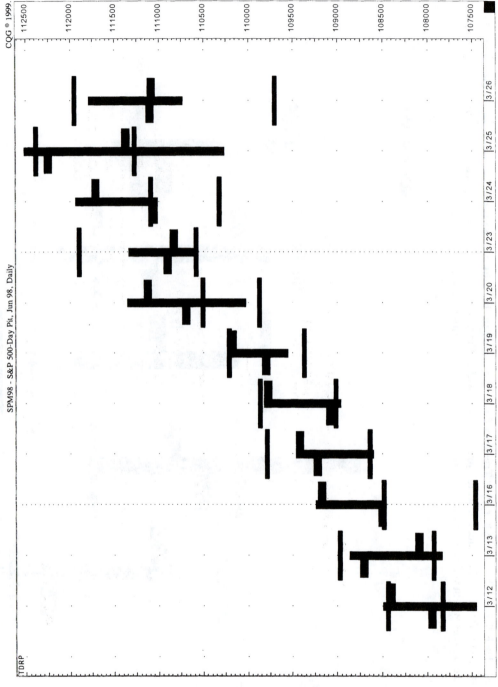

SPM98 - S&P 500-Day Pit, Jun 98, Daily

CQG © 1999

Figure 9.15 displays a daily chart of the S&P 500 June 1998 future. The majority of the projected ranges for each day effectively contained the daily price highs and the lows. Any movement outside the projections was very minor and resulted in a reversal in the underlying price. In each instance, by the close of that trading day, price returned within the projected range area.

10

PULLING IT ALL TOGETHER

N *OW THAT WE HAVE DESCRIBED how these indicators identify low-risk price reversals on a long-term and a short-term basis, let's combine these various techniques into a seamless trading methodology.*

The pace of life has accelerated in recent years but it pales when compared to how conditions have changed within markets around the world over the past 25 years. Barely a generation ago, the volume on the New York Stock Exchange averaged 6 million shares a day. We recall in the summer of 1973 when the market closed early just to handle the additional paperwork associated with the increase in volume of a mere 1 to 2 million shares a day. Daily moves in the Dow Jones Industrial Average of 20 to 30 points were rare and whenever weekly declines exceeded 50 points, portfolio managers were frozen and quick to anticipate a replay of 1929 or some other serious market calamity. To prevent similar financial disasters, most market officials were reluctant to introduce new products and relied upon legislation introduced since the Depression of the 1930s to protect the economy.

The introduction of capitalism and markets worldwide, as well as the acceptance of derivative markets by conservative trust departments, endowments, pension accounts, and government agencies has been an encouragement to investment pioneers to experiment and expand trading opportunities and horizons. The growth of the various trading vehicles and the acceptance and appetite of the trading community for these products have been astonishing. Despite this incredible growth, one factor has remained constant and that is the psychology of those individuals who trade these various markets. The same emotions which drove the individual trader to make certain decisions in the stock market throughout the years still affect those who trade the commodities, financial futures, equity, and options markets today, but now they may be more exaggerated due to the leverage involved in these markets. Often the tools used to evaluate these markets have been developed by professors and market research quantitative think tanks. Their techniques to calculate realistic price valuations are a testimony to the importance of technical market models, as well as the acceptance of this sort of methodology.

Despite the widespread interest in these new markets, there is one aspect which has lagged in this rapid growth, and that is data reporting and availability. Although the overall data-reporting process has improved tremendously since the days of old, there are still many pockets where the process is lacking. In fact, the effort to write this book illustrates this one deficiency loud and clear. Whereas we have made numerous observations regarding option day trading throughout the years, many difficulties arose when we attempted to document and test them. Unfortunately, there are only a few providers of stock and commodity option data and those who do provide them do not necessarily provide the same information. The information lacks both consistency and accuracy. In addition, due to the enormous amount of data, as well as the frequency of price errors, extensive work is required by these providers not only in data storage and management, but also in data cleansing. While one data vendor may provide daily option high, low, and closing bid and ask and no close, another may provide open, high, low, and close; the one or two other stock option providers will merely report the close and perhaps only report the statistics for the nearby option expiration and strike price. Surprisingly, even the exchanges fail to make available the data. As far as futures option providers, the problems are no less serious. There are few data sources and those who do supply option data to the public are at the mercy of the various exchanges who do not necessarily correct bad data reports.

Now if one were to overlook the occasional bad data, testing of the various option trading techniques could be done. We conducted some of our own indicator testing but became exceedingly frustrated. In fact, to illustrate examples of TD Dollar-Weighted Put-Call on an intraday basis is futile, let alone impossible. To do so, one must obtain accurate indications of trading volume and price activity which occurs at specific times during the trading day—in other words, one requires data that one just can't obtain. To illustrate examples hypothetically based on market tendencies that we have seen is much more realistic and sensible. This concern applies equally, only to a lesser extent, to TD % F, since we found the daily highs and lows are sometimes reported incorrectly. Nevertheless, we believe the concept of TD % F is most critical and can be tested by following the option markets real time and paper trading the indicator. And, with additional experimentation with this option market-timing technique in real-time scenarios, a trader can further enhance both its performance and its utility. The critical factor is to open one's mind to these methods designed to assist option traders.

A TRADING GAME PLAN

There are many considerations that must be brought together in order to determine the best way to trade options. Following the markets throughout the years has enabled us to make numerous observations concerning the trading activity of underlying securities as well as their related option markets. While we do not proclaim to be experts in the ways of option trading, there are certain items that we look for before we will trade a particular option market. Our plan of attack is not necessarily correct but it is mechanized, enabling us to participate in a variety of markets with consistent results.

When evaluating and arriving at an ideal low-risk entry price level, the relationship between the option and the underlying security must be in synchronization. Despite the fact that the option markets are mature exchanges, it does not alter the fact that trading volume may be light or even nonexistent in a particular option. When a small group of large individual traders or a large group of small traders have an interest in a market, liquidity exists; without this feature, trading is erratic and unpredictable. That is why it is important that, before traders even consider trading an option, they compare the underlying security to the respective option to determine how the two instruments move together and whether the market can be traded effectively. It may just so happen that the option activity is so slow that the contract hasn't been traded for hours, or even days, meaning any trade that occurred would require the trader to make considerable price concessions. If a market is inactive, most often it is best to avoid day trading in that option altogether. Consequently, make certain that the option is liquid and that any comparisons to be made between an option and its underlying asset are based upon trades which occur within the same time frame. By comparing the two when an option has not traded for a period of days and the underlying security has traded consistently produces a distortion in comparative results. Furthermore, one must be wary when comparing the closes of the option and the underlying security, for the underlying may have traded consistently into the close while the option may have gone hours without trading. In addition, the fact that the underlying security opens prior to the options anywhere from one to several minutes later can also give a misrepresentation to any comparisons which may be made. Just to be safe in these scenarios, always note the time of each security's last trade.

We prefer to select our option trading opportunities from those options which are close to expiration and trading at- or slightly in-the-money in order to eliminate as much of the time value from the premium as possible. This way, we are essentially trading an option's intrinsic value and are unaffected by some of the negative impact of time decay. Generally, we like to concentrate upon those options which are within two to three weeks of expiration. Before we enter into any option position, careful consideration is always given as to our level of exposure. We feel that it is important for traders to avoid overextending their capital commitments in any one market, as any adverse price movement or lack thereof will have a deleterious effect on their option positions. Therefore, when day trading, we typically limit our option purchases to a fraction of what we would pay to own the security outright. We tend to go with exposure percentages of 2 percent of our total portfolio value for day trading options, and 4 percent for position trading options. As with long-term investing, one should always look to spread risk across a variety of investments and diversify one's portfolio. Our intentions in presenting these percentages are not to determine the exact number of option contracts we feel a trader should buy based upon a mathematical formula—after all, each trader is different—rather it is to ensure that traders are cognizant of the risks inherent in option trading. To find success in option day trading and position trading, timing is the key, not size. Also, we always trade out of our option positions, rather than exercise them—after all, who's ever heard of a successful option day exerciser? By trading out of our position, we save on commission costs, we don't lose the option premium, and we receive the intrinsic value of the option as well as the additional time value, thereby maximizing our potential profits.

We also make several considerations as to when we should purchase our options. It is also important to consider the day of the week in which one should enter the option market. Specifically, one should be wary of holding positions from Friday to the following Monday, as many option theoreticians recalculate their volatility and delta numbers once a week to determine an appropriate value for the time premium, usually after the close of trading on Fridays or over the weekend. This can have a negative impact upon the price of one's long option position, particularly as the option approaches expiration. It is also wise to avoid purchasing call options just prior to a stock going ex-dividend. Because call options do not entitle the holder to any cash dividends, the value of one's call option will decline upon the ex-dividend date. It is important that a trader be aware of the ex-dividend date prior to initiating a long call position. Additionally, since most of our indicators dictate that the timing for option entry depends upon the price activity of the underlying security, the exact time of entry is unpredictable, but when day trading we look for and select option trades whose low-risk call- or put-buying opportunities occur earlier in the trading day. These trades will give the market adequate time to develop and perform. We also avoid purchasing options after a trend has been established, particularly when day trading, as trend followers miss out on the initial expansion in call premiums following a price low and put premiums following a price high. We prefer to utilize market-timing indicators to anticipate intraday price reversals and maximize our option profits.

Most of the market-timing techniques we describe can be applied to the options themselves as well as to the underlying securities. Since the data is more readily available for the underlying securities and this information includes corrections, we suggest applying the techniques to the underlying securities as a proxy for the options. We presented a number of techniques which enable a trader to enter a market at the open of trading, at the close of trading, or at any point inbetween. If one were a day trader, obviously, the thought of entering a trade at the open and the potential of exiting any time during the trading day is most appealing since it maximizes the game clock to its absolute limit. Not only are the specific entry techniques we suggest critical, but so are the various methods we present for exiting the market other than the old day trading stand-by: on the close.

Our intent is to introduce you to an assortment of various market-timing techniques, and we encourage you to apply them to both the option—provided you have confidence in your data—as well as the underlying security, and then trade the option intraday with a profit objective in mind. Since we are suggesting one utilize these indicators on such a short time frame, gains may be small relative to the profits that can be expected over greater time frames. To account for this, we suggest that, if possible, traders have larger stakes in some option markets in order to make these trades worthwhile, particularly if the options are relatively inexpensive. Our work does not preclude a trader from extending the trade past the boundaries of that specific trading day or even trading in the underlying security itself. The "options" available to the trader are manifold.

Alignment is a practice we like to apply to our trades. *Alignment* relates to the juxtaposition of an indicator over a series of time periods. Ideally, we like to see each indicator confirm a low-risk trading opportunity on several different levels. Specifically, if the overall market environment is conducive to a trend change, we want to be there as soon as we can, meaning finding the point of inflection on the smallest time frame possible. For example, it would be appropriate for a daily, hourly, or 30-minute chart to be consistent with the direction in which a one-minute trade is about to be elicited. Typically, we start our indicator search on greater time frames to establish the overall trading environment. To day trade, we then move to smaller and smaller time periods in search of shorter-term indications which confirm these results (although we will occasionally take low-risk call-buying or put-buying indications that go against the bigger picture every now and then). Once our entry point has occurred, we then repeat the process to locate an ideal low-risk exit point. We're not implying that this process of confirmation be as stringent and complex as unlocking a safe, but we are emphasizing the fact that a confirming, overriding indicator will enhance the prospects for trading success.

In addition to alignment, we also like to confirm one indicator with another or a series of others. This is an extremely important requirement that we make for ourselves when trading. There is a distinct comfort level when numerous indicators all confirm an impending trend reversal. However, as is the case with alignment, it is important that traders not overextend themselves in terms of adding too many variables to their trading decisions, as these could conflict with one another, leaving the traders indecisive as to what the next move should be. Oftentimes, when too many indicators are applied to a market, with some conflicting with others, market readings become overloaded. Therefore, to combat the possibility of conflicting indicator readings, we suggest that traders determine which indicators establish precedence and take priority over others, and use those to overcome any uncertainty.

We are very mechanical in our approach to trading. Whether we intend to trade options or their underlying securities, we examine markets with an indicator checklist, noting which market-timing techniques are speaking for which markets. Once we obtain a general picture of the market, we can make our option trades and our security trades accordingly. The following paragraphs include some of the most important indicators we use when loading our trading shopping cart. While we will include some of the basic option strategies we would use in the event of a low-risk entry or exit, traders can substitute any other strategy they deem appropriate. This includes the strategies outlined in Chap. 2 and those which we were unable to address, but are heavily documented in other option literature, such as covered call- and covered put-writing strategies, butterfly spreads, ratio strategies, and synthetic trading.*

Option Buying Rules. We recommend before a trader purchases an option, be it a call or a put, that the market has fulfilled as many of the four option buying rules as possible. These rules are extremely important when applied to day trading.

- *Rule no. 1: Buy calls when the overall market is down; buy puts when the overall market is up.* To determine whether the overall market is up or down, we examine the advance/decline index, or a comprehensive market average such as the S&P 500 or the New York Stock Exchange Composite. When the overall market trades lower, call option premiums typically decrease. Therefore, by requiring the market index to be down for the day at the time a call is purchased, the prospects for a decline in a call's premium are enhanced. Similarly, when the overall market trades higher, put option premiums typically decrease. Therefore, by requiring the advance/decline market index to be up for the day at the time a put is purchased, the prospects for a decline in a put's premium are enhanced similarly.
- *Rule no. 2: Buy calls when the industry group is down; buy puts when the industry group is up.* Just as most stocks move in phase with the market, so too do most industry group components move together with their industry counterparts. When one stock within an industry group is down, chances are the others are down as well.

---

* See Larry McMillan's *McMillan on Options* (John Wiley & Sons 1996).

- *Rule no. 3: Buy calls when the underlying security is down; buy puts when the underlying security is up.* In order to time the purchase of calls, we look for the price of the underlying security to be down relative to the previous trading day's close, as most traders believe this implies that the down trend will continue. To make this rule more strict, we will also relate the stock's current price with its opening price level. Either comparison ensures that the market's outlook is perceived bearish by most traders. In order to time the purchase of puts, we look for the price of the underlying security to be up relative to the previous trading day's close, as most traders believe this implies that the up trend will continue. To make this rule more strict, we will also relate the stock's current price with its opening price level. Either comparison ensures that the market's outlook is perceived bullish by most traders.
- *Rule no. 4: Buy calls when the option is down; buy puts when the option is down.* The option's price, be it a call or a put, must be less than the previous day's close. As an additional requirement, it may also be less than the current day's opening price level as well. Of all rules listed, this requirement is singularly the most important.

The combination of the preceding rules removes one's emotions when trading options to make the process of option buying more mechanical and objective. Occasionally, we will make these trading rules more stringent by comparing the current trading bar's close to the current trading bar's open, as well as the current trading day's close to the prior trading day's close.

TD % F. The first indicator we rely upon when trading options is TD % F. We feel this is one of the simplest and most effective option trading indicators to use when day trading options. What we are looking for with TD % F is for a current day's call or put option to decrease to approximately no less than half of the prior trading day's value, as calculated from the previous day's close. When a call option's current price declines to 48 to 55 percent of the previous trading day's call option closing price level, we obtain a low-risk call-buying zone for the following trading day. Similarly, when a put option's current price declines to 48 to 55 percent of the previous trading day's put option closing price level, we obtain a low-risk put-buying zone for the following trading day. Our exit point is determined by our expectations for the option and the underlying market. If we are uncertain as to what the underlying security will do over the course of the day, we will use the profit-targeting low-risk exit levels that are calculated by multiplying the previous day's close by 190 and 204 percent. On the other hand, if we believe that the market will continue to move in the direction that is favorable to our option position, be it a put or a call, and can exceed 208 percent of the prior trading day's close, indicating that additional upside price movement should occur, then we may elect to maintain our position longer than intended without a profit target. In these cases, we look to the other indicators which can be applied intraday to indicate a possible price reversal and the need to exit our position, such as TD Sequential, TD Combo, and TDST. Our stop loss levels are determined by how much we paid for the options. If the options are cheap, and we have not acquired too large of a position, we will not include a stop loss level—our long option contracts act as an inherent stop. However, if the option contracts are expensive, or if our option position is large, then we will consider exiting our position if the market trades less than between 42 and 48 percent of the prior trading day's close, as additional downside price movement should occur. If one is uncertain as to whether a TD % F reading will hold, a trader could always trade a long call spread or a long put spread.

TD Dollar-Weighted Options.   We also apply TD Dollar-Weighted Options analysis to the options themselves to arrive at a measure of market sentiment. TD Dollar-Weighted Options analysis differs from, and addresses the shortcomings of, the traditional method of calculating put/call ratios, where the volume of puts is simply divided by the volume of calls. We apply this indicator on a daily basis and on an intraday basis and then coordinate our option purchases at some point during the trading day with our other indicators as well. This sentiment indicator first measures the dollar value of the nearest expiration and strike options, by multiplying the call volume by the call price and by multiplying the put volume by the put price, and then divides the put activity by the call activity. When the dollar-weighted put volume exceeds the dollar-weighted call volume, by recording a put/call ratio of 2.00 or greater on an intraday basis, or 1.25 or greater on a daily basis, then the call option becomes more attractive and a low-risk call-buying opportunity presents itself. When the dollar-weighted call volume exceeds the dollar-weighted put volume, by recording a put/call ratio of 0.50 or less on an intraday basis, or 0.75 or less on a daily basis, then the put becomes more attractive and a low-risk put-buying opportunity presents itself. These readings identify the trend of the overall market environment.

A more comprehensive view of the market's condition can be obtained by performing a more thorough put/call comparison by also using open interest. We first calculate the dollar-weighted put/open interest ratio by dividing the put volume by the put open interest, and then multiplying this ratio by the put's market price; similarly, we calculate the dollar-weighted call/open interest ratio by dividing the call volume by the call open interest, and then multiplying this ratio by the call's market price. Once these final dollar-weighted volume/open interest values are determined, the put value is divided by the call value to indicate the overall market environment. When the dollar-weighted put volume as a percentage of open interest exceeds the dollar-weighted call volume as a percentage of open interest, by recording a put/call ratio of 2.00 or greater on an intraday basis, or 1.20 or greater on a daily basis, then the call option becomes more attractive and a low-risk call-buying opportunity presents itself. When the dollar-weighted call volume as a percentage of open interest exceeds the dollar-weighted put volume as a percentage of open interest, by recording a put/call ratio of 0.50 or less on an intraday basis, or 0.80 or less on a daily basis, then the put becomes more attractive and a low-risk put-buying opportunity presents itself. These readings identify the trend of the overall market environment.

If this fraction on an intraday basis is greater than or equal to 2.00, meaning the put volume as a percentage of open interest is at least two times larger than the call volume as a percentage of open interest, then traders are more bearish than bullish, and the market should rally—this occurs for the same reasons we mentioned earlier, specifically, because traders aren't expecting the market to move higher and their selling campaigns are close to exhaustion. On the other hand, if this fraction on an intraday basis is less than or equal to 0.50, meaning the call volume as a percentage of open interest is at least two times larger than the put volume as a percentage of open interest, then traders are more bullish than bearish, and the market should decline—this occurs for the same reasons we mentioned earlier, specifically, because traders aren't expecting the market to move lower and their buying campaigns are close to exhaustion. These ratios can be reduced to 1.20 for put options and 0.80 for call options when making a dollar-weighted put/call comparison as a percentage of open interest, on a daily basis.

In either instance, a dollar-weighted put/call ratio or a dollar-weighted put/call ratio as a percentage of open interest do not provide a definitive entry point, per se. Therefore, we typically apply the indicator on a daily basis and an intraday basis and then await another daily or intraday indicator to confirm the reading, such as TD % F, TD Lines, or any of the other indicators presented throughout the book. This process is what identifies a specific entry point for our option purchase. With TD Dollar-Weighted Options, our exit point is usually obtained when a short-term, intraday indicator reading in the opposite direction is recorded, usually TD Sequential, TD Combo, and TDST. Our stop loss level is either nothing at all in cases where the options are cheap or we don't have a large position, or simply a dollar loss in cases where the options are expensive or we have a large position. Long spread positions can also be taken in the event of market uncertainty to reduce the cost of the option debit.

TD Sequential and TD Combo.   Trading with TD Sequential and TD Combo on an underlying security provides us with much trading versatility and freedom. Throughout the trading day, a large number of TD Sequential and TD Combo trades surface across various time frames, enabling a trader to select from numerous possibilities. Because there are so many trading opportunities, we limit our low-risk trading choices to a small set of time frames (such as 1-, 5-, 10-, 15-,

30-, and 60-minute charts) to ensure that we are trading responsibly, not just actively. We can trade based upon a daily low-risk trading opportunity, and then time our entry intraday; or we can simply trade intraday based upon any of our preferred time periods. Whether we decide to trade merely a completed Setup series or a completed Countdown series depends upon the indicator's interaction with other indicators, such as TDST lines and TD REI with TD POQ. In either case, a low-risk put-buying opportunity would occur following the completion of a sell Countdown phase, and a subsequent entry indication if we were trading conservatively, for TD Combo and for either of the two possible TD Sequential settings; and a low-risk call-buying opportunity would occur following the completion of a buy Countdown phase, and a subsequent entry indication if we were trading conservatively, for TD Combo and for either of the two possible TD Sequential settings. If we were trading more aggressively, we could bypass the entry techniques and trade the options based simply upon the completion of the Countdown phase.

A similar trading situation occurs for completed Setups, particularly when a Setup is unable to exceed the previous TDST in the opposite direction, indicating the market may not run to the completion of the Countdown phase. A low-risk put-buying opportunity would occur following the completion of a sell Setup phase and a low-risk call-buying opportunity would occur following the completion of a buy Setup phase, provided each Setup fails to exceed the prior TDST line in the opposite direction. Because completed Setups and Countdowns can be quite powerful indicators, we would only trade low-risk trading opportunities with call and put options to ensure that our maximum gains are unlimited. We wouldn't trade these readings with spread orders because they would limit our gains. When trading intraday, our exit point is obtained once a profit objective is reached or when a Setup or a Countdown has been, or is just about to be, completed on either the same or a different time frame. Our decision depends on our trading bias at that time. Our stop loss during these day trading sessions are, again, nothing in cases where our options are cheap or we have a small option position, and usually just a dollar loss if the options are expensive or our position is large.

The greater the time frame in which a low-risk TD Sequential or TD Combo Countdown buying (call-buying) or selling (put-buying) indication occurs for the underlying security, the greater the likelihood we will extend the holding period of our trade. As a rule of thumb, any completed low-risk TD Sequential Countdown or TD Combo Countdown indication occurring on a 30-minute basis or greater suggests that price will sustain an extended price reversal, over a number of price bars. Because these larger time frame indications typically last longer than shorter-term indications, with any longer-term intraday trade that we initiate, we will always evaluate our position prior to the close to determine whether we feel the market will continue its price movement prior to a price reversal, in which case we would hold our option position for at least one additional trading day.

Depending upon the situation, we may also trade options using any of the four indicators which can be used to initiate entry into a trade following a completed Countdown phase, specifically TD Open, TD Trap, TD CLOP, TD CLOPWIN (see Chap. 6). In these cases, we would use the indicators on a daily price chart and time our option purchases once the indicator rules are fulfilled. Unlike many of the other indicators, option entry for these four market-timing techniques can only occur intraday. We would look to buy calls when the market fulfilled the requirements for a low-risk buy opportunity and to buy puts when the market fulfilled the requirements for a low-risk sell opportunity. Our exit point is obtained when our profit objective is reached or when an indicator reading in the opposite direction has occurred. Our stop loss during these day trading sessions are nothing in cases where our options are cheap or we have a small option position, and usually just a dollar loss if the options are expensive or our position is large.

TDST, TD Lines, TD Retracements.   Each of these three indicators identify breakout levels for the underlying security that can be traded as a trend-following technique or faded in cases where the levels are either disqualified (in the case of TD Lines and TD Retracements) or were not held on a closing basis, an opening basis, and then trade at least one tick beyond that level. We typically utilize these indicators on a daily chart and use their daily levels as low-risk intraday entry points, but they can be applied to intraday charts with effectiveness. As the time frame to which these indicators apply becomes smaller and smaller, we pay more and more attention to the qualified breakouts, as opposed to the disqualified breakouts (which are more important on a daily scale). If the market exceeds a buy TDST, a qualified TD Supply Line, or a qualified TD Retracement level upside, on a closing basis, the next bar's opening price, and then trades at least one tick higher than the opening, then a low-risk call-buying opportunity is presented—although, we personally don't often participate in these trend-following moves. If the market exceeds a sell TDST, a qualified TD Demand Line, or a qualified TD Retracement level downside, on a closing basis, the next bar's opening price, and then trades at least one tick lower than the opening, then a low-risk put-buying opportunity is presented—again, we personally don't participate in these trend-following moves very often.

If the market holds a buy TDST on a closing basis as well as the following trading bar's opening, or exceeds a disqualified TD Supply Line or TD Retracement level upside (meaning none of the four qualifiers are met), then a low-risk put-buying opportunity is presented—on a daily chart, these are the type of option buying indications we are seeking. If the market holds a sell TDST on a closing basis as well as on the following trading bar's opening, or exceeds a disqualified TD Demand Line or TD Retracement level downside (meaning none of the four qualifiers are met), then a low-risk call-buying opportunity is presented—again, on a daily chart, these are the type of option buying indications we are seeking. A trader could also enact a long spread to reduce the debit if one were so inclined, but that is up to the discretion of the individual. Because there is no definitive exit point aside from the closing price (unless other indicators insinuate that it would be desirable to extend the holding period of the option beyond the current day's close), we utilize other indicators, including TD Sequential and TD Combo, to confirm a low-risk exiting point. Yet again, the stop loss level is arbitrary, depending upon the investor. For us, our stop loss during these day trading sessions is nonexistent in cases where our options are not expensive or we have small positions, or is a dollar-stop if the options are costly or our position is large.

TD Line Gap and TD Line Gap REBO.   These two indicators work much like typical TD Lines, only without the necessity of qualifiers. TD Line Gap and TD Line Gap REBO are indicators that construct TD Lines from a TD Point to a subsequent price gap or price lap. An upward-sloping TD Line Gap line connects the most recent TD Point Low to the low of the most recent price gap or price lap upside; conversely, a downward-sloping TD Line Gap line connects the most recent TD Point High to the high of the most recent price gap or price lap downside. Once a TD Line Gap upside breakout occurs above a downward-sloping line, a low-risk call-buying opportunity is presented. The only qualifier states that the current price bar's opening price must open in the direction of the breakout, meaning it must be greater than the previous price bar's close. Conversely, once a TD Line Gap downside breakout occurs below an upward-sloping line, a low-risk put-buying opportunity is presented. The only qualifier states that the current price bar's opening price must open in the direction of the breakout, meaning it must be less than the previous price bar's close.

TD Line Gap REBO takes things a step further to confirm TD Line Gap breakouts. TD REBO works by taking the price range of the prior trading day and multiplying it by a percentage—such as 38.2 percent—this value is then added to and subtracted from the current day's opening price. In the case of an upside breakout indicating a low-risk call-buying opportunity, price must breakout above both the downward-sloping TD Line Gap line as well as the upper TD REBO level. The low-risk, trend-following entry point would occur at the higher of the two levels. Additionally, traders could also choose to enter at both price levels, purchasing a portion of their call positions at the first breakout level and the balance of the call position at the second breakout level.

We typically use TD Line Gap and TD Line Gap REBO on a daily basis. The most obvious reason is that intraday charts do not leave many price gaps. Unless a market is illiquid, where the spread between the bids and offers is wide, intraday price activity moves consistently without many price holes. They can be applied intraday on a larger scale, but these instances are typically used with any resulting price laps as opposed to price gaps. Therefore, we use the daily momentum levels of these two indicators as our intraday entry points. For both of these indicators, our exit point occurs when our profit objective is attained or when we receive a conflicting reading from a different indicator. If our position is large, our stop loss is placed at a level that corresponds with the most we would care to lose on the trade.

TD REI and TD POQ.   We utilize TD REI and TD POQ together and predominantly on a daily basis or a longer-term intraday basis in the underlying security. If the TD REI records an extreme oversold reading, meaning the TD REI has resided below –45 on the TD REI oscillator for a period of six or more trading bars, then price should continue to decline; a trend follower could use this opportunity to purchase put options. Similarly, if the TD REI records an extreme overbought reading, meaning the TD REI has resided above 45 on the TD REI oscillator for a period of six or more trading bars, then price should continue to advance; a trend follower could use this opportunity to purchase call options. If the TD REI records a mild oversold reading, meaning the TD REI has resided below –45 on the TD REI oscillator for a period of five or fewer trading bars, then TD POQ can be applied. If in the underlying security, before an overbought reading is registered, the market records an up close that is followed by an opening price that is less than the up close bar's high, and then trades at least one tick higher, then a low-risk trend-following call-buying opportunity is presented at the breakout price above the high. If the open is above the up close day's high, but not above the high two price bars ago, and the close is above the open, then a weaker, but nevertheless low-risk, call-buying entry is indicated upon the close. If the TD REI records a mild overbought reading, meaning the TD REI has resided above 45 on the TD REI oscillator for a period of 5 or fewer trading bars, then TD POQ can be applied. If in the underlying security, before an oversold reading is registered, the market records a down close that is followed by an opening price that is greater than the down close bar's low, and then trades at least one tick lower, then a low-risk trend-following put-buying opportunity is presented at the breakout price below the low. If the open is below the down close day's low, but not below the low two price bars earlier, and the close is below the open, then a weaker, but nevertheless low-risk, put-buying entry is indicated upon the close.

We prefer to day trade disqualified TD REI and TD POQ oscillator readings, although both qualified and disqualified indications can be equally powerful. The only problem exists with the fact that a qualified TD REI indication is a trend-following trade and therefore the option's premium will already reflect some of the market's psychology before one even enters the trade. For a disqualified TD REI and TD POQ indicator reading following a current mild oversold reading and an up close, TD POQ requires that the open of the price bar of the underlying security after the up close be above both of the two previous price bar highs in order to warrant a put-buying opportunity. In these instances, the opening price has been exaggerated upside and the market will typically decline, most often filling in downside any price gaps. For a disqualified TD REI and TD POQ indicator reading following a current mild overbought reading and a down close, TD POQ requires that the open of the price bar of the underlying security after the down close be below both of the two previous price bar lows in order to warrant a call-buying opportunity. In these instances, the opening price has been exaggerated downside and the market will typically advance, most often filling in any upside price gaps. These trades can be entered intraday following the current bar's opening price which indicates whether the trade will be disqualified and require a trader to fade the indicator or whether the trade will be qualified and require that the trader follow the trend of the market.

Our exit point for qualified or disqualified, extreme or mild readings is usually obtained when a short-term, intraday indicator reading in the opposite direction is recorded, usually TD Sequential, TD Combo, and TDST. You can see the importance of indicator alignment with one another. Our stop loss level is either nothing at all in cases where the options are cheap or we don't have a large position, or simply a dollar loss in cases where the options are expensive or we have a large position. Long spread positions, similar to those mentioned in Chap. 2, can also be taken in the event of market uncertainty to reduce the cost of the option debit. In addition, option positions can be extended beyond the current trading day if other indicators support that action.

TD Fib Range, TD Exit One, TD REBO Reverse, TD Camouflage. Each of these four indicators are applied to daily price charts or long-term intraday charts of the underlying asset to arrive at a trading outlook for the option. Qualifiers can be introduced to each market-timing technique to enhance its results, but for the sake of simplicity, we'll just present the indicator in its most basic form. TD Fib Range states that daily price range movements of 1.618 times the previous trading day's true price range or 1.618 times the average of the previous three days' true price range, when added to or subtracted from the previous trading day's close, oftentimes corresponds with market exhaustion. When the market closes outside these points of exhaustion, an ideal low-risk call-buying opportunity in the case of a price decline below the lower TD Fib level, or an ideal low-risk put-buying opportunity in the case of a price advance above the upper TD Fib level, is presented at the close of the price bar or the following price bar's open. We prefer to use this indicator together with TD % F and TD Dollar-Weighted Options, as they work well in conjunction with one another.

In the case of a TD Exit One low-risk call-buying opportunity, the market must first record three consecutive down close days, and then the current day's open must be greater than the close one day ago and the current day's low must trade less than the close one day ago. In addition, the price range one day ago must be greater than the true price range two days ago. The low-risk call-buying opportunity occurs one tick less than the close one day ago, or at the low one day ago, depending upon whether TD Differential says the underlying market should move lower or not: if the difference between the close one day ago and the low one day ago is greater than the difference between the close two days ago and the low two days ago, then the low-risk call-buying level is one tick below the previous day's close; and if the difference between the close one day ago and the low one day ago is less than the difference between the close two days ago and the low two days ago, then the low-risk call-buying level is one tick below the previous day's low. If price should rally after trading one tick below the prior day's close, then we will purchase our call option position at that point; however, if price should rally after trading to the prior day's low, then we will purchase a portion of our intended call position at the prior day's close and the balance at the prior day's low. The low-risk put-buying opportunity occurs one tick greater than the close one day ago, or at the high one day ago, depending upon whether TD Differential says the underlying market should move higher or not: if the difference between the close one day ago and the high one day ago is greater than the difference between the close two days ago and the high two days ago, then the low-risk put-buying level is one tick above the previous day's close; and if the difference between the close one day ago and the high one day ago is less than the difference between the close two days ago and the high two days ago, then the low-risk put-buying level is one tick above the previous day's high. If price should decline after trading one tick above the prior day's close, then we will purchase our put option position at that point; however, if price should decline after trading to the prior day's high, then we will purchase a portion of our intended call position at the prior day's close and the balance at the prior day's high.

TD REBO is a momentum indicator that measures the previous trading day's true price range, multiplies this value by either 38.2 or 61.8 percent (or any other percentage with a reliable history of effectiveness) and then either adds this value to or subtracts it from the current day's opening price to establish a low-risk option entry. If the underlying asset's price trades above the upper TD REBO level, then a low-risk (trend-following) call-buying opportunity exists at that price level; if the underlying asset's price trades below the lower TD REBO level, then a low-risk (trend-following) put-buying opportunity presents itself. TD REBO Reverse, on the other hand, is trend anticipatory. In the case of a low-risk call-buying entry, if the current day's open is above the previous three days' closes and the entry price is above the prior three days' highs, then buying at a price level which is calculated by multiplying the greater of the two previous trading days' true ranges by a percentage—such as 61.8 or 38.2 percent—and adding that value to the current day's open would be too aggressive, and rather than purchase a call upon the TD Reverse REBO breakout, we would purchase a call. In other words, if the current bar opens greater than the close of each of the three prior days, and the entry price is greater than the high of each of the three prior days, then one would fade the perceived REBO upside breakout. Conversely, in the case of a low-risk put-buying entry, if the current day's open is below the previous three days' closes and the entry price is below the prior three days' lows, then buying at a price level which is calculated by multiplying the greater of the two previous trading days' true ranges by a percentage—such as 61.8 or 38.2 percent—and subtracting that value from the current day's open would be too aggressive, and rather than buying a put upon the TD Reverse REBO breakout, we would purchase a call. In other words, if the current bar opens less than the close of each of the three prior days, and the entry price is less than the low of each of the three prior days, then one would fade the perceived REBO downside breakout.

TD Camouflage is used on larger time frames and identifies patterns that are indicative of a possible market reversal. TD Camouflage requires that, for a call-buying opportunity at a suspected market low, the current day's low must be less than the previous day's low and the current day's close must be less than the previous day's close, but at the same time the current day's close must be greater than the current day's open. In this scenario, we would look to execute a small portion of our low-risk call-buying position at the close of the pattern day and the balance at the opening of the following day. Conversely, for a put-buying opportunity at a suspected market high, the current day's high must be greater than the previous day's high and the current day's close must be greater than the previous day's close, but at the same time the current day's close must be less than the current day's open. In this scenario, we would execute a small portion of our low-risk put-buying position at the close of that day and would purchase the balance on the next day's open. In each instance, the critical price relationship and comparison exists between the current bar's open and close, whereas most traders concentrate upon the less-important and -relevant relationship between consecutive closes.

Our primary trading style with TD Fib Range, TD Exit One, TD REBO Reverse, and TD Camouflage is to simply buy the call or put option outright upon reaching these price levels and objectives. However, if these indicators conflict with the overall market picture, we will consider trading a long option spread so we do not have to put up as much money and can still participate in the market's move. Our exit points are obtained once a profit target is reached or, if one were so inclined, once an intraday indicator reading in the opposite direction is recorded. Our stop loss levels are either nothing at all in cases where the options are cheap or we don't have a large position, or simply a dollar loss in cases where the options are expensive or we have a large position.

TD Range Projection.   We utilize TD Range Projection to approximate the following day's price range. While this indicator can also be used intraday, we prefer a broader time frame, such as hourly charts, and prefer to use this indicator to project daily ranges. To arrive at TD Range Projections, three mathematical formulas are applied depending upon the current day's relationship between the close and the open. While we can use TD Range Projections to make trading decisions outright, it is primarily used to confirm other indicators and form opinions as to the probable direction and price activity of a particular market.

How one trades TD Range Projections is determined by the opening price relative to the projected high and low. If the market opens within the projected high and the projected low, a trader can expect resistance at the projected high and support at the projected low. In this instance, when price exceeded the projected high to the upside, a low-risk put-buying opportunity occurs; conversely, when price exceeded the projected low to the downside, a low-risk call-buying opportunity occurs. If the market opens outside the projected range, meaning it opens above the projected high or below the projected low, it qualifies as a possible price breakout, provided price follows through by at least one price tick in the direction of the breakout. In this instance, an option trader can trade in the direction of the trend breakout, by buying calls upon opening above projected high breakout, or by buying puts upon a downside projected low breakout. However, this practice would be described as trend-following and the option premiums would more than likely have already been affected. In addition, if the opening price exceeds the projected high to the upside, then this level would now provide support and should be held on a closing basis; similarly, if the opening price exceeds the projected low to the downside, then this level would now provide resistance and should be held on a closing basis. When trading with TD Range Projections, our exit points are obtained once we are satisfied with our profits or once an intraday indicator reading in the opposite direction is recorded; our stop loss levels are either nothing at all or a dollar loss, depending upon the size and the value of our position.

GAME PLAN SUMMARY

In each trading example highlighted in the preceding section, once we have utilized at least one of the prior 20 or so indicators to enter into a trade, we are on the lookout for a low-risk intraday signal in the opposite direction to indicate that we should exit the trade. The best indicators that do so intraday are TD Sequential, TD Combo, and TD Setup Trend, all of which can be applied effectively anywhere from daily charts to one-minute charts; and TD Lines and TD Relative Retracements, where qualified intraday breakouts are preferred over disqualified intraday breakouts. This doesn't mean the other indicators cannot be applied intraday, especially on larger time frames, such as hourly charts, but they are not tailored to identify the types of price momentum swings that the former five indicators do. Unless we receive a long-term indicator informing us not to, and unless we have not already done so, we typically exit our day trades prior to 15 to 30 minutes before the close of that trading day, since most of the day trading public and floor traders tend to exit their positions around that time, which can cause an unexpected adverse price swing in the market. However, keep in mind that we do not require that one must exit one's position that trading day, as most of the indicators presented—especially when applied to daily charts—are effective for more than simply one price bar, or day, of activity.

Therefore, to summarize, what we are looking for in selecting an ideal trading candidate is an option that is liquid, is close to expiration, and trading at-the-money or slightly in-the-money. We will also consider trading options that have a low total cost in order to have a lower level of risk. Additionally, option trades resulting from low-risk entry indications that have sufficient time to develop, are in alignment over several different time periods, and are synchronized with other indicator readings increase the likelihood of success.

OTHER OPTION TRADING TIPS

We have presented a series of indicators designed to make a trader's job of identifying market turning points simpler. Not all may suit your trading needs and some may require adaptation before their implementation. We encourage you to research and establish a level of trading comfort with at least a few of these techniques. Make certain you understand their intricacies and the nuances associated with each. Apply the methods to the market on paper before trading with your own funds. Try to integrate the indicators into your own trading regimen. Once completely understood, follow the plan religiously and detach your emotions from any decision making. Once trading has begun, establish intervals of trading evaluation and only then begin to introduce any enhancements and revisions to your methodology. Once again, the testing phase should be extensive before any deployment of assets. Trading survival is crucial and traders must avoid any interference which may jeopardize or place into risk a substantial portion of their capital at any one time.

For those who trade as a hobby as opposed to a full-time profession, we recommend that one shy away from using these indicators on an *intraday* basis. To be a successful day trader, one must devote an extraordinary amount of time and effort to following the markets, evaluating each of several different market situations as they unfold. Unfortunately, day trade options or the underlying security with these indicators is just not for everyone. However, this does not preclude or prevent one from utilizing these market-timing techniques altogether, it simply means one must alter one's time horizon. In fact, for those who can't afford to day trade for one reason or another, we encourage you to apply these indicators to daily price charts to see how they can enhance your investing abilities over the following days, weeks, or even months. The beauty of these indicators is that they are versatile and are not limited strictly to one time frame—they can be applied on both a daily and an intraday basis, each with consistent and effective results. If one does not wish to take on the larger risks inherent in, or the greater time commitments required for, day trading, one can become a longer-term position trader, or an investor, and reduce each of these items considerably. These indicators can provide the framework, the structure, and the discipline to analyze and trade the markets; it's just up to you to decide what you will choose to do with them.

We realize that trading options is a game of chance and statistics. By including various proprietary indicators, as well as our market-timing experience and insight in this book, our goal has been to tilt the option playing field in your direction rather than in favor of the option writers. We attempt to provide you with a perspective on the overall market environment and from there to make certain that you are anticipating trend reversals properly. Our entire concept is to buy weakness and to sell strength, thereby removing the emotional premium attached to so many trend-following trades. We are not implying that one should buy (buy calls) whenever the market is down or sell (buy puts) whenever the market is up, regardless of the reasons the markets have perpetuated these moves, we are simply saying that in these environments one should look for low-risk opportunities in which to initiate these contratrend positions. The common denominator of most all of our market-timing approaches to option trading is a theme of price exhaustion or antitrend analysis. Each approach is designed to be purely objective and mechanized. It has always been our belief that our research work is an unfinished project. We do not want to force our settings and qualifiers for the various indicators upon any user, rather we encourage others to experiment and perfect our techniques. This is not to imply that the work is unfinished or indecisive, by any means, but we are open-minded to the possibility that you may be able to contribute to the enhancement of these indicators. If we had presented this information as systems, then the impression would be that they are turnkey and complete and not subject to any chance of improvement. This is not the case. We have found and continue to be firm believers that results derived from creativity and development are unpredictable and oftentimes very rewarding. Unless an approach is near perfect, there is always a need to perform additional research to improve it. So, our invitation is extended to you to work with the concepts we provide, paper trade them, put them into effect, and further research and upgrade these techniques. In time, doing so should greatly improve one's trading success.

EXPANDING YOUR HORIZONS

Having read this book, a reader may conclude that to arrive at a number of option trading possibilities many of the indicators must first be applied to the underlying security. One could ask, "Well, why can't I simply day trade the underlying security itself?" Well, the truth is, you can. The majority of these indicators were created prior to the advent of the options market to predict price movement in different securities markets. It was only once standardized, publicly traded options came into existence and became popular that we realized these indicators which applied to the securities markets could be used as well to initiate positions in a derivative securities market such as options. In other words, for those indicators that are not directly applicable to options trading, one can use the results obtained from applying the indicators to the underlying security. The primary reason we are recommending trading options based upon our indicators is because they provide a structure which allows traders to limit their risk, keep their rewards unlimited, and allow them to control more size for less money. However, this does not mean traders should necessarily trade options exclusively. If traders feel more comfortable day trading the underlying asset, then they should by all means do so.

Likewise, a trader is not restricted to day trading when applying many of these indicators. We appreciate the fact that not all of our readers are either prepared or capable of enduring the emotional and physical demands of day trading. Additionally, the time commitments for day trading either options or the underlying securities are great. Therefore, for those of you who are not ideal candidates for short-term day trading, we suggest applying these indicators in the context of position trading. Because all of our indicators are dynamic and apply equally well to all markets, regardless of the time frame in which they are utilized, traders can expand their time horizons and become position traders in either options or securities, as opposed to simply day traders of options or securities. Because these indicators are so versatile, traders can customize the work to meet their trading needs.

Also, there is nothing in our work that says one can't find a balance between day trading and position trading. What may begin as a day trading position can, and oftentimes will, evolve into a longer-term position—this added dimension will increase one's trading opportunities and profits dramatically. By trading rigidly, traders limit their rewards—always. Traders must be willing to experiment with and rationalize trading positions. This practice will make a successful trader.

For those of you new to trading, either options or securities, the path you choose is up to you. However, the questions you must consider are many and can have a drastic impact on your livelihood. If you feel unsure about the trading style you should take, our suggestion is that you start on a longer-term time frame, analyzing daily charts and applying the indicators to positions over a period of days or even weeks, and consider trading small. Once a level of comfort in the options and/or securities markets is attained, you can gradually increase your participation and your exposure. Taking small losses and letting profits run is much easier to manage, both financially and emotionally, than taking large losses and then trying to recover. Keep in mind that the name of the trading game is to live to see the next day of trading. In the investment business, there is no life after financial death.

The important fact is that readers understand we are not providing them with a trading prescription, rather we are offering a new way of analyzing and trading existing markets. Hopefully, they will find the most ideal means of implementing this work into their trading arsenals in a way that is harmonious with their trading styles.

Conclusion

FOR SO MANY YEARS the stock market has defied the laws of gravity. Any and all pullbacks were perceived correctly by investors as opportunities to buy. From the corner grocer to the teachers at school, everyone was participating in this meteoric market rise. Almost each and every stock market investor, regardless of gender or age was on an unprecedented historic financial roll, making money hand over fist in the process. Mutual funds, bursting with cash inflows at a record pace, were the vehicle of choice for most preoccupied investors; whereas independent-minded investor entrepreneurs challenged themselves to the task of investing their own money. The testimony to their successes is chronicled each and every day in the financial pages of the press.

Needless to say, a secular tide into the stock market of record proportions has been afoot and has made even the most reckless, unsuitable, and ill-timed investment decisions appear near genius. By definition, as the market records all-time highs, no previous buyer will have incurred a loss. The question posed by this audience of investors has not been how much longer this perpendicular market rise would perpetuate itself, rather it has been how long it would take the market to exceed each 1000-point threshold barrier. Throughout this unprecedented move, the only concerns expressed were those of veterans of past bear markets. However, it became clear that the barometers and the benchmarks these professionals applied successfully to markets past had no bearing, application, or relevance to this record-breaking stampede. Fortunately, for the sake of the public's portfolios, the concerns and admonitions of these pros by and large fell upon deaf ears. Investing was never intended to be this lopsided and easy!

In hindsight, it appears to have been preordained and inevitable that many investors would perceive the evolution from investor to trader as a natural progression, requiring no additional abilities or experience, only more time and access to information. The first handful of defectors from the ranks of investors were described by their compatriots as pioneers. It was only a matter of time before other investors exhibited similar yearnings to become traders. The resulting success and wealth that investors have enjoyed has served to foster cravings to acquire more quickly even more success and wealth. The pattern is predictable and, unless properly prepared, a trader is doomed.

As Bob Dylan had groaned prophetically so many years ago, "the times, they are a changin'." Indeed, not only have the dynamics of the market changed but so too have the composition, mood, and outlook of its constituents. All the major obstacles of the past which precluded broad, active public participation in trading, such as high commissions and research costs, have been dismantled or removed. The supply of research information, news, and data has been made available on a timely basis to large and small investors alike. We have observed that a fledgling trader's market behavior is initially subdued and controllable. However, the distinct risk to a trader exists that the lure and the expectations of large and immediate profits become irresistible. Unless a trader is properly prepared to deal with these temptations, failure is a foregone conclusion.

The accounts of a day trader who sits in front of a quote machine barking trading instructions to a broker and making obnoxious amounts of money have been embellished over time to include exorbitant cash payments for vacation villas, private jets, yachts, and other trappings of the rich and famous. While these and similar outrageous stories permeate this industry and infiltrate an investor's psyche, no one has produced any documentation describing the process whereby traders can educate themselves to become such enviable market trading mavens. The mystique and reverence attached to these few legendary trading deities borders on a mania and hysteria which surpass those associated with modern-day cults. Such individuals do exist but their population is limited to but a rare few. Within the investment community, this frenzy conjures up fantasies more elaborate and personal than those enjoyed by children awaiting Christmas morning.

However, traders are human and are held victim by their emotions—this message is delivered every day by the ultimate judge, the marketplace. Don't you think that if all traders were destined to be successful, trading would be the profession of choice? Despite the perceptions you may acquire from exaggerated media accounts, movies, or acquaintances, the potential rewards associated with trading are just too great for this exercise to be so easy. In life, as in physics, there is a direct correlation between energy exerted and productivity. Successful trading not only requires the intelligence and the knowledge to select suitable trading candidates, but it also requires the emotional wherewithal to act and react prudently and reasonably, independent of the activities of other traders. An element of street sense is a nonquantifiable but essential quality, which often distinguishes a mediocre trader from a great trader.

To graduate from an investor to a day trader is a feat accomplished by very few. It's easy to construct a profile of a successful trader, detailing the trader's skills and attributes, but just as it is difficult to reproduce a recipe for grandma's famous apple pie, the formula for creating the ideal trader is likewise vague, inexact, and nondescript. Granted, it is virtually impossible to transform an investor into a trader by following a prescription in a book, but there are certain prerequisites which are obvious and essential and can be communicated.

One way to accelerate a trader's education is to provide a series of objective techniques which should facilitate the trading process. That is our role and in order to fulfill it we expanded the original scope of our book to include numerous market-timing indicators. The best way for a trader to accomplish the implementation of these methods is to avoid as much external interference as possible. This includes prudent and sound money management principles. Above all, traders should avoid at all costs relying upon their trading successes to support their lifestyles. Adherence to such a practice invites tendencies and excuses to wander and deviate from one's trading game plan. Other admonitions include the establishment of a trading structure, the refusal to be influenced by others, and the practice of trading discipline. We also suggest that a trader establish a psychological balance between the challenge of trading and winning, and the necessities of earning a comfortable living.

If you have read this book to this point, you are likely the type of individual who possesses the mental discipline, interest, and wherewithal to trade options successfully. We must admit that our first few perusals of books on option trading were bland, dry, and unappealing episodes. We recall using a magic marker to highlight those areas of text which we believed to be the most important or were unclear and, lo and behold, upon the conclusion of the book we realized that we had unknowingly painted the entire book yellow. This was certainly a backhanded testimony to our lack of understanding and utter confusion. Hopefully, by providing an option trading process from the perspective of the option buyer, we have piqued your interest in the subject matter of day trading options and, at the same time, kept the discussion sufficiently simple and educational.

To simply declare oneself ready to pursue the profession of day trading is the easy part. To be disciplined and control one's emotions and to install the necessary money management skills are essential components of success and are difficult to acquire. To install trading indicators and to apply and follow them objectively is likewise difficult. Day trading stocks or futures is no simple task, but to day trade options on these securities poses other greater risks since these instruments are more leveraged and can expire. Timing is the key to success, as is the preservation of capital. We believe success in trading options is a result of timely anticipation of trend reversals. Prior to the reversal of a trend, if a trader wanted to position him-

or herself against the prevailing trend, option premiums would be low since trading interest is concerned with the outstanding market trend. That is the ideal time to evaluate trading opportunities. We have presented a series of indicators we believe to be helpful in identifying pending trend reversals. Although no person or market model is infallible, we believe following an objective game plan or strategy gives a trader a tremendous edge, as well as reduces the strain he or she would likely feel blindly trading without a market-timing compass.

Appendix

OPTION CODES

Shown on the next page are the codes for the various expiration months and strike prices. While it is not essential that one memorize or even consider these codes in order to trade options, they are helpful to know. Among other uses, these codes are used by brokers to place orders or write up order tickets and are listed on client trading statements. Now, many readers may be wondering what all of these letters and numbers mean exactly. These codes for the different expiration months and strike prices are combined to create a technical option reference definition. When written out, the option code is as follows: underlying asset, expiration month code, and then strike price code. For example, the code IBM G K would refer to an IBM July 55 Call, 155 Call, 255 Call, or 355 Call, depending upon where the market price for IBM stock is currently trading; similarly, the code MSFT O P would refer to a Microsoft March 80 Put, 180 Put, 280 Put, or 380 Put, depending upon where the market price for Microsoft is currently trading. Please note that the strike price codes presented are not applicable for all options, such as currency options and DJX options, so contact your broker to see which options are excluded.

IS OPTIONS TRADING RIGHT FOR YOU?

As we mentioned earlier, day trading options, or even position trading options for that matter, involve risk and are not suitable for every investor. What determines suitability, you ask? Among other things, a trader's required capital commitment and financial goals and needs. The CBOE offers a document entitled, "Characteristics and Risks of Standardized Options," that provides a prospective option trader with the important components of option trading; this risk disclosure document must be provided to a potential option trader when opening an option trading account and prior to buying or selling an option. Speaking with a registered broker will let you know if option trading is right for you. For further information or questions on option trading, please contact any of the exchanges where option contracts are listed and traded.

Expiration Month Codes

	Jan	Feb	Mar	Apr	May	Jun	Jul	Aug	Sep	Oct	Nov	Dec
Calls	A	B	C	D	E	F	G	H	I	J	K	L
Puts	M	N	O	P	Q	R	S	T	U	V	W	X

Strike Price Codes

Key	A	B	C	D	E	F	G	H	I	J	K	L	M	N	O	P	Q	R	S	T	U	V	W	X	Y	Z
Strike Prices	5	10	15	20	25	30	35	40	45	50	55	60	65	70	75	80	85	90	95	100	7½	12½	17½	22½	27½	32½
	105	110	115	120	125	130	135	140	145	150	155	160	165	170	175	180	185	190	195	200	37½	42½	47½	52½	57½	62½
	205	210	215	220	225	230	235	240	245	250	255	260	265	270	275	280	285	290	295	300	67½	72½	77½	82½	87½	92½
	305	310	315	320	325	330	335	340	345	350	355	360	365	370	375	380	385	390	395	400	97½	102½	107½	112½	117½	122½

344

The Chicago Board of Options Exchange (CBOE)
400 S. LaSalle Street
Chicago, IL 60605
www.cboe.com
1-800-OPTIONS
(1-800-678-4667)

The American Stock Exchange (AMEX)
86 Trinity Place
New York, NY 10006-1881
www.amex.com
1-800-THE-AMEX
(1-800-843-2639)

Pacific Stock Exchange
301 Pine Street
San Francisco, CA 94104
www.pacificex.com
1-800-825-5773

Philadelphia Stock Exchange (PHLX)
1900 Market Street
Philadelphia, PA 19103-3584
www.phlx.com
1-800-THE-PHLX
(1-800-843-7459)

OPTION DATA VENDORS

CQG 1-800-525-7082
Commodity Systems 1-800-274-4727
Data Transmission (DTN) 1-800-475-4755
Deltasoft 800-250-7866
Genesis Financial Data 1-800-808-3282
MJK 408-456-5000
Moore Research 541-484-1774
TBSP 1-888-827-7462
Telescan 1-800-324-8246

OPTION ANALYSIS SOFTWARE

Option Oracle 1-800-250-7866
Option Station 1-800-328-1312
Option Vue 1-800-733-6610

BIBLIOGRAPHY

DeMark, Thomas. *New Science of Technical Analysis.* New York: John Wiley & Sons, 1994.

DeMark, Thomas. *New Market Timing Techniques.* New York: John Wiley & Sons, 1997.

McMillan, Larry. *McMillan on Options.* New York: John Wiley & Sons, 1996.

McMillan, Larry. *Options as a Strategic Investment.* Englewood Cliffs, N.J.: Prentice Hall, 1992.

RECOMMENDED READING

Caplan, David. *The New Options Advantage: Gaining a Trading Edge over the Markets.* Probus Publishing Co. 1996. ISBN 1557388636.

Fontanills, George. *The Options Course.* John Wiley & Sons. 1998. ISBN 0471249505.

Frost, Ron. *Options on Futures.* Probus Publishing Co. 1995. ISBN 1557385165.

Natenberg, Sheldon. *Option Volatility and Pricing.* Probus Publishing Co. 1994. ISBN 155738486.

Schaeffer, Bernie. *The Option Advisor.* John Wiley & Sons. 1997. ISBN 0471185396.

Smith, Courtney. *Option Strategies.* John Wiley & Sons. 1996. ISBN 047111555.

Trester, Ken. *The Complete Option Player.* Bookworld Press. 1997. ISBN 0960491422.

Special Demo Disk Offer

FREE TD INDICATORS DEMO DISKETTE TO READERS OF THIS BOOK
You can receive a free copy of this informative software for Windows end-of-day, Window on Wall Street, DTN TradeStation/SuperCharts, Bloomberg, Dow Jones, and Bridge TradeStation, or TradeStation/SuperCharts by calling 714-731-3384 or by sending your name and address to

TD Indicators c/o Investment Software
1742 Amherst Road
Tustin, California 92780
or by e-mailing iss-dandavis@att.net or duanedavis@att.net,
or by visiting our Web site, www.marketsadvisory.com

DeMark Indicator Studies are now available on the following networks:

Aspen Research
800-359-1121
970-945-2921

Bloomberg
828-628-7879
714-731-3384
e-mail: duanedavis@att.net or iss-dandavis@att.net

Bridge
1-800-325-3282
714-731-3384
e-mail: duanedavis@att.net or iss-dandavis@att.net

Bridge/Dow Jones TradeStation
828-628-4222
714-731-3384
e-mail: duanedavis@att.net or iss-dandavis@att.net

CQG
800-525-7082

Deltasoft
800-250-7866
e-mail: dsoft@west.net

DTN
800-475-4755
e-mail: duanedavis@att.net or iss-dandavis@att.net

FutureSource
1-800-621-2628

TradeStation or SuperCharts
828-628-4222
714-731-3384
e-mail: duanedavis@att.net or iss-dandavis@att.net

Window on Wall Street
800-998-8439
e-mail: duanedavis@att.net or iss-dandavis@att.net

Window Stand-Alone
828-628-4222
714-731-3384
e-mail: duanedavis@att.net or iss-dandavis@att.net

For more information, visit our Web site, www.marketsadvisory.com.

THOMAS R. DEMARK

Thomas R. DeMark Sr. has spent his entire business career in the investment business. From 1972 to 1978, he was an officer of National Investment Services (NIS), a multibillion dollar pension fund manager. From 1979 to 1982, he was president of Financial Markets Consulting, a market-timing consulting subsidiary of NIS. In 1982, DeMark founded DeMark Investment Advisory, an advisor to many of the largest and most successful hedge funds, fund managers, mutual funds, and investment counseling firms. His clients included George Soros, Goldman Sachs, Union Carbide, IBM, Minnesota Mining, Steinhardt Partners, Atlantic Richfield, First Investors, Hoisington Investment, among many others. In 1988, DeMark became executive vice president of Tudor (Paul Tudor Jones), a multibillion dollar hedge fund. In 1990, DeMark established a partnership with Chicago Board of Trade Treasury Bond legend Charlie DiFrancesca ("Charlie D"). In 1990, DeMark and multibillion dollar fund manager Van Hoisington formed Devan Futures, a $40 million fund. In 1994, DeMark served as special advisor to Leon Cooperman, a $5 billion hedge fund manager. At the same time, DeMark formed Market Studies, a provider of DeMark's suite of market-timing software to data vendors, such as CQG, Window on Wall Street, Bloomberg, Bridge, Aspen Research, FutureSource, Data Transmission, Omega Research, and private label. Currently, he provides consulting services to large funds. Formerly, he was chairman of Logical Information Machines (LIM). Previously, he wrote two highly successful books on market timing, *The New Science of Technical Analysis* and *New Market Timing Techniques*. He has been a featured speaker at many conferences, has appeared regularly on TV and radio, and has contributed numerous articles to financial magazines. His professional career was the cover feature article for *Futures* magazine and he was described by the magazine as "a trading system developer without peer."

THOMAS R. DEMARK JR. (T.J.)

Thomas R. DeMark Jr. (T.J.) has also spent his entire career in the investment business. Upon graduating from Williams College, T.J. worked on the floor of the Chicago Mercantile Exchange for Dean Witter. Subsequently, he joined Merrill Lynch and became the youngest licensed Futures and Stock registered representative. In 1998, he left to trade on the floor of the Chicago Board of Trade for his own personal account with John DiFrancesca, a successful bond and index futures floor trader. Currently, he is a trader at a large, successful hedge fund. T.J. has conducted numerous seminars on his proprietary trading indicators throughout the Far East, Europe, and the United States on behalf of Dow Jones. He also co-authored a series of 12 articles published in *Futures* magazine.

INDEX